Legend:
- National Frontiers
- Provincial Boundaries
- Railways
- Rivers
- Land over 3000 feet

INDIAN OCEAN

ATLANTIC OCEAN

Tropic of Capricorn

Sofala
R.SABI
Bulawayo
Francistown
R.LIMPOPO
Serowe
L.NGAMI
Gaberones
Mateking
BOTSWANA
Windhoek
WEST AFRICA
Walvis Bay
Luderitz
ORANGE
Vryburg
Kimberley
ORANGE FREE STATE
Bloemfontein
TRANSVAAL
Pretoria
Johannesburg
SWAZILAND
DELAGOA BAY
Lourenço Marques
NATAL
Durban
LESOTHO
Fish R.
East London
Port Elizabeth
CAPE PROVINCE
Cape Town
CAPE OF GOOD HOPE

0   500
Miles

AN INTRODUCTION TO THE
HISTORY OF CENTRAL AFRICA

An Introduction to the

HISTORY OF
CENTRAL AFRICA

THIRD EDITION

A. J. WILLS

London

OXFORD UNIVERSITY PRESS

1973

Oxford University Press, Ely House, London W.1

GLASGOW NEW YORK TORONTO MELBOURNE WELLINGTON
CAPE TOWN IBADAN NAIROBI DAR ES SALAAM LUSAKA ADDIS ABABA
DELHI BOMBAY CALCUTTA MADRAS KARACHI LAHORE DACCA
KUALA LUMPUR SINGAPORE HONG KONG TOKYO

Hardbound edition ISBN 0 19 215648 9
Paperbound edition ISBN 0 19 215649 7
© Oxford University Press, 1964, 1967, 1973

First edition 1964
Second edition 1967
Third edition 1973

*Printed in Great Britain by
Hazell Watson & Viney Ltd.
Aylesbury, Bucks*

PREFACE

THE termination of the brief career of the Federal state of 1953 is significant for it implies a shift in the balance of power, and one that will probably endure. It does not necessarily mean an end to federalism in the region. It has not been the intention to treat it as the climax of this book, which was started, and more or less completed, before the fate of the Federation was decided.

Bushmen have lived in Central Africa for upwards of ten thousand years. Africans have inhabited the region for over fifteen hundred. Asiatic races have traded on its periphery for close on ten centuries, Europeans for more than four. Recent events cannot compare in importance with the Bantu migrations of the first millennium A.D. and the European settlement of two generations ago. The Central African territories are not organic nation states that have matured through centuries of common heritage, but artificial creations of external forces. Their future form and the future relationship between them must alter and adapt as the realities beneath the surface of contemporary politics assert themselves. This is an age of transition, nowhere more so than in Africa. The rapidity of the change is bewildering, and a sense of proportion is greatly needed among the people of all races whose lives are caught up in the maelstrom of change.

The principal purpose of this book has been to provide material for students and teachers of history in the Rhodesias and Nyasaland. Until a few years ago it was difficult to teach local history at all owing to the lack of available works on the subject. Recently a large amount of literature, mostly specialized, has appeared. I hope that there is still a place for an account that tries to give a balance to the story of the African peoples before the advent of the European, and to each of the three Central African territories, whose historical association cannot be destroyed by the break-up of its present political form.

A book of this length can only be an introduction to its subject, and a reasonably extensive bibliography is therefore provided. It is not original research, and I have relied heavily on the work of historians, anthropologists and economists whose books and articles are listed. In particular I am gratefully indebted to Roger Summers for advice and help on the sections concerning the early Shona and the Portuguese, though he is in no way responsible for the final presentation. I have received great courtesy and help from the staff at the Colonial Office Library, and at the library of Rhodesia House, London. I wish to thank the High Commissioner for Northern Rhodesia for permission to see a map illustrating land distribution in the territory. I am more grateful than I can say for the help and encouragement given me by many other people and by my family at home. Finally I should like to thank the publishers for their invaluable suggestions and co-operation.

London 1963 A.J.W.

PREFACE TO THE THIRD EDITION

When this account originally appeared, it was with the hope of giving a greater balance to the background of the African peoples than had been customary in general texts. It has of course been overtaken by a vast amount of research into African history relating to both the colonial and the pre-colonial periods. In this edition I have tried to introduce a little of that new wine into an older flask, especially as regards the prehistory of Africa and the Iron Age in Mashonaland. In this respect I am much indebted to Dr Patrick Carter of Downing College, Cambridge, for his advice and encouragement.

The opportunity has also been taken to add two sections on events since 1965. I regret that it has not been possible in the time available to deal more than cursorily with developments in Malawi. For the rest, it should be added that to write of contemporary events involving living people, some of whom bear heavy responsibility, calls for moderation as well as insight; and that anyone claiming however boldly to be an historian must, when dealing with irreconcilable points of view, temper his own commitment and seek an approximation of the truth in an otherwise less justifiable detachment.

Norwich, January 1973 A.J.W.

CONTENTS

MAPS

A NOTE ON THE USE OF AFRICAN NAMES

As far as possible the plural prefix has been dispensed with when using the names of African tribes.

With regard to the Ndebele of Southern Rhodesia, this form has been preferred, but the earlier 'Matabele' has been employed when quoting from contemporary sources and when referring to the Matabele Mission of the London Missionary Society.

I

INTRODUCTORY

Background

AFRICA is at once the oldest and the youngest of the world's continents. The oldest, because its overall geological structure has not been significantly altered during the observable period of geological time; not, that is, as in Europe and Asia through the folding of mountain ranges, the submerging of land masses, and the carving by ice ages of fresh forms upon northern land-scapes. Across the deep forests and wide savannas of Africa there exist varieties of animal life that are survivals of the fauna inhabiting the planet before man appeared to master his environment. A primeval atmosphere communicates itself even today to the newcomer from Europe who is acquainted with a visible historical process, with material change both slow and sudden but mostly man-made. But if in these terms Africa presents itself as the oldest of the earth's surfaces, in human terms, south of the Sahara at least, the world is still young. Age, unless measured simply in years, is the result of accumulated experience. If the experience of more 'advanced' human societies, the product of progressively developing reasoned thought, is today being grafted on to the awareness of diverse peoples, it has not extinguished the freshness of outlook and expression that belongs to communities who for time beyond memory have relied upon oral tradition, and while evolving complex social structures have throughout had to contend with the problems of food, shelter and defence in their more immediate forms.

The generalization 'Africa' embraces wide variety. Travellers south of the Sahara have discerned common factors in contemporary human tradition, in climate, vegetation and animal life. Such common factors undoubtedly exist, due both to the geographical position of the continent that lies across the equator and duplicates its climatic conditions north and south, and to the originally migratory character of its indigenous peoples who, though spread over a vast area, possess a related origin. Generalization cannot however eradicate infinite diversity, and is made less justifiable by recent events. The impact of exotic cultures has tended to divide where an over-all unconscious unity existed. Until a century and a half ago, the most noticeable division in human terms south of the Sahara was that between west and east, the latter being distinguished by its more recent range of settlement, and by closer contact with the Hamitic north-east. Subsequent immigration and conquest from Asia and Europe have created more divisions in language and religion, in the character of race relationships and political structure, and in forms of economic productivity. While old varieties have been submerged in new uniformities by communications and by the coverage of predominantly 'western' traditions, former similarities are tending to disappear through the fragmentation of organic African societies on a new scale and on new levels.

In tropical Africa, say between the Sahara and the Limpopo, this fragmentation according to the present pattern is unlikely to be more than a temporary phase. Already tentative moves towards federal combinations have been made among new 'states' defined by frontiers of the most artificial kind from the communal and economic points of view, and the pan-African conference of 1958 is unlikely to have been the last. None the less, throughout its long future the history of Africa will bear ineradicably the marks of Islamic penetration and of the 'western' colonial period, and if the consequences of the former go deepest, having been longest established, those of the latter will be more widely spread and more outwardly evident.

Despite the very long period of the association between East Africa and the Orient, it was by Europe, with its technological achievement in medicine, weapons and communications, that Africa was subdued. In spite of originally closer cultural affinity with eastern peoples, it is by western thought and tradition that the new Africa, by and large, has been infused. Until the present, this impact of Europe upon Africa has passed through two phases, while a third recently begun is still in process. The first, during the post-Renaissance age of discovery, saw the establishment of trading settlements, principally Portuguese but also Dutch, English and French, along the coast from Cape Verde in the west to the horn of Africa in the east. As with the Islamic settlements on the east coast, the primary impulse was economic, being a consequence of the new capitalism of the emergent nation states; of ideology or humanitarianism there was little, though since the burning religious rivalry that accompanied the reformation was a feature of the new nationalism and a vital part of sixteenth- and seventeenth-·century European society, missionaries generally sailed with the merchant adventurers. The immediate effect on Africa, economically and socially, was slight, and as will be seen in the case of the Portuguese on the lower Zambezi, of a more or less temporary nature. Only at the Cape was a settlement of lasting significance established during this phase, and the stamp of its seventeenth-century thought was to set it apart from the quality of subsequent colonization.

Aside from the Cape, only the Portuguese colonies at Angola and Mozambique passed unaltered into the second phase, Dutch and French stations on the west coast being withdrawn or changing hands. The new phase, developing with startling rapidity during the last quarter of the nineteenth century, was a consequence of the new nationalist imperialism arising out of the industrial revolution and the French revolutionary theories that accompanied it. Again the impulse was primarily economic, though in this case instead of gold and spices to enrich the treasuries of the maritime powers, the new generation of traders sought raw materials and markets to satisfy the multiplying machinery of the factory age. This time technological advance, a hardly questioned confidence in the supremacy of white civilization, and the pressure of an expanding population in Europe wrought an absolute change in the economic, political and social structure of the continent. A distinctive feature of the new phase was the role of ideology which went hand in hand with commerce—sometimes a pace ahead, sometimes following close behind; this combination a contemporary, perhaps too cynically, described as philanthropy plus five per cent. Part evangelist, part humanist, often both together, the idealism in European imperialism could not justify but helped to mitigate the harsher consequences of an inevitable economic drive.

The final stage of this second phase, called variously colonial-ism or imperialism, is still with us and has overlapped with the third, a phase that has developed since the war. In this case while the object is economic, it is overlaid with ideological conflict; and while Europe by virtue of its prior influence has the lead, it is playing a secondary role in the contest for the mind of Africa that is being waged between the western and the communist worlds. The ideologies of each, both capitalist and socialist, are European in origin, but those European governments which possess or formerly possessed African territories, principally Britain and France, are compelled to play an ambiguous role. While they have to stage a political withdrawal, rapid or gradual as the situation and their policies demand, they yet find it necessary to preserve as best they may the tenets of western liberalism, or at least try to prevent African states from falling within the communist grasp. Both the reason for and the consequence of such a policy is the retention and development of their economic links with the African continent. African governments can auction their development programmes to the highest bidder and neither east nor west can afford to ignore opportunities for investment. The result is a new economic imperialism on a vaster scale in which the former colonial powers and the United States have a long lead; but it is one which they will have to work hard to maintain. The ideological implications are equally vast, for Africa's two hundred and thirty million people stand on the frontier between eastern and western philosophies. Facing this challenge, they possess a fundamental realism which is not easily deceived.

Seen in this light, the European settler communities in Africa are both an asset and a liability to the western cause; an asset since their ties of loyalty are to the west, and a liability since, tending to be politically to the right of colonial or ex-colonial western governments, they provoke harsh nationalist and potentially anti-western reactions that may in time prove overwhelming.

The area with which the present book is concerned has played a leading role in all three phases of European influence. It has also held a significant place in African history for two other reasons. The highlands north of the Zambezi and particularly along the eastern escarpment formed the classic migration route for East African Bantu as well as pre-Bantu peoples. The plateau formed the only feasible passage between the arid region of the Kalahari and the fever-ridden plain bordering the Indian Ocean, its savannas providing grazing for the herds of the predominantly pastoral tribes from the north east. Moreover into the resulting mingling of peoples the gold of Mashonaland early attracted oriental and Arab influences. Secondly, the Zambezi river was thereafter to prove the meeting point of contrasting policies—the protectorate colonial policy of the British government in the north and east, and the principle of European domination and racial separatism coming up from the south. The Central African states are therefore faced with many features of the contemporary African problem: militant nationalism; the development of African government in an economically and educationally backward community, one which moreover is subjected to the pull of the Moslem coast and to that of a possible East African federation; the evolution of a multi-racial society, and in particular the position of a white community that is subjected to the pull of the white-dominated south; problems of land distribution and of land tenure in a changing economy; the adaptation of tribal institutions to the requirements of modern administration; the growth of large urban populations out of a rural society; and the utilization and just distribution of wealth from enormous mineral and power resources.

The Long Dawn of History

Africa, like Europe and Asia, has seen well over a million years of recognizably human life. Indeed, it is now believed that, long before this, the first creatures ancestral to *homo sapiens* evolved in Africa itself, and spread thence to other continents. During this vast period of time there occurred throughout the south and east of the continent successive types of early man in stages which roughly approximate to those in other parts of the world. Inevitable differences in this development arose, since environment conditions the nature of life, and whereas in colder northern latitudes the advance and retreat of the ice-cap marked crises in human existence in response to which new techniques slowly evolved, the corresponding phenomenon in tropical and sub-tropical Africa was the period of increased rainfall, or

regional wet phase followed by a long dry period, during which
the habitable portions of the continent receded. It is thus on
the fringes of the more arid areas, for example along the line
dividing the sandy regions of the Kalahari and South West
Africa from the wetter lands to the east, that evolutionary
trends have been distinguished; many of the most profitable
discoveries have been made along river valleys such as the Vaal,
and the Zambezi above the Victoria Falls.

During these million or more years, four major climatic
changes were followed by two lesser humid phases, the present
relatively dry period being subsequent to the last of these. The
earlier Stone Age in southern Africa evolved during the very
dry stage following the first or Kageran climatic period. At this
remote age in human pre-history, the 'australopithecines' or
southern apemen first became established as tool and weapon
makers in stone, possibly owing to a need to change from a
vegetable diet to one of meat. The country favoured for this
type of existence was that where the forest fringed on drier open
country, since before fire was discovered south of the Sahara,
trees formed a valuable refuge from dangerous game. Evidence
shows however that later in the Early Stone Age the use of fire
had become known in this region, layers of ash having been
found in Early Stone Age sites at Potgieter's Rust and at the
Kalambo Falls in North-Eastern Zambia.[1]

Hunting techniques were limited. Tools were very simple,
being first of unworked sharp stone, wood and unworked bone:
later in the period stones were worked by flaking. The zenith
of the Early Stone Age was reached with a culture the equivalent of the early Acheulian of Europe, of which traces have
been found principally in Northern Angola and the Katanga,
and also in North-Eastern Zambia. The characteristic tools
were the hand-axe and the cleaver, a sort of primitive stone
knife, used in carving wood and meat. There was no other
specialization, but late in the period there was a marked improvement in the standard of stone flaking. Meanwhile the
second (Kamasian) and third (Kanjeran) climatic changes had
advanced and retreated during a period of some three hundred
thousand years. So far, very few human remains have been
unearthed from the deposits of these wet phases, and it is
from the evidence of developing stone industries that the

course of human evolution in southern Africa has had to be inferred.

When the rainfall again declined about fifty thousand years ago, men gradually moved out of the more arid regions into watersheds and areas of thick forest. Fossil records of this intermediate period reveal, for the first time, human types with modern *homo sapiens* characteristics. These are exemplified by the skeletal remains discovered in 1913 at Boskop in the Transvaal; Boskopoid man is believed to have been a direct ancestor of the Bushmanoid type. The wider range of settlement was accompanied by increased regional specialization, and the development of new ideas and techniques which belong to the period described as the Middle Stone Age. The use of fire and the knowledge of how to make it was by this time probably universal in southern Africa, opening wide new possibilities in bush-clearing, hunting methods and the working of wood. The use of artificial traps for game, both pits and fall-traps using sharpened stakes, probably dates back to this period, together with an increased organization of communal hunting in areas of more open country. These developments were accompanied by a greatly increased variety of tools and of materials with which they were made, including stone, skin, sinew, bone, wood, bark and resin, though in most cases only bone and stone have survived. Stone tools such as axes were now provided with hafts, no doubt to protect the hands from sharper cutting edges, while implements were generally smaller and more finely made. The use of pigments, not yet for rock art but rather to ornament the body, was now originated. The two main types of culture during this dry period were the Fauresmith, with its typical habitat in more open country, as in the south and west in the Transvaal, Bechuanaland and the western Cape; and secondly the Sangoan, belonging to more forested regions such as the Zambezi and Luangwa valleys and the Congo Basin. The skull of *homo Rhodesiensis* discovered at Broken Hill Mine was that of a man living early in this period, though he was of a type which among several others was later to become extinct.[2]

As the rainfall increased during the fourth or Gamblian climatic change, these Middle Stone Age cultures advanced again into less inhabited regions, until their communities were established over most of south and central Africa. No sites have been found in the Kalahari or in the eastern coastal region, but many have been unearthed all across the tableland from Mossel Bay in the Cape Province to the Kalambo Falls near Lake Tanganyika, not to mention the Congo basin. The greatest concentration of known sites is in Matabeleland, notably the cave at Bambata in the Matopos, and along the Zambezi valley between Chirundu and the Falls, as well as across the Tonga plateau.

The Middle Stone Age period had lasted some forty thousand years when the Gamblian phase began to come to an end, and with the growing aridity there commenced a general stir of activity, leading to an admixture of cultures and to contacts between groups that had previously been widely separated. Included in these movements were possibly some from much further north as the frontiers of the dry Sahara region advanced. It is possible that by this means finer stone-working techniques derived from the by now more advanced cultures in Europe and Asia, were conveyed to east and southern Africa. On the other hand it is equally true that great progress in stone working had been made by the existing cultures in Africa itself. It was probably a combination of both these developments that led to what has been called 'the microlithic revolution' in southern Africa.[3]

This great stride forward in the standard of tool and weapon manufacture was made during the dry period between twelve thousand and six thousand years ago and was the work of cultures classified as Magosian. They have much the same characteristics all the way from Uganda to the Cape. The principal feature was the making of much smaller, finer flakes or blades of stone, wood and bone, frequently of beautiful and symmetrical craftsmanship, and the use of these in composite tools and weapons. The result was greatly increased efficiency in hunting as well as in woodworking, together with leather and other craft. In Rhodesia, sites classified as Magosian have been found at the Victoria Falls, at Khami near Bulawayo, and at Mtemwa rocks near Marandellas, but they appear to have been less widely distributed than the earlier cultures of the Middle Stone Age period, many of which still survived.

Thus about six thousand years ago the human communities south of the Sahara, now of generally Bush-Boskop type, progressed to that stage of more advanced techniques and marked regional specialization which we call the Later Stone Age. This cannot, however, be equated with the Neolithic period in the Near East. It is true that some polished stone tools of like standard have been unearthed among African sites, but the Later Stone Age African communities were much slower to attain the revolution in economic life represented by the change from food-collecting to food-producing that evolved in the river valleys of Egypt and the fertile crescent. No communities possessed domestic animals apart from the dog, and nowhere so far as we know, with one possible exception in the region of the Upper Niger, was food obtained by cultivation. Until this time human progress in tropical Africa had been roughly parallel with that elsewhere, and the divorce that now occurred was to have far-reaching consequences. With the development of the dry phase a period of isolation, perhaps the most complete in the entire history of the continent, began. 'It was then that Africa south of the Sahara fell decisively behind the north and most of Eurasia, and acquired that character of technical and cultural backwardness which even the advent of the Iron Age could not entirely alter.'[4]

Nevertheless the Later Stone Age, of which the Bushman communities distributed across the subcontinent prior to the Bantu invasion were the most recent survivals, was a tremendous advance upon earlier achievement. It was partly one of craft technique, and partly one of social organization. From the point of view of stone manufacture, two main cultures have been distinguished: the Smithfield, to be found more to the south and east, with larger implements of macrolithic type, and the Wilton, partly in South Africa but more concentrated north and south of the Limpopo, using more purely microlithic flake stone tools. These included polished axes, drills, perforated stones, many varieties of scraper, grindstones and pestles, and differing styles of arrowheads. Bone implement manufacture was also well-developed, and a cave in the southern Matopos has yielded a number of bone arrowheads, needles, discs and ornaments. Generalization is impossible, however. Regional specialization is a feature of the Later Stone Age, and the type of product within the Wilton culture complex varies from one place to another. That in Matabeleland appears to have been adapted to open country, while the Wilton products of Mashonaland were more suited to life in the more wooded country to the east. In all cases the requirements imposed by the local hunting method appear to have been the determining factor.

Great strides were also made in the structure of society. Since existing Bushman communities are survivals of the Later Stone Age period it has been possible, by combining studies of such communities with the examination of remains beneath the floors of cave dwellings, to form an impression of the prevailing way of life. This was certainly more tribal in organization, though only northern peoples seem to have had chiefs. Tribal organization and leadership meant tribal laws, institutions and ceremonies. Specialization in manufacture led to barter or trade, and it is likely that goods often travelled across wide distances in the course of changing hands. Groups were nomadic, and thus did not build even semi-permanent dwellings but erected windbreaks of leaves and branches as Bushmen often still do today. In areas strewn with kopjes, shelter was often found in caves and beneath overhangs in the rock. Societies were generally monogamous, and social life was according to strict rules. Both within the family and within the group a clear division of labour was practised. There is little evidence of conflict between Later Stone Age peoples. Their numbers were few, and there was apparently no need for competition in gathering food from the abundant natural environment.

The practice of rock painting developed, it is believed, in Later Stone Age or even Magosian times. Pigments had already been used for decorating the body for thousands of years, but no reason can be divined with certainty for the evolution of styles of rock decoration. Similar styles began to occur in Europe at the same time, but there is no evidence that rock art in southern Africa was other than entirely indigenous. Progress in this field has taken place in different parts of the world separately but on parallel lines.[5]

The earliest paintings, of which there must have been some executed as long as eight thousand years ago, have long since disappeared, but surviving works of more recent times, chiefly the product of Bushman artists, show that the purpose was generally magical or ceremonial. Some paintings may have had totemic significance. Others, particularly in the later period, represented events of critical importance to the clan. South of the Zambezi—where paintings are found in rich profusion among the granite kopjes of the Matopo hills and the outcrops of the Mashonaland plateau, not to speak of the wide distribution of paintings and engravings in the Transvaal, along the Orange river, in the Drakensberg and the Cape—all over this region rock art, though passing through fairly well-defined stages of development, is naturalistic. Well-drawn, clearly recognizable species such as cheetah, buffalo, rhinoceros and lion in reds, browns and ochres are to be found, sometimes in caves but more often on rock walls sheltered from rain by overhangs but facing out into the open. North of the Zambezi, towards Lake Mweru, along the Muchinga escarpment, and across the watershed separating the Luangwa and Lake Nyasa, rock art is less common, and is schematic in design, consisting of indecipherable shapes and patterns for which no satisfactory explanation can be given, though some magical or ceremonial purpose is again assumed.[6]

The naturalistic paintings that survive appear to fall into three phases: an earlier period indicating a peaceful traditional existence, largely occupied with hunting; later, a period showing an interest in the arrival of new peoples, perhaps Hottentot or Bantu, who seem to be living side by side with the existing race, not destroying them but nevertheless disturbing their established outlook and way of life. Signs of this infiltration appear earlier in Mashonaland than Matabeleland. Lastly occurs a fairly brief phase during which the standard of art degenerates either through loss of technique or through inferior imitation by an alien people.

It is to the events indicated by the second of these phases that we must now turn our attention. By this time, that is to say during the first millennium of the Christian era, the scattered population of southern Africa comprised Later Stone Age people of Bushman-Boskop stock; among them were related Hottentot groups, probably a variant of Khoisan type, who had moved southward during preceding centuries.

II

EARLY INVASIONS IN MODERN TIMES

Iron Age Peoples and the New Era

THE diffusion southwards towards central Africa of iron-working, food-producing cultures early in the Christian era marked the greatest economic change in the continent prior to the industrial age. Principally it was ideas and techniques that were generated or transferred, though there were also shifts of population. At a time when the Sahara region was better watered than it is today, established trade routes crossed from the Nile to the Chad area and beyond to the middle Niger. All along this route therefore, there existed during the three millennia before Christ an interchange of ideas and culture. These were centuries during which communities along the middle Niger and on the plateau between the Niger and the Benue evolved the working of gold and perhaps of copper learned from Libya in the north, the technique of pottery, representational art. On the Nile, dynastic Egypt rose and flowered, and extended its empire to the south, into the land of Cush beyond Nubia. Across the dusty savannas of equatorial Africa heterogeneous communities, part Negro part Hamitic, pursued a pastoral existence with a Later Stone Age culture, mingling now with the Negroid peoples of the forest belt, now with the aboriginal inhabitants scattered over the highlands that skirt the Congo basin.[1]

During the last three centuries B.C. a number of circumstances was combining to disturb these fringe communities and push them southwards, some into the forests of the Congo and its tributaries, others, the more pastoral and Hamitic, towards the great lakes, the rift escarpment and the East African highlands. What these circumstances were we must largely speculate, but three were most probable: the further desiccation of the Sahara, a process already centuries old in the present phase, a background trend; second, the southward shift of the Cushite power in the sixth century B.C. following the Assyrian conquest of Egypt; and lastly the spreading knowledge of iron, the Iron Age revolution, brought to Egypt by the Assyrians, and absorbed as a feature of the Cushite economy on the upper Nile by the fourth century B.C.[2]

It should not be too readily assumed, however, that Africa owes its Iron Age, with its concomitant agricultural economy, entirely to the brilliant advances of Egypt and the fertile crescent. The iron-working techniques that appeared on the Nok plateau of northern Nigeria by the late sixth century B.C. may have had a spontaneous origin. By the first century B.C. knowledge of its use had spread thence to the communities north and south of Lake Chad and in the central Sudan. There is also evidence of iron-working having commenced by about 300 A.D. at isolated points in east and southern Africa.[3] Invariably the discovery must have provided its users with undreamed of means of subduing new environments and of attaining an unquestionable superiority over the Later Stone Age peoples, Negroid or Khoisan, Cushitic or Nilotic, who were thinly scattered across the tropical zone. Crop cultivation would lead to more food, to larger communities, to the search for more land, and so to the gradual infiltration of small groups into areas most favourable for farming, to be frequently welcomed for their superior abilities and techniques, rather than resisted, by the indigenous hunter-gatherer inhabitants.

The lines of this development are hard to trace, and hardest of all in terms of physical type. Broadly speaking, the sub-Saharan Iron Age of the first millennium A.D. is associated with the Bantu-speaking peoples, but these are represented by a wide variety of physical characteristics.[4] A clearly Negroid origin associates them unquestionably with the Negro inhabitants of equatorial West Africa.[5] A large proportion of the proto-Bantu stock, that is of Negroid peoples ancestral to the Bantu, originated in the savanna lands north of the Congo rain forest. During the last centuries B.C. and the first centuries A.D. groups appear to have crossed thence to the south of the forest belt, to find a similar habitat in the southern Congo. Meanwhile by the end of the first millennium B.C. peoples that have been described as Afro-Mediterranean, perhaps ancestral Nilotic groups, pastoralists with sheep and cattle rather than cultivators, had settled in the rift valley of East Africa.[6] Intermarriage between Negroid and Khoisan communities south of the Congo produced a hybridization of physical characteristics that was later compounded by further mixture with Cushitic and Nilotic elements in the eastern half of the continent. It is not therefore possible to talk of a Bantu physical type, the skin-colour of Bantu-speakers alone ranging from near-black to pale bronze.

Apart from linguistic patterns and traditions of family organization, the most fruitful lines of development for research lie in the use of iron itself, in the spread of different crops such as sorghums and millets followed by the later adoption of Asian food plants, and in the manufacture of pottery in styles characteristic of the developing Iron Age.[7] Analysis of these lines suggests that the working of iron had become general in the southern Congo highlands before 1000 A.D. and that the consequent population expansion and proliferation of tribal units led to competition for land and to the movement of Bantu-speaking groups eastward of the great lakes. In due course there developed new forms of tribal organization whose principal characteristics were widely diffused and widely similar: a more advanced and complex social/political structure based on the extended family; the possession, under strict control by the tribal authorities, of artificial furnaces for the working of iron, sometimes of copper and even gold; the cultivation of crops, of which millet was the most common, according to the system of 'slash and burn' that was to have such widespread effects on the vegetation pattern of the south-eastern savannas; and sometimes, mainly towards the east and only in tsetse-free areas, the herding of long-horned cattle and fat-tailed sheep. Early in the second millennium, due to the stresses of movement, war and land-settlement, there emerged a new type of kingship, often associated with monotheistic cults, culminating notably in the Luba empire to the north of the Zambezi and the Mutapa empire to the south.

A further stimulus to the agricultural, mineral, industrial and building activities of these slowly forming societies was provided by trade with the east coast. Long before the Christian era, the East African coast had held an important place in the network of trade that was spread across the Indian Ocean. Hindu traders, who brought the coconut palm to grace the East African lagoons, had by 600 B.C. and probably before learnt to trust their boats to the monsoon and the open sea. With them came merchants in succeeding centuries from the Red Sea, Arabia and the Persian Gulf, and from as far east as the Indies. Towards the end of the first century A.D. a Greek navigator compiled a geographical account of the Indian Ocean, the 'Erythraean Sea', which lists the capes, harbours and islands of the African coast as far as the Rufiji river, 'beyond which the unexplored ocean curves round to the west . . . and mingles with the western sea.'[8] The presence was recorded of Arab traders, and of primitive inhabitants with whom they traded for wax and ivory, rhinoceros horn, tortoise shell and even palm oil. Arab trade was at first mainly confined to the coastline north of the equator but, while Iron Age communities were settling east of the Rift, Arab merchants were probing south along the seaboard till by A.D. 750 they were trading from their furthest outpost, Sofala—beyond Cape Corrientes the monsoon ceases to blow—from which in due course they began to export gold to Europe, Arabia and India. It was at about this time, in the eighth century, that they began to establish permanent settlements, the colonial movement springing in part from the upheaval caused by the religious whirlwind of Islam. The Omani traders centred on the rocky harbour of Muscat, separated from Mecca by a thousand miles of sand, rebelled against the new movement. Many fled across the sea to the African coast, already known as Zinj-el-bar, the land of the black people. Though the authority of the coastal sheikhdoms such as Mogadishu, Mombasa, Kilwa and Pemba never extended far inland, Arab blood was to mingle with that of the coastal tribes and with plantation slaves to form the Swahili peoples. A consequence of this long history of coastal trade was that oriental wares such as pottery and glass made their way inland. The unearthing of such more permanent relics, combined with radio-carbon dating techniques applied to remnants of indigenous industry, enable us to arrive at tentative conclusions about the approximate dates of early Iron Age societies in south-central Africa.

The first traces of such societies long precede any exotic influence. An early Iron Age site dating from the fourth century A.D. has been found at Machili on the eastern borders of Barotseland, seven hundred miles from the sea. South of the Zambezi the discovery of dimple-based ware at type-sites named after Gokomere and Ziwa in Mashonaland have revealed the presence of Iron Age farmers there as early as the third century. Other recent finds suggest that the Gokomere people had settlements all the way from the Inyanga highlands to the northern Transvaal and north-eastern Botswana well before A.D. 500. For some time they or a related people were the first Iron Age occupants of the Zimbabwe site. During the second half of the first millennium two other Iron Age groups arrived in the area—the Leopard's Kopje culture people, whose type-site was near Bulawayo and who later spread south from Matabeleland to Mapungubwe, and some further settlers of unknown origin who were in occupation of the Zimbabwe site until about 1075 and whose culture included the manufacture of human and cattle figurines.[9] These Period II people at Zimbabwe were probably responsible for the first gold-mining in the area, which dates back to before A.D. 1000.[10]

While a continuously developing pottery tradition suggests the integration of earlier communities with later settlers, the influence of a new wave of immigrants, classed as Period III at Zimbabwe and identified as Karanga or early Shona by historians, is marked by the commencement of dry stone construction here and there on the Mashonaland plateau. Competition for grazing and hunting rights must by now have been growing more acute. The granite outcrops strewn over the high veld no doubt suggested a means of fortification reminiscent perhaps of a distant northern tradition. Parts of the valley walls and some of the foundations of the 'acropolis' at Great Zimbabwe date back to the eleventh century. At the same time there is evidence of more strongly constructed pole and mud huts, of spinning and weaving, of gold trading with the Arabs coming up from the distant coast. Excavations at Ngombe Ilede in the Tonga valley north of the Zambezi also indicate a trade in exotic materials by the early eleventh century.[11]

Thus from the eleventh century to the fifteenth a thriving, pioneering Bantu-speaking society occupied Mashonaland.

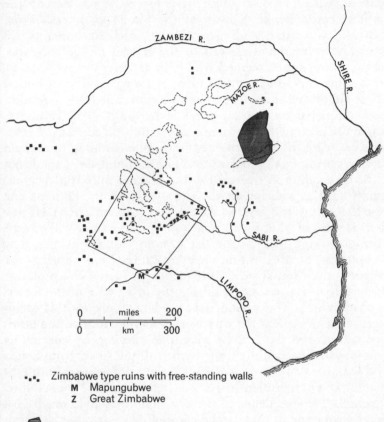

ZAMBEZI R.

SHIRE R.

MAZOE R.

SABI R.

LIMPOPO R.

| 0 | miles | 200 |
| 0 | km | 300 |

•.•. Zimbabwe type ruins with free-standing walls
  M Mapungubwe
  z Great Zimbabwe

Area in which Inyanga terraces occur

Areas of ancient gold workings

Area in which gold ornaments have been found buried

Ancient Gold Working & Stone Building

There can now have been little question of peaceful co-existence with the aboriginal hunter-gatherers still subsisting on the plateau, whose arrows would have played havoc among the settlers' cattle herds. Known to the Shona as *mwandionerepi*, 'how did you catch a glimpse of me?', such Bushmen as still remained retreated westward to the fringes of Lake Ngami, whose swamps then teemed with wild game.

At some time during these three or four centuries of Period III at Great Zimbabwe the stone structure called the 'acropolis' was completed on the kopje called Mwanha Hill. Doubtless originally occupied for defence, the outcrop's natural characteristics were now augmented by stone walling, the main rampart being finally topped by a line of rounded pillars. If not at first, certainly in due course, the place acquired a religious significance as a shrine for the cult of *Mwari*, the divine being worshipped by the Shona. At the very end of Period III the first stones of the Great Enclosure, sometimes called the 'Temple', were laid on the flat ground east of the hill. The completion of this astonishing structure came during the zenith of the Zimbabwe culture known as Period IV, probably in the late fifteenth century during the first phase of the Rozwi predominance. The period is marked not only by this architectural achievement but also by the manufacture of fine bowls and tall-necked pottery, by soapstone carving, by continuing gold-production, and by trade both with the Arabs from Sofala and with the copper industrialists of the Luba empire in distant Katanga. The elliptical enclosure is however the outstanding triumph. The excellence of the dry stone masonry, much of it greatly superior to that on the acropolis and at other sites, has suggested that the builders must have developed their technique elsewhere; but the method, without bonding, was not of the Arab style. Certainly the ground plan is inescapably African.[12] The final product, grand but grotesque, seems to combine the expression in stone of the typical Bantu royal enclosure with the projection of the style used in the 'acropolis' fortification such as its rounded profiles, narrow entrances and lookout platforms.

Our conceptions about the ethnographic and cultural situation during these centuries early in the second millennium should not of course be confined within the limits of Mashonaland and Matabeleland. Among the Sotho tribes of Botswana, for example, there is evidence that ancestors of the Bafkeng and Barolong crossed the Zambezi as early as the eleventh century. Evidence from pottery remains suggests that they may have been related to the Period II people at Zimbabwe, but that their settlements extended well south of the Limpopo before the time of the early Shona arrival on the plateau about 1075.[13] There they will have come among descendants of the earlier Gokomere people and Leopard's Kopje people before making their way south towards the Drakensberg and south-west to the Orange River, ultimately to mingle to a considerable extent with Bushman and Hottentot communities.

The distinctive characteristics of the Mashonaland plateau, however, with its sweeping downs and granite outcrops, its mineral resources and its access to the coastal trade, were to provide the setting for an African state whose maturing Iron Age culture-complex was to be unsurpassed in southern Africa for over three hundred years.

The Early Shona Kingdoms

With the flowering of early Shona society at the commencement of what is called Period IV during the fifteenth century, events come more clearly into focus. Principally this was due to the fact that the new phase concided with the appearance of the first Portuguese settlements on the east coast. If the picture becomes clearer, however, its nature also changes, for we no longer have to rely entirely on the evidence of material remains. Hitherto we have chiefly observed the African scene through the eyes of the archaeologist with his terminology of Iron Age, culture type, industrial technique. The contribution of archaeology continues to be fundamental, but it is overlaid by the recorded evidence of the contemporary European eyewitness, with a less scientific and more biased vocabulary. In the study of a society without written records, the names of places and tribes, details of custom and behaviour, for the first time become available.

Portuguese evidence was in fact often misleading not only because of inherent bias but also as a result of their own misunderstanding of the situation of the Mashonaland plateau. Their convincing descriptions of the dominant place held by the 'Empire of Monomotapa' south of the Zambezi gave rise to exaggerated legends which were told and believed in Europe as late as the nineteenth century. In fact by the time that the Portuguese were in regular contact with the Mutapa kingdom this picture, deliberately fostered by the northern Karanga, was already far from the truth.

Nor can the Portuguese records cast much light on the origins of the early Shona people. The country is referred to on Portuguese maps as *Mocaranga*; one of the Shona tribes of today in the district to the east of Salisbury preserves the name Karanga and claims descent from the Mutapa's people. Further south another group, the Kalanga, still survives. In spite of oral tradition, however, it seems that the early Shona who crossed the Zambezi in the mid-eleventh century did not then call themselves Shona, but later acquired the name from the plateau across which they established their settlements. We know of two local tribes, the Manyika and the Lungwe, who have taken their names from the country in which they have settled, and the invaders as a whole may have done the same.[1] The word 'Shona' is a linguistic term applied generally to the ancestral Karanga, Rozwi and other groups who were the bearers of the Period III culture. Von Sicard has suggested that an early Shona settlement gave its name to Sena on the lower Zambezi; even that the people had northern Hamitic connections, remnants of such traditions being most purely preserved among the present-day Lemba people.[2] Some aspects of Period III culture, such as soapstone birds and bowls and decorated pottery illustrating long-horned cattle, have suggested a Hima relationship.[3] However fanciful these conjectures may be, there is a Portuguese account which describes the Karanga people as being taller and lighter-skinned than the coastal tribes, 'a noble race and respected among the Kaffirs'.

Research into oral tradition, while giving only imprecise evidence, supports a northern origin. A Karanga headman has told us that 'the ancestors of the first Mwene Mutapa, who was called Mutota, came from a country far to the north, beyond the great lake. After a period there was no longer sufficient room for all of them, so some migrated south, past the great lake, and crossed over the Zambezi. They then spread out to the south and west and occupied most of the area between the Zambezi

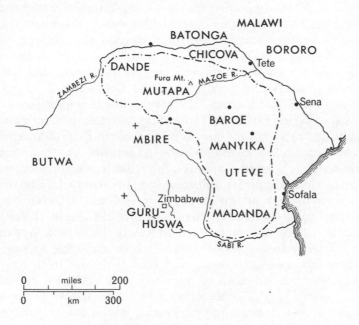

.–·–·– Boundary of Mwene Mutapa Confederacy (estimated by Fernandez 1512–14)

• Portuguese forts and trading posts

+ Relics of Portuguese habitation

BAROE Tribal territory

Early Shona Kingdoms and Portuguese Settlements

and the Limpopo, leaving the valley of the Zambezi to their vassals, the Tonga and the Tavara.'[4] A more specific tradition suggests that Mutota was descended from an almost mythical leader Nembire, genealogical founder of the Rozwi clan, whose people, perhaps originating on the Congo-Zambezi watershed, crossed the Zambezi about 1325.[5] If this was so, the Rozwi had within a century become the predominant clan among the Shona/Karanga of Period III, had established their hegemony in Guruhuswa on the southern part of the plateau, and were the new generation of builders at Great Zimbabwe.

It was at this point, around the year 1450 which marks the beginning of Period IV on the archaeological scale, that the *mambo* Mutota (c. 1420–50) led an expedition north from Zimbabwe to the headwaters of the Mazoe tributaries. According to tradition the object was a search for reliable salt supplies, but a more widely imperial ambition can be assumed. The title of *Mwene Mutapa* or 'great plunderer' is said to have been conferred upon Mutota by the Tavara of the Zambezi valley whom the Shona now subjugated. Similarly the Tavara gave the name *Korekore* to the Shona people, whose regiments appeared to them like locusts covering the land.[6] Mutota then was a Rozwi mambo, member of a ruling and probably priestly family, controlling a confederation of Shona tribes. These he now by dint of outstanding personal qualities welded into an empire extending from the Zambezi to the Limpopo. Inheriting the praise-name of Mwene Mutapa, his son and equally able successor Matope (c. 1450–80) consolidated and extended this empire from his new capital at Fura mountain. The provinces were governed by close relatives, perhaps sons, of the Mambo. During the reign of the next and less effective Mwene Mutapa Nyahuma, however, the conflicting ambitions of these subordinates led to the break-up of the state. Changa, a son of Matope by a slave wife, governed Guruhuswa from the old capital of Zimbabwe and controlled most of the mineral resources. Probably with the support of Arab traders, who were already well established in the country, he attacked the northern Karanga in 1490, killing Nyahuma and gaining outright control. Four years later Nyahuma's son Kakuyo regained the independence of the north, but from this time central as well as southern Mashonaland remained under the rule of Changa and his successors, henceforth owing to Arab influence carrying the praise-title of Changamire.[7]

This then was the situation when a European first entered the country in 1512: an already disintegrating confederacy of Shona kingdoms, each ruled over by a royal family of Rozwi stock, with the Shona themselves established in an aristocratic relationship to an earlier-settled Iron Age population whom they employed in the mining of gold and perhaps for building in stone. The visitor that year was Antonio Fernandez, a Portuguese *degredado* sent to report for his government on the origin of the gold exported from Sofala. Fernandez' account was subsequently drawn upon by the chronicler Damaio de Goes in a description of some features of Shona life on the plateau. 'In the middle of this country is a fortress of heavy stones inside and out; it is a very curious and well-constructed building, as according to report no lime to join the stones may be seen. . . . In other districts . . . there are other fortresses built in the same manner, in all of which the king had captains.'[8] Thirty years later de Barros, another chronicler, added that 'the natives of this country call these edifices *Symbaoe*, which according to their language signifies court, and they say that, being royal property, all the king's dwellings have this name.'[9] It seems however that *zimbabwe* generally meant 'stone place', and could even refer to a kopje that was used as a place of defence. Further descriptions from de Goes, and again from Joao dos Santos sixty years later, give a contemporary picture of the Shona way of life recognizably similar to that of the better organized Bantu societies of recent times, notably the Lozi. References are made to the quantities of game in the region, and to the cattle and crops of the people. The chiefs 'are not called kings by the kaffirs, but *nkosi* or *mfumo*'. They have no idols, but 'they have a confused knowledge that there is a great god, whom they call *molungo*'.[10] Witchcraft is common and severely punished, and for seeking out offenders they use 'the oath of *lucasse*, which is a cup of poison that the accused is called upon to drink, with the assurance that if he is innocent the poison will leave him safe and sound.'[11] Portuguese judgements were not always unsympathetic, for de Barros wrote that the Shona had 'many customs strange to us which appear to be dictated by good policy, according to their barbarous ideas'. Dos

Santos expressed the view that their language was 'the best and most polished of all the Kaffir tongues that I have heard spoken. . . . They speak in metaphors with very just comparisons, used most appropriately for their purposes and interests, to which all their designs are directed.'[12]

Portuguese accounts of the socio-political structure of the Mutapa kingdom, of which alone they developed an intimate knowledge, were probably typical of most of the other Rozwi-governed states of Mashonaland. It is evident that the Mwene Mutapa derived much of his political authority from his religious, indeed priestly, function as sole communicator with the *mhondoro* or ancestral spirits of the tribe, who were required to intercede with Mwari if the rains or crops should fail or other disaster befall. From this function, and from his own future spiritual destiny, the king had acquired a semi-divine significance. His illness threatened the welfare of the state. His life, while it continued, was symbolized by a royal fire, burning at his capital throughout his reign; from it embers were taken to keep alight subordinate fires that symbolized the unity of the nation.[13] Court ritual was elaborate. The Mwene Mutapa's authority over life and death was expressed by three wands, to let one of which fall was the signal for execution. No commoner could speak with him face to face but from the ground, with face averted, slowly clapping the palms of the hands, and then only through intermediaries. The Portuguese found these regulations irksome, but impressive enough.

The Portuguese were of course principally interested in the acquisition of gold, and their records give numerous descriptions of the methods by which the Shona obtained it, and of the richness of the deposits right across this great tract of country. Many reports were wildly exaggerated, and served to deceive not only their own contemporaries in Portugal but also, through the haze of legend, the Rhodesian pioneers who came three centuries later. Nevertheless, taken altogether many millions of pounds worth of gold were extracted prior to the modern European occupation, most of it between the twelfth and seventeenth centuries. Two principal methods were used. 'The first and most usual,' wrote dos Santos, 'is to make deep holes and mines, from which they dig into the earth and along the veins which are known to them, and bring out the gold, washing it in bowls.' This method was dangerous, the walls and shafts often collapsing. In recent years, examination of ancient workings shows that while one or two mines, such as that near Gwanda, were excavated to a depth of 150 feet or more, most were less than fifty feet deep.[14] The early miners were in any case only interested in ore yielding several ounces to the ton, which was usually found near the surface, ore being broken down by fire heat and by crushing. Another limiting factor was seasonal flooding. Gold was mined in Manicaland all the year round, but further west in more level country the workings were often flooded by the rains. A second method, which yielded the purest metal, was by recovering the alluvial gold from streams, especially along the Revua, the Ruenya and the Angwa rivers in the north-east.

Much skill was shown by the prospectors of this and earlier times in discovering ore-bearing ground. Little was left unexploited. In modern times, with the exception of gold reefs near Great Zimbabwe and in the Felixburg area north of Fort Victoria, practically every gold claim has been sited on an ancient working.

What purpose lay behind this methodical and long-continued industry? The immediate answer is trade, the Shona and their predecessors being anxious to buy cloth and exotic ornaments from coastal merchants, principally Arabs but later Portuguese. It is not the whole answer. Gold was worked to a small extent before the Arabs reached Sofala to provide a steady market. Finely manufactured gold objects such as bowls, amulets and ankle rings, nails and emblems have been found in graves at Zimbabwe and Mapungubwe. There is little evidence that the Period IV people used gold for such purposes; the Shona evidently mined gold for export rather than for use. It seems we must assume a tradition of gold mining and craftsmanship established by early Iron Age settlers, to be exploited by successive conquering peoples for different ends.

In attracting alien influences from the distant seaboard, gold was to become one of the factors that would undermine and ultimately destroy the progressive character of Iron Age society in Mashonaland. The schisms from within might have been resolved had they not been exploited by Portuguese and Arabs from without. Family feuds, endemic since the end of the fifteenth century, flared up again in 1565 when Chikanga, mambo of Manyika in the eastern highlands, challenged the title of Mwene Mutapa Mokambo. Both were killed in this war, which was still smouldering when a Portuguese force under Barreto first entered Manyika in 1569. Thereafter the Portuguese employed the route along the lower Zambezi and thence south direct into Mutapa country, and from the end of the century the Mwene Mutapas relied on Portuguese assistance to maintain a sometimes precarious independence against the eastern states as well as against the Changamires in the south. Nor were they free from external attacks by wandering military groups such as, possibly, the Jaga originating in Kasai[15] and, more certainly, the Zimba, a ferocious horde of unknown origin who roamed unchecked in the lower Zambezi valley towards the end of the sixteenth century, and then left to spread a trail of fire and slaughter as far north as Mombasa. Their presence in the region also threatened the Portuguese, weakened Arab influence in the interior, and may have been responsible for driving Kiteve's people for the first time up into the highlands of Inyanga. The departure of these marauders permitted an uneasy security to return. Arab and Portuguese influence, in mutual rivalry which itself contributed to the general discord, was reasserted. The northern Shona chiefs came increasingly to rely on external support to keep their power. In 1629 Mwene Mutapa Kapararidze attempted a national revival in the hope of driving all foreigners, white men and Arabs, into the sea; but the attempt was foiled and Mavura, a baptized Portuguese nominee, was installed in his place. It was a precarious position, however, since the power of the Portuguese itself was waning. Meanwhile the kingdom of Guruhuswa in the south, about which we know little since the Portuguese seldom came into direct contact with it, had grown in strength. In 1693 Changamire Dombo, a veritable Shaka of his day, destroyed the trading post at Dambarare on the Hunyani river, and attacked Tete. The Portuguese were forced off the plateau, the Mwene Mutapa was reduced to the level of a district chief, and by 1700 a new Rozwi empire, once more centred upon the south, had emerged.[16]

It was at about this time, and possibly because of the southern Rozwi offensive, that the inhabitants of the Inyanga region

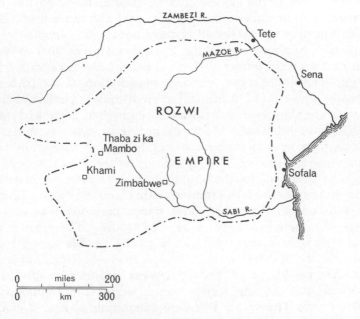

ZAMBEZI R.

Tete

MAZOE R.

Sena

ROZWI

Thaba zi ka
Mambo

EMPIRE

Khami

Zimbabwe

Sofala

SABI R.

0 ____ miles ____ 200
0 ____ km ____ 300

—·—·— Boundary of Rozwi Empire 1700–1834
• Portuguese forts and trading posts

The Rozwi Empire

were driven for a second time to take refuge among the high-lands, where they maintained a precarious existence for two generations or more. Partly for shelter and partly for defence, they constructed stone ramparts around pits dug into the ground, while the kraals for their livestock were also roughly built of stone. Eventually they were able to return to lower and slightly more fertile slopes, though their neighbours did not permit them at once to inhabit the level and more hospitable veld. On many of these hill slopes stones and boulders lay in profusion, and anyone wishing to cultivate would first have to clear off a great number of them. That they were piled in lines along the hillsides is the probable explanation of the Inyanga terraces whose remains are still evident today. Timber at that level is not abundant, and once the supply had been used up it would have been natural for the people to resort to stone, of which there was an unlimited supply for building walls and encircling settlements. The expedition to the Inyanga ruins in 1950–51 declared that 'it was a shortage of building material rather than a desire for permanence that led the Inyanga people to depart from the more usual Bantu materials—wood and mud—for building their huts and walls'. The eighteenth century has been suggested as the most probable time for the construction of these terraces.[17]

Other pre-Shona or related groups fled north across the Zambezi or, like the Venda, south across the Limpopo to settle in the Transvaal. The new generation of Rozwi would appear to have sacrificed creativity to military aggression and the fruits of spoil. An eighteenth century account stated that the people were much devoted to their chief, but that 'they pass their whole lives in indolence and spoliation, hold agriculture and commerce in contempt, and consider themselves superior to other races. Plunder is their sole object . . . and they have compelled the entire populations of several districts to flee to the north side of the Zambezi.'[18] This judgement was probably distorted. Nineteenth century observers were to comment later on the unique standards of craftsmanship and religious organiza-tion still maintained by the eastern Shona clans. Gold produc-tion, however, declined, perhaps owing to the difficulty of mining at deeper levels. During this Period V on the archaeo-logical scale, the stone forts of the south were kept in good repair, and in some places, as at Khami and Dhlo Dhlo, new ones were constructed; but the work was roughly accomplished and never of the former quality. Half-caste traders still made their way up the escarpment to exchange cloth for gold dust, though in greatly diminished amounts—a trade from which the chiefs still derived some benefit and which they were reluctant to surrender when the Rhodesian pioneers arrived.

Before that time, however, the Rozwi state was to be violently disrupted, though not totally destroyed, by incursions from the southern Bantu who had migrated northwards away from the turmoil of Shaka's wars. In 1834 Zwangendaba's Ngoni stormed the Great Zimbabwe, cleared the Shona defenders from many of their forts, and drove the last apparent ruler of the Rozwi system to his death on the hill since called Thaba Zi Ka Mambo.[19]

The Portuguese Settlements

The Portuguese had arrived on the east African coast, as we have seen, at about the same time as the Shona were establishing themselves on the plateau south of the Zambezi. Indeed, most of what we know of the early Shona has come down to us through the records of Portuguese observers. Although these first European traders had no lasting influence on the tribes inland, the fact that they were the first of their race to have contact with the Bantu in this area demands that their story should be known. Their records are of great value to us. The reasons for their successes as well as for their failures are significant.

Portugal, a very small country it should be remembered, on the Atlantic coast of the Iberian peninsula, had then a population of a few hundred thousand, a large proportion of whom derived their living from the sea. In the fifteenth century, following the Spanish lodgement on the north coast of Africa at Ceuta, Moorish and Arab tales began to circulate of gold resources beyond the Sahara. To attempt to venture there by sea appeared the obvious, indeed the only way. Inspired and financed by the great geographer and navigator Dom Henriques, a grandson of John of Gaunt, a succession of sailors made exploratory voyages along the west African coast. The passing of Cape Verde in 1455 proved that the Sahara gave way again to lands of natural vegetation. Further probes round the coast, reaching Sierra Leone in 1467 and the mouth of the Congo in 1482, disappointed their promoters by revealing inhospitable forests, deadly fevers, and little promise of mineral wealth. By this time, however, the prospect of finding a sea route to India, where the sources of a rich trade were known to exist, was exciting the minds of the Portuguese. Pedro da Covilhao, who had reached Ethiopia from the north in 1488, sent despatches home including this advice to Portuguese captains: 'Keep southwards. If you persist, Africa must come to an end; and when ships come to the eastern ocean, let them ask for Sofala and the island of the Moors (Madagascar), and they will find pilots to take them to Malabar.'[1]

Already in 1486 Bartolomeo Dias' expedition with three ships had rounded the southern cape, and sailed along the south African coast as far as the Fish river. Fearing that to venture further would be to court disaster, they turned back, without realizing that the worst part of the voyage to India had been made. Ten years later, Vasco da Gama's little fleet set sail from Lisbon, passing the Cape of Storms in 1497, and then proceeding eastwards and northwards. The first Europeans to gaze on the east African coast for over a thousand years, they kept within a few miles of the shore, coming to their surprise upon a number of fine Muslim towns. Da Gama expressed astonishment at the material standard of civilization now unexpectedly discovered, at the luxurious attire of the Sheikh of Mozambique, the fine stone buildings of Kilwa and the 'noble city' of Malindi. Visits on this and subsequent voyages revealed towns laid out with regular streets, houses with large windows and terraces, and mosques such as that at Zanzibar dating back to the eleventh century, decorated with exquisite Persian art.[2] At Malindi the Portuguese found a pilot to guide them across the Indian Ocean to Calicut. The sea route to India had been opened.

Upon da Gama's return to Portugal, arrangements were prepared for further expeditions, the prelude to ten years during which the Portuguese were to gain control over the chief Arab towns as far north as Mombasa. Meanwhile interest in Sofala's reputed wealth had been aroused. It was on da

Gama's third voyage, in 1502, that he decided to have a closer look at the place, and sending the rest of his ships north to refit, stopped there for some days. Sofala is a few miles from the present-day port of Beira, and was the southernmost of the Arab trading towns. Da Gama found that the harbour with its sand bars was difficult for his ships, which had a deeper draught than the Arab dhows. The town was built close to fever-ridden swamps, and consisted only of a large residence for the Arab governor, behind which were scattered about a thousand huts. The Portuguese on this occasion stayed only long enough to prove the presence of gold in the district, which had been acquired from inland. But the Arabs, probably for reasons of prudence, had shown no hostility, and further visits followed.

The reports of gold aroused a great stir in Portugal. The acquisition of wealth from spices and precious metals was the main object of colonization. While the Guinea coast in West Africa had not proved altogether a disappointment, Ashanti gold could not compare with the output from the South American mines that crossed the Spanish main. Rumours derived from Arab sources suggested that this might be the Old Testament's 'Land of Ophir' from which Solomon had obtained his gold. Exaggerated tales were told that the metal was in common use by the people. Diogo d'Alcacova reported in 1506 that at least a million mithcals were shipped abroad every year. On Sofala, now and for some years to come, Portuguese hopes were concentrated.

In 1505, Francisco d'Almeida was appointed Portuguese 'Viceroy of India', with his headquarters at Goa, and with authority over any Portuguese settlements that might be established on the East African coast. During the same year Kilwa was occupied by the Portuguese, and Mombasa plundered. Within a few years Portuguese hegemony was established over most of the Arab coastal towns as far north as Malindi. Relations with the Muslims was generally to prove bad, and Mombasa was to be the scene of repeated Arab rebellions till Fort Jesus was built in 1592. But the Arabs were never united, and the Portuguese were generally on amicable terms with the people of Malindi, traditional rivals of Mombasa to the south.

In the same year that d'Almeida was sent to India, an expedition commanded by Pedro d'Anaia landed at Sofala with the object of making a settlement there. The Arabs connived with the local Africans to drive them out, but the attack was beaten off. Within a few months the garrison had been reinforced from both Portugal and India, and a senior officer appointed commander-in-chief. The latter had complete authority over the Portuguese in Sofala, and others who were converted to Christianity there, and received tribute from the Muslim inhabitants. The local Bantu and Bushmen, however, were independent of his control.[3] After 1509, Portuguese trading vessels called at Sofala every year. Sometimes they were waiting for the south-west monsoon, which only blew from March or April until October, to carry them to India. Gardens at this and other coast stations were planted with maize, millet and melon, brought from the colony in Brazil and now introduced into southern Africa for the first time. None the less, Sofala was poorly placed as a departure point for the Indian crossing and never became an important Portuguese station. Instead a fort and hospital were built at Mozambique, which became the headquarters on the southern part of the coast.

Between 1509 and 1560 the principal developments in the area were the establishment of posts at the mouth of the Quilimane river which bypassed the Zambezi delta, at Sena about a hundred miles up the Zambezi, and at Tete another hundred and fifty miles upstream. Thus far the Zambezi is navigable without difficulty once the sandbanks at the delta have been passed, and for a long time it was as far as the Portuguese managed to progress inland. The settlements were small, the only stone buildings in each case consisting of a simple church, a small fort and a warehouse in which traded goods could be stored until it was time for them to be shipped to the coast. The inhabitants led miserable lives, isolated in an inhospitable climate. Despatches to Portugal had for administrative reasons to travel via India, waiting on the monsoon, so that at least two years must pass before a reply could be received.[4]

Until 1560, though some contact had been made with the Shona inland, no concentrated attempt had been made to colonize the country, or to mine gold there. Isolated journeys had been made into northern Mashonaland. The most notable were those of Antonio Fernandez, a *degredado* commissioned to redeem himself by completing the dangerous mission of reporting on the tribes and resources of the country. Travelling directly inland from Sofala in 1514, Fernandez circumvented the Inyanga highlands where Kiteve's villages defied entry, passed round the southern end of the Chimanimani range, and entered the Sabi valley. The route taken thereafter is not precisely known, but it is certain that he reached the Mazoe river at a point, says the chronicler, 'which was five days' walk from the Monomotapa's town, both the Mazofe and the Monomotapa's territory being rich in gold'. Fernandez from this and a subsequent journey brought back accounts of the stone forts or 'zimbabwes', of the gold mining in progress, and of the suitability of the country for European settlement. He urged on the authorities the need to establish forts and trading posts in the interior in order to secure the gold trade.[5] The Portuguese at Tete, Sena and Sofala, however, were too concerned with clinging to their unhappy lives as they were to consider advancing into the interior. Their chief solace was the arrival of the annual ship from home, bringing fresh faces and fresh supplies, and perhaps a chance of returning to Europe. The impulse to move further inland must come from Portugal itself.

That impulse came first from the Church. From the spreading of exaggerated tales, the strength and extent of the 'Empire of Monomotapa' had grown very large in the imagination of the Portuguese at home. Hitherto the Jesuits and other missionary bodies had made their main field of work in India, where St. Francis Xavier had laboured until his death in 1552. The idea of converting the Mwene Mutapa's people now began to win support. About 1556 the son of a Shona headman who had settled among the Tonga on the coastal plain south of Sofala visited Mozambique and was baptized a Christian. He asked for missionaries to be sent to his village. News of this request reached Don Gonçalo da Silveira, a Jesuit who had been sent to Goa in that year. In January 1560 Silveira crossed the sea at the head of the first Christian mission to southern Africa in history.

The missionaries spent over two years at Gamba's village,

near the coast about fifty miles from Inhambane. They had the advantage of an assured initial welcome, and of previous experience of oversea work in India. To begin with, all went well. After a few weeks, all the residents at the chief's village had accepted the new faith, and Silveira left the country confident that he left behind him a seed well sown, unaware that it had produced no root. As the months went by at the village, the missionaries began to become unpopular with the people as they tried to turn them to new ways. They denounced polygamy, and proclaimed the inheritance of a dead man's wife by his brother to be a mortal sin. They declared that the traditional practice of making rain was an empty ceremony and an ungodly superstition. These things were close to the hearts of the people, and woven into the pattern of their existence. The new converts steadily ceased to attend the mission services. They no longer listened to the teaching of the Portuguese. The priests had to admit that their work had failed, and packing what little they had with them, made their way back to Inhambane and Sofala, and thence to India.

This setback is not hard to understand. The Portuguese had made little attempt to study the people whom they came to teach, or the significance of their customs. It is good manners among the Bantu to agree with an invited guest. This apparent agreement the missionaries supposed to be genuine conversion, and they were more concerned with the quantity than with the quality of their converts. Even Livingstone, three centuries later, met the same problem. 'They indeed receive us with a show of apparent friendship but . . . do not want our Gospel, for it teaches men to put away their wives, and this they are determined not to do. Most of their people, taking courage from the countenance of their chiefs, are bitter scorners and opponents.'[6]

Silveira meanwhile was preparing a more ambitious expedition into the interior. In September 1560 he passed through Quilimane and Sena to Tete, pausing on the way to administer to the Portuguese at these posts, some of whom had not seen a priest for years. Thence he travelled west on to the plateau. The welcome at Fura mountain was friendly, and Silveira was offered gifts of gold, cattle and slaves, all of which—a typical error—he declined. His work was rewarded with the same story of early success, including the conversion of the paramount himself, to be followed by a rising tide of opposition to his insistence on the Christian custom in marriage.

There was resident at the capital at this time a number of Arab traders, some of them refugees from the Portuguese occupation of Mozambique. None of them, being Muslim, had any cause for friendship with the missionary, but above all they feared Portuguese interference in their monopoly of the gold trade. Their warnings that Silveira was not only a sorcerer but an enemy who would bring the Portuguese to conquer the country proved an influence which a Portuguese trader, Antonio Coiado, then staying at the village and well known to the Shona, could do little to counter. Silveira was ordered to leave the country. He refused, baptized fifty new converts the following day, and was murdered the same night on the chiefs' orders, together with the recently baptized people.[7]

The news of the martyrdom aroused great enthusiasm in Portugal for missionary work among the Shona. In subsequent years a number of priests, mostly Dominican friars, came out to preach in the country. Some success attended their efforts, but it was impermanent. Many were quickly discouraged, and in 1605 a royal decree forbade Dominican missionaries to return to Europe, in the hope that this would 'increase their zeal'.[8] But difficulties were almost insuperable. Apart from physical obstacles and inter-tribal feuds, Muslim influence extended through much of the area. Lastly the momentum of Portuguese colonization itself began to fail. During the seventeenth century their hold on the coast grew weaker, and their political influence with the tribes inland was not maintained. By the end of the seventeenth century, missionaries who died were not being replaced, and even before the time of troubles that followed, the old tribal beliefs had asserted themselves throughout.

Eight years after the death of Silveira, the first large-scale attempt was made by the Portuguese to gain access to the gold resources of the country. Sebastiano, King of Portugal in 1568, a man of extravagant intentions, expressed his resolve to create a vast dominion in central Africa south of the Zambezi. In 1569 Francisco Barreto was sent out to be the first independent governor of the Portuguese East African stations. Every effort was to be made to reach the Mwene Mutapa and to negotiate for the mining of gold. The expedition was lavishly equipped with soldiers, arms, trek animals and stores of all kinds.

In view of the notoriously unhealthy conditions in the lower Zambezi valley, many of the party favoured striking directly inland from Sofala. Barreto, however, advised by the chaplain to the expedition, decided less wisely on the Zambezi route. Landing with its heavy equipment at Quilimane, the expedition made its way slowly over the hundred miles up river to Sena. Camp was established there in the great heat of November. With the onset of the early rains, many of the white men went down with fever. The sickness was first blamed on the muddy waters of the rising Zambezi, and then on the local Arabs who, suspected of poisoning a well, were slaughtered to a man. The death rate was mounting by the time that the envoy sent to the Mwene Mutapa's a hundred and fifty miles to the west returned. His news revived flagging spirits. The paramount agreed to welcome the Portuguese provided they would support him against Chikanga's people, a rival branch of the Shona occupying Manicaland.

Agreeing to this proposition, Barreto assembled those of his force who were fit and set out southwards towards the highlands of Inyanga. In the foothills the party came upon the regiments of Mongasi, one of Chikanga's indunas, spread across a slope awaiting their approach. When an encounter was imminent an old woman ran in front of the assembled Shona and threw dust in the direction of the Portuguese, crying that the white men would be struck blind. The Shona, coming on confidently, were sharply disillusioned by the fire of the Portuguese flintlocks and were driven off. A second battle two days later was more fiercely fought, the Shona using the crescent-shaped formation later made famous by the Zulu. In a third fight Barreto's men, depleted in number and weakened by sickness, were compelled to defend themselves behind a stockade. Though the Shona again failed to overcome the little force and made no further attack, the Portuguese found progress impossible, and struggled back to Sena.[8]

After some weeks of rest, a party was sent north of the Zambezi into country where silver mines were reputed to exist. Nothing was found, and the garrison that was set up in the area of search was wiped out by an African attack. Shortly afterwards Barreto himself died.

Despite the disastrous failure of this expedition Barreto's successor, Fernandes Homem, resolved the following year (1571) to make a new attempt to reach the gold mines. Withdrawing the remnants of the expedition to Sofala, he stayed there for some weeks to refit and finally set out directly inland with a small party more lightly equipped. This time the Portuguese managed to reach Chikanga's in the vicinity of the Vumba mountains. Gold was found being mined there, but an historian writing forty years later described the disappointment which accompanied this long-awaited discovery: 'When (they) found themselves in the land of gold, they thought they would immediately be able to fill sacks with it, and carry off as much as they chose; but when they had spent a few days near the mines and saw the difficulty and labour of the Kaffirs, and with what risk and peril of their lives they extracted it from the bowels of the earth and from the rocks, they found their hopes frustrated.'[9] After concluding a treaty with the chief by which the Portuguese would send a supply of cloth annually in exchange for the right of entry into that part of Shona country, Homem returned to the coast and to Mozambique.

Though no further government expeditions were sent out for some years, chiefly owing to the death of Sebastiano in 1578 and to the inclusion of Portugal in the kingdom of Spain in 1580, individual traders came out prospecting on their own, and by 1600 a number of them was scattered across Mashonaland as well as in the Zambezi valley. Their existence must have been extremely hazardous, particularly during the 1580s when the marauding Zimba appeared in the Zambezi valley. During these incursions the Portuguese at Tete supported the local Africans, and in consequence Zimba bands attacked the settlement in 1592, killing or driving out the inhabitants. A relief force was defeated near Sena the following year. Not until the Zimba left the district were the Portuguese able to reoccupy both trading posts.

Up country to the south, Mwene Mutapa faced his own difficulties from rebel vassals. The chieftainship at the time was held by Gatsi Rusere (1596–1627), who was the first of the line to buttress the authority of the paramountcy with European support. The Portuguese first went to his aid in 1599, then more frequently after 1608, extracting important trading and mining privileges in advance.[10] An effective coalition against Rusere was broken up, and from 1612 to 1616 a successful campaign was waged against Chikova up river on the Zambezi, where silver ore was believed to exist. A report from Portugal in 1608 indicates the interest with which the revival of fortunes was received at home: the king of Spain was 'aware of the importance and riches of the gold and silver mines of the kingdom of Monomotapa. . . . Conquest and exploration could not (formerely) be undertaken as the land was not sufficiently known, and (because of Arabs) who greatly impeded Portuguese trade; which difficulties are not felt at present, as the Arabs have all disappeared in those parts, and the Portuguese have penetrated far into the interior, where they are well received by the natives and carry on with them a constant trade. The king of Monomotapa is at present very weak, at war with neighbouring chiefs and vassals, and greatly desires the intercourse and favour of the Portuguese, offering in return the silver mines of the territory.'[11]

Dos Santos makes an interesting comment on reports of trade with the Portuguese in Angola. Such reports were doubtless true 'as Kaffir merchants from Abutwa brought a blanket to the kingdom of Manica to sell it, which blanket had come through Angola, and was bought by Portuguese in Manica, and I saw it in Sofala'.[12]

Belief in the existence of silver ore north of the Zambezi inspired Gaspar Bocarro's exploratory expedition of 1616. Hopes of silver were disappointed, but passing through 'Bororo' country Bocarro reported the wide use of copper for bracelets and currency. He reached Lake Nyasa. 'Near the town of Moromba is the great river Manganja, or a lake which looks like the sea, from which issues the river Nhanha, which flows into the Zambezi below Sena, and there is called the river Chiry.' Crossing the lake, Bocarro travelled down the line of the 'Rofuma', reporting the coastlands deserted after recent Zimba raids. He reached Kilwa fifty-three days after leaving Tete.[13]

The increased activity of the Mozambique administration in Mashonaland brought a sharp reaction in 1629 when Kapararidze, who had succeeded Rusere, attempted to drive all foreigners from the country. By 1630 there were only five European survivors in all Mwene Mutapa's territory and only seven in Manicaland. Diogo da Meneses' punitive expedition of three hundred Portuguese troops and (reported) twelve thousand African spearmen acted with exceptional firmness, burning Chikanga's principal village in 1632, defeating and executing Kapararidze at Fura mountain, and setting up a puppet chief Mavura in his place. Mavura consented to a treaty which gave sweeping concessions. Mwene Mutapa was to consider himself a vassal of the Portuguese. Traders were given wide freedom, and there was to be no restriction on mining. Privileges were extended to the Portuguese officer at Masapa, the trading post near Fura mountain, who was to be entitled 'Captain of the Gates'. Churches were to be built and mission work carried on without interference. The chief was no longer to require obeisance and handclapping from official Portuguese representatives.[14]

The renewed conquest by local commanders coincided with a fresh burst of interest in Portugal. Rumours had reached Lisbon that an English ship was being fitted out to probe the Mozambique coast. The king at once despatched Joao da Costa to see to the fortification of the Zambezi mouths. Da Costa, having arrived in 1633 and placed his guns, proceeded up river to Sena and surveyed the situation there. His subsequent report, extravagantly phrased, suggests that he had the vision of a Cecil Rhodes, though not his resources. Karanga and Manica were rich in gold and silver. 'Your Majesty can have more profit than from all the Indies of Castile.' All that was required was white settlement. 'The land lacks for nothing else, and with this your Majesty will be lord of all the world as you deserve to be.'[15] The report created a sensation in Lisbon. A detailed and masterly settlement scheme was worked out, providing for a thousand selected immigrants, married couples, with troops in support. But implementation was delayed for two years while the situation in Portuguese India grew unfavourable. Further investigations ordered to the Zambezi suggested that the gold reefs, though numerous, were not after all so rich. The settlers at Tete and Sena, entrenched in large *prazo* estates with a profitable slave and ivory trade, continued to place every discouragement in the way of the proposal. At length in 1635 the expedition, no doubt wisely, was diverted to India, where the need for immigrants was believed to be greater. Thus was the planting of the first comprehensive colony in southern Africa averted.

Portuguese influence on the plateau after 1632 was sufficient to make and unmake chiefs as important as Mwene Mutapa and Kiteve. The Mutapas from Mavura onwards were baptized by resident Dominicans, but the effect of the ceremony appears to have been superficial. The country continued unsettled for several years and the following account by a trader in 1634 indicates that the position of Europeans was often insecure: 'The Portuguese,' he wrote, 'have many forts in the empire of Monomotapa; for by treaty with the emperor, in return for presents, they have free passage to trade in his lands, and buy and sell all the gold that is found therein. They have to depend chiefly on their flintlocks, which each person keeps ready; for in Kaffir country where trading goes on, rebellions often break out, and then each one's best defence is his gun . . . The power of the natives is vastly greater than that of the Portuguese in this country.' The return of Muslim influence is also evident. 'Many Arabs dwell in the empire of Monomotapa. They are opposed to us always and everywhere. When we raised Mavura, a Christian, to be the chief on condition that he should expel them, they stirred up the tribes to make war on us.'[16]

At this period there were sometimes as many as forty Portuguese residents at Tete, with perhaps six hundred Christian Africans and half-castes living in the district. Most of the trade with the Monomotapa's people passed through Tete, while Sena was the centre for that with the tribes of the eastern highlands. Kiteve traded directly with Sofala. The Portuguese had a number of trading posts, or 'fairs', in Mashonaland even as far west as Dhlo Dhlo. Among the more important of these were those at Dambarare, probably on the Marodze river, Masapa and Bukoto, both on tributaries of the Mazoe river, and Luanze, probably on the low veld a hundred miles south of Tete.[17] All trade entering and leaving the country had to pass through one of these posts. Joao dos Santos, who travelled through the region at the beginning of the century, wrote this account of Masapa: 'The captain at Masapa has jurisdiction . . .

over all the Kaffirs who come to Masapa, and those who live on his lands or within his borders. He has power to give verbal sentence in all cases, and can even condemn the guilty to be hanged. This authority has been given him by Monomotapa. He serves as agent in all matters between the Portuguese and Monomotapa . . . (and receives) all the duties paid to him by the merchants, Christian or Arab, which are one piece of cloth for every twenty brought into these lands to be sold.'[18] Some of these trading posts had stone ramparts for defence, but in most cases buildings were simply of pole and mud, whose traces have since entirely disappeared. Rectilinear foundations have been found on some sites, as well as relics of china and glass.

During the middle years of the seventeenth century, the gold trade was at its height. Statements vary concerning the amount of gold being exported, but one estimate has placed it at about 2,000 ounces for some years. Whatever the truth, it is doubtful whether the government gained more from the gold trade than sufficed to balance the expenditure on forts and warehouses and on official salaries at Sofala and elsewhere.[19]

After 1680 the Portuguese position began once again, and for the last time, to crumble. Their superiority over the African population derived from their possession of firearms, combined with the willingness of tribal groups to make use of them as allies. As time went on local captains exercised their power less on behalf of the king of Portugal and more for their own self-interest. Senior administrators, endeavouring to assert their authority, risked unpopularity with the settlers; on one occasion, the commissioner at Tete, having decreed a rise in customs rates, was fired upon by the outraged inhabitants and died of his wounds. Portugal was too distant to give adequate support in emergency, while help from Goa could only come when the monsoon was favourable. Meanwhile individual Portuguese grew arrogant and frequently treated Africans with injustice. As the century advanced to its close resentment against the white men increased until a surge of common feeling overcame the tribesmen's sense of inferiority in arms. Memory of the defeat in 1629 must have caused Monomotapa to call in Changamire's Rozwi. It was an ill-advised decision, but this time the African victory was complete. The settlement at Dambarare was attacked by Rozwi in 1693 and its residents annihilated. Raids on other posts followed and the Portuguese, reduced in numbers and with no organized leadership, were defeated piecemeal. By the end of the century they had disappeared altogether from the plateau.[20]

The collapse of white settlement was not entirely due to the obstacles faced by the pioneers in Africa itself. An important factor was the situation in Portugal. In 1580 the country had been absorbed into the kingdom of Spain, which was too concerned with religious wars in Europe and with colonial expansion in South America to pay much attention to the east coast of Africa. Competition from other countries also intervened. After 1600, East India Companies were formed in England and Holland, and later in France. Though their ships generally left East Africa alone, and sailed directly across the Indian Ocean, the growing trade which they built up in India and the East Indies caused the Portuguese to pay more attention to the defence of thir own interests there. The Arabs of course took note of these developments, and were not slow to strike at the weakening hold of the Portuguese. There had never been more than a hundred Europeans on the whole of the coast north of Cape Delgado. In 1631 there occurred the first of a new series of revolts against them. At the end of the century an Arab leader, Imam Seif bin Sultan, drove them out of Mombasa, Pemba Island and Kilwa. By 1700 the Portuguese hold over the coast north of Mozambique was entirely at an end.[21]

The small size of Portugal's population should also be remembered. Despite the courage and enterprise displayed by the Portuguese adventurers in the fifteenth and sixteenth centuries, the great period in the country's history, there were not enough people to build up and maintain trading settlements all over the colonial empire. Increasingly the Portuguese Government had to staff its garrisons and administrations with *degredados*, sometimes political offenders of birth and education but more often criminals of all kinds being punished by transportation abroad. With few exceptions such men did not make resourceful and enterprising pioneers.

During the eighteenth century, the period of Rozwi dominance on the highlands, the Portuguese knew little of what was happening among the tribes of the interior. Exaggerated memories of the Monomotapa lived on, so that right up till the nineteenth century this title was being written on 'guesswork maps' across great areas of southern Africa. Meanwhile the demoralized Europeans at the remaining little settlements continued their fever-ridden and dreary existence, now mainly occupied with the traffic in slaves and ivory. A small quantity of gold was still being produced, a fraction of the former amount; when Livingstone visited Tete in 1856 less than 140 ounces were passing through each year.[22] Slaves came mostly from north of the Zambezi. A small post was established at Zumbo in 1714, and occupied for a time, at the junction of the Zambezi and Luangwa rivers. Portuguese half-castes extended their 'prazos' into the lower Luangwa valley. Lake Nyasa had been visited at least once, in 1616, but its existence and extent were only vaguely realized. An occasional trader succeeded in penetrating to Lunda country in the far north-west, but no permanent post or regular trade was established there. No attempt was made to revive Portuguese fortunes in this part of Africa until Lacerda's journey to Kazembe's village in 1798.

The Dutch at the Cape

Since the voyage of Dias in 1487 the Cape, despite its name of *buena esperança* bestowed for the great hope it gave of discovering the Indies, had a bad reputation for dangerous storms. The Portuguese seldom made use of Table Bay as a refreshment station, and were further discouraged from doing so when Francisco d'Almeida met his death at the hands of Hottentots after putting ashore there on his way to Europe in 1510.[1] Instead, St Helena provided a staging post while others were found further round on the East African coast, and the Cape remained unoccupied save by the Bushmen and Hottentots who for centuries had made the district their home.

By the end of the sixteenth century the Portuguese control over their empire was weakening both of its own accord and in face of foreign rivalry, principally that of the Dutch. The annexation of Portugal by Spain in 1580 had made all Portugal's overseas territories the prey of the enemies of Spain. Of the latter the Protestant Netherlands were the most inveterate, having thrown off their allegiance to Philip II in 1579, and consequently found the port of Lisbon, vital to their trade, closed to them in 1581. Dutch sailors were thus forced to trade themselves in eastern waters, which they proceeded to do, encouraged by Drake's destruction of the Spanish battle fleet in 1588. Soon there were four Dutch companies trading in India, and in 1602 these were combined into the Dutch East India Company. Dutch sailors now penetrated rapidly the far eastern preserves of the Portuguese and founded stations at Bantam, the Moluccas and Java, Amboyna and Timor, with their headquarters at Batavia; while in India itself they made settlements on the Coromandel coast and at Surat. An unsuccessful attempt was made on Mozambique, but after 1609 they left the Portuguese East Africa stations alone, and laid their outward and homeward course across the South Indian Ocean. The Cape therefore made a convenient landfall, and Dutch and English ships frequently put in there for water during the first half of the seventeenth century. In 1645 Holland wrested St Helena from the Portuguese, but the island was not much favoured, and when in 1647 a shipwrecked crew spent a year ashore at the Cape their reports of conditions were encouraging enough for the Company in Amsterdam to set up a permanent station. So it was that on 6 April 1652 three Dutch ships under the command of Jan van Riebeeck dropped anchor in Table Bay, and the history of European settlement in South Africa had begun.

This Dutch settlement differed from that of the Portuguese at Sofala a century and a half earlier in two respects. Whereas the Portuguese were in search of gold, and had as their chief object trade with the indigenous inhabitants and later penetration of the interior in order to mine themselves, the Dutch East India Company regarded the Cape as a port of call for their ships bound to and from the east, and explicitly instructed van Riebeeck at the outset to confine his dealings with the natives to the necessary minimum, and not to colonize inland. In contrast to this, the second difference lay in the nature of the land. Whereas the sultry tropical climate of the East Coast boded ill for European settlement, the Mediterranean conditions prevailing at the Cape were eminently suitable. It was inevitable, therefore, that sooner or later an agricultural and pastoral European community would establish itself in the Cape district.

The Company disliked this prospect. It was reluctant to assume the responsibility and expense of administering a settled community when its interest was solely confined to controlling its monopoly with the eastern spice trade; and it feared the complications that would follow from any conflict with the native inhabitants. Here indeed the instincts of the Company were true. The Cape at this time was inhabited by Bushmen and Hottentots. The Bushmen, relics of the Stone Age, still scattered across central and southern Africa, were unprepossessing in appearance and unreliable as neighbours, being nomads and hunters, and as such thieves of domestic cattle. The Hottentots, later comers than the Bushmen, were thinly scattered from what is present-day South-West Africa to Natal. Taller than the Bushmen and lighter skinned, they were considerably more advanced, being pastoralists whose wealth lay in cattle. The Company's policy was one of strict non-interference with the Hottentots, but van Riebeeck needed cattle for meat, and was bound to trade with them, which led to misunderstanding and mistrust, or to graze his own cattle on their land, which led to affrays. Within a few years of European settlement the problem of land, which was to bedevil relations between white and black for many generations, had plainly intruded on the scene.

It was war with England in 1665 and with France in 1672 which drew the Dutch East India Company to revise its policy and strengthen its grip on the Cape by assisting immigration and encouraging settled farming. Under Simon van der Stel (Governor 1679–99) the colony expanded into the hinterland, and in 1688 its population was enlarged by an influx of Huguenot refugees. During the eighteenth century the frontier slowly moved eastwards, pushed out by frontiersmen or 'trekboers'. These men formed an outlook compounded of features that have been firmly stamped on the character of their descendants until recent times. They grew to love the freedom of the open veld. They also grew to mistrust and dislike a government at the Cape, directed from overseas, which pursued a contradictory policy of extending its authority over all further settlement, an outcome of the Company's determination to maintain its monopoly over trade and produce, and of refusing to give adequate support and protection, the result of its original view that the Cape was no more than a naval station, and must not become an expensive liability. Thirdly the frontier Boers perpetuated a tradition of hostility towards native peoples which derived from the original contact with Bushmen and Hottentots, and was fed by the Company's unwise action in the early eighteenth century of permitting the importation of black slave labour to the Cape. An early period of mixed marriages with Hottentots and slaves had produced after two generations a sizeable coloured population at the Cape, and the sharp reaction of the new colonists against this practice, that threatened to submerge their race, led to strict injunctions from Calvinist Church and government enjoining segregation.

The Dutch already held these ingrained attitudes when they first met the advancing Bantu in the region of the Great Fish river during the last quarter of the eighteenth century. They saw no reason to change them when the problems experienced by their forebears at the Cape were repeated in their own contacts with the Xhosa beyond the Fish, nor when the British Government, in permanent control of the colony after 1806, continued the irritating policy of nagging control of the frontier. The British took over the administration at a time when native policy, apart from vagrancy, was no longer a difficulty in the west; and when, at home, the evangelical revival was beginning to stir the conscience of government and public towards the condition of black peoples generally, slave and free. Thus it was that the Boers, finding no longer any place for their beliefs and way of life in the new scheme of things, trekked away from the Cape and, it is said, from the nineteenth century, across the Drakensberg, the Orange river and the Vaal.

By chance their movement followed closely upon the great migrations of the Southern Bantu, resulting from the hammer blows of Shaka's tyranny in Natal. In consequence the trekkers came either upon country swept clear of inhabitants by the warrior hordes emanating from Zululand and inhabited by cowed and frightened remnants, or upon the fighting tribes themselves, marauding and aggressive, unwilling to make any terms with the newcomers, but only to wash their spears in blood. The fate of Retief's party at the hands of Dingaan's Zulus in Natal, and of other trekker parties who met the Ndebele north of the Vaal, served to make yet more indelible the impression on the Boer mind of the black race as one to be subdued and maintained in subjection.

South African history in the nineteenth century followed a varied and dramatic course which there is no space here to describe, and the brief account of which has already taken us ahead of schedule. It had, however, a powerful influence on affairs north of the Limpopo. In the first place, the Ndebele settlement in their final home north of the Matopo hills was a direct consequence of their clash with Potgieter's party in 1836 and of their wish to withdraw beyond reach of the white man. Less direct but more far-reaching was the creation within South Africa of a community pledged to segregation and white supremacy, whose views were to affect the outlook of all Europeans in the subcontinent. Though a contrasting tradition continued at the Cape, and though it was this tradition that was transmitted to Central Africa through Cecil Rhodes, the Boer outlook set a standard that came largely to be associated with white South Africa, and which was emulated to a varying extent north of the Limpopo.

III

LATER INVASIONS IN MODERN TIMES

The Nyasa Tribes

WHILE the developments that have been described were taking place south of the Zambezi, great events were in progress in the north. Other groups of Iron Age Bantu, then and later passing through the east African highlands, had been settling around the shores of Lake Nyasa and along the coastal plain of Mozambique.

Of the tribes migrating to the Nyasa region, the first about whose early history we know anything for certain are those belonging to the pre-Luba Malawi group called by the Portuguese 'Maravi'. Reference to them was made by the traveller Gaspar Bocarro, who in 1616 made an exploratory journey up the Shire valley, round the lake, and down to Mozambique.[1] Nyasa was subsequently marked as 'Lake Maravi' on the Portuguese maps of the period. Bocarro formed the opinion that the Maravi tribes had arrived in the area at some time in the previous century; it is probable that, coming down either the east or the west side of Lake Tanganyika from the great lakes in the north, they reached the Nyasa-Tanganyika plateau about the end of the fifteenth century. They must have had contact with the Luba at one time, for 'Ulua country' and 'Mwata Yamvo' are remembered in their traditions. From the plateau, under chiefs whose hereditary names even in that early period were Undi, Karonga, Mkanda and Mwase, they moved in the sixteenth century along the west shore of Lake Nyasa, some groups settling down there. By the seventeenth century there were considerable numbers at the south end, still generally calling themselves Malawi.[2]

At some time in the eighteenth century, a considerable portion split off towards the west, forming a distinct tribe or group of tribes known as Cewa, while the people remaining by the lake came to be called Nyanja, or Mang'anja, meaning 'lake people'. Of those taking part in this further migration, some continued neighbours of the Mang'anja, living in the present Blantyre-Ncheu district, while a powerful group led by Mwase moved in a north-easterly direction and settled down near Kasungu.³ It was with these people that the Bemba came into conflict when they crossed the Luangwa for a short time about 1750. Between present-day Fort Jameson and Lundazi, there settled a third group under chief Mkanda; while lastly, to the south-west along the Kapoche river, chief Undi and his successors ruled over a fourth Cewa group. By the end of the eighteenth century, the Portuguese at Tete believed that the Maravi formed a great empire in the triangle between the Luangwa, the lower Zambezi and the lake, but this conception was exaggerated. There is no evidence that any chiefs became paramount over a powerful kingdom such as had once existed south of the Zambezi.

At some time after 1800, Undi's Cewa began to hunt and settle across the Luangwa, in territory which was at that time occupied or used by the Lala and Lenje people under chiefs called Mukuni. It was sparsely inhabited country, and there was little fighting; rather, through intermarriage with these strangers, a new branch of the Cewa was formed, coming to be known as Nsenga.⁴ The first of their chiefs, who are called Kalindawalu, ruled about the year 1820, and fifteen years later some of them recrossed the Luangwa to make villages in the district around Petauke. Here the Ngoni found them after fording the Zambezi in 1835.

The Cewa and related peoples were not aggressive. They herded sheep and goats rather than cattle, and were hard-working agriculturalists. A description of the Mang'anja by Livingstone, quoted in a later chapter, gives a glimpse of their way of life. In the nineteenth century, however, they became the prey of Arabs, Yao and Ngoni, not to mention the slave-trading activities of the Portuguese half-caste traders in the lower Luangwa valley.

Much less is known of the Yao, the Makwa and the east coast tribes in early times. We can give no dates to the appearance of their predecessors in these latitudes, though it was probably

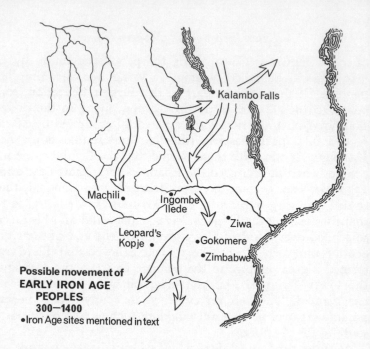

**Possible movement of
EARLY IRON AGE
PEOPLES
300–1400**
●Iron Age sites mentioned in text

Kalambo Falls

Machili ●

Ingombe
Ilede

Ziwa ●

Leopard's
Kopje ●

● Gokomere

● Zimbabwe

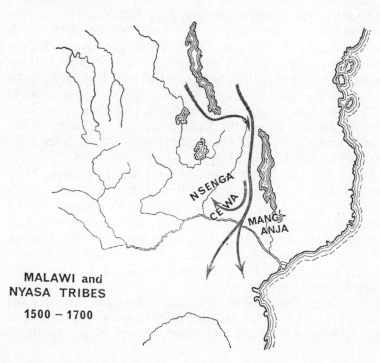

NSENGA

CEWA

MANG'-
ANJA

**MALAWI and
NYASA TRIBES**

1500 – 1700

around the first millennium A.D. They have no traditions of origin, apart from a general conviction that they came from the north. The lack of tradition is most likely due to the disintegrating effect on their societies of commercial contacts with foreigners on the coast, and more certainly to the slave trade, with its consequences of war and the usurpation of authority by men of mixed blood, who were unable to carry out the chief's customary responsibilities.

The Portuguese had contact with some of them near Mozambique early in the sixteenth century, and dos Santos wrote in 1609 that 'the Kaffirs on the mainland of Mozambique are Makwa, heathens very barbarous, and great thieves. . . . Their mode of speaking is in a loud harsh voice. . . . They file their lower and upper teeth.'[5] The Makwa remained in the district for the next two hundred years, benefiting from the passage to and from the interior of trading caravans, and consequently coming into conflict in the mid-nineteenth century at least with the Yao south of the Rovuma.

The Yao themselves say that their traditional home is between the Lujenda and the Rovuma rivers, east of Lake Nyasa.[6] It is probable that they had contact with the Arabs on the coast for as long as two hundred years before the Portuguese arrived, and that their ancestors were among the tribes of 'Zinj' found by the Arabs inhabiting the coastal plain. From the Arabs they learned trade. Isolated examples have been found on the plateau, north and south of the Zambezi, of beads and fragments of pottery and glass, and it must have been such tribes as the Yao who, acting as middlemen, were responsible for bringing these exotic goods into the interior. Our first definite record is in the diary of Lacerda (1798) who stated that a people called Yao (Ajawa) were trading inland and buying ivory from markets that had hitherto been the preserve of the Portuguese. Sixty years later, in Livingstone's time, they were beginning to compete with the Arabs themselves, both for ivory and for slaves.

It was at some time in the 1850s, perhaps because they were attacked by the Makwa, or because of the irruption of the Ngwangwara Ngoni led by Zulu Gama coming south round the north end of the lake, or perhaps because of internal dissension, that the Yao left their home of many generations and moved, some west to the higher ground around the source of the Rovuma, others, in four groups, south towards Lake Chirwa, where Livingstone encountered them, and where they presented the early missionaries with a dilemma they were unable to resolve. By 1876 they were the ruling tribe on the upper Shire, slaving and raiding, and the Shire highlands became empty of people as the result of their persistent attacks. They were of large physique and aggressive nature, and though they did not have the warrior discipline and highly developed political structure of the Ngoni, they had the advantage of guns bought from the Arabs. By the end of the nineteenth century the tribe had lost much of its traditional form. Their chiefs often had Arab blood in their veins, and many of their people were Muslim. It was not till after 1891, when the country was declared a British protectorate, that they were finally subdued after several years of fierce fighting.

The Luba Dispersal

The Malawi tribes have been described as a pre-Luba group. It is to the migration of the Luba peoples themselves, similarly matrilineal and without cattle, who were to populate large areas of Northern Rhodesia, that we now come.

The early Luba had probably left the region west of Lake Victoria at some undetermined date between the tenth and twelfth centuries. The name, possibly derived from the same root as Yoruba, may indicate a West African origin. Skirting the thick forests of the Congo basin, they passed to the west of lakes Kivu and Tanganyika, till they were settled, more as a loose federation than as an empire, in the area between the Bushimaie and Lualaba rivers.[1] This is where we find them in the sixteenth century, when they first appear in Portuguese records. Though a Luba tribe still existed, taking its name from the original stock, a number of clans had separated to the west, south and east. These, though speaking Luba dialects, were differently named and followed increasingly different customs. None kept cattle; all lived by the cultivation of millet, and obtained their meat by hunting. Some were skilled at the mining of copper and iron. Unlike the Shona and other more easterly tribes, they had had no dealings with Arabs or Portuguese, until the end of the sixteenth century when they made contact with the Portuguese on the west coast at Benguela and Loanda, so that a small ivory trade commenced. A century later rumours were to reach them of the Portuguese in the lower Zambezi valley; but when efforts were made to promote a trade in that direction also, other events intervened, notably the great increase in the Arab slave trade.

It is likely that at the time of the irruption southwards from the upper Congo tributaries, which is described in succeeding paragraphs, most of the country between Tanganyika and the Zambezi was empty of people, apart from scattered groups of Bushmen of whom traces remain on the Bemba plateau and around Lake Mweru.² It was in fact the Luba tribes who exterminated the Bushmen in these parts, or who drove them into the swamps and islands of Mweru and Bengweulu. About 1550–60, following the Malawi who had traversed the Tanganyika plateau and moved down the west side of Lake Nyasa, other pre-Luba groups, forming communities from which such tribes as Lala, Lenje, Soli and Ila are descended, were probably establishing themselves west of the Luangwa before the main body of the Luba migration took place. It has, however, been suggested that the Soli and the Ila, like the plateau Tonga, stemmed from the very earliest Bantu settlers who arrived in the lower Zambezi before the Shona period. It may also have been at this time that the Luyi people, forerunners of the Lozi, were finding their way south from the Congo tributaries, across the watershed into the upper Zambezi valley.

It was not until after 1650 that the north-east and north-west of what is present-day Rhodesia experienced the invasion of the Lovale, Lunda, Bemba and other tribes of Luba stock. Concerning the origins of the Lunda there are differing legends, especially between the northern Lunda and southern Lunda versions, but all agree that they sprang from the Luba territory which at the end of the sixteenth century lay in the area between the Kasai river and Lake Tanganyika. There is a story widely told that shortly after 1600 dramatic events with far-reaching consequences occurred among a Luba clan called Tubungu.³ The chieftainship, falling upon a woman Lueji, was disputed by her brothers Chinguri, Chinyama and Dyulu. Her position was strengthened by her marriage to a visiting Luba hunter,

Ilunga, a man of strong character who, taking possession of the royal *lukano* bracelet, bow and drums, assumed the powers of chieftainship. Refusing to submit but not daring to risk a conflict, Chinguri left the country with a section of the tribe and migrated to the west, making contact with Portuguese from Loanda in 1609 before turning back to settle on the banks of the Lui, a tributary of the Congo. Chinyama, another brother of Lueji, took his own clan westwards at about the same time and settled on the Luena river on the upper Zambezi. This group was to become the Lovale tribe, who still occupy that area today partly in the Congo, partly in Angola, and partly in the Mwinilunga district of Northern Rhodesia.

At about this time the people of Lueji and Ilunga were calling themselves baLunda, and were growing in strength. When a grandson of Lueji, Iavo Naweji, inherited the chieftainship he styled himself the Mwata Yamvwa, which is said to mean 'lord of wealth' and has been continued as the title of the Lunda emperors in the southern Congo down to the present day.[4] Aware that Chinguri's people were proving a threat from the west, the Mwata Yamvwa decided to consolidate his position by securing the country to the south and to the east of the Congo-Zambezi watershed, which was uninhabited at the time. Four captains, perhaps five, were despatched on this mission, among them Kanyembe (or Kazembe) Mutanda, who settled a little to the south of the Mwata Yamvwa; Musokantanda, who founded a chiefdom in what is now the Musonoi district in the Katanga, and in eastern Mwinilunga; Kanongesha, who went further west, originating the Ndembu tribe between the Lunga and upper Zambezi rivers; and Shinde, who took his group west and south again, towards the Lufwiji, becoming neighbours of their cousins the Lovale. Their descendants, even today, pay customary tribute to the Lunda Paramount in the Katanga.

By the beginning of the eighteenth century the southward Lunda expansion was completed, and the Mwata Yamvwas were looking eastwards towards the Luapula only eighty miles from their capital at Kabebe, beyond which it was hoped to establish trading relations with the Portuguese. Here lived a tribe of early Iron Age settlers, the Shila, ruled by their chiefs Nkuba, who had themselves driven out pre-Bantu occupants called Bwilile and established a kingdom in the Luapula valley and round Lake Mweru to the west.[5] Soon after 1700 a Lunda regiment under Bilonda crossed the river, inflicting a defeat on the Shila, and ranged onwards across the Tanganyika plateau. The expedition returned and after Bilonda's death Kanyembe, who styled himself Kazembe II, completed the subjugation of the Luapula valley by 1740, defeating Nkuba a second time and making an alliance with his sister. The Shila were allowed to remain on the land, but have subsequently paid annual tribute to the Kazembes. In this second half of the century one or two Portuguese half-caste traders reached the Luapula. Lunda envoys were sent to Tete in 1790. Kazembe V was ruling the tribe when Lacerda came to his village in 1798.

Early in the eighteenth century the Bemba, too, were appearing east of the Luapula. The closeness of their connection with the Lunda is uncertain but they, like the Lunda, were of Luba stock. Bemba tradition says that as early as 1550 the proto-tribe from which they later emerged was situated in 'Kole', which was probably the dispersal area on the plateau in the north of modern Angola. In 1670 they were living on the Lualaba river under a chief who had the title of Mukulumpe or Mulopwe, 'the great one'. This despotic ruler put out the eyes of his son Katonga and threatened a similar fate against Chiti, another son with whom he had quarrelled. Many of the people appear to have been discontented owing to the irksome burden of forced labour they were required to do, and to escape the tyranny they willingly followed Chiti and his brother Nkole south and eastwards, crossing the Luapula at a place called Kashengeneke.[6]

Some time after 1740 the Bemba met the Lunda in the Luapula valley. There were conflicting theories as to whether they fought, and Lunda tradition has no confirmation of the Bemba story that one of their own chiefs was set up in Kazembe's place. Both the Bemba and the Luapula Lunda speak the same (ciBemba) language, which is different from that of the other branches of the Lunda in the west. It has been suggested that both tribes acquired their present speech from the peoples, principally Shila, whom they conquered in the Luapula region. At any rate the Bemba did not remain in the area for more than a few years. Proceeding eastwards in approximately 1760, they passed round the northern end of Lake Bangweulu, at which point certain clans split off from the main group to form new tribes including the Chishinga and Unga. A further division occurred after the Chambeshi had been forded at the Safwa rapids, the dissident section forming the Bisa tribe, which moved away south-westwards to the country between the Bangweulu and Luangwa rivers where Lacerda found them when he passed through the country in 1798. Yet another section, which became the Senga, broke away at about this time, crossed the upper Luangwa eastwards between 1780 and 1800, and settled in the country west of the Nyika and Vipya plateaus. In the hills they encountered the primitive Tumbuka, descendants of ancient settlers from the earliest Bantu migration, and to their astonishment found that among these upland people the value of ivory was unknown, roughly hewn tusks being used for everyday purposes. The Senga in the nineteenth century were to become the victims of Bemba, 'Arab' and Ngoni aggressions, and were rescued in a parlous condition by the B.S.A. Company's forces in 1897.

Meanwhile the Bemba continued their restless search for a home. During the 1760s, still led by Chiti and Nkole, they crossed the Muchinga hills and came on the Cewa in the Luangwa valley. These people were the descendants of that section of the early Malawi who had moved up to the Luangwa under their chief Mwase. Tradition relates that a dispute over a woman led to a hand-to-hand combat between the two leaders, as a result of which Chiti died. At any rate, before long the Bemba were retracing their steps to the north, carrying with them the body of their dead chief, till on the banks of the Katonga stream south of the Chambeshi they came on a patch of thick forest. Here they buried Chiti, and gave the name Mwalule to the place, which remains the burial ground of the paramount chiefs to this day.

Their next move, which was their last, took the Bemba across the Chambeshi and on to the high ground between Lakes Bangweulu and Tanganyika. There they sited the chief's village not far from the present-day government station of Kasama, while Mwamba, a subordinate chief, went further north still. By 1800 the Bemba were living roughly where they do now. During the nineteenth century their power increased, partly through the purchase of guns from the Arabs, after 1860, in exchange for ivory and slaves. Surrounding the Bemba, and especially to the south-west of them, were grouped Bemba-speaking tribes of similar matrilineal custom. Before the coming of the white man at the end of the century it seems that Chitimukulu held sway over the whole of the country between the great lakes of Tanganyika, Mweru and Bangweulu, north-east to the sources of the Luangwa, and south into present Lala and Lamba country.[7]

Concerning the origins of the Luyi, forerunners of the Lozi in the far north-west, there is much tradition but little certainty. It is generally agreed that the Luyi, which means 'river people', came south from the Congo-Zambezi watershed along the Kabompo river, having once lived among the Congo tributaries. Some Luba ancestry is probable. During the seventeenth century they were moving southwards into the upper Zambezi valley, compelled perhaps by the Lunda migration which formed the Lovale tribe. The Luyi found the plains occupied by early Bantu such as Subia and Mashi, as well as Bushmen, all of whom were driven out to the south and south-west. During the eighteenth century they were adjusting their economy to the annual floods, and learning the use of cattle and a variety of crops and other pursuits from neighbouring tribes, many of which were absorbed into the dominant political system. By 1800 there were something like twenty-five tribes grouped under Luyi authority, the Luyi themselves being concentrated mainly in the flood plain area. Early in the nineteenth century Mbunda immigrants from the west settled on the higher ground east of the plain, a movement which has continued sporadically since, and which has been joined by the coming of other tribes from the west of the Zambezi, classed by the Lozi as Mawiko or 'westerners' and including Mkoya, Mbowe, Lunda, Luchazi and Chokwe people.

The Paramountcy of Mulambwa, greatest of the Luyi chiefs, from 1812–30, marked the highest level of Luyi history prior to the Kololo conquest. Mulambwa is remembered for the firm justice of his rule, and for the making of laws on a wide range of subjects including tax collection, the punishment of thieves, the provisioning of armies and the care of relatives of men killed in war.[8] Legislation of this nature suggests a settled and well-organized society, and in fact by the nineteenth century the Luyi formed one of the most highly organized and progressive Bantu states in southern Africa. The only local tribes powerful enough to meet them in the field were the Lovale and the Ila, of whom the former were generally on friendly terms with the Luyi, paying a tribute as a token less of submission than of goodwill, though hostilities occurred at least once during Mulambwa's reign; while the latter were broken up into a cluster of disintegral clans with no overall authority. From the Ila, then, despite their remarkable fighting qualities, and from the Tonga and Toka to the south, the Luyi were able regularly to drive away great quantities of cattle in order to replenish their own herds.

It was in Mulambwa's time that the Mambari slave traders first came to the Zambezi from Bihé country to the west, being in contact with the Portuguese stations on the Angola coast. Mulambwa would have nothing to do with them, thus setting a standard to which subsequent rulers of Barotseland generally adhered.

In 1830, by which time the Kololo were already making their first forays north of the Zambezi into Toka country, Mulambwa died, and after his death the succession of the chieftainship was disputed. The tribe was thus in a divided state when the Kololo entered the plain from the south in 1833, and within five years the Luyi, or the Lozi as the Kololo called them, had been overthrown.

The Return of the Southern Bantu

At the last quarter of the eighteenth century the southern Bantu tribes, following a pastoral and intermittently nomadic way of life, had extended as far as the borders of the present-day Cape province. On the tableland north-west of the Drakensberg as far as the edge of the Kalahari sands lived a series of Sotho-speaking tribes, while along the coastal lowlands the Nguni groups were making their way towards the Great Fish river, beyond which they were soon to clash with advance parties of the first white settlers.

Between 1780 and 1785 Dingiswayo, a chief of the Mtetwa clan, occupying lands in present-day Natal, conceived the ambition to unite under his own rule a number of independent peoples, among them an insignificant section which bore the name of Zulu. Soon after 1800 a young member of this section, Shaka, obtained a position of authority in one of Dingiswayo's regiments, and subsequently engineering the death of Dingiswayo, made himself the chief of the increasingly powerful Mtetwa tribe. The latter took on the name of Zulu, a suitably proud-sounding name derived from a root word meaning 'sky'.[1]

Shaka's military despotism was perhaps the most extraordinary event in Bantu history since the beginning of the migration a thousand years before, and had far-reaching consequences throughout south-east Africa. Within a few years the Zulu developed a military society of a Spartan kind which was not only a political achievement, but made an irresistible fighting machine. Up till this time, however, the Abenguni had been loosely grouped, with an instinct for a pastoral, nomadic life. Though Shaka and his Zulu imposed unity for a time, it was not likely that they would hold together for long. Shaka did not absorb other clans into his own group, but ruled by force and fear. Independent leaders were bound, sooner or later, to break away. When they did so an upheaval was caused which resembled the chain reaction in a nuclear explosion. Not only were the enormous grasslands north and south of the Vaal to be temporarily cleared of people, with important effects on the policy of the Boer trekkers who established themselves there after 1836, but more important from the central African point of view was the violent irruption northwards of three or four aggressive groups that were to become dominant over wide areas north of the Limpopo.

After leaving Natal in 1821 Mzilikazi, of whom more later, attacked the Sotho in the Drakensberg who, led by Moshweshwe, retired to the mountain retreat of Thaba Bosigo and repulsed the invaders. Though Mzilikazi then made his way northwards across the Orange river, the Sotho were disturbed and restless. A number of them, led by a woman named Mantatisi, rebelled against Moshweshwe and broke off to the west, pillaging and murdering as they went. They were not a tribe, but a mixed body of bandits gathered from several tribes. After crossing the upper Vaal in order to plunder the

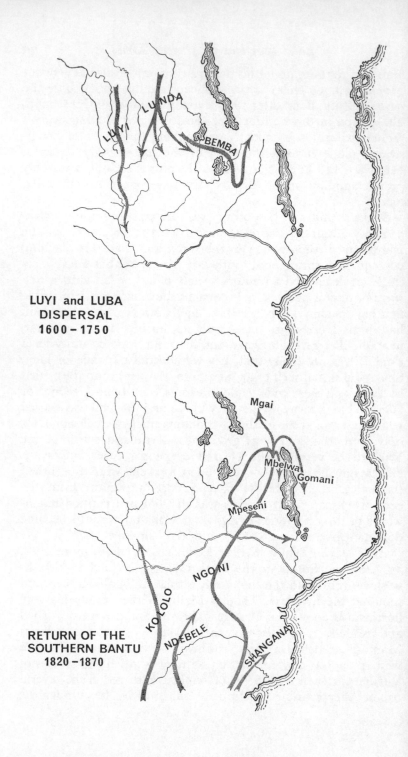

LUYI and LUBA
DISPERSAL
1600–1750

LUYI
LUNDA
BEMBA

RETURN OF THE
SOUTHERN BANTU
1820–1870

Mgai
Mbelwa
Gomani
Mpeseni
NGONI
KOLOLO
NDEBELE
SHANGANA

Tswana, Mantatisi's horde was routed near Kuruman in 1824 by an armed force of Griquas called up from the south, to defend the Tswana, by the government officer at Griquatown and the missionary Robert Moffat. The invading force was split up like a shattered rock. At the head of one small group, the Kololo, which set out for the north, was a young warrior named Sebitwane, not himself a chief but related to the ruling house of the Sotho.

There followed seven eventful years for the Kololo, during which they defeated a combination of Tswana tribes, fell foul of the Boers, had several encounters with the Ndebele, and lost numbers of men and cattle in the wastes of the Kalahari. By 1831 the tribe, now a diverse collection of Sotho people hardened into an organized fighting force, had reached the Zambezi near its confluence with the Chobe.

Across the river the land rose gently into the Toka plateau. This was excellent cattle country, and in a few weeks the Kololo were over the Zambezi, Sebitwane had married a daughter of Musokotwane, and the Toka had submitted to the new overlordship; though on the Kafue plain beyond the plateau the cattle-rich Ila defended their homes with bitter ferocity. But even so far north the Kololo were not secure from the Ndebele, whose impis ranged widely across the Limpopo and raided beyond the Zambezi in successive years. The Kololo went in mortal fear of the Ndebele, a fear which was later intensified when Mzilikazi brought his people to the highlands north of the Limpopo in 1838, and which was to govern their attitude towards other tribes and towards missionary and commercial influences in the second half of the century. When persistent rumours reached Sebitwane of the fat cattle and fertile grasslands of the Luyi plain he determined, in 1833, to make the country his own.

By this time, all was not well in the state of the Luyi. Mulambwa had died in 1830, and the succession had been disputed between two claimants, Silumelume and Mubukwanu. Though the former had been killed, and Mubukwanu was paramount, the country was still divided when the Kololo approached, creating an opportunity which Sebitwane seized at once. His fighting force, seasoned by ten years of war and travel, moved up the Zambezi into the Barotse plain. The Luyi met them for the first time in the Kataba valley, ten miles east of the river, where, using his cattle as a decoy, Sebitwane wiped them out. In three more fights successively further north at Ngundu, Liondo and Limolwe, where the crocodiles joined in the slaughter, the Luyi forces were decimated and the remnants of their army, retreating north beyond the plain, built a fortified village at Lukulu. There Mubukwanu shortly died, the Kololo invested the village, the starving defenders were compelled to eat their dogs, and the new chief Imasiku only just managed to escape across the Kabompo before Lukulu surrendered and the Kololo were masters of Barotseland. The year was 1838.[2]

Sebitwane made his capital at Linyanti south of the Zambezi, appointing officers at various headquarters in the plain itself. He ruled the conquered Luyi with generosity and firmness, and Livingstone, who met him shortly before his death in 1851, regarded him as one of the greatest of the African chiefs he had known. In his account the missionary wrote: '(Sebitwane) was about forty-five years of age, of tall wiry form, of coffee and milk colour, and slightly bald. He was cool and collected, and more frank in his answers than any other chief I ever met. He was the greatest warrior ever heard of beyond the colony, and always led his men into battle himself.' . . . 'The Makololo are by far the most intelligent and enterprising of the tribes I have met.'[3]

The wise policy of treating the conquered tribes of Barotseland on equal terms with his own Kololo was not continued by Sebitwane's son, and discontent gathered among the Luyi. Those who had gone into exile north of the Kabompo bided their time. After Imasiku was killed by the Mbunda in a local foray, Sipopa, a son of Mulambwa, was called to lead the Luyi in Lukwakwa country. By this time the Kololo capital had been transferred to Naliele on the plain, they were well established, and the Luyi, in an astonishingly rapid change, were taking generally to Kololo (Sotho) custom. It was at this time, too, that they changed their tribal name to Lozi, which was what the Kololo called them. Coillard, the missionary, wrote thirty years later: 'It was from the Makololo chiefs, of whom they (the Lozi) always speak with affection and the highest respect, that they . . . formed their ideal of the dignity, manners and power of a sovereign. The warrior tribe of the Lozi, once subdued, had become devoted to all the interests of the Makololo; and if Mpololo, the cousin and successor of Sekeletu, had not shown himself so capriciously cruel, they would not have thought of revolting. But once resolved to free themselves, there was no atrocity they would stop at.' Concerning the Kololo influence on the Barotse tribes, he added: 'We hear everyone around us speaking Sesuto. . . . The same customs, the same manners, the same dress, the same sociability and official code of politeness, great herds of cattle and abundance of milk. It really requires an effort of mind to believe oneself on the Zambezi.'[4]

But the days of the Kololo were numbered. The fatal expedition of the London Society missionaries in 1860, and Livingstone's subsequent disillusionment with the Kololo and theirs with him are described elsewhere. The rapid descent from the pinnacle of warrior statesmanship achieved by Sebitwane can perhaps be ascribed to a lack of a common tradition among the Kololo, a heterogeneous group born in disintegration and held together only by the personality of a great leader. Taking advantage of the unpopularity of Mpololo, and of divisions about a successor, Sipopa led an invading force southwards in 1865. The people on the plain and on the Toka plateau rose with them, and the Kololo were exterminated to a man. But it was because the women and children were spared that the process of grafting Sotho custom and speech on Luyi tradition was able to continue to its completion.

During the years of the Kololo migration, two groups of Nguni stock had also been moving northwards away from the turmoil of Shaka's wars. Leading the first was Mzilikazi, son of Mtshobana of the Kumalo clan, one of Shaka's captains. Mtshobana, after a successful raid, had omitted to hand over all the cattle he had taken, and was put to death by Shaka. Mzilikazi, however, was largely to blame for this disobedience. Fearing a similar fate, he gathered some followers together and escaped across the Drakensberg.[5] After being repulsed by the Sotho, they marched north-west across the Orange river, scattering the tribes, laying waste the country, following Shaka's methods of keeping the children, the young women and the fittest of the young men from the defeated communities as they went. It was at this time in the region between the Drakensberg and the Witwatersrand that they came to be known as Ndebele, which probably means 'those who bear long shields'. By 1830 they were raiding across the Vaal, among their victims being the Mangwato and other Tswana tribes, and still further north the Kololo who were by this time on the banks of the Zambezi. In 1829 Mzilikazi first met Robert Moffat, whose station at Kuruman was not far from his headquarters; but though he liked and admired the missionary he paid no attention to his teaching then or later.

By 1832 the Ndebele chief was across the Vaal river with his capital at Mosega, and from here he twice raided Boer trekking parties that came up in 1836. The Boers took their revenge by attacking and burning his kraal. The Ndebele, invincible in open country against people traditionally armed, could not stand against the muzzle-loading guns of the Europeans even though they outnumbered them by a hundred to one. Once more they departed northwards. Fording the Limpopo, they passed through the fringes of the Kalahari, raiding the Ngwato on the way. On reaching the locality of the Matopo hills, Mzilikazi settled a branch of his tribe there and went ahead with the rest towards the Zambezi. It was probably his intention to cross the river and make his home on the north side; but though he several times raided the Kololo/Lozi and the Toka, the prevalence of tsetse fly in the Zambezi valley and the Lake Ngami region discouraged him. After several months' absence he returned to the Matopos to rejoin the Mnyama section. Here he found that the indunas, seeking a chief of their own, had decided to elect Nkulumane, Mzilikazi's eldest son. Enraged by what he regarded as treachery, the king had these indunas punished, some say by death, on the hill since called Thabazinduna not far from Bulawayo. His sons were allowed to escape to the south, though their ultimate fate is in dispute. Mzilikazi himself settled down some distance to the north, building a new capital near Inyati.[6]

About twenty years of prosperity followed for the Ndebele. The society of the tribe was at this time divided into three sections—the *abezansi*, the true Ndebele from the south; the *abenhla*, from the various peoples incorporated on the trek north; and lastly the *amaholi*, these of the western Shona who inhabited the area now settled by the Ndebele or who were captured in raids, to serve as herdsmen or weapon-bearers, perhaps eventually as soldiers. Outside this immediate area the Shona had to adapt themselves to the forays of Mzilikazi's young warriors, often by rebuilding their villages among inaccessible caves and boulders and by devising subtle alarm systems. Most avoided the harshest fate by agreeing to pay tribute; others resisted, usually to suffer loss of life and cattle, occasionally as in the case of the Hungwe to defeat the raiders; while some, in eastern Mashonaland, never experienced Ndebele raids at all. Here much of the religious and industrial character of Shona society was preserved. At the outset of Lobengula's reign in 1868 there was an intensification of raiding activity, but subsequent expeditions never reached far into Shona territory. While there is no question that the Ndebele continued as a disciplined military despotism to live by raiding round all points of the compass, later European accounts, aiming to justify the occupation of Mashonaland by claiming to have rescued the Shona, tended to exaggerate the extent and savagery of Ndebele power.[7]

Whereas Mzilikazi and his original force were the product of Shaka's statecraft and military training, Zwangendaba and his group, who broke away two or three years in advance of the Ndebele, had never been absorbed into the Zulu system. After the death of Dingiswayo, the Ndandwe chief Zwide was Shaka's greatest rival. Zwangendaba, head of the smaller Jere clan, had on one occasion fought against Zwide, defeated and captured him; but in treating him generously by sending him home with a gift of cattle, had cemented an alliance. Now Zwide and Zwangendaba stood out together against the rising Zulu power. Battle was joined, and Shaka triumphed. Many of Zwide's warriors changed sides. Zwide was taken captive and put to death, and Zwangendaba with his surviving followers made his escape to the north-west.[8]

This small but well-knit fighting force now set out on a migration which was to prove one of the longest ever achieved by a Bantu tribe in two generations. During the first fourteen years, which took them as far as the Zambezi, a new nation was formed, when children grew to manhood and fresh blood was

brought into the group from conquered peoples. The tribe
came to be known as Ngoni, though many other names were
to be accorded to its various branches throughout east Africa
from the Orange river to Lake Victoria.⁹ At first some time
was spent in the coastal region north of Delagoa Bay, till the
tribe turned eastwards towards the Mashona highlands. Here
they caused such havoc among the Shona tribes that when the
Ndebele arrived a few years later the charred remains of
burnt-out villages could still be seen, marking the path that
Zwangendaba had taken. Even today there is many a Shona
legend that begins 'in the time of Zwangendaba'. Later on
however, Shona ex-captives were to play an important part in
the politics of the northern Ngoni. After a year or two passed
in this way, the Ngoni proceeded northwards to the Zambezi,
which they reached at a point near Zumbo in 1835.

The crossing of the Zambezi was an event of such consequence that legendary stories of it are still told in Ngoni
villages. A circumstance that evidently made a remarkable
impression on the minds of those taking part was that a total
eclipse of the sun occurred in mid afternoon, plunging the
world in darkness. The river here, though shallow at that time
of year, is very wide, and a number of cattle were drowned.
Great powers of leadership and organization must have been
displayed by Zwangendaba in the successful conclusion of this
difficult operation. It is said that just after the event, a son
called Mbelwa was born to Zwangendaba's great wife.
Another, Mpezeni, now a boy of perhaps five years, had been
born in Mashonaland.¹⁰

North of the river, the Ngoni moved into Nsenga country, in
the angle between the Luangwa and the Zambezi, which they
occupied for about five years. Then, still plundering wherever
opportunity offered itself, they advanced north-east, and by
1840 were among the Tumbuka in the area of the Rukuru
valley and the Vipya highlands. Restless as ever, they then
moved still further north to the country called Ufipa between
the northern end of Lake Nyasa and the southern end of Lake
Tanganyika. It was here in the year 1845, at a place called
Mapupo, that Zwangendaba died.¹¹ It is said that before his
death he prophesied that a race of white men would come into
the country. He was buried, according to Ngoni custom, in his

cattle kraal. He had brought his people over two thousand miles from Natal.

Disputes about the chieftainship followed, as was so often the case after the death of a great leader. There was, however, no civil war. The Ngoni, unlike the Luyi, had not found a settled homeland from which they were unwilling to disperse, and commanders of independent groups were free to go where they pleased. Zwangendaba's children were still young, the eldest, Mpezeni, being not more than fifteen years old. The old chief's brothers therefore inherited his authority. Ntabeni led his clan northwards up the west side of Lake Tanganyika, while Ntuta took another section north as far as Lake Victoria where, disappointed in the quality of the land, he turned and came back to the region of Unyanyembe, the Tabora district of today. A large proportion of the tribe remained where they were under a third brother, Mgai. Upon his death some time in 1850, a further division of the tribe took place. Although Mpezeni was the eldest of Zwangendaba's sons, Mtwalu had been nominated as the heir to the chieftainship. Many of the people, however, preferred a younger son, Mbelwa, to either of these. In the end, the matter remained undecided, and the tribe disintegrated. One commander, Zulu Gama, who was not of royal descent, led a group round the north end of Lake Nyasa and thence southwards, till he met with the Maseko Ngoni, a splinter group who had arrived there after crossing the Zambezi twenty years before. Mbelwa, after an unsuccessful attempt to follow and assert his authority over Zulu Gama, turned south with Mtwalu to the highlands west of Lake Nyasa. Here they wrought havoc among the local tribes, particularly the Henga, Tumbuka and Nkamanga, who had to retreat to a hungry existence in inaccessible hills, or hide themselves among the rocks along the lake side.[12] Livingstone, travelling up the lake in 1861, described the human bones and rotting corpses lying on the beaches. This reign of terror in west Nyasa country, intensified after a Tonga revolt in 1875, continued until the Ngoni were gradually pacified by the civilizing influence of the Livingstonia mission. Mbelwa himself lived until 1891.

Mpezeni's section, which comprised the remainder of the tribe, also turned south, to the upper reaches of the Luangwa river. Crossing the river to the westward, he came to the plateau inhabited by the Bemba, who had settled there fifty years before. In the war that ensued about 1856, the Bemba had the advantage of guns obtained from 'Arab' traders who were already penetrating thus far west, and the Ngoni suffered a reverse. Deciding not to press the matter further, Mpezeni turned south-west through Bisa and Lala country, and spent some time in the Muchinga hills. Then, about 1865, having crossed the Luangwa, the Ngoni devastated Cewa country. Chief Mangombe took refuge with his people on a hilltop north of the Mpongwe range but, surrounded by the Ngoni, they began to starve and had finally to surrender. Nor was Mpezeni yet content. Moving on south-west to Nsenga country, he dealt fiercely with the people. It was not till after 1870 that this branch of the Ngoni finally established themselves in the hill country around the source of the Lutembwe river, close to the Portuguese border, not far from where the present chief's village stands today.[13]

Thus the Ngoni are found today living east of Lake Nyasa— the Ngwangwara Ngoni—and to the west of it, in Malawi; and also in eastern Zambia around Chipata. By the end of the century, though the political system and much of the old fighting discipline remained, the old Nguni stock had largely disappeared through the constant intake of new blood from conquered tribes. The old Ngoni language, too, was disappearing and today has all but completely gone, being used only to sing the chief's praises on ceremonial occasions. The Ngoni speak the tongues of the peoples whom they conquered— Tumbuka, Nsenga, Cewa, Mang'anja and Yao.

IV

THE DARK CONTINENT

'Viagem à Contra Costa'

By the end of the eighteenth century the Portuguese on the lower Zambezi were, as we have seen, in a sorry condition. Heat, malaria, dysentery and sleeping sickness had rotted ambition, while the hope that springs from health and opportunity had withered away. The slave trade had become the means of existence for many.

The march of events elsewhere in southern Africa, however, was now to stir again the adventurous spirit of the Portuguese. Since 1652 the Cape of Good Hope and its hinterland had been in the hands of the Dutch, the health and vigour of whose settlements contrasted strongly with the condition of Angola and Mozambique. The eighteenth-century wars in Europe had been partly contests for colonies overseas. Interest in Africa was just beginning to grow, both as a source of refreshment for merchant ships, and as a possible supply of raw materials. It was not difficult for far-sighted men to see the importance of Africa for European trade during the coming century. Dr Francisco de Lacerda was such a man. To him the opportunity was now clear for Portugal to make good her claim in Africa, staked long ago by her east and west coast settlements. If these could be linked together by a great trade route, a *viagem à contra costa*, across the continent, a new future might commence for the commerce of his country.

Lacerda was well-educated, a Doctor of Mathematics and at one time the Portuguese Astronomer Royal.[1] As an administrator he had served with great merit in Brazil. His interest in Africa was known. In 1797 he was transferred to Sena as Governor of that station, where he spent a year making plans for an exploratory journey into the interior. Rumours of the power of the Kazembes on the faraway Luapula had for some years been reaching the Portuguese. Lacerda determined to visit the Lunda chief, and then to continue westwards to Loanda. He found it difficult to obtain support from the people at Sena and Tete, and wrote despondently that they were 'men who choose Royal service as a profession that pays, rather than men who love glory and would be useful to the state'.[2] Perhaps it was feared that the new trading enterprise would interfere with the profitable traffic in slaves. Doubtless they resented the demands made by an energetic newcomer upon their flagging energies. Whatever the reasons, volunteers were hard to find, traders cheated Lacerda, and the prazo owners refused him slaves for porters. Lacerda himself fell ill. Persisting none the less, by July 1798 he had an expedition organized, consisting of a priest called Pinto, sixty-two troops including one or two Portuguese officers, four hundred slave porters, and some guides.

From the outset, the party met difficulties. While they were still in the Luangwa valley, many of the porters deserted. The Cewa tribesmen, whom the Portuguese still knew as Maravi, were hostile. Lacerda's fever returned. By the time he had reached the higher ground of the Muchinga hills beyond the Luangwa, his numbers were depleted and his followers discouraged. His own lack of understanding of the Africans and of sympathy with their ideas must have made his troubles twice as hard to deal with. Of the beginning of one day's march he wrote in his diary: 'Tortured with (fever) which attacked me at 5.0 a.m. I set out three hours later. Nothing is more miserable than to have to do with men wanting common sense like these Kaffirs, who are absolutely indifferent to good and evil, who feel only when they suffer, and who cannot allow themselves to be persuaded. . . .'[3] And later in the same vein: 'A Kaffir's mouth never opens without a lie slipping out. It is a people wholly regardless in matters concerning the truth.'[4] Men with longer experience in Africa than Lacerda have made this error of judgement. Others with more understanding of a people with an entirely different background and way of life have taken a rather different view. On the other side of the coin, a great African chief at a later date, complaining of the apparent duplicity of Europeans, protested that 'the white man does not know how to tell the truth'.

Lacerda, like many of the earliest missionaries who came

sixty years or more later, lived in an age when no study had been made of Bantu custom, and the Africans themselves had little or no experience of Europeans. His courage as, weary and ill, he struggled on across the plateau demands admiration. His interest in the appearance and customs of the people through whom he passed finds expression in his diary. Like all early European travellers in Africa, he was struck by the power of witchcraft that prevailed. 'There (is) a belief in this part of Africa (even among many whites, as I saw in Mozambique) that no man ever dies except by sorcery. Whenever a Kaffir accused of his crime denies his guilt, he undergoes the "mwavi" ordeal. It consists in administering the tincture of some bark . . . and the wretch generally dies in horrible pains.'[5] Of the Bisa he noted that he saw 'not an inch of cotton cloth, all being dressed in fibre fabrics', and that though millet and occasionally beans, groundnuts and sweet potatoes were to be seen growing, the people were very short of food. The Bantu custom in greeting also caught his attention: 'They clap palms in measured time, after which they enter into conversation.'

During much of the journey Lacerda, being unable to walk, had to be carried in a litter, but the dry season was well advanced, and once on the plateau the expedition made better progress. Passing round the northern fringe of the Bangweulu swamps, without seeing the lake, they continued north-west and entered Lunda country. On 3 October, Kazembe's village was at last reached. Here came a setback, for the chief refused to see them. In view of the traditional desire of this tribe to make trading contact with the Portuguese, this cool reception is hard to understand. Certainly it was the custom not to receive visitors immediately (though Livingstone, at Shinde's in 1856, found the opposite to be true), but this Kazembe, who was Lukwesa, fifth of the line, kept the Portuguese waiting for eight weeks before granting an audience. The party camped by the Chunga stream north-east of the village and settled down to wait. Lacerda, however, had grown increasingly ill, and died on 18 October without seeing Kazembe.

Father Pinto, the second in command, though not as educated a man as his leader, did not lack loyalty or perseverance. He continued to wait through the blazing heat as the rain season approached till, at the end of November, Lukwesa agreed to see him. The chief now seems to have been reasonably friendly, and willing to trade; but when the Portuguese asked if they might soon proceed on their way to Angola, permission was refused. This refusal, wrote Pinto, was followed by a feast 'to celebrate having closed once for all the Angola road, so as to increase the connection with Tete, whence all their best things come'. It seems that the Lunda were not on good terms with the tribes, particularly the Shila, across the river, and wished to deny them any advantage. Moreover, Lukwesa wanted the gifts that the Portuguese had intended for the Mwata Yamvwa, and in the end had his way.[6] Pinto waited for a further eight months, well into 1799, but with no success. Meanwhile the discontent of his followers mounted. Many deserted, and finally the troops mutinied and set off back to the coast without him. As they went, they spoke against Pinto to the chiefs through whose country they passed, in the hope that he might be killed and the story of their defection not be told.

By July 1799, the priest had finally given up hope of completing the journey to Angola. With the handful of his party who had remained loyal, and with only four months of dry weather left, he turned back for the nine-hundred-mile journey to Tete. Villages in Bemba and Bisa country, that had greeted them the year before, were now hostile. Often in danger of attack, the party lost many of its stores to thieves. On one morning when a raid occurred, a number of carriers threw down their loads and fled; Pinto himself had to go back to recover valuable papers, and narrowly escaped with his life. After crossing the Luangwa and traversing Cewa country he at last reached Tete, in an exhausted condition, in November 1799.

For thirty-two years, no further expedition of importance was sent into the interior by the Portuguese. Between 1802 and 1811, however, a remarkable journey was made by two Portuguese half-castes, Baptista and Jose, generally known as the Pombeiros. These men were of poor education, but one knew how to write, and kept a rudimentary diary. In 1802 they were despatched by the Governor of Loanda on a trading expedition to the interior, and succeeded in being the first known travellers to make the journey from coast to coast.

Held up for some reason not far inland from the east coast

for three years until 1805, they managed to reach Kazembe's village in 1806. Lukwesa's son was ruling at this time, considerably harsher and more despotic than his father. Baptista wrote: 'The Kazembe is powerful in his capital, and rules over a great many people. His place is rather smaller than the Mwata Yamvwa's.' Kazembe, it appears, was well-accustomed to half-caste traders, 'who trade in seed, cassava flour, maize, beans and fish. Ivory comes from the other side of the Luapula, and is brought as tribute by the (Shila) people. Green stones are found in the ground, called "katanga". Bisa and other tribes come and trade. There is much salt in the district.' Again: 'The trade of the Kazembe's country consists of ivory, slaves, green stones and copper bars.'[7] When the tribes in any way interfered with traders coming through to the Luapula from the direction of Tete, Kazembe would punish them, wanting the monopoly for himself, and was in fact at war with the Bisa when the Pombeiros passed through. For some reason again not clearly explained, Baptista and Jose waited another four years at Kazembe's before completing the journey to Tete which they reached in 1811. In his report the Governor of Sena remarked cryptically, 'According to their capabilities, they did a great deal'. Not content with this feat, the two men turned back to the interior, and eventually arrived in Loanda after crossing the continent a second time.

A further effort, which turned out to be the last, by the Portuguese to stimulate trade with the interior, was made by two army officers, Monteiro and Gamitto, in 1831. They managed to reach the Luapula, but Portuguese hopes of extending their commerce into the region were to be disappointed. The slave trade was already increasing throughout this part of Africa, to the detriment of ordinary trade.

The Slave Trade

It is not known for certain when the Arabs started trading for slaves along the East African coast. Arab settlements were being founded by A.D. 700 and it is possible that slaves were being exported by 750. There is, at any rate, clear evidence of a slave trade from Kilwa and Mombasa by 915.[1] It was a trade which differed radically from its later counterpart in the West. The latter had for its object the supply of the New World, where slavery was also new, limited in extent, and as events were to show, shallow-rooted. The East Coast trade, on the other hand, supplied countries in Arabia, the Persian Gulf and further east, whose social and economic system was based on slavery, where there was no abolition movement nor any hope of one, and where the Christian governments fighting the evil had no chance of exercising the necessary power. Since the markets in these countries could not be closed, the only alternative was to suppress, by force if need be, the trade itself which supplied them.

Even here the system was firmly entrenched. Arab colonization was linked with the rise of the Islamic religion and empire, and this was also true of the slave trade that went in its train. The 'Land of Zinj' provided an inexhaustible supply of slaves to Muslim countries where, as the demand grew, the local supply automatically diminished. This was not the original reason for the descent on the coast of Arab colonists, who were in part refugees and in part, increasingly later, traders. Certainly they were not empire-builders, but rather sought wealth where they could find it, and only established political organization with this end in view. Their chief objectives were gold, copper, ivory and sandalwood, but as Europeans were later to discover on the west coast, these were often not in sufficient quantities to be profitable in themselves. The ivory and metals, particularly the former, that were obtained from the interior had, moreover, to be carried on foot sometimes hundreds of miles from the inland plateau down to the coast. All these circumstances, together with the essential factor of African co-operation, combined to create conditions for a lucrative trade in slaves.

It was, however, only in the nineteenth century that sources of supply in the interior were tapped. Even then, not all slaves were exported. At many Arab coast settlements tropical cash crops were grown, of which the most notable were the clove plantations in Zanzibar; the labour was provided by slaves brought down from the interior. The economy of the sultanate of Zanzibar rested entirely on slavery. Not only did the wealthy Arabs own many slaves for domestic and plantation use, but others operated solely in the slave traffic, and a slave market grew up which came to be the largest on the whole coast, though there were others at Mogadishu, Malindi, Mombasa, Kilwa, Mozambique and Sofala, to mention only the greatest. The rapid increase in the traffic in the nineteenth century occurred during the energetic Sultanate of Seyyid Said (1806–56), and owing to the expanding demand for ivory in Europe, so that by Kirk's time it was estimated that as many as 20,000 slaves a year were being exported from Zanzibar alone.[2]

The routes along which slave caravans were conducted to the coast had by that stage become regular highways which annually extended more deeply into the interior. Mombasa and Malindi were the principal slave markets for the region around Lake Victoria, while Zanzibar drew mainly on the inhabitants around the highlands and lakes of Tanganyika. Slaves from the Nyasa region were exported through Mozambique where the Portuguese for long, despite British protests, turned a blind eye to the traffic. A caravan usually included at least fifty slaves, and often many more. Frederick Moir gave a vivid description in 1885 of a party he had met on the Tanganyika plateau which, including guards, was about three thousand strong: 'First came armed men dancing, gesticulating and throwing about their guns as only Arabs can do, to the sound of drums, panpipes and other less musical instruments. Then followed, slowly and sedately, the great man himself . . . his richly caparisoned donkey walking along nearby; and surely no greater contrast could be conceived than that between the courteous and white-robed Arab, with his . . . silver sword and daggers and silken turban, and the miserable swarm of naked squalid human beings that he had wantonly dragged from their now ruined homes. . . . The men were driven, tied two by two, in the terrible "goree" or taming stick, or in gangs of about a dozen, each with an iron collar let into a long iron chain, many even so soon after the start staggering under their loads. The women (were) fastened to chains or thick bark ropes. Many, in addition to their heavy weight of grain or ivory carried . . . babies. The double burden was almost too much, and still they struggled wearily on.'[3] The evident pride of the caravan leaders is also plain from Livingstone's reports. A caravan which he met in the Shire valley in 1861 was led by black (Yao) drivers who, 'armed with muskets and bedecked with various articles of finery, marched jauntily in the front, middle and rear of the line, some of them blowing exultant notes on long tin horns. They seemed to feel that they were doing a very noble thing. . . .'

Callousness towards the lives of their human property aroused Livingstone's surprise as much as his disgust. 'Two of the women had been shot the day before for attempting to untie the thongs. This, the rest were told, was to prevent them from attempting to escape. One woman had her infant's brains knocked out, because she could not carry her load and it; and a man was despatched with an axe because he had broken down with fatigue. Self-interest would have set a watch over the whole rather than commit murder; but in this traffic we increasingly find self-interest overcome by contempt of human life and bloodthirstiness.'[4]

Though pure Arabs ruled the sultanates and owned most of the plantations and slave markets on the coast, it was usually men of mixed blood who travelled in the interior. Johnston in 1895 estimated that in the whole of the British Central Africa Protectorate, which at the time included North-Eastern Rhodesia as well as Nyasaland, there were not more than fifteen 'white' Arabs all told.[5] The notorious slave hunter Mlozi, who operated at the north end of Lake Nyasa 1885–95 was of mixed Bantu and Arab blood, as also were Jumbe and Kopa Kopa. Mushida, chief of the Yeke people beyond the Luapula, had Arab blood in his veins, as also did many of the Yao slaving chiefs in the Shire region. The overseers of the caravans were sometimes themselves Bantu slaves, and sometimes half-castes whose object was to become wealthy and retire to the luxury of plantation life at the coast. 'Arabs' such as Mlozi had similar aims, but established themselves in the interior especially after 1885, partly to step up the supply of slaves by waging controlled warfare from a regular base, and partly to counteract if possible the growth of European influence in the interior. The caravan described by Moir in the passage quoted had been formed by an 'Arab', Kabunda, who had settled in the fertile Lofu valley for about ten years and now determined to return to Zanzibar with the ivory he had amassed. 'So he picked a quarrel with Kalimbwe, the chief, and took all his cattle; then organized a sudden raid throughout all the valley, and every man, woman and child who could be found was seized and tied up.'

If the Arabs controlled the slave traffic along the Tanganyika plateau and across the north and centre of Lake Nyasa, the principal slave hunters in the Shire region south of the lake were the Yao who had recently moved towards that district from the upper reaches of the Rovuma, and by the 1880s were even penetrating as far west as Cewa country in the Luangwa valley. Unlike the Arabs, these people had no interest in coast plantations, and traded in slaves which they sold indiscriminately to Arabs and Portuguese, for the purpose of acquiring cloth and more especially guns and powder to aid them in the period of conquest and land settlement in which they were engaged.[6] They also, like some other Bantu tribes, kept slaves for domestic purposes. They came into conflict with the Christian missions on the one hand and the non-slaving warrior Ngoni on the other, and were finally checked and subdued by the imperial forces under Johnston in the last decade of the century.

The Portuguese in the lower Zambezi valley, far from resisting the Yao, were by 1870 openly dealing with them, either directly along the Shire or through their Chikunda connections in the Luangwa valley. Since 1645 when, losing their grip on the Shona plateau, they were beginning to confine their attention to the Zambezi lowlands and the coastal strip, they had exported slaves from Mozambique to Brazil. When slavery was abolished there in 1888 they continued the traffic by sending them to Réunion Island in the Indian Ocean as well as to San Thomé in the Bay of Benin. Their source of supply was not only from the Yao—a fairly recent development—but also for a longer period the 'prazo' holders along the southern Luangwa. Livingstone commented that while in general the Portuguese were tolerably humane—'when they purchase an adult they buy, if possible, all his relations and thus secure him by domestic ties'[7]—the half-caste prazo owners were much less merciful. Known to the Africans as Chikunda, they held large estates on condition of sending regular caravans of ivory and slaves down to Tete. Portuguese control was negligible, and in practice they acted as independent chiefs; probably the most formidable was Matakenya, with headquarters and extensive property in the

Zambezi valley between Zumbo and Tete. Men such as these were responsible for a great deal of the war and desolation that disturbed the Zambezi valley in the nineteenth century. South of the Zambezi there was little slave trading, both Arab and Portuguese influence having long disappeared from Mashonaland. In the coastal district in the Manica highlands and the sea, however, a former Goanese mercenary captain, Gouveia, also called de Souza, had established himself as a tribal leader and, used by the Portuguese in the 1890s to extend their influence inland, also raided the local tribes for slaves, which were sent down to the coastal ports.

In the north-west, too, a slave trade existed springing from the Portuguese colony in Angola, which was the chief source of supply of labour for the cocoa plantations at San Thomé island. Here, together with half-caste Portuguese known to the Bantu as Mambari, the intermediaries were the Mbunda tribe, an Angola group which, however, was only concerned with trade and not, like the Yao, with conquest. They ranged inland to the upper Zambezi and even as far as the Katanga and the Luapula, and though the Lozi generally refused to deal with them, other tribes in the region, particularly the Lunda, suffered widely from their depredations, which continued after the slave traffic in the north-east had been brought to a standstill. Colonel Harding travelled through much of North-Western Rhodesia in 1901 and wrote that 'owing to the persistent slave raiding of the Valovale and Mambari, the Lunda are in a constant state of armed resistance. Most of the villages are stockaded, and on our arrival the natives rushed away into the bush like rabbits.' He added that Lunda villages 'are destitute of young men, while decrepit and palsied veterans of both sexes are seen in abundance throughout the kraals'.[8] West of the upper Zambezi and north of Barotseland the story was the same. 'Every day I see signs of the slave trade; the trees literally hung with the shackles which are used to put the hands of the slaves in at night, some of them large enough to hold three slaves. These are left behind, often on the corpses of the unfortunate prisoners.'[9] It was not until after 1910 that the last slave caravans disappeared from the Congo-Zambezi watershed.

The African response to the slave trade varied from tribe to tribe. It is a common feature in African history, not only in this region, that the traffic, which fastened on societies like a parasite in the blood, seldom aroused a violent reaction on any scale. The Arabs, like the west coast traders, never met with a concerted opposition; in the disturbed conditions of those days most of the chiefs, unable to prevent the evil, chose to live with it, gaining what they could. Livingstone blamed the Africans as well as the Arabs for what was happening. Unity alone, however, could have barred the intruders, and a united front based on territorial and political organization was impossible in Africa at that time. The Nguni groups and the Lozi alone came near it, and without it resistance to the Arabs, for long armed with guns and with breech-loading weapons in the latter part of the nineteenth century, was out of the question. There was an insatiable demand for the purchase not only of such weapons, which were the key to local mastery as well as defence, but also of the cloth which the Arabs could supply. 'What would we do without Arab cloth?' the Yao asked Livingstone.[10] Equally important perhaps was the fact that to sell a man into slavery was a convenient means of dealing with a prisoner taken in war, or even a troublesome member of the tribe. Mirambo, an Ushi chief in the bend of the Luapula, complained to Harrington in 1898: 'Now you have turned out all the Arabs, what am I going to do with the bad characters in my country? I have no prisons like you, and no askari to guard them. When any of my people got troublesome I sold them for calico to the Arabs.'[11] This was bad enough; it was only a short step to picking a quarrel with a neighbouring village, or paying off an old score.

Different tribes had their particular reasons for their degree of participation.[12] The plateau inhabited by the Bemba was of a sandy infertile soil, so that to obtain sufficient crops the people evolved the destructive slash-and-burn *citimene* system of agriculture. They kept no cattle, and most years were short of food. In war therefore they were not disposed to keep their captives whom they could not afford to feed, and used to put them to death, thus gaining a reputation for ferocity unrivalled in the region. To sell them into slavery for guns and powder appeared a more merciful and was certainly a more profitable course. The Lovale on the Congo-Zambezi watershed, another high

plateau of poor soil, used similarly to sell their war captives to
the Mbunda and the Portuguese. Kazembe's Lunda on the
Luapula on the other hand traded in slaves for different
reasons. Controlling a strict monopoly of elephant hunting,
the Lunda had for generations exported ivory to the coast
through Bisa and other intermediaries, and from the mid-
nineteenth century through the Arabs, to whom they supplied
not only the ivory, and copper, but also the slaves required to
carry it. The trade in ivory increased vastly at this time owing
to the expanding demand in Europe.

Notable among the tribes which stood aloof from the slave
trade, for different reasons, were the Ngoni and the Lozi.[13] The
former, both during the long march from Natal and subsequently in the different groups into which the tribe had disintegrated, had increased their numbers and sustained their
strength by recruiting, from the tribes they conquered, the
young men as warriors and the women as wives. They were a
cattle-owning people, and generally settled in fertile country,
so that not often being short of food, they neither wished nor
needed to sell their captives to the Arabs. The Lozi, a more
settled and complex society, were among the most advanced
socially and politically of any of the southern Bantu, and by
1800 were occupied in a wide variety of skills, including fishing,
cattle raising, agriculture and boat-building, as well as iron
work and other crafts. This variety, which resulted from their
occupation of the Zambezi flood plain, was achieved by the
absorption into their society of tribal groups which had individually made progress in these directions. Though they had a
firmly rooted institution of domestic slavery, the Lozi almost
invariably, including the period of Kololo rule, refused to
deal with the west coast traders. 'I do not sell my people like
cattle', Lewanika told a Mambari expedition in 1899.[14]

Of the profound effects of this trade upon the native population north of the Zambezi, the most apparent was the de-
population following on devastated villages, slaughtered
people and ruined crops. Burton, exploring the Tanganyika
region in the 1850s, estimated that in order to obtain one
slave caravan of fifty-five women, ten villages had been raided
and destroyed and about two hundred people killed in each.[15]
Perhaps this was an exceptional slaughter. Nevertheless when

we consider that of these fifty-five, several would have died before they reached Zanzibar, and when we recollect that for a considerable period twenty or thirty thousand slaves were sold annually in the slave markets, the total loss of life staggers the imagination. Secondly, though petty fights had always been carried on, their violence was sometimes intensified by the introduction, steadily inwards from the coast during the nineteenth century, of guns and powder. This did not necessarily render fighting more destructive; a raid from the Ngoni with spear and knobkerry against another tribe traditionally armed could cause great loss of life. Livingstone indeed wrote that 'the universal effect of the diffusion of the more potent instruments of warfare in Africa is the same as among ourselves. Firearms render wars less frequent and less bloody. It is exceedingly rare to hear of two tribes having guns going to war with each other.'¹⁶ The advance of the 'gun frontier' rather had the effect of altering the balance of power, giving dominance to those tribes supplied with firearms (the Bemba, for example, could not have withstood the Ngoni onslaught in 1856 without weapons obtained from the Arabs) and encouraging them to make war on those who were not so equipped. Within the tribe, too, the traditional structure was broken up when a man could gain a chieftainship by force of superior arms instead of by rightful succession; as frequently happened among the Yao.

A tragic consequence of the slave trade for African peoples was the degenerating effect upon the character of individuals, if not of whole societies. Livingstone repeatedly asserted his opinion that the character of a man was permanently debased by enslavement, and wrote while returning from Manyuema: 'The strangest disease I have seen in this country seems really to be broken-heartedness, and it attacks free men who have been captured and made slaves.'¹⁷ Moreover separation from his family and tribe was in many ways the worst disaster that could befall an African, worse than the fact of slavery itself, and those who were subsequently liberated, only to be submitted to the discipline of organized life on a mission station or other settlement, found themselves in little better case.

Perhaps an equally serious consequence in the long term was the effect on the general view of the African unquestioningly

accepted by many Europeans. The practice of enslaving
Negro Africans, dating back through the classical to the Egyptian
period, was so time-honoured as to make it appear in the
natural order of things that the black race belonged to an
inferior caste. If the Dutch Calvinists could quote the authority
of the Old Testament for this convenient assumption, the long
tradition of slavery had a far more subtle and deeply permeating effect, which even to this day has not perhaps been
completely eradicated from the European and for that matter
the Asian consciousness. Yet it was the new phase of European
expansion, taking place in a new age of spiritual and humanitarian enlightenment, that was to rescue the African peoples
from this malignant traffic in human life—a traffic which,
over a vast terrain, was holding up, even reversing, the progress
towards a more settled and organized existence which some
African societies at least had been making.

Livingstone

The destruction of the slave trade in East Africa, in so far as
it was a product of the humanitarian spirit in Victorian Britain,
depended upon an awakened public opinion. David Livingstone more than any other man was responsible for arousing
the public conscience and bringing a vast array of facts into
the open.

Livingstone started his life in Africa as a missionary, and
though his experience extended his vision, and enlarged his
ambition, his life work from the time that he set foot on the
continent was a continuous if developing theme, devoted to
bringing Christian civilization to the region for the benefit of its
indigenous peoples. The charge that he was abandoning his
calling for the appeal of exploration seems to have troubled his
mind, for he found it necessary to protest that 'the end of the
geographical feat is the beginning of missionary enterprise'.
Again, 'I would not be content to be an explorer only, but a
missionary first and a geographer by the way'. Towards the
end of his life, when the obsession to discover the Nile source
had taken hold of his mind, he wrote in the same vein: 'The
discovery of these sources would only serve to open my mouth
among men.' However Livingstone might seek to resolve the

contradictions in his character, he has been described with some truth as the greatest geographer that Africa has ever seen.

The significance of his career as a missionary, to which in his own mind his scientific achievements were subordinate, lies in his practice of two revolutionary ideas that were to become the twin foundations of missionary policy during the last quarter of the century. The first of these was that though conversion to the Christian faith was vital for the individual, infinitely more important was the influence upon African society generally of the 'wide diffusion of better principles'. In mid-Victorian England where mission work, generally supposed to consist of talking to a native under a tree, or as Livingstone put it, 'going about with a Bible under the arm', this theme struck the right note. The second novel idea was that the territories of the far interior should be reached by mission enterprise at once, instead of gradually advancing the frontiers of areas already being worked. That this belief sprang from personal inclination as much as from experience was revealed in a letter written soon after Livingstone's arrival at the Cape in 1841, in which he declared, 'I would never build on another man's foundations. I shall preach the Gospel beyond every other man's line of things.'[1] His early years at an established mission station, however, served to confirm him in this attitude of mind. He considered that too many missionaries were crowded in the Cape Colony; nor did he find the companionship of 'the brethren' at Kuruman an easy one, thus revealing an individualism that was to appear even more plainly during the expedition to the Zambezi in 1859.

Livingstone had been born in Blantyre, a small industrial town near Glasgow, in 1813. His parents were a class of people whom he described as 'the honest poor', and his later childhood was spent working long hours in a cotton mill. Having early conceived the ambition to devote himself to mission work overseas, he saved money to study for a medical degree, which he obtained in 1840. It was an early indication of realism. In the same year he left England for South Africa to join Robert Moffat, who was working in Griqualand for the London Missionary Society.

Although over ten years elapsed before Livingstone set out

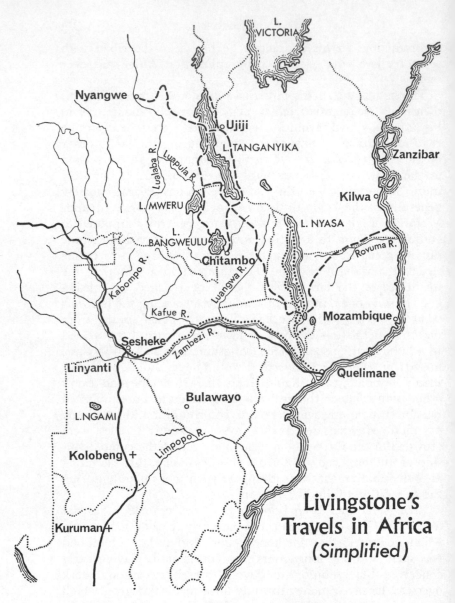

L. VICTORIA

Nyangwe

Ujiji
L. TANGANYIKA

Zanzibar

Lualaba R.
Luapula R.

Kilwa

L. MWERU

L. NYASA

L.
BANGWEULU

Rovuma R.

Chitambo

Kabompo R.

Luangwa R.

Kafue R.

Mozambique

Sesheke

Zambezi R.

Linyanti

Quelimane

Bulawayo

L. NGAMI

Kolobeng +

Limpopo R.

Kuruman +

Livingstone's
Travels in Africa
(Simplified)

.... Present Day Boundaries

—— Livingstone's First Series of Travels

••••••••• Livingstone's Second Series of Travels

– – – – Livingstone's Last Series of Travels

on the first of his exploratory travels north of the Zambezi, they formed a valuable apprenticeship to life and travel in Africa. The first eight and a half years were spent teaching among the southern Tswana tribes. Ranging beyond Kuruman he set up outstations at three places, the last of which was Kolobeng in 1847, where for a short time he made his home with his wife Mary, Robert Moffat's daughter. The following year he wrote of the far interior, as Rhodes might later have written: 'All my desires tend forwards, to the north. . . . Why, we have a world before us here.'[2] It was from the Tswana near Kolobeng that Livingstone heard accounts of the land beyond the Kalahari, forest country well-watered by the tributaries of a great river. He wrote later of this news that 'the prospect of a highway capable of being traversed by boats to an entirely unexplored and very populous region grew from that time forward stronger and stronger in my mind'.

It was a prospect hitherto unimagined. Until the 1840s, Kuruman had been regarded as the northern frontier of permanent white settlement, of which Kolobeng was an uncertain extension three hundred miles beyond. Setting forth from this outpost in 1849, Livingstone with two European companions crossed two hundred and fifty miles of desert and reached Lake Ngami, then a fine sheet of water. On a further expedition in 1851 he succeeded in meeting Sebitwane, the Kololo chief from the upper Zambezi. Sebitwane had on this occasion come a hundred miles to see Livingstone, it having been an ambition of his life to speak to a white man. Each was impressed with the other, and Livingstone later devoted five pages of his journal to the chief. He was making plans for founding a mission station among the Kololo, when Sebitwane fell ill and died. It was an embarrassing circumstance. After making his way as far as the Zambezi at Sesheke, Livingstone returned to the south. Two important ideas had, however, arisen in his mind. The first was that the Zambezi might form the highway for which he was seeking. The second was that 'if the slave market were supplied with articles of European manufacture by legitimate commerce, the trade in slaves would become impossible'.[3] He determined to explore the country further himself.

The London Society approved of his plan and agreed to

look after his wife and children during his travels. Livingstone spent a short time in Cape Town at the end of 1851 preparing for his journey, and there took the opportunity to learn from the Astronomer Royal the technique of making geographical observations. Leaving for the north in June 1852, he reached Linyanti in May the following year. Again there was a friendly welcome from the Kololo, now ruled by Sebitwane's son Sekeletu; but Livingstone's closer acquaintance with Kololo life and custom led him to revise more favourably his opinion of the work of established settlements in the south. He searched in vain for a mission site in the swampy country surrounding the Kololo capital. Rather than turn back and report that 'the door was closed', he resolved to put into execution the second part of his plan and, by reaching the Congo tributaries, open up a path to Loanda on the coast.

Sekeletu provided him with twenty-seven men, some of whom were to be with him for several years ahead. Mostly Kololo, they included Luyi, Toka, Subia and Mbunda. He was supplied with three muskets, a rifle and a shot gun. For presents he carried twenty pounds of beads worth forty shillings. There was one box of clothes, another of medicine, and a third containing among its contents three books—a Nautical Almanac, some logarithm tables, and a bible. A sextant, a compass and a thermometer, a small tent and some blankets completed his supplies. It was light equipment for a journey of over two thousand miles through unknown country.

Passing the confluence of the upper Zambezi and Kabompo rivers, Livingstone came to the plateau of the Congo-Zambezi watershed, and there encountered the branch of the Lunda people ruled by Shinde, whose ancestor had come from Mwata Yamvwa's country nearly two hundred years earlier. The chief had never seen a European before, though half-caste slave traders from Portuguese coastal settlements used regularly to visit his capital. On his arrival at the village, which was of considerable size, Livingstone waited a day before speaking to the chief. On the second day, he wrote later, 'Shinde soon came, and appeared a man of upwards of fifty years of age, of frank and open countenance, and about the middle height. He seemed in good humour, and said he had expected yesterday that "a man who came to him from the gods would have approached and talked to him." That had been my intention in going to the reception, but when we came and saw the formidable preparations . . . I yielded to the solicitations of my men, and remained by the tree opposite to that under which he sat. His remark confirmed my previous belief that a frank, open, fearless manner is the most winning with all these Africans.'[4]

Livingstone was now leaving Zambezi country, and crossing the upper reaches of the Congo tributaries, making his way over the hilly plateau towards Loanda on the distant coast. Here there was more evidence of the slave trade, and the tribes were at best grudging in their assistance and at worst openly hostile. Livingstone suffered from bad attacks of fever and ran short of food, and was very ill when he staggered into Loanda at the end of May 1854. His men were amazed at the sight of the sea, and exclaimed: 'Then it is not true what the ancients taught us, that the world has no end! All at once it says to us, "I am finished. There is no more of me." ' The Portuguese gave Livingstone a most friendly welcome, and he stayed with Gabriel, the British Commissioner for the Suppression of the Slave Trade, at whose house he was nursed back to health during four months. Resisting persuasion to return to England by sea, he insisted on going back into Central Africa, having promised to see his bearers safely home.

In September, therefore, he set out again for the interior. Learning before long that the ship carrying his journals from Loanda to England had been sunk and all his papers lost, he stopped with a Portuguese trader for some months, writing them up again from memory. While travelling, he noted again the effects of the slave trade, and also the amount of superstition prevailing among the people. 'A great number of persons are reported to lose their lives annually by the cruel superstitions to which they are addicted. . . . A person when accused of witchcraft will often travel from distant districts in order to assert her innocency. They . . . drink the infusion of a poisonous tree, and perish.'[5] Elsewhere he wrote by contrast of the natural beauty of the country. 'How often have I beheld on still mornings . . . green grassy meadows, cattle feeding, goats browsing, women wending their way to the water, men sewing under banyan trees. . . . Such scenes, flooded with sunshine, and enlivened with the songs of the birds before the heat of the day becomes intense, form pictures which can never be forgotten.'[6]

Progress was slow on the return journey; perhaps seven miles a day were covered over the enormous distance. Back at last in the region of the Zambezi tributaries and away from the tracks of the slave trade, the 'kindly spirit of the people' reappeared. The Luyi and Kololo were delighted to see their friends again. By October Livingstone was at Linyanti, handing to Sekeletu the Portuguese Governor's gift of a colonel's uniform. Sekeletu wore it for a church service and, says Livingstone, 'it excited more attention than the sermon'.

There remained the exploration of the Zambezi, a thousand miles to Quilimane. Soon after leaving Linyanti, the explorer had his first view of the great falls of 'mosi-o-tunya', which he named after Queen Victoria. From there, rather than descend through the valley and gorges, he travelled over the Tonga plateau to the north, crossing the Kalomo river and visiting Chief Monze's village. 'We rather liked Monze,' he wrote, 'for he soon felt at home with us.' The country of the plateau Tonga, besides, was healthy and fertile and seemed to offer good prospects for a mission centre and for white habitation. This judgement later proved an accurate one. After crossing the Kafue near Chirundu, however, he found the people astride the lower Luangwa, victims of Chikunda slave raids, less friendly, and the aggressive behaviour of Mpembe's tribesmen caused him to fear for his life. A gift of meat, and the statement that he was 'Inglesi', gained him safe passage.

Beyond the Luangwa, Livingstone came on the ruins of the old Portuguese post at Zumbo, and a few days later reached Tete where he was well cared for by Major Sicard, the Portuguese Commandant. From him he learnt the welcome news of the fall of Sebastopol in the Crimean War. The account of Tete in the journal gives a good picture of this three-hundred-years-old trading village, though 'compared to what it was, Tete is now in ruins'. A note on the gold trade is of some interest. Nearby, there were six washing places. 'To the south-east lie the gold washings of the Mashona; still further east those of the Manica, where gold is found more abundantly. I saw gold from this quarter as big as grains of wheat. The people only work gold when they want a little cloth; when they find a piece, they often bury it, from the idea that this is the seed of the gold. ... Besides gold, there is iron in this district, of excellent quality.'[7] From Tete, Livingstone went down the Zambezi by boat, always observing its navigability. At Sena he found 'stagnation and ruin. ... Nowhere else does the European name stand at so low an ebb.' By the time he reached Quilimane he was sick with malaria and dysentery. When he boarded the ship for England after waiting a further six weeks, leaving behind his Kololo who had insisted on staying with him thus far, he had completed a journey of over four thousand miles, that had taken over four years to accomplish.

It was a feat which was to have far-reaching effects on the history of Africa. Back in England, Livingstone was given a hero's reception, which he found both gratifying and embarrassing. Before a world increasingly thirsty for knowledge of all kinds, he had laid open a great tract of country and human society hitherto blank on the map. His geographical observations were of the greatest consequence in the understanding of the continent, the lie of its rivers and the structure of its land mass.[8] His loyalty to his African carriers, and theirs to him, aroused fresh interest in the African peoples, raised them to a new level in the public esteem, and revived the old resentment against the slave trade. His book, *Missionary Travels and Researches in South Africa*, received wide attention, and over twelve thousand copies of the first edition were sold immediately.

The journal contained a statement of missionary policy which is worth recording here as a clear account of Livingstone's views on the subject in his middle years: 'Sending the gospel to the heathen must ... include much more than is implied in the usual picture of a missionary, namely, a man going about with a Bible under his arm. The promotion of commerce ought to be specially attended to, as this, more than anything else, demolishes that sense of isolation which heathenism engenders, and makes the tribes feel themselves mutually dependent on and mutually beneficial to each other. ... Those laws which still prevent free commercial intercourse among the civilized nations seem to be nothing else but the remains of our own heathenism. My observations on this subject make me extremely desirous to promote the preparation of the raw materials of European manufacture in Africa, for by that means we may not only put a stop to the slave trade, but introduce the Negro family into the body corporate of nations, no one member of which can suffer without others suffering with it. Success in this, in both Eastern and Western Africa, would lead, in the course of time, to a much larger diffusion of the blessings of civilization than efforts exclusively spiritual and educational confined to any one small tribe. These however it would of course be extremely desirable to carry on at the same time at large and healthy stations, for neither civilization nor Christianity can be promoted alone. In fact, they are inseparable.'[9]

Livingstone himself spoke in public on several occasions. The most effective of these was at Cambridge University, where he warned that in a few years he would be 'cut off' in Africa. The last words of the address were delivered at the top of his voice: 'I go back to try to open up a path to commerce and Christianity. Do you carry on the work that I have begun.'

Lord Palmerston, then Prime Minister, had throughout his career shown hostility to the Atlantic slave trade. He now gave his sympathetic support to an expedition which should combat the traffic in East Africa. On this occasion therefore, Livingstone was able to travel in an official capacity. The London Missionary Society's hesitant disapproval of his activities from 1853–6 had made him resolve to leave its service, though without rancour. He was instead commissioned as British Consul at Quilimane, with further instructions to make contact with African chiefs in the interior. The principal object was to open up lines of communication. The government wanted trade routes. The churches wanted mission stations. Livingstone wanted both. He was well supplied with funds, a steamer for the river, and five European companions. The expedition sailed in March 1858, and in May had reached the mouth of the Zambezi.

The first object was to study the navigability of the lower Zambezi; but here hopes were dashed when the Kebrabasa rapids proved insuperable. Turning aside to the Shire, the expedition was more fortunate, and the steamboat sailed up and down it

two or three times as far as the cataracts named by Livingstone
the Murchison Falls. On 18 April 1859 he saw Lake Chirwa for
the first time and commented on the beauty of the Shire highlands landscape. On a third trip up the river during June, he
reached Lake Nyasa itself. There was abundant evidence of
the slave trade, and the lake itself clearly provided one of the
great slave routes inland. 'By means of a small steamer above
the cataracts, the slave trade in this quarter would be rendered
unprofitable.'[10] In later years the trade was to show itself less
easily subdued, but in 1857 when the Arabs had only recently
established their grip on the west shore, Livingstone may have
been right. To the south of the lake, the principal offenders
were the Yao. These were already raiding the villages of the
Mang'anja and other tribes, and selling captives to the Arabs,
periodically terrorizing the population of the highlands.

Of the Mang'anja at this time Livingstone wrote an interesting account. They were, he said, an industrious race. 'In addition to working in iron and cotton and basket-making, they
cultivate the soil extensively. All the people turn out to labour
in the fields. It is no uncommon thing to see men, women and
children hard at work, with the baby lying close by beneath a
shady bush. Iron ore is dug out of the hills, and its manufacture
is a staple trade. Each village has its smelting house, its charcoal
burners and blacksmiths. They make good axes, spears,
needles, arrowheads and bracelets. Many of the men are intelligent looking, with well-shaped heads, agreeable faces and high
foreheads. We soon learned to forget colour.'[11] The passage is
expressive of Livingstone's own caste of mind and of his mid-
Victorian outlook.

Early in the dry season of 1860, Livingstone set off on a
journey up the Zambezi to Barotseland. He hoped there to
make contact with the London Society mission due to have
arrived from the south. He regarded himself, besides, as
'honour-bound' to return to their homes those Makololo who
had served him on his first expedition, and who had awaited
his return from England in 1858. His relations with the other
Europeans of the party had not been easy, and now Kirk alone
from their number accompanied him. Together they set off up
the river along its north bank.

Livingstone enjoyed these weeks of travel away from the

slave trade, through country he knew, and wrote cheerfully. The Makololo, too, were happy, and would talk late round the camp fire in the evening. Part of one such conversation was recorded in the journal. A champion of the common man held forth: 'We could govern ourselves better, so what is the use of chiefs at all? The chief is fat, and has plenty of wives, whilst we, who work hard, have hunger, only one wife, or more likely none. This must be bad, unjust and wrong.' This challenge to authority is met with a chorus of approval, but the defender of divine right speaks out: 'The chief is the father of his people. God made the chief.'[12] Politics, if this rudimentary discussion may be called such, formed then as now an inexhaustible topic among Africans; but, as Livingstone elsewhere reflected, thought and discussion had brought little progressive advantage hitherto. 'Men of considerable ability have arisen among them from time to time, and have attracted much attention by their wisdom; but the total absence of literature leads to the loss of all former experience, and the wisdom is not handed down.'[13]

On reaching Toka country, Livingstone learned of the disastrous fate of the London Missionary Society's expedition to the Kololo at Linyanti. He was greeted at Sesheke by Sekeletu. Despite his unfriendly treatment of Price and Helmore the previous year, the sick chief now expressed a warm wish that an English settlement should be established on the Toka highlands. Such a settlement, if led by a man of the Doctor's calibre and fame, would serve his policy; but Livingstone and Kirk were still intent on discovering a practicable trade route to the interior. Plans were already afoot, besides, for establishing a mission in the Shire highlands. The rains were now two months away. Keeping this time to the course of the Zambezi, the party made its way back to the east, having narrow escapes in the Kariba gorge and at the Kebrabasa rapids on the way.

At the mouth of the river they met their new boat, the *Pioneer*, bringing the members of the Universities' Mission to Central Africa's (U.M.C.A.) mission party led by Bishop Mackenzie.[14] A few weeks later, all set out up the Shire to look for a suitable site for a settlement. The slave traders had been more active than ever in their absence, and it was on this occasion that they met the slave party described in the previous chapter. An account of the vain attempt to build a station among the Mang'anja is given later. Its failure, together with the deaths of several in the mission party, was only one of the many disappointments attending Livingstone on this expedition. The greatest personal loss was the death of his wife at Shubanga in 1862. He was involved in constant friction with his European companions, with whom he always found it difficult to work in harmony. There was, besides, a lot of trouble with the first river boat, which burnt quantities of wood without developing much power, and early sprang leaks in its metal plates. The *Pioneer* gave better service, but the mission it had been brought out to establish met with no success. Geographical knowledge of enormous importance had been gained, but the only immediate outcome was that the Portuguese, making use of Livingstone's experience, were able to extend their contacts with slave traders in the Shire area. None the less, it was with regret that he received notice of the expedition's recall in April 1863.

After an adventurous voyage across the Indian Ocean to Bombay in the expedition's third boat, the *Lady Nyasa*, Livingstone reached England in 1864. Here the writing of the *Narrative of an Expedition to the Zambezi and its Tributaries* occupied some months, which were immediately followed by preparations for a return to Africa. This time, he was to go alone. His aims were largely geographical, for the sources of the Congo and the Nile were still in doubt; but in his own mind he was still a missionary, 'doing geography by the way'. Palmerston died in 1865, Russell was less friendly, and in any case the Government considered that the cost of the previous expedition had borne an inadequate return. Livingstone was now therefore independent of both Government and mission societies, and money was raised by friends and from the sale of his book. It was with less lavish equipment that he arrived in Zanzibar in March 1866, leaving in a few days for the Rovuma river and the interior.

This, the last of Livingstone's journeys in Africa, was the longest, at least in time, continuing from 1866 until his death in 1873. It is the story of the heroic wanderings of a man driven by grim determination. When he set out, he was already fifty-three years old. His difficulties commenced at the outset, when his transport animals died, and many of the new men he had employed, some Indians and some freed African slaves, deserted. By the time he had travelled up the Rovuma and passed round the southern end of Lake Nyasa, he had only nine followers left. This made for better speed and discipline, but made load-carrying harder, and lessened the party's importance in the eyes of the people they met. Passing by the area of the present Fort Jameson, where Mpezeni's Ngoni were harrying the local Nsenga, Livingstone crossed the Luangwa and entered the Muchinga hills. Here, in January 1867, his box of medicines was stolen. This loss was to prove fatal to him, and he wrote, 'I felt as though I had received sentence of death'.[15] He might have turned back, but instead went on his way to explore the lakes of Bangweulu and Mweru, of which the latter had been seen by the Portuguese in Lacerda's time, seventy years previously. Despite the setback to his fortunes, his humour did not desert him. Of existing maps a passage in the journal states: 'One bold constructor has tacked on 200 miles to the north-west end of Lake Nyasa, a feat which no traveller has ever ventured to imitate. Another has placed a river in the same quarter running 3,000 or 4,000 feet uphill, and named it the 'New Zambezi', because, I suppose, the old Zambezi runs downhill.'[16]

He was now in Bemba territory, which he had been planning to visit at the time of his recall in 1863. He recorded of them: 'The Bemba are decidedly more warlike than any of the tribes south of them. Their villages are stockaded, and have deep dry ditches round them.'[17] It was in fact Arab influence and the slave trade that had thus laid its mark on the Bemba way of life. The condition of the area was so disturbed that Livingstone had to spend some time at Kazembe's village. There the visits of Pereira and Lacerda were still remembered. 'The present Kazembe,' wrote the Doctor, 'has a heavy uninteresting countenance, without beard or whiskers, and somewhat of the Chinese type. . . . He smiled but once during the day, and that was pleasant enough, though the cropped ears and lopped hands, with human skulls at the gate, made me indisposed to look on anything with favour.'[18] Here too Arabs were permanently stationed in the district, and Livingstone found himself dependent on some of them for supplies. At last in 1869, travelling in company with some Arabs, and sailing part of the way up Lake Tanganyika, he reached Ujiji. His strength was low. From this town, regularly visited by Arab caravans from Zanzibar, he hoped in due course to establish communication with home.

The remainder of his journeyings make a story of struggle against physical obstacles and despair, which is related in pages of his journal that lack most of his earlier enthusiasm. The widespread atrocities of the slave traffic, increasing even as he travelled into areas hitherto untouched, depressed his spirits, while malaria and dysentery made him increasingly weaker. After resting at Ujiji, he crossed the lake and moved slowly west through Manyuema country, till he managed to reach the Lualaba at Nyangwe. Here he was a chance witness of a violent atrocity in which Arab traders, new to the town, shot down in full daylight over three hundred people, including women and children, who had come to buy and sell at the market. Horrified by the episode, Livingstone resolved to retrace his path to Ujiji. Arriving there after a hard and painful journey in October, all his hopes concentrated upon the expectation of relief, he was met with a series of crushing disappointments. There were no letters, his stores had been plundered, and his medicines had not arrived. To him it must have appeared a miracle that, when he had been there for just over a fortnight, his servant Susi should come running up to announce that an Englishman was about to arrive. This was Henry Moreton Stanley, a hard-headed journalist commissioned by the *New York Herald* to find the explorer for a world that feared him dead. Stanley was extravagantly equipped. For a few weeks the two men explored the north end of Tanganyika, and Livingstone's health greatly improved. But he refused to return to Europe, and in the end Stanley left him to continue his wanderings until he died.

At Nyangwe, Livingstone had seen the Lualaba flowing northwards. Uncertain whether these waters flowed into the Congo or the Nile, he none the less determined to find their source. The need to map the river had become an obsession. The accomplishment would at once complete and justify the work of his life. He planned to move southwards towards Bangweulu and the copper mines of the Katanga, where the river was rumoured to spring, and thence to turn and follow the outflow to its mouth. But this was beyond his strength. In September he was again ill. By the time the rains commenced he was crossing the Bemba plateau, and in January 1873 trying to travel round the south end of Lake Bangweulu. An inaccurate reading from a damaged sextant had brought him too close to the lake, and the 'sponges' of the swamp were to defeat him. Unable to walk, he had to be carried through the floods and pelting rain. Though till mid-April he was making notes on the flora and fauna that he observed, he was growing weaker. On the 10th he wrote: 'Oh! how I long to be permitted by the Over Power to finish my work.' On the 29th, 'knocked up quite', he reached Chitambo's. He died there at about four o'clock in the morning of May 1st.

It is not the least remarkable event in Livingstone's story, that his African servants now determined to carry his body to the coast so that it could be conveyed to England for burial. Through many weeks of danger they made the journey northwards to Unyanyembe (Tabora) and then east to Zanzibar. The leaders were Susi and Cuma, and a freed slave called Jacob Wainwright, who alone of them all attended the funeral in Westminster Abbey. There, the inscription on Livingstone's tomb quotes his own words: 'All I can say in my solitude is, may Heaven's rich blessing come down on everyone—American, English, Turk—who will help to heal this open sore of the world.' His appeal had not gone unanswered; already, within a month of his death, the slave market at Zanzibar had been closed for all time.

The significance of Livingstone's monolithic career is not only found in his influence towards ending the slave trade, nor in his geographical discoveries. It was no less a part of his achievement that he understood the Africans in a way that no other man of his time, even Moffat, had done, and showed them to the world as having qualities, failings and emotions no different from those of people in more familiar societies. His sympathy for many of their customs and beliefs, extending to respect for much of their medical practice, endeared him to Africans right across the continent. So also did his unfailing sense of humour. To them he was 'Ngaka,' the Doctor. 'He was a god. There was no other man like him,' an old Lozi tribesman told François Coillard years later. His reputation, legendary as it became, accounted as much as anything for the tolerant reception granted by most Africans north of the Zambezi to the pioneer missions in the last quarter of the century.

The Pioneer Missions

Livingstone saw his own life work as an extension, though a revolutionary one, of the field of operations already in existence in the south. Subsequent events, in the long run, were to justify his methods, though only after arduous struggles and initial failures. It was as a direct result of his first journey, and of the appeals which he made in Britain on his return, that the first two missionary expeditions to the Zambezi were despatched. Indeed the whole character of his work, with his insistence on medicine, practical pursuits and healthy trade, left its stamp on later enterprise. Moreover since the pioneer missions in Central Africa preceded commercial interests let alone administrative authority, they influenced the impact of both on indigenous African society. Their influence was greatest in Nyasaland and Barotseland, and least in Southern Rhodesia, and this fact was to mark indelibly the subsequent course of events even to this day.

The background to this phase of the missionary advance was the evangelical revival in Britain, which generated new currents in church schooling for the growing industrial population and helped to swell the tide of reform that included the emancipation of slaves in the British Empire in 1833. Though many radicals of Benthamite persuasion expressed scorn for humanitarians among the new commercial middle class, whose lively conscience towards the negroes of the West Indies and the peoples of Africa yet allowed them to be so tough with their own labour at home, the missionary movement was to gather momentum throughout the century. It had chiefly been active through the Society for the Propagation of the Gospel and the Church Missionary Society (1776) in West Africa, India and more recently in New Zealand. There the conflict of interests between colonists and Maori bore many similarities to the situation in South Africa, where the London Missionary Society had been at work since 1799. The frontal missionary attack on Africa as a whole was not to begin till after the formation of the Evangelical Alliance in 1846, which aimed to unite all English Protestants, Anglicans and Nonconformists alike, in common resistance to the ultramontane Roman Catholic revival, and which infused new energy into the missionary spirit.[1]

Livingstone's epic journeys and crusade against the slave trade, occurring during the great years of Britain's prosperity between 1850 and 1874, therefore burst upon the world at a crucial time. It is no wonder that a premature enthusiasm gave rise to the tragic expeditions of the 1860s, nor that after 1875 a new series of enterprises steadied into a permanent stream.

The first mission towards Zambezi country was the London Society's expedition to the Ndebele in 1859. Robert Moffat had then been twenty-eight years in South Africa, twenty-two of them at Kuruman. He had left England after the war, aiming to advance mission work inland from the newly acquired British colony of the Cape. There William van der Kemp, joined by John Philip in 1819, was in conflict with the Cape Dutch in his efforts not only to evangelize but also to secure the political and social emancipation of Africans and Hottentots. Moffat left them after ten years to work among the Tswana tribes in the hinterland north of the Orange river. A man of strong personality and unshakeable convictions, though lacking the imagination of Livingstone, he was greatly respected by the Tswana chiefs and had a profound influence upon Khama of the Mangwato. His first encounter with Mzilikazi was in 1829 when the Ndebele king, his headquarters at Mosega still unmolested by the Boer trek that was yet to come, was occupying the country south of the Limpopo.[2] Other visits were made, the latest being to the new capital at Inyati near the Matopo hills, by which time there existed a strong mutual regard between the two men. In 1859, believing that the time had come for the establishment of a station among this, one of the most powerful and dreaded of the southern African tribes, Moffat despatched a party northwards, equipped with stores sufficient for two years. Apart from himself, the expedition included his son John Smith Moffat and two other English families.

The distance from Kuruman to Inyati was some seven

hundred miles, at first through semi-desert country, where the wagon wheels dragged through deep sand, and later across the northern tributaries of the Limpopo where the slow and back-breaking task of pulling the transport through drifts had to be performed many times. These were conditions which were commonplace to all pioneers, missions and traders alike, but were overshadowed by the uncertainty of the reception at the journey's end. 'There lies before us,' wrote John Moffat, 'an uninhabited region for another two hundred miles before we can reach the southernmost outposts of the Matabele, a people so warlike and predatory in their habits that no one can live near to them in peace.'[3] Several weeks out the trek oxen developed an infectious lung disease and the elder Moffat, not wishing to bring infected cattle into Matabeleland, sent a request to the king for help. Mzilikazi sent first a troop of warriors to pull the wagons and then, when this proved too slow, his own team of oxen, a gift from Moffat himself on an earlier occasion.[4] On the border of Ndebele territory the expedition was obliged to endure a long wait through the mounting summer heat, while the king and his indunas debated the wisdom of allowing it to come through. In December, when the rains had already started, the permission at last arrived and the party on arrival was provided with a site on good land by a spring of water a mile or two from the royal kraal.

The elder Moffat returned to Kuruman in July 1860 after extracting a promise from Mzilikazi that the missionaries, dependent on the Ndebele for their lives, would be looked after. The king, and his son after him, never broke this promise. On the other hand he gave the Europeans little assistance in their teaching, and steadfastly refusing conversion himself, discouraged leaning towards it among members of his tribe. Though Ndebele were allowed to listen to the missionaries' sermons, which were regularly preached, their reactions had to be of careful indifference if not open scorn. John Moffat thus described an incident while he was addressing about a thousand Ndebele at Inyati: 'I pointed to the compact crowd in front of me and said, "You men can every one of you speak to God for himself and God is willing to listen to you." I told the boys and girls that, even when they were alone in the gardens or herding cattle in the veld, they could speak to God and he would hear them. By this time I noticed that there were signs of uneasiness. I looked round at the chief, whose seat was a couple of yards from me. He had risen up and stood trembling with rage. He shouted in a stentorian voice, "You are a liar!" This was followed by a roar of applause from the audience. Again he said it, and again there was a thunderous cheer. I waited for the dead silence that fell upon all and said, "Chief, I am not speaking my own words. I am speaking the words of God." The chief slowly subsided into his chair.'5

Matters did not improve with the years. In 1862 a headman, Mongebe, whose interest had grown too strong, was put to death with all his people and his village burned to the ground. The following season, after more than three years of un-stinted endeavour, Emily Moffat wrote: 'We see little of the people. Our Sabbath congregations are small.' She added that one member of the party had taken to bribing the people to attend 'for more than we can approve, and now they expect pay for listening to a service'.6 Sindebele booklets were prepared and printed, but the king absolutely forbade any of his people to learn to read. When Coillard passed through Inyati in 1876 he wrote: 'You will ask me what influence the Gospel has had up till now in this savage nation. Apparently none whatever. (They) have laboured for twenty years in this country. . . . In spite of all efforts and sacrifices, there is no school, no church, not a single convert.'7 It is true that in some ways the mission exerted a considerable influence over the years. Gradually the Ndebele became more familiar with the white men, and less suspicious of their intentions and their ways. Principally through influence on the mind of the king, some political and social changes were brought about so that by 1880, in the time of Lobengula, harsh punishments for minor misdemeanours were less casually inflicted, and the rule restricting marriage to those who had killed in war was to some extent relaxed. But these changes were slender. Among all the Central African tribes, the Ndebele were the most uncompromisingly resistant to new ideas, and through their inflexibility were later to be broken.

John Moffat left Inyati in 1864 and went to work at Kuruman, where he succeeded his father in 1870 when the latter retired to England at last. That was the year of Lobengula's accession, and the missionaries were allowed to open a second station near the new chief's capital at Bulawayo. The mission was reinforced by the arrival in 1875 of Charles Helm, and of David Carnegie in 1882. In that year a Roman Catholic priest, Father Bartholomew Kroot, S.J., came to Matabeleland, and before his death three years later achieved the first Ndebele convert, who was a leper. Meanwhile European traders and concession seekers were beginning to enter Matabeleland, and the London Society missionaries were in demand as interpreters and advisers to Lobengula in the difficult negotiations that in the late 1880s were taking place. No other Mission Society entered Matabeleland or Mashonaland, apart from Coillard's 'through passage' in 1876, until after the British South Africa Company had begun to administer the territory.

If the Matabele mission endured many years of disappointment and failure, at least no disaster befell them. The fate of the London Society's expedition to the Kololo, by contrast, was tragic and swift. Setting out in July 1859 under the leadership of James Helmore, with Roger Price and their families, the party struck north through the Kalahari. Their aim was to settle among that Zambezi tribe who had so impressed Livingstone and who, the Doctor had assured them, would welcome a Christian mission with open arms. It was hoped that Livingstone, who the previous year had returned to the lower Zambezi, would travel up the river and be at Linyanti to introduce the newcomers. Helmore and Price were fresh to the country. The rigours of the desert journey tried them hard. By the time they reached Linyanti, several of the party were weak and ill. Sekeletu, contrary to their hopes, offered them no sort of welcome. His main reason for desiring a resident missionary at his capital seems to have been that he would thereby have an intermediary or adviser who would in some way discourage the Ndebele from making their dreaded forays. For this purpose he had hoped that either a Moffat, whose family he knew stood high in Mzilikazi's regard, or Livingstone himself, would decide to come.[8] The two new arrivals, ignorant of the language and of the ways of the country, were a bitter disappointment. Sekeletu denied them permission to move to Sesheke or up to the Tonga plateau where healthier conditions prevailed.

Obstinately refusing to turn back, Helmore resolved to await Livingstone's expected arrival at Linyanti. The fever of the low-lying place at once began to take its toll. Within a few weeks Helmore and his wife and two of their four children had died, together with a number of servants in the party. Price made up his mind to withdraw. He was short of food, which the Kololo refused to provide, and Sekeletu had made away with most of Helmore's supplies. Gathering his weakened party together, Price started south for the Kalahari in April. Before he had reached its drier, healthier air, his own wife and child succumbed. Weary and broken in spirit, he was found at Lake Ngami by John Mackenzie coming north in his support. Together they made their way back to Kuruman.

Though the expedition had been expensively equipped, the disaster was chiefly caused by insufficient medical supplies. Livingstone, who on reaching Sesheke the following year expressed his bitterness towards Sekeletu for the shameful way in which the missionaries had been treated, declared later that there should be a medical member of every missionary expedition to Zambezi country. In fact, the expedition was steeped in errors of judgement from the beginning, which Moffat might have prevented had he not been preoccupied with the mission to Matabeleland.[9] It was also a misfortune that the Kololo state was on the verge of disintegration and already under the insidious influence of Mambari slave traders. The Kololo seem later to have regretted their part in the incident. Their own troubles were not far ahead. Sekeletu died in 1865, and a few months later occurred the Lozi revolt in which all Kololo men lost their lives. A long period of disturbance followed in Barotseland. Twenty years were to pass from the time of the London Society's attempt, before another missionary expedition arrived on the upper Zambezi.

Meanwhile, on the lower Zambezi, another enterprise met with tragedy the following year. The Universities' Mission to Central Africa, itself a response to Livingstone's Cambridge appeal, despatched a party whose arrival at the mouth of the Zambezi in 1860 has already been described. Its leader, Bishop Mackenzie, was a resolute, even saintly spirit, but regardless of prudence in pursuing what he believed to be the right course.[10] Accompanied by Livingstone, who had just returned from Sesheke,

he proceeded up the Shire to look for a mission site. Beyond
Chibisa's they found the slave traffic on the increase, for the
Yao, having made contact with the Portuguese on the Zambezi,
were raiding and burning Mang'anja villages in the Shire
valley. It was a Mang'anja chief, Chigunda, up country east of
the Shire and north of the Ruo not far from present-day Zomba,
who invited the expedition to establish its station near his
village. It soon became evident that these Mang'anja were
frequently the subject of Yao attacks. Mackenzie conceived the
optimistic plan of meeting the marauders peacefully and
persuading them to leave the Mang'anja alone. The only outcome of the encounter was a scrap between the Yao and the
Mang'anja in the European party, in which the Europeans
were compelled to join for their own safety. In the weeks that
followed there were further affrays and Yao activity made
mission work impossible. Although, in consequence of two
vigorous reprisals, a Yao chief declared his wish for peace with
the English, any ground gained by this temporary settlement
was soon lost to another enemy. In April, Mackenzie died
of fever, and a number of Africans at the Magomoro station
also went down with it. Soon a second European succumbed.
Food supplies ran short, and the remaining members of the
party decided, unwisely, to retreat to lower ground by the
Shire, where two more deaths quickly ensued. In the face of
these blows the surviving missionaries still persevered; but the
following year, 1863, a successor to Mackenzie arrived, Bishop
Tozer, who at once moved the station south to Mount Moram-
bala near the junction of the Shire with the Zambezi. This was
a healthier place, but the local population was negligible and
offered little scope for mission work. Despite Livingstone's
bitter disappointment—he called it, unjustly, a 'cowardly
retreat'—Tozer finally decided to withdraw from the Nyasa
region altogether, and eventually settled at Zanzibar.

The early 1860s were thus years of failure in the mission
field, though the London Society's settlement at Inyati continued its lonely existence among the Ndebele. The trouble
was above all due to physical obstacles. Malaria was still the
greatest enemy. Medical knowledge was insufficiently advanced
for Europeans to survive for long periods in any but the drier
parts of the plateau. Geographical discovery was still in a

primitive stage. Secure and regular routes to the interior across the vast and difficult terrain did not exist, so that support for the outstations could not easily be maintained. News and supplies took weeks or months to reach their destinations. For one reason or another the African peoples themselves were not in a position, or else were unwilling, to give the newcomers the assistance that, in those difficult times, they vitally needed. The circumstances of the Matabele mission were no exception to these conditions. Had it not been for Robert Moffat's long acquaintance with Mzilikazi, dating back to the early days of the Ndebele migration, there is little doubt that the settlement at Inyati would, like the rest, have been extinguished. Lastly, in the Nyasa region, the slave trade and the wars it produced made life hazardous and continuous work almost impossible. More money, men and experience were required, more commercial and political support had to be provided, before the pioneer missions in the Zambezi region could be securely and confidently established.

But relations between Europe and the 'dark' continent were speedily altering. Rumours concerning the natural resources of the interior were beginning to grow. The competitive spirit was being aroused, and men were awakening to new opportunities of science, commerce and power as well as of philanthropy. Forerunners of the new expansion, traders and hunters, as isolated individuals, were beginning to make their way towards the open veld and the great rivers. The white man, the sight of whom in Livingstone's day would often send women and children crying into their huts, though still a rarity over most of central Africa, was no longer in many parts an unheard of spectacle. The slowly advancing influence of the European, early foreseen by such leaders as Zwangendaba and Sebitwane, came dimly to be recognized over the area as a whole. The distinction between the European and the light-skinned Arab or half-caste, and the different type of trade he had to offer, came also to be known. These slow changes began gradually to operate during the 1860s and 1870s. The revival of missionary activity after 1875, stimulated principally by the death of Livingstone, benefited from these circumstances and from wider experience of African travel.

The first of the new mission society operations in central

Africa was to have a decisive influence on the course of events in the country around the upper Zambezi which came to be known as Barotseland, and later as North-Western Rhodesia. That this was so fell out by accident. The Société des Missions Évangéliques de Paris, a Protestant body at work in Basutoland, proposed in 1875, in response to Livingstone's appeals, to send an expedition to Mashonaland. The London mission at Inyati was still continuing its arduous existence but the Ndebele, now ruled by Lobengula, were resisting efforts to bring new parties and establish new mission stations in his territory. Ignorant of this invincible hostility, the Paris Mission equipped and despatched an expedition led by François Coillard and Adolphe Mabille.

Setting out northwards from Basutoland in April 1877, Coillard did not make for the 'missionaries' road' from Kuruman, but passed directly through the Orange Free State and the Transvaal, crossing the Limpopo just east of the Macloutsie river. Some hundred and fifty miles north-east, not far from the Great Zimbabwe, they came upon a Shona clan whose unfriendly welcome was mainly concerned with efforts to acquire blankets, powder and guns. Messengers arrived from Lobengula expressing the king's displeasure at this unauthorized visit to a subject people. Proceeding westwards under escort to Bulàwayo, Coillard met Lobengula. The king took a liking to him personally but resented the intrusion, objected to the presence of Sotho servants, old enemies of the Ndebele, in his party, and told him summarily to take his expedition out of Matabeleland altogether.

Sensing failure and retreat, the party left Bulawayo along the track south-west and arrived at Soshong, the capital of Khama, Christian chief of the Mangwato. Here Coillard heard talk of the Lozi beyond the Kalahari, among whom the influence of the Kololo, originally Sotho people, was said to remain. For linguistic reasons this seemed a suitable field of operations. Early in the dry season of 1878, Coillard's party struck out into the Kalahari.

The situation in Barotseland can now be summarized.[11] After the destruction of the Kololo during one night of massacre in 1865, the restored Lozi chief Sipopa proved a cruel autocrat and was forced into exile and death. His nephew, Ngawina, succeeded him. But a challenger to the title arose in the young

Robosi, a grandson of Mulambwa, whose family since the Kololo conquest had been living in refuge north of the Kabompo among a Luyi tribe, the Lekwaka. In 1870 Robosi gathered his supporters and in quick conflict drove out Ngawina and established himself as paramount chief. Owing to the insecurity of his circumstances, his rule was severe. Lozi hegemony over surrounding tribes including Ila and Lovale, which had lapsed during the Kololo period, was soon restored, but much resentment was felt against the new chief, especially in the southern neighbourhood of Sesheke. A rebellion occurred in 1884, organized by an ambitious commoner, Mataa. A young man of royal connection, Akufuna, was declared chief, with Mataa as Ngambela, principal councillor. The following year, however, Robosi counter-attacked successfully. Known from that time forward as Lewanika, this great man, who came increasingly under the influence of Coillard, ruled Barotseland without further disturbance until his death in 1916.

Coillard's arrival at Leshoma on the Zambezi in August 1878 was thus at an inopportune time. Robosi sent a message that he was building a new capital, and asked the missionaries to return the following year. The rains were imminent and Coillard, remembering Helmore, resolved to make the long journey back to Basutoland. It was six years before he was back on the Zambezi, after spending the intervening period in Europe and South Africa gaining support for the enterprise.

At Sesheke in 1885, the French party witnessed the scenes of the counter-revolution that restored Lewanika to power, described by Coillard as 'one of the bloodiest'. Thereafter Lewanika, firmly in the saddle, was anxious for the mission to stay in his country. This was of particular significance, for in 1884, prior to the Mataa rebellion, a powerful delegation from Lobengula had arrived at Lealui, inviting the Lozi chief to form an alliance in resisting the advancing tide of the white man. Lewanika courteously declined this offer, which he may have seen as a subterfuge. Instead he made overtures to Khama who, though a chief of less standing than Lobengula, had recently accepted the protection of Great Britain. Khama suggested that Lewanika, instead of opposing the white man, should join forces with him against the white man's drink.[12] A contributory factor had been the presence at Lealui from 1882–4 of Frederick Arnot. A free-lance Scottish missionary and disciple of Livingstone, Arnot recommended the example of Khama and spoke on Coillard's behalf.

The Paris mission founded its first station on the edge of the Barotse plain by the Sefula river, a few miles south of Lealui. A school was started and a church built, but response was slow to appear. For years witchcraft investigations, trials by ordeal and summary executions were 'almost a daily occurrence'. Lewanika nevertheless did not withdraw his support, and the European and African members of the mission gradually won the respect and friendship of the people. In 1892, permission was given for a station to be opened at Lealui itself. The site offered was a mound on the plain close to that on which the royal kraal was built. 'The mound,' wrote Coillard, 'is the sorcerers' hillock, locally called Loatile. It is there that sorcerers are executed, being first poisoned, and then burnt alive. . . . The brushwood and thorn bushes are the home of every imaginable venomous insect. . . . Under these thorns lie broken bows and assegai shafts, and human bones bleached by the sun and discoloured by damp.'[13] The mission had by this time been reinforced by the arrival of Adolphe Jalla and his wife. Leaving them to take charge of Sefula, Coillard himself went to live at Lealui.

It is clear that Lewanika held the Frenchman in high regard, and increasingly deferred to his opinion. Though he felt bound to hold to the traditional beliefs, he allowed his son and heir Letia to be baptized in 1898. Use of the *mwavi* ordeal was forbidden in the capital, though not elsewhere, in 1893. It was directly as the result of the missionary's persuasion that the great raid against the Ila planned for 1897 was called off at the last minute. Lewanika never set out on another. The activities of witchdoctors were checked by a law of 1897 which tried to make at least witch-finding illegal, and condemned the witchdoctors of Lealui to sweep the streets of the village.[14] The period 1894–8 has been described as one of 'spiritual awakening' among the Lozi. While conceding the great influence of the Paris mission already indicated, the destruction of Ndebele power in 1893 should not be overlooked. Security, the great boon of European administration, helped here as elsewhere to bring about a revolution in African life.

The missionaries did their best to remain aloof from politics, but it was impossible to stand aside from the stream of events. Late in the 1880s concession hunters had been appearing at Lewanika's court, and in 1890 Lochner, Rhodes' representative, arrived. He was unable to stay for long, and Rhodes tried subsequently to make use of Coillard. The latter described his own position: 'I cannot serve two masters. But if, without any official title, I can be to your Company of any service as a medium of communication, and until you get the proper man, I willingly place myself at your disposal.'[15] It is certain that Coillard's influence, as well as consultations with Khama and observation of Lobengula's predicament, weighed with Lewanika in accepting British protection. Coillard lived until 1904, and was buried beside his wife's grave at Sefula.

Not every pioneer mission was so placed as to affect the course of history. To the remote and exceptionally hostile Ila, known widely as Mashukulumbwe, there came in December 1893 a small party of Methodist missionaries led by Arthur Baldwin. They had already had sufficient discouragement. Reaching the Zambezi at Kazungula four years earlier, they had been held up by the Lozi, who resented this approach by white men to their traditional foes, a semi-subject people from whom tribute was sporadically exacted. At length, largely owing to the support of the Paris mission and to the arrival of Frank Lochner, permission came for the Methodists to proceed as far as the Lozi capital. After a further delay of two years, while they stayed at the Sefula station, the party was at last able to venture eastwards to Ila country. The first station was founded on the Nkala river, a tributary of the Kafue. Five Europeans died between 1893 and 1905. The discovery of copper in the bend of the Kafue after 1900 brought prospectors to the region, and when mining began the mission was brought into closer contact with the outside world. With an ingrained tradition of independence, however, the Ila did not take kindly to new ideas; above all lack of tribal unity made it impossible for mission influence to spread widely.[16]

Meanwhile, far away to the east in the region of Lake Nyasa, 'Livingstone's country', the Scottish churches had been active. Here the situation was vastly complicated by the slave traffic. Two years after Livingstone's death, the Free Church organized an expedition led by Commander Edward Young and Dr Robert Laws. The character of the enterprise from the beginning was coloured by the slave trade and Livingstone's belief that it must be driven out by healthy trade. Dr James Stewart, of the African school at Lovedale in the Cape, had inspired the present mission, which was to be 'both industrial and educational'. Laws, who led the mission for fifty years, was gifted not only as an evangelist but also in a wide variety of pursuits from printing to bricklaying, and was well suited for such a task. He possessed, moreover, the strength of character and diplomatic powers required in the extraordinarily difficult state of tribal politics then prevailing.

Arriving at the mouth of the Zambezi in July 1875, the expedition travelled up the Shire in a small steamer, the 'Ilala', which was taken to pieces at the Murchison cataracts and reassembled on the lake. The first station, named Livingstonia, was at Cape Maclear, selected for its anchorage. It was an unhealthy district; in five years, as many Europeans had died. Owing to the regular passage of slave caravans, besides, it was thinly populated. In 1881 Laws decided to move north to Bandawe, half way up the lake on its western shore. This was the country of the lake Tonga who, as soon became violently clear, were cowed to a state of terror by the raids of Mbelwa's Ngoni living in the highlands above. The Tonga rebellion of 1875, partially successful, still rankled with the Ngoni, though in fact their power was beginning to decline. Laws realized that an approach must be made to the Ngoni themselves, and went to see Mbelwa. The chief was arrogant, angry that the missionaries should have chosen to settle among his rebellious 'subjects' by the lake shore. 'Why do you not come up and live with us? Can you milk fish? We will give you cattle. We are the rulers.'[17] This was the attitude of Lobengula, and that of Lewanika, once more expressed by the chief of a dominant people. The presence of Europeans at the capital was to be a source of prestige, an advantage to be gained. That it should be granted to underlings was an intolerable rebuff. Unlike Coillard, Laws had a convincing argument to hand: supplies came by water, so that a mission must be close to the lake shore. In time, when staff increased, a teacher would be sent to the Ngoni in the hills.

Laws made a strong impression on Mbelwa. When William Koyi, an African trained at Lovedale, of Nguni stock and able to converse with the Ngoni in their own language, went to work at Mbelwa's in 1882, he was accepted by the chief. Two Europeans later joined him. But for the chief's protection the missionaries would very likely have been killed by the hostile tribesmen, who at first treated them with hatred and scorn. Gradually as the years passed confidence was gained, first with medical work and later with a school. The raids on the Tonga and other local tribes continued. Mbelwa's brother Mtwalu wanted to destroy the Bandawe settlement as it was offering sanctuary to Tonga refugees, and in 1887 the position was dangerous. Peace was finally secured by Laws' own intervention, and a substation opened at Mtwalu's village. Mbelwa died in 1891, the year in which British protection over the Nyasa districts was proclaimed; Mtwalu, who succeeded him, followed in 1897. The next chief, Mtwalu's son, was a Christian and an elder in the native church. In twenty years the tribe had become a changed people, unrecognizable to Tonga and Henga remnants returning cautiously to evacuated villages.[18]

South of the lake, in the Shire highlands, the Established Church of Scotland founded their own settlement, also in 1875. The mission was yet a further response to Livingstone's appeal, and its headquarters were named Blantyre after the explorer's birthplace in the valley of the Clyde. The site was a strategic one, on healthy uplands overlooking the Murchison cataracts; commanding the line of the water route, it was later to form a bulwark of British interests against Portuguese expansion.

For a few years the mission ran into difficulties, neither its leadership nor its organization being equal to the enormous problems to be faced.[19] In an attempt to instil into the local population, who for years had lived in conditions bordering on anarchy, a respect for the mission and its authority—in the absence of any other—those in charge resorted to harsh discipline which they were temperamentally unsuited to exercise. Their conduct aroused concern in various quarters including the Foreign Office. The leader of the mission was recalled and his place taken by David Scott. The new instructions strictly confined Scott to missionary work. He was to make no attempt to found a British colony, or to act as 'ruler in the land'; the Imperial government was in 1880 still anxious to avoid at all costs any extension of its responsibilities in Africa. Scott re-organized the mission, and built a neat settlement of well-constructed houses. A large and dignified church of burnt brick lifted its stately head above the trees. A substation was opened near Domasi in 1884, and work on another on Mlanje mountain began in 1890. 'An English arcadia' was Johnston's description of Blantyre when he arrived to take up his duties as H.M. Consul that year. He found the mission, in spite of the Foreign Office, creating an unanswerable case for a British Protectorate.

The Blantyre mission, resisting the Portuguese in the south, and the Livingstonia mission, fighting the Arab slavers in the north, were closely linked with the trading concern started in 1878 by James Stevenson, a Glasgow merchant and a member of the board of the Church of Scotland Mission. Originally the Livingstone Central Africa Trading Company, this later became the African Lakes Corporation. Though short of capital, the Company acted as an important counter to Arab influence and extended its trading operations across the Tanganyika plateau.[20]

On that plateau, the last of the pioneer missions to enter the area was at work. In 1890, extending their field of activities southwards from Uganda and Tanganyika country, the White Fathers, a Roman Catholic order founded originally by Cardinal Lavigerie in 1848 for work in Algeria, made a settlement at Fwambo on the Stevenson Road. Unlike the Protestant missions, this Roman Catholic movement was not inspired by the heroic exploits of a missionary explorer, nor by the ambition to destroy the slave trade, but rather from a continuing tradition of Jesuit work and the need to compete in a field where the Protestants were taking the lead. Apart from unsuccessful Jesuit enterprises in Matabeleland and Barotseland in the 1870s, this was the first Roman Catholic mission to the Central African highlands since the disappearance of the Portuguese Dominicans from Mashonaland in the eighteenth century.

The continual movement of the slave traffic along the Tanganyika plateau made missionary work among the Mambwe difficult. For this reason, and because he conceived the ambition to convert the much feared Bemba into 'valiant and upright Christians', Father Dupont, the mission leader, made plans for moving further south into Bemba country. It was well known that Chitimukulu had given orders against any white man being received into his territory on pain of merciless reprisal. In spite of this threat, Father Van Oost in February 1894 resolved to make a reconnaissance visit to Mukasa's, and somewhat to his surprise was well received throughout his journey. Preparations were made for a new station, but soon after a second visit in May 1895 Van Oost died of blackwater fever. Dupont set out in his place, and in spite of vacillation on the part of Mukasa, threats of fire and slaughter from Chitimukulu, and a warning from Daly at Fife that the Company authorities could guarantee no sort of protection, the station at Kayambi Hill near Mukasa's was founded in July.

Two years later Dupont, who had by this time gained the friendship of some of the headmen, made a bold visit to Mwamba's, but his situation there, partly owing to Arab influence, was so dangerous that he withdrew. In 1898 he was in touch with Chiti himself, when news came from Mwamba's that the chief was ill and wanted medical aid. Mwamba died soon after the mission party arrived on the scene. The people, terrified of the customary funeral massacre, flocked to the camp three miles from the village. Though there was bloodshed and violence in the surrounding country, the refugees were unharmed, and the grateful population christened the site of the new mission station 'Chilubula', or 'the place of escape'.[21]

It is now possible to assess the part played by the pioneer missions during these transitional years in central Africa. The earliest enterprises had been launched during the later years of the period of exploration. The last of the pioneer expeditions on the other hand overlapped the commencement of European administration. By 1875 the big tribal migrations were almost ended. Into this recently formed pattern of peoples the missionaries were the first to come to stay, making their concern the people themselves rather than the topography or the discovery of natural wealth. In this they were the vanguard of the administrators rather than the commercial interests of the twentieth century. Their lines of advance anticipated those of both political and commercial development. The construction of railways over the turn of the century rendered the pioneer approach routes obsolete, and in fact marked the end of the pioneer period.

One of the most notable of the achievements of the missionaries was the personal influence exerted by some of their outstanding leaders on chiefs of the dominant or military tribes. Moffat and Khama, and again Mzilikazi, Livingstone and Sebitwane, Coillard and Lewanika, Laws and Mbelwa, these are examples of the impression made upon autocratic and superstitious rulers by peaceful and dedicated men. Chiefs such as these were intelligent leaders who had inherited a system of tribal mastery and conquest that had become a part of the social fabric, and were exercising authority in circumstances where inflexible cruelty was necessary for survival. They were far from incapable of understanding the ideas the missionaries brought them; of the examples given, only in the case of the Ndebele, inheritors of Zulu ways, was tradition finally too strong. Those missions which worked among 'subject' tribes, or tribes less closely bound under the rule of one strong chief, had in some ways a more difficult task. In the tribe, the chief was the guardian of tribal belief and religious practice. For this reason he was seldom subject to conversion, but if the heir could be won over before inheriting the chieftainship, half the battle in the tribe was gained. Among Ila, Shona and Mang'anja, for example, support had to be obtained piecemeal. Here too the material was more often freed slaves—'detribalized Africans in the midst of a tribal society'.

In some instances, missions were the instrument of pacification; more often they benefited from the order created by administrations in the nineties. Co-operation between missionaries and commercial companies or imperial representatives was easy and inevitable in those days. There could be little conflict of interests between men of a common civilization isolated far beyond its frontiers. It was free co-operation, not an enforced alliance. In 1895 Coillard refused Rhodes' invitation to become the Chartered Company's representative in Barotseland. Laws did not always walk in step with Johnston, who would have liked to treat Mbelwa's Ngoni with a firmer hand. The missionaries realized none the less that their own work could only advance in an atmosphere of peace and security, and themselves shared the late Victorian view of benevolent imperialism as a means towards the millennium of a universal Christian order. Only later were their interests to diverge, when European settlement increased, and government policy widened towards the dual mandate.

The Traders

If men such as Robert Moffat, Coillard and Laws came in search of the hearts and minds of men, others came looking for wealth in this vast region, and for the hard, free and adventurous life which the quest could give. At first, ivory as the prize took pride of place. In those days the highlands of Africa from the Orange river to the fringes of the Sahara teemed with great herds of elephant. For a long time, but increasingly in the nineteenth century, ivory had been purchased by Arabs and exported through the east coast to Europe and the middle and far east. It was alongside this trade that the traffic in 'black ivory', slaves who would carry the tusks, was maintained. But the numbers of elephant that fell in this way to the spears and traps of the Bantu had not seriously depleted the herds. It was not till the European hunters began to penetrate the country at the end of the nineteenth century, with their efficient and accurate rifle fire, that elephant began to disappear altogether from great areas of central Africa.

Ivory hunters first appeared in Matabeleland in the early 1850s. One of them, Edwards, travelled north with Robert Moffat on the latter's visit to Mzilikazi in 1854. A frequent visitor to the mission at Inyati after 1860 was Edward Chapman, who often used to bring up supplies and carry mail. After 1861, more such hunters began to enter the country. Two of these were George MacCabe and Jacob Hartley, who farmed in the northern Transvaal. The latter had injured his feet, walked with difficulty and always hunted on horseback, but none the less claimed twelve hundred elephant in one year. Some hunters went in great fear of the Ndebele and their chiefs, and all were subject to petty thievery, hindrances and arrogance from the young tribesmen when they came across them. Others, however, by their open, friendly and courageous nature, won respect and friendship. George Phillips, who hunted in the country from 1864 until 1900, was well-liked by the Ndebele, who nick-named him the 'playful elephant'. Two of the most famous of the Boer hunters were Jan Viljoen and Piet Jacobs, who after one expedition came back with 10,000 lb of ivory. Another hunter of repute, William Finaughty, once shot ninety-five elephants in a day, obtaining tusks to the weight of two and a half tons. In these early days, elephant were still learning the danger signal that was the report of a gun.[1]

The life led by these men, though dangerous, was free and often rewarding. Their wagons, like those of all travellers at this time, were much the same as those used for generations in South Africa, and which had served the trekkers of 1838. They had no springs, but were built loosely to take the unevenness of the ground. None the less, breakages in shafts, axles and wheels were frequent, and much time on trek was spent in carrying out repairs. A team of oxen usually numbered twelve, but others were driven alongside to replace those that died of disease, thirst, fatigue or poisoned water. Progress across even country was in any case slow, which gave men leisure for thought, and to those with education, time for study and diary writing. Many days, however, would be strenuously occupied in cutting trees from the line of advance, and in crossing rivers at drifts. Here the steepness of the river bank had often to be cut away, the wagon dismantled and floated across the water, and reassembled on the other side. In game country, days were spent away from camp on horseback. Ivory had to be carried by bearers to the camp. In the evenings, guns had to be cleaned and repaired, used bullets recast and new ones made. After the hunting season was ended, or perhaps after two or three seasons in the interior at a stretch, the party with its tattered and sun-bleached equipment would jolt and roll slowly over the hot, thirsty journey of several weeks back to the south, where the ivory and ostrich feathers would be sold, and new supplies purchased for another expedition.[2]

Mzilikazi was unwilling to allow white hunters into Mashonaland, less to protect the game for his own use, than because he feared the Europeans would sell guns to the subject tribes.[3] Some hunters, however, were on good enough terms with him to be granted this privilege. In 1865 Viljoen, Jacobs and Hartley penetrated Shona country north-east as far as the Umfuli river. It is probable that they were the first Europeans to set eyes on this region since the departure of the Portuguese one hundred and fifty years before.

It was on this occasion that Hartley observed old gold workings no longer in use, and it was his reports, and those of the German hunter and geologist Karl Mauch who travelled in Matabeleland in 1867, which led to rumours of gold reaching the south, to the discovery of gold at Tati in 1867, and to the ephemeral 'gold rush' the following year. Sir John Swinburne, chairman of the London and Limpopo Mining Company, obtained permission to survey Tati in 1869, but exceeded his rights by grazing cattle and laying claim to land. His successor, Levert, did the same, and the Ndebele had their first experience of the thin end of the wedge.⁴ Another gold seeker in 1867 was Thomas Baines. Back in England in 1864 after Livingstone's second expedition, he had been invited to South Africa by Mann of the South African Goldfields Exploration Company, and went north intending to explore in the Eastern highlands, having heard tales of 'ruined stone buildings— apparently Egyptian but perhaps early Portuguese, with gold workings nearby'. After visiting Matabeleland in 1868 during the interregnum, Baines obtained a concession in 1871 from Lobengula, to prospect between the Gwelo and Hunyani rivers. It is noteworthy that Lobengula in this document was careful not to alienate from his kingdom 'this or any other portion of it, but retain intact the sovereignty of my dominions'.⁵ Baines found gold, but lacked support in London, failed to float a company, and died in South Africa in 1873. He left behind him however a valuable collection of water-colour drawings of the contemporary central African scene. Meanwhile, mining at the Tati concession did not prosper. Gold was not found in great quantity, and transport costs made its working unprofitable. A number of prospectors returned to the south, a further reason for this exodus having been the death of Mzilikazi in 1868; many Europeans feared that with his grasp on the nation relinquished, the Ndebele would restrain themselves no longer.

A few hunters remained in the country, however, and no harm came to them. Lobengula continued the policy of his father towards the white man, which was influenced in no small measure by the presence of the missionaries at Inyati and Hope Fountain, and also by the instinctive knowledge that the power of the Europeans, behind and beyond these first isolated few, was greater than most of his people realized. So through the 1870s and 1880s the hunters continued to make their expeditions into the 'far interior', some now crossing the Zambezi and roaming further north. The most notable during this period was Frederick Courteney Selous. Arriving in South Africa in 1871 at the age of seventeen, he spent a year hunting in the Transvaal, finding elephant as far south as Kuruman. In 1872 he reached Matabeleland, where he had his famous encounter with Lobengula.[6] Believing Selous to be too young to make a hunter, the king granted him permission to hunt freely where he wished in Matabeleland and Mashonaland, an opportunity of which he made full use. After a visit to England in 1876, Selous returned and spent much time in the country around the headwaters of the Mazoe river. It was at this time that he discovered the grotto caves at Sinoia, and coming upon Fura mountain near the former capital of the early Shona chiefdom, renamed it Mount Darwin. At his instigation the 'hunters' road' from Bulawayo to the Hartley hills was cut, so that wagons could be brought in for ivory. More than once he hunted north of the Zambezi, and on one dangerous occasion narrowly escaped with his life in an Ila, or Mashukulumbwe, village.

By 1880, elephant was becoming scarcer in Mashonaland, the herds being either shot out, or else retreating south-east to the Sabi valley and the coastal plain, or north across the Zambezi. Over the river there was plenty of game, but transport difficulties in this more thickly forested country discouraged most from going so far. George Westbeech, however, spent most of the years from 1872 to 1888 in Barotse country. Brave and friendly in character, he learnt a number of the local languages, and was on good terms with the Lozi including Robosi, later to become Lewanika. His influence at the paramount's court was of material assistance to Coillard and his party when they came to the country in 1878 and 1884.

In the Nyasa region, there were fewer individual hunters, and early trading operations were from the outset closely in accord with mission enterprise. In 1878, as an embodiment of

Livingstone's belief that a healthy trade would drive out the slave traffic, a commercial enterprise was founded by two Scotsmen, John and Frederick Moir, called the Livingstonia Central Africa Company Ltd. This was later to become the African Lakes Company, and was known to the Africans as 'Mandala' after the nickname given to John Moir, who wore spectacles. The Company was founded with benevolent intentions, as well as for profitable purposes; it did not, in fact, pay any dividend for several years. It would not sell guns or ammunition to the Africans, and was opposed to the drink traffic. Its managers, the Moir brothers, have been called 'fearless hunters and undaunted explorers', and also muddleheaded and miserly businessmen. Lugard, at any rate, wrote that John Moir was never a man to give in; 'I always had the greatest admiration for his indomitable pluck.' Certainly both men played a considerable part in the founding of Nyasaland.

The first object of the Company was to have a boat on the lower Zambezi and another on the lake, and a trading post next door to the Livingstonia mission. From Cape McLear, and after 1881 from Bandawe, native requirements such as calico were sold in exchange for ivory and other produce of the country, and labour. Activities were also extended through the Shire highlands south of the lake from a post at Blantyre, and to Karonga at the 'north end'. Meanwhile in 1878 the London Missionary Society had founded a mission at Ujiji, and rather than continue to use the arduous nine hundred mile route overland from Zanzibar, its leaders decided to establish a 'water route' from the mouth of the Zambezi and through the great lakes. To complete this route, the construction commenced in 1881 of a road that was really more of a rough track, across the Nyasa-Tanganyika plateau from Karonga. This track came to be known as the 'Stevenson Road', after the Glasgow merchant, a chairman of the African Lakes Company, who contributed £4,000 towards its cost. Though it was properly cleared for a distance of only seventy miles, the route was functioning in 1885. By this time the London Society had moved its headquarters to the south end of Lake Tanganyika, and in 1887 a new mission station was opened, on the line of the Stevenson Road, at Fwambo.

During these nine years, the African Lakes Company expanded its operations. Although there were many complaints of its inefficiency, and there were objections to its methods of discouraging competition from other trading concerns, it gave a lot of support to the Scottish missions, and also helped materially to reduce the power of the Arab slave traders. These were years when the slave trade appeared to be declining. In 1875, the Sultan of Zanzibar had issued proclamations against the slave traffic inland, particularly from Nyasa country, and these laws, though not fully enforced, had some effect. By 1887, however, the influence of the Sultan was weakening, and Arab power together with the slave trade was about to flare up violently. At the same time, Portuguese efforts to make good their claims to the interior were being revived. These were circumstances for which the Moir brothers were not fitted to deal. Their enterprise was not backed by the enormous resources that later gave the British South Africa Company freedom to exploit its opportunities regardless of opposition, nor were they blessed with such dynamic powers of leadership. Their later pretensions towards the exercise of the powers of a chartered company on the Nyasa-Tanganyika plateau made them unpopular with both missions and Government. It is to their credit, however, that grappling with the problems of climate, staffing and marine transport, they succeeded in bringing a measure of trade into that disordered and strife-torn region.[7]

Meanwhile in Matabeleland a fresh wave of prospectors and concession seekers was appearing. Though Tati had proved disappointing, tales were being told in the Cape and the Republics of rich gold to the east of Ndebele country. Karl Mauch had reported the existence of the Great Zimbabwe ruins in 1873, and of the old gold workings round it. The discovery of diamonds at Kimberley in 1871 and of gold in the Zoutspansberg in 1872 had brought to South Africa a host of prospectors and miners many of whom, frustrated in their first hopes, were willing to try elsewhere. Individuals and syndicates began to approach Lobengula to ask for the right to mine in his country, held to their lonely posts through dangerous weeks in hope of enormous rewards. North of the Zambezi, too, men were seeking from Lewanika concessions to obtain minerals from Barotse country.

V

THE OCCUPATION—
(1) SOUTH OF THE ZAMBEZI

Europe and Africa in the New Phase

FEW African leaders in the 1870s could be expected to foresee the revolution in political control that was to overtake almost the entire continent during the coming whirlwind decade. Great changes had, it is true, already taken place. Most noticeable perhaps was the advance of the 'gun frontier' through dealings with the Europeans in the south and east, and with the Arabs in the east. The slave trade had intensified; why this was, none could know even if they paused to consider. Significant but less striking was the appearance in the interior of a few isolated missionaries, the occasional hard-travelled hunter, even more rarely the explorer's caravan. What did it all portend? Change in Africa, even when perceptible, had usually been gradual. For most the path to the next village led beyond the horizon, and the horizon for the warrior tribes had always been their own.

African leaders were not altogether alone in their unawareness of impending events. To European statesmen in the late seventies Africa was still 'the dark continent'. Livingstone's work had revealed much south of the equator, but no government, least of all the British, thought to act on his discoveries. Kirk at Zanzibar pressed in vain for official action against the slave trade, and William McKinnon the philanthropist could obtain no government support for a commercial concession in East Africa in 1877. The overture to the coming drama was rather played by Stanley with his journey across the continent and down the Congo river from 1876 to 1879, an overture that was conducted by the wily and opportunist king of the Belgians. Leopold had seen what greater statesmen, their anxious eyes on the balance of power in Europe and the mounting crisis in the

Near East had failed to observe, that Africa was to be the new storehouse for the industrial world, and a new market for its exports.

A floodgate was opening. This was not, however, an entirely new phase in world history. The expansion of Europe was already centuries old, and in this very century, since the settlement of 1815 had brought peace to a world in which Britain was the unrivalled industrial leader, there had been a growing stream of European emigrants, though Africa, even South Africa, had been mainly passed aside. Nor was the fight with slave trading a new development. The seaborne traffic from the west coast had been more or less stamped out by the 1840s, and in that same decade the British Government had intensified British naval operations against Arab slave dhows in the Indian Ocean, though to little effect. Mission enterprise abroad had commenced a new wave of activity as early as the end of the eighteenth century; though mostly directed at the Far East and the Pacific, British societies had worked in southern Africa since the 1820s, while in the north the White Fathers of Cardinal Lavigerie began their work in 1848. What now marked a new turn of events was the combination of three factors: the discovery by 1870 of feasible routes into the African interior, of great lakes and healthy uplands; the growth of economic nationalism in Europe and North America, closing the doors on traditional markets for British manufactures and creating new national industries seeking raw materials and assured markets of their own; and the beginning of a new struggle for power in Europe, or at least for a balance of power, led by Bismarck's Germany united after victory in 1870 over France.

Britain was to take no lead in the coming stampede for overseas territory. Disraeli, despite his panegyric on Empire in 1872, and his concern with India and the security of the canal route, gave no thought to a new empire in Africa. In the west, the long fight with the slave trade was over. The trading post at Lagos was declared a British protectorate in 1862, but in 1865 a Parliamentary committee expressed the view that Britain should withdraw rather than extend its influence in the region.[1] Now that quinine was widely used, ships plied the coast for ivory and palm oil, but competitors were few, and free trade governments were not inclined to establish monopolies. In the north, it is true, control of the Suez canal involved a reluctant British Government in the administration of Egypt in 1881, but this was with every express intention of withdrawing at the first opportunity; certainly there was no thought yet that the exercise of power at the delta must mean control of the Nile source more than two thousand miles southward. In the east, operations against the Arab slave trade were strictly confined to the blue waters of the Indian Ocean.

All this was to change. It was not the British Government which changed it, but the commercial ambitions of Peters and the German Colonial Society, of William Taubman Goldie and his National Africa Company in the Niger delta, of Leopold in the Congo; then of the French Government in North Africa, incensed with the British coup in Egypt, and of the Portuguese, dreaming of reviving past glories. Above all perhaps of Bismarck, seeking Germany's security by involving her neighbours in colonial conflicts—Bismarck who, when referred by the explorer Eugen Wolf to a map of Africa in 1884 replied, 'My map of Africa lies in Europe. Here lies Russia, here lies France, and we are in the middle; that is my map of Africa.'[2] The remark was no idle one, and events were often to show that despite all efforts by 'men on the spot', colonial frontiers in Africa were to be drawn as the situation in Europe dictated.

Bismarck had his opportunity with the international conference on Africa, arising out of a border dispute between Leopold's Congo and Portuguese Angola, which was held at Berlin during 1884–5. The conference delimited spheres of interest between Germany, France and Britain in the bend of West Africa, and declared a free trade area right across the continent from the mouth of the Congo in the west to the Zambezi delta in the east.[3] The boundaries of the Congo Free State were roughly outlined. By 1886, Germany was laying claim to East as well as South-West Africa, and Britain was embroiled with France in the north and north-west. Much of the ground lost by Britain was due to the unwillingness of Gladstone's Liberal governments from 1880–5 to extend British responsibilities in the imperial field. The year 1885, a critical one in Africa, had seen Britain beset by crises at home and abroad: agonizing reappraisals about Ireland, disaster at Khartoum, the imminence of war with Russia over a remote Afghan frontier post. With the establishment of Salisbury's strong Unionist administration in 1886, a firmer policy commenced. Spheres of interest for Britain and Germany were marked out in East Africa in the 1886 agreement, and a charter given to McKinnon's enterprise, now at last formed as the Imperial British East Africa Company. Salisbury, his own Foreign Secretary, was not a man of grand designs, rather of cautious diplomacy; but he was not inhibited as Gladstone had been by a reluctance to use means inconsistent with principle, for an end perhaps expedient for national greatness now but questionable for the future. Limited instead only by the threat of isolation in Europe, and by Parliamentary insistence on economy at home, he had a real sympathy with the philanthropists working for peace in East Africa, and from 1890 a growing concern for control of the upper Nile as an anchor for the British position in Egypt.[4]

In this, Salisbury was moving with the tide of British opinion. Since the seventies, Ruskin and Froude had been lecturing at Oxford, the former on the contribution to world civilization that it was the island race's unique opportunity to make, and the latter on the benefit that the country would derive from the establishment of a commonwealth bound together by strong if invisible links; of colonies in which its urban populations, condemned now to live amidst 'foul drains and smoke blacks and the eternal clank of machinery', could instead be reared 'in the exercise of plough and spade, in the free air and sunshine'.[5] Such sentiments accompanied a renewed spate of emigration to North America and Australasia, where new enthusiasms awoke for the British connection; but in Africa as always the complex situation presented different problems. Gold seekers, flooding to the Rand after 1886, paved the way for new tensions between Britain and the South African Republic. In Central, East and West Africa, the exploits of traders and concession seekers called forth a warning from W. T. Stead, the clear-sighted and influential editor of the *Pall Mall Gazette*. While giving sympathetic recognition, he wrote, to the building up of new empires beyond the sea, and to 'the peopling of waste and savage continents with men of

our speech and lineage', it was the duty of the Imperial
Government 'to follow the adventurers with its authority, and
to restrain the violent impulses of its hardy frontiersmen'.
'We can at least act as the outside conscience of the colonists,
reminding them of the stress and strain of local temptations,
of the higher law of justice and morality, and of right.'[6] This
indeed was the policy most closely followed by Salisbury in
carefully balancing, on the fulcrum of national policy, the
powerful forces with which he was faced: the visionary imperialism of Rhodes, the humanitarian pressure of the churches
and the Aborigines Protection Society, and the outspoken
criticism of Radical Little Englanders such as Henry Labouch-
ere, editor of *Truth*, the magazine that gave so much offence to
the Rhodesian pioneers after 1890.

In Africa, from Cairo to the Cape, these conflicting policies
met and mingled. In the north, German pressure on Uganda
from the east, Italian exploits in Eritrea, and French penetration from Equatorial Africa in the west, awoke Salisbury's concern for the Nile source, and his sympathy for the I.B.E.A.
Company's claim made by Frederick Jackson in defiance of
German efforts, to control of the disputed interior. To the southward, most of East Africa had been consigned to the German
sphere in 1886. The London Missionary Society, however, was
active at the north end of Lake Tanganyika, providing a
nucleus of hostility to the slave trade and a possible hope that the
wasp's waist for Rhodes' Cape to Cairo communications might
be preserved. Further south still, along Lake Nyasa and the
Shire, the voice of national policy was hardly heard. This land,
'Livingstone's country', was rather the acknowledged preserve
of the Scottish churches, and by 1890 the scene of a combined
attack on Arab slave trading and Portuguese imperialism in
defence of Christian evangelism and the welfare of its strife-torn
native peoples. Lastly in South Africa, Cecil Rhodes proclaimed
a policy of federation within the British Empire, that would
eliminate 'Krugerism' in the Transvaal; this to be achieved by
surrounding the Republic, to the west as had been done by the
annexation of Bechuanaland in 1885, to the north by treaty
with Lobengula and the settlement of Mashonaland, and to the
east by the cession to Britain of Delagoa Bay, and the acquisition of as much else of Portuguese territory as might be won by

force or fraud. Beyond this, Rhodes dreamed of an all red route to Cairo and the establishment of a British sphere at least as far as Tanganyika lake.

Central Africa therefore, particularly the wide territory between the Zambezi and the Tanganyika plateau, was the meeting place of Rhodes' imperialism coming from the south, backed by his political position in the Cape Government, his influence in London and of course the millions of De Beers; and the humanitarian interest penetrating from the north and east, intent on eradicating the slave trade and intertribal war, and establishing a peaceful administration under which the African peoples could prosper. This interest was supported by the British Government, at once more powerful and more pettifogging than Rhodes. Throughout the area therefore policies were bound to clash, and the Imperial Government inevitably must find itself restraining 'the violent impulses of its hard frontiersmen', if not yet acting as 'the outside conscience of its colonists'. The latter was a role to be delayed for the best part of two generations, for in the meantime pressure from foreign governments, hostility to barbarism, and the exigencies facing men with common problems in wild and open country, enforced a co-operation between commercial enterprise and benevolent imperialism that often cracked but never sundered.

The Converging Forces of Imperialism

The supreme exponent of nineteenth-century commercial enterprise in the colonial field was Cecil Rhodes, fifth son of an English country clergyman. Measured in millions his exploits rivalled those of the Barings with their investment empires in Canada and the Argentine, and the Rothschilds dominating the stock exchanges of London, Paris and New York. Unlike these, Rhodes was a self-made man, and, moreover, used his wealth not to create more again but to further vast designs of his own. He had come to South Africa at the age of seventeen to join a brother who was planting cotton in Natal. The reason for his emigration was a sickly constitution caused by a weak lung, though Rhodes liked afterwards to claim that it was 'the eternal cold mutton' that drove him abroad.

South Africa at this time provided an exceptional climate but indeterminate prospects.[1] Its separate states struggled individually with severe difficulties that they could better have handled as one. The Cape Colony clamoured for internal self-government which the United Kingdom, fearing domestic recriminations over the surrender of native policy, was unwilling to give. Expensive 'kaffir wars' on the eastern frontier meanwhile drained the resources of home and colonial governments. In Natal the growing of sugar and cotton had led to the import of Indian labour with its attendant problems and the small European population, ever anxious of the Drakensberg tribes, was years away from managing its own affairs. The Free State was perennially beset by quarrels with the intractable Basuto, while to the north of the Vaal the coffers of the republican government at Pretoria were empty. The scattered farms often lay neglected while the Boers served on commando to guard the southern frontier against renascent Zulu power. Indeed, the African threat to white settlement was greater at this time than ever before or since, for the impoverished European communities beyond the western Cape were greatly outnumbered by a militant African population among whom firearms had spread widely in recent years. Rhodes' arrival in the country thus occurred at a critical time in its history. Within two decades the balance was to be sharply reversed in favour of European dominion.

Two years previously, in 1868, a diamond had been picked up in a riverbed in Griqualand West beyond the Orange. The news had rippled round the world. A colony of diggers gathered on the backveld farm. In October 1871 the young Rhodes, responding to the first of many calls of opportunity, crossed the Drakensberg and the wide plains of the Orange Free State to this centre of rough life, broken men and sudden fortunes. His capacity for driving a hard bargain through determined persuasion speedily emerged. He became a well-known figure among the hundreds of men, black and white, digging and sifting on the claims. Often he was to be seen sitting on an upturned bucket, watching his Africans at work, brooding on wider schemes. A visit to his brother, prospecting in the Zoutspansberg two hundred and fifty miles away, opened his eyes to the empty condition of the seemingly limitless north. He grew to love the harsh invigorating country with its brilliant colours and wide skies. At Kimberley he advanced his interests by tenacity and enterprise. The yellow diamond-bearing ground was giving way to blue. Many thought the blue ground held no diamonds, and sold their claims. Rhodes bought them, convinced the pessimists were wrong. The excavations deepened, competition dislocated the work, and the need for a combined organization became clear to the leading rivals including J. A. Robinson, Barney Barnato and Rhodes himself.

As his wealth increased his ambitions widened. He was to play a leading part in the affairs of Kimberley, perhaps of the Cape and all South Africa. Aiming to enhance his status by completing his interrupted education in the traditional way, he returned to England in 1873 and entered Oriel College, Oxford. There he studied till 1878, visiting South Africa every year as much for his health as to supervise his business.

These were formative years for Rhodes. The double life at Oxford and Kimberley served to emphasize the dual nature of his personality which made him so controversial a figure during and after his lifetime. To the challenge of the commercial world he instinctively responded. Money itself did not interest him, it was the game that mattered. He had discovered that it was a game he could win by force of his vehement personality and sound business judgement. An opponent could always be 'squared' by dint of enthusiastic persuasion backed by financial resources and, if necessary, by the *fait accompli*. At the same time he was never quite able to throw off the idealism and self-dedication instilled into him by his childhood in a country vicarage. Here Oxford provided the missing factor. John Ruskin's inaugural lecture was recently remembered: 'Have a fixed purpose of some kind for your country and yourselves. . . . Make your country a royal throne of kings, a sceptred isle, for all the world a source of light, a centre of peace. . . . This is what England must do or perish: she must form colonies abroad as far and fast as she is able.'[2] In place of an orthodox religious belief Rhodes developed theories of his own; their basis was a form of mystical Darwinism derived at second hand from Wynwood Read's *Martyrdom of Man*. To his rather boyish imagination, the English-speaking race represented the highest level to which humanity had yet evolved. The divine will, if such existed, must be that through this chosen instrument a state of society based upon justice, liberty and peace would be created. His own purpose in life must be to further this state of society. In an early will he left his entire estate to the Secretary of State for the Colonies, for the establishment of an organization whose aim should be 'the extension of British rule throughout the world, the perfecting of a system of emigration from the United Kingdom, and the colonization by British subjects of all lands where the means of livelihood are attainable by energy, labour and enterprise'.[3] Though the will was modified in his maturer years, he never abandoned altogether these vague and vast idealisms, which provided grandiose canopy for his ambitions and for his brilliant conquests in the world of affairs.

His love of Africa, its open spaces, and his own foothold on the continent, gave his ambitions practical scope. Having obtained his degree in 1881, he settled down in earnest to his South African career. At Kimberley he gathered round him reliable friends, including Alfred Beit, diamond merchant and building speculator, and Starr Jameson, his doctor. With them, during long discussions in his Kimberley shack, he shared his plans. These already extended beyond the Limpopo. Indicating on a map the huge area between the Orange river and the central African lakes, he exclaimed one day: 'I want to see all that red, British red; this is my dream!'

Such a dream was in conflict with the aims of Afrikanerdom. Rhodes always recognized that the Afrikaners were a permanent and leading element in the European population of South Africa. On his journey to the northern Transvaal in 1871 he had come to like the Boer farmers of trekker descent for their slow deliberate speech, rough but steady ways, and simple but rock-like faith. When now in 1881 he gained election to the Cape parliament, surprising its dignified members with his casual Oxford tweeds, it was as member for Barkley West, a predominantly Boer district. Before long he was friend and political partner of Jan Hofmeyr, who was to capture the Afrikaner Bond in the Cape and turn it from its anti-British aims. Throughout his life, and in spite of his part in the Jameson Raid, which was an expression of hostility to Krugerism rather than to Afrikanerdom itself, he stood for the sharing of South African leadership between the two peoples.

Union in South Africa, Rhodes believed, should come through federation under the British flag and a system of imperial defence. In fact, though others such as Cape governor Sir George Grey in the 1850s and Lord Carnarvon more recently in Disraeli's ministry of the 1870s had favoured the federal solution, the year of Rhodes' entry into politics was an unpromising moment. The dispute over Griqualand still rankled with the Boer State, the British annexation of the Transvaal had been managed badly, and the Boer revolt of 1880 had been followed by their victory over the British at Maiuba Hill. The earlier disaster to British arms at Isandlwhana in the Zulu war had also contributed to the decline in British prestige, and it seemed unlikely that either force or friendship would win the co-operation of the Dutch republicans.

Meanwhile, the north lay open. Rhodes saw that British control of the lands beyond the Limpopo would cut off the Transvaal from northward extension and by three-quarters surrounding it, compel its absorption into a British South African system. It now became his primary purpose to persuade the Cape leaders and the British Government of these facts and of the need to act on them. He was, moreover, impelled by his dream of imperial expansion, which had now grown into an idea of an all-British route from the Cape to Cairo. This determination was reinforced by reports from Frederick Selous and other travellers into the interior, of the suitability of the land, at least as far north as the Zambezi, for European use if not occupation, and of the mineral wealth that was believed to exist there. With increasing insistence Rhodes hammered home to the authorities, through Sir Hercules Robinson, High Commissioner at the Cape, that time was short and becoming shorter. The Transvaalers, taking advantage of a tribal dispute among the Tswana, were moving in to occupy land astride the missionaries' road around the source of the Limpopo north of Griqualand West. In 1882 they declared two independent republics, Stellaland and Goshen, which Paul Kruger upon election as President of the Transvaal in 1883 forthwith recognized. A rival was also appearing from another direction. Determined not to be backward in the scramble for African

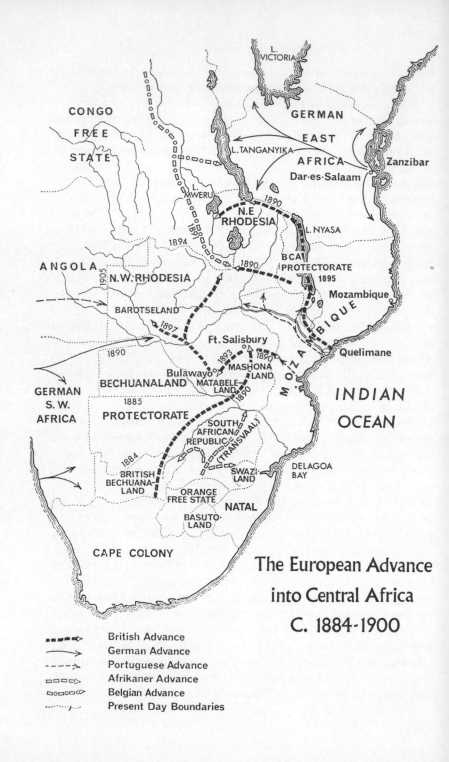

The European Advance
into Central Africa
C. 1884-1900

▪▪▪▶	British Advance
⟶	German Advance
‑‑‑‑➤	Portuguese Advance
◻◻◻▷	Afrikaner Advance
◦◻◦◻◦▷	Belgian Advance
·······⌐	Present Day Boundaries

territory that was about to begin, a German company took possession in 1884 of the small harbour of Angra Pequena on the south-west coast a hundred and fifty miles north of the Cape Colony border. A few months later, in default of any objections from London, Bismarck's government proceeded to lay claim to all of Damaraland and Namaqualand which cover the area of present-day South-West Africa. Kruger paid a visit to Berlin in the same year, and it was widely supposed that he hoped to link the Transvaal with the new German territories and cut off the British at the Cape.

Such an outcome would be fatal to Rhodes' plans. The track from Kuruman was the way north. He harangued the Cape Assembly: 'I look upon this Bechuanaland territory as the Suez Canal of the trade of the country, and as the key to its road to the interior.' The colonial government shied at the expenditure, but after unsuccessful negotiations with the two new republics in 1883 an imperial expedition under Sir Charles Warren gained control. In 1885 the British Government established Southern Bechuanaland as a Crown Colony, and declared a protectorate over Northern Bechuanaland as far as the Zambezi. Rhodes had hoped to act through the Cape Government and to dispense with British assistance. 'We want to get rid of the imperial factor in this question, and deal with it ourselves, jointly with the Transvaal.'⁴ He mistrusted the vacillation and delays of the Colonial Office which had already let slip South-West Africa to Germany; and considered perhaps that Cape controlled territory would be a better base for his next step. Such a declaration, besides, was calculated to win over Cape Dutch and northern Boer opinion for a British dominion free from interference from overseas. But the Cape Government had been unwilling to bear the cost. Ten years later Rhodes was to try to obtain the transfer of Bechuanaland to his Chartered Company administration; again without success, but for different reasons. Meanwhile he had to be content with the considerable advantage gained.

Rhodes met Kruger for the first time during the Bechuanaland negotiations and tried to win him over to his idea of a South African federation that could make a combined advance to the north. But Kruger sensed an enemy to Boer freedom, and would not come to terms.

The President of the Transvaal was in fact playing his own game. The west being now closed to him, he would have liked to drive south-east to Swaziland and Delagoa Bay, but public opinion compelled him to look north. The London Convention of 1884 confirming the independence of the Transvaal had left its northern boundary open.[5] In 1887 Pieter Grobler left Pretoria for Bulawayo with a treaty whose terms amounted to an alliance between the Transvaal and the Ndebele nation, and provided for permanent Boer representation at Lobengula's court.[6] The king, probably unaware of its real significance, signed this agreement, which was the first of its kind with which he had been called upon to deal.

The news disturbed Rhodes profoundly. Once more he faced the reluctant Robinson with the need to act. 'Where will you stop?' asked the High Commissioner; but Rhodes won the day. John Moffat, the former missionary recently appointed Assistant Commissioner for Bechuanaland, at present visiting Matabeleland, was instructed to inform Lobengula that the Grobler Treaty was invalid. The emissary was a suitable choice, for Lobengula trusted Moffat as an old friend. In February 1888 he signed a substitute agreement, which he understood little better than Grobler's, by which he averred perpetual amity with the British Queen and promised not to treat with any other power without the assent of Her Majesty's High Commissioner.[7] The north was kept open for Rhodes, but at a cost. Lobengula had learned to distrust the white man's documents, and the first doubts had crossed his mind about the honesty of his friends.

It is probable that the Ndebele king had in his mind a rough but sound impression of the South African political scene, and was growing aware of the new forces that were converging on the granite kopjes and thorn-stunted veld of Matabeleland. He knew by instinct if not yet by experience the latent power of the Europeans. How they would come to his country, what use they would try to make of the land and for how long, he could not be sure. The Boers had dispossessed the Africans of their land. So had the English in Natal. The Sotho on the other hand were still free in the occupation of their traditional homeland. The Tswana tribes appeared to be secure in theirs. Besides, it seemed that it was gold the white men were after in

Mashonaland. Sometimes they came for a time and mined gold, and then it was finished and they went away. They had not stayed for long at Tati; the broken-down shacks and abandoned, derelict equipment beside the deserted workings were, perhaps, a hopeful sign. This indeed was something the Ndebele could understand for they, like other African peoples, regarded the land as something to be used and occupied rather than to be owned. Thus Lobengula would consider a mining concession before surrendering rights in land.

To recent events, Lobengula reacted with caution. He was aware of the closing of the ring. He compared his predicament with that of a fly before a chameleon, 'that advances very slowly and gently, first putting forward one leg, then another, until at last he darts out his tongue'.[8] He knew that to fight the intruders would be useless. His own people, especially the regiments of young warriors, wanted to drive all white men out of the country once and for all. This rising impatience he had with all his might to restrain. The Europeans would come and 'eat up' his land and people. Yet they might be held off, bargained with, their demands moderated. By every means short of force they must be kept from taking Matabeleland, and that to the Ndebele meant Mashonaland as well. Khama, as all men knew, had accepted the protection of the British Queen; but this line of action was not open to the Ndebele, for it would impose an enforced peace on the protected area and mean the end of the wars and raids to which the tribe was bound by inclination and long tradition, and without which the structure and organization of its society would collapse. The king must therefore stand and bargain for his rights in the open market where, in that day and age, inevitably he must lose.

Lobengula wanted to trust the Europeans, and wanted them to trust him. He was, and proved himself within wide limits, a man of honour. He was fond of the Ndebele proverb, 'There is a wall around the word of a king'.[9] Moffat and his like he believed he could trust; many of the hunters and travellers that first came to Matabeleland were respectable men. The traders Fairbairn and Dawson were in turn entrusted with the keeping of the royal elephant seal, a supreme mark of confidence. Later comers, however, did not appear to be so respectable or so reliable. By 1888 there were over a dozen white men camping round Bulawayo, including Renny Tailyour representing the German financier in Johannesburg, Edward Lippert, and ˙E. A. Maund, well-connected in the United Kingdom, on behalf of the Exploring Company. In September 1888 there were added to their number three representatives of Rhodes, of whom Lobengula now probably heard for the first time.

When news of the Moffat treaty had reached Grahamstown, Rhodes had been galvanized into activity. As it happened, his financial affairs had been prospering greatly in recent months. The old De Beers Company, which he had formed in 1880, had acquired something like half the diamond production of the Kimberley and neighbouring fields, and Rhodes was already planning a merger with Barnato, his last remaining rival. On the Witwatersrand, discovered in 1886, he had also, after some hesitation, bought up a number of valuable properties and formed the Consolidated Goldfields Company; though he never had the faith in gold that he had in diamonds. Confident in these already huge resources, he sent north three emissaries to negotiate at Bulawayo—Charles Rudd, an associate of long standing at˙Kimberley and a member of De Beers, Rochfort Macguire, a lawyer and compatriot from Oxford, and Francis Thompson, a South African experienced in Ndebele language and custom.

When they arrived at Bulawayo in September, already late on the scene, the atmosphere was dangerous, the king having difficulty in restraining his *matjaha* warrior recruits from outright rebellion. In the *matjaha* system, the Ndebele had forged a weapon of such force that it might in certain circumstances be difficult to control. Lobengula's accession twenty years before had been disputed, and even now any apparent failure of audacity on his part could breed a dangerous mood. Shippard, writing in October, described the 'insatiable vanity' and 'almost incredible conceit' of the 'restless and bloodthirsty Matjaha', whom he considered largely responsible for the prevailing raid system.[10]

Rudd and his companions stayed at Bulawayo for five weeks through the dust and mounting discomfort until October. That they were finally rewarded with success was not altogether due to Thompson's repeated insistence that Rhodes was not interested in land, nor to the inducements in the form of military equipment that he was prepared to offer. An important factor was the overt support given to Rhodes by men whose opinion Lobengula respected. Sir Sydney Shippard, Commissioner for Bechuanaland, though not greatly liked by the Ndebele, had unchallengeable authority as the most senior representative of the great Queen whom they had ever met. Without openly supporting Rudd's party, Shippard, one of Rhodes' old Oxford friends, succeeded in discrediting Maund, who claimed to have the backing of the Colonial Office.[11] John Moffat was known to favour Rhodes. What Lobengula did not know was that the former missionary, after long years at Inyati, was of the opinion that 'the Matabele are a miserable people, and have made myriads of other people miserable too', and that at this very time he was writing that 'as a military power it will be a blessing to the world when they are broken up'.[12] To this opinion, latent in the minds of all European negotiators, was added the belief that the sojourn of the Ndebele in Matopo country might not be more than a temporary one. It had been known for years, stated John Mackenzie, that the destruction of the surrounding country was compelling them to look for another homeland which would probably be on the other side of the Zambezi.[13] Whatever the truth of this opinion, which bears a resemblance to Johnston's later assessment of Mpezeni's Ngoni, it could not justify duplicity. 'Do not mistake me,' John Moffat added, 'I would not do anything . . . to break such faith as there may be between us and them.' It is possible that he still believed in Rhodes. Charles Helm, then leading the London Society's Matabele Mission, certainly put in a word for Rhodes, whom he believed to be the most responsible of the various contestants in the field. Lotje, the induna closest to the ear of the king, was of the same view. Deeply worried by the need to obtain the best terms for his people, flattered by the court paid by so many white men, tempted by the payments offered, Lobengula at length made up his mind.

The concession, witnessed by Helm and signed with the king's mark over the royal elephant seal, was a brief document. The king, his heirs and successors, were to be paid £100 a month, and were in due course to be supplied with a thousand breech-loading rifles and a hundred thousand rounds of ammunition. A further and bizarre stipulation, as an alternative to part of the money payment, was the offer of an armed steamboat on the Zambezi, of which nothing more was heard. In return, Lobengula granted Rhodes' representatives 'complete and exclusive charge over all metals and minerals . . . in my kingdom . . . together with full power to do all things they may deem necessary . . . to procure the same . . .' and undertook to grant 'no concessions of land or mining rights . . . without their concurrence.'[14] This agreement, in the light of subsequent events, has been called Lobengula's death warrant. It is certain that it spelt the doom of the Ndebele nation. It is equally certain that Lobengula was not aware of this fact, and that Rhodes and his associates knew it. The Ndebele way of life was bound to go, for the world itself was changing. Whether it passed through fraud or fair dealing might seem to make little practical difference. The two parties to the negotiation lived in different worlds; between them there was no common ground. Mutual understanding was hardly possible. But the subsequent suspicion among the Ndebele that they had been outwitted hung like a cloud over the country in later years.

From this time Rhodes and Lobengula, having at a critical moment come to an agreement, began to move apart. Lobengula, on his side, regretted what he had done and tried, so far as he could, to withdraw. Rhodes on the other hand exploited his position to the full in order to obtain advantage which, even at the time of signing, Lobengula never intended him to have. In his own world, he held the key to the north. The door could only be unlocked in London, but before leaving for England he spent the best part of five months making sure of his position in Africa. After a night-long argument he persuaded Barnato to sell the Kimberley mine to De Beers for over £5¼ millions, thus forming De Beers Consolidated Mines Ltd with control of the entire South African diamond fields. His colossal personal fortune was now sufficient for his needs. Meanwhile in Bulawayo his rivals tried to persuade Lobengula that he had been deceived, and Rhodes found it necessary to pay some of them to drop their claims. Maund was more successful, and by January 1889 had induced Lobengula to send two of his headmen to England to discover the truth of

Rhodes' relations with the Queen's Government. Rhodes' influence at Cape Town was able to delay their embarkation, but
in March the king's misgivings overwhelmed him. Seeking a
scapegoat, he ordered the death of Lotje with all his clan for
having supported the concession policy. Jameson, who had
already once treated Lobengula professionally, went north
again; but though he could relieve the king's gout he could do
little to appease his anxiety, which was not diminished by a
letter from the British Government warning him that a man
'gives a stranger his ox, not his whole herd of cattle'.[15]

Rhodes could delay his departure for London no longer. He
wrote to Jameson: 'Our enemies may bowl us out if I do not go
at once to headquarters. Our concession is so gigantic, it is like
giving a man the whole of Australia.'[16] The words clearly reveal the broad interpretation he was prepared to give to his
agreement with the Ndebele king.

The political scene at the time of his arrival in March 1889
was not unfavourable. Lord Salisbury had replaced Gladstone's
Liberal administration and the Conservative Prime Minister,
in any case more sympathetic towards Empire, had been faced
during three years of office with the need to keep pace with the
scramble for African territory by European powers. His decision
in 1888 on a prolonged occupation of Egypt converted the
whole Nile valley into a prospective British sphere of interest.
A persistent obstacle was the reluctance of Parliament to vote
funds, but the use of the chartered company principle, recently
abandoned in India, was revived to enable government to off-
load the cost of pacification and administration. Gladstone
had already followed this course in the case of Borneo (1882)
and the Niger (1885). Salisbury now secured the British hold on
East Africa by granting a charter to Sir William McKinnon's
Imperial British East Africa Company, thus setting a clear
precedent for Rhodes.

The aim of the imperialists, in southern Africa, had been to
expand British influence northwards through the agency of the
Cape Colony, so avoiding a head-on clash with the German and
Transvaal Governments. This policy had failed owing to the
inability of the Cape Government to bear the cost. Rhodes'
appearance in London in 1889 thus appeared a piece of
remarkable good fortune. 'And who may be this Mr Rhodes?'

asked Salisbury in April, and discovered that here was a man who could and would solve the problem—who would carry the cost of administering Central African territory, contain the Transvaal without embarrassment to Britain, and build the railway essential to the success of the project.

Rhodes was working against time. Any day the news might reach London that Lobengula had rescinded the concession. Although the first instalments of gold had been accepted, the fact of protest would strengthen the hand of political opponents of the charter. He had first to deal with rival syndicates. It was not difficult to purchase the Tati Concession from Swinburne. Even Maund and the Exploring Company now surrendered to the threat that money was no object. An amalgamation, the United Concessions, was formed as the nucleus of the British South Africa Company, for whose charter negotiations now commenced. Here Rhodes' passage was less easy. The project was attacked by radical Little Englanders, who opposed expansion outright, by the South Africa Committee who preferred direct control from the United Kingdom, and by Exeter Hall who claimed that the Government was once more shirking its responsibilities. John Mackenzie warned that the Chartered Company would involve the Government in tribal wars. Many like him deplored the sale of guns to the Ndebele, and doubted the wisdom of consigning tribal territory to the control of a gold-seeking joint stock enterprise. The free traders on the other hand, objected to the monopolistic terms of the charter.[17]

Rhodes' enthusiasm however made a marked impression in high quarters. He dined at Windsor and left the Queen, a shrewd judge of men, convinced that here was one who could overcome the many obstacles. At Whitehall he carried the day with Salisbury and Knutsford, who succumbed with remarkable ease to the casual theory that rifles were less brutal than assagais, and that Africans were not capable of adjusting the sights. The bulk of the Unionist party would vote for this opportunity to acquire thousands of square miles of territory with no charge on the Treasury. A paradoxical gift of £10,000 to Parnell for the cause of Irish home rule, which for Rhodes epitomized his theory of imperial federation, gained him the Irish vote. Waverers were convinced when the Duke of Fife, son-in-law of the Prince of Wales, the Duke of Abercorn and Earl Grey, all considered 'safe' men in official quarters, agreed to serve on the board of directors. It was generally known that the Company, backed by Rothschild, De Beers and Consolidated Goldfields, owned a share capital of £1 million. On 29 October 1889 the Charter was granted.

The rights which it conferred came direct from the Crown, and did not merely confirm the privileges conceded by Lobengula; moreover the area which it covered extended far beyond the confines of Matabeleland and Mashonaland. The Company was required to promote civilization and good government in the regions north of Bechuanaland and west of the Portuguese territories, and was given the right to 'make treaties, promulgate laws, preserve the peace, maintain a police force and acquire new concessions'.[18] These were very great powers and converted a plain mineral concession into practically sovereign rights. It was understood that they could be exercised only with the approval of the Ndebele or other Central African tribes concerned, but Rhodes was convinced that somehow such approval would be gained. Relations between the Company and the Africans was subject to supervision by the Secretary of State, and the Government reserved the right to cancel the Charter at any time, but no official resident was provided for in the Company's territory to give effect to these reservations.

As soon as the Charter was assured, Rhodes sailed for Cape Town. Meanwhile in Bulawayo the position had gone from bad to worse. In order to restore the situation Jameson went north again in October and met Thompson, who had remained bravely at his post for over a year, hastening south in fear for his life. Jameson's persuasive personality and charm this time had their effect in steadying Lobengula, and in reminding him of all the arguments of necessity that had caused him to sign the concession originally. In January 1890 news reached Matabeleland that the Charter had been granted, and a few days later a small troop of Royal Horse Guards in full uniform arrived at the capital with a letter from Queen Victoria advising Lobengula to work with the Chartered Company. Information that the Portuguese were now laying claim to areas of eastern Mashonaland further helped to turn the king back on to the course he had already begun. Having thus re-established the Company's interests in Bulawayo, Jameson left for the south in February, to help in the organization of the Pioneer Column.

Settlement and Conquest

Since the Rudd Concession had been signed the previous year, preparations had been going forward for the recruitment of a pioneer force that would found a settlement in Mashonaland. The selection was carried out with considerable care. Rhodes insisted that every member of the expedition should have had South African experience, and that a good proportion should be of Afrikaner extraction. About two thousand applications were received, some from as far afield as Canada and Australia, and from them two hundred were chosen. Most of these were well below thirty years of age, and included representatives of a wide number of trades such as would be needed in a new community—blacksmiths and bakers, printers and carpenters, as well as storekeepers, farmers and miners. The party was to be led by Major Frank Johnson, with Captain Heany and Lieutenant Borrow as second in command, and for the duration of the march was to be organized on a military basis. A squadron of four hundred mounted men, commanded by Colonel Pennefeather, who were later to form the nucleus of the British South Africa Police, were to accompany the column for further security. During the march, each trooper in the Column was to receive seven shillings and sixpence a day, and on arrival in Mashonaland each man would be allowed to mark out a three thousand acre farm, and peg up to fifteen gold claims.[1] The expedition was well-equipped, its supplies amounting to a hundred and seventeen wagon loads, with herds of livestock to be driven alongside. Early in 1890, parties began to assemble in Kimberley and Mafeking, and in March the whole force moved north to Fort Cecil on the Macloutsie river, to undergo a final period of preparation.

News of these events was not concealed from Lobengula, who was again growing restive. In April Jameson made yet another visit to Bulawayo, to explain the object of the Pioneer Force. On this occasion his good humour contained more than a hint of firmness, and the king was compelled to concede a grudging assurance that the white men coming to dig for gold would be allowed to 'have the road' and to pass through his country, as they must, to reach the goldfields. The High Commissioner for South Africa, now Sir Henry Loch, also wrote assuring Lobengula that 'the men assembled by the British South Africa Company are not assembled for the purpose of attacking him, but on the contrary are assembled for a peaceful object, namely searching for gold. . . . They are ordered to travel at a distance from the Matabele kraals.' No mention was made of the occupation of land. The territory in question was Mashonaland, which in Lobengula's eyes belonged to the Ndebele. The value of the ambiguity deliberately drafted into the concession was now becoming apparent. This was the more so in view of the broad meaning given to the words 'searching for gold', which Lobengula was right to suspect. When on 6 June Loch gave his consent for the expedition to set out, the object was declared to be 'the peaceful occupation of Mashonaland'.²

Three days after the Column had crossed the Macloutsie river on 27 June, they were met by a party of Ndebele with a message from Lobengula: 'Has the King killed any white men, that an impi is collecting on his border? Or have the white men lost anything they are looking for?' Jameson sent back reply that this was the working party, on its way to Mashonaland on the road already arranged. On 11 July the Pioneers crossed the Shashi river and were within the confines of Ndebele territory, though still in the low veld away to the south of their settlements. Four weeks later came another protest, and it was Pennefeather this time who replied: 'I cannot stop or return. I have my orders to go to Mashonaland and must obey them. If the King wishes to fight or attack us, I cannot help it. You gave this road, and I am avoiding your kraals and people.'⁵ In Bulawayo and the neighbouring Matopo hills a hundred and twenty miles to the north, the Ndebele nation seethed with discontent. There was real danger that the king would be defied. With 18,000 armed men, few doubted that the six hundred whites slowly skirting the Limpopo valley could be overwhelmed. All had heard of Isandlwhana. But Lobengula knew that to gain such a victory would be to lose all, and the tribal tradition of military discipline stood the test of this crisis. In the end, no attack was made.

Each day the Column advanced, sometimes as far as twelve miles. Scouts were always out to the front and rear and on the left flank, and at night a searchlight's beam pierced the darkness. Two parallel tracks were cut, so that a defensive laager could speedily be formed. The troops took turns to make the road ahead, levelling the ground and felling trees. Many streams had to be crossed, first those flowing into the Limpopo, among them the Umsingwane, the Nubye and the Nuanetsi. Later, as the expedition began to turn north, the Lundi and the Tokwe, tributaries of the Sabi, and forming roughly the borderline between Matabeleland and Mashonaland, had to be forded. Over a hundred wagons had to be floated or dragged across these drifts. The Tokwe was crossed in August, and the struggle began through the escarpment that leads out of the thick, rough country of the low veld and up on to the open plateau. Finding a suitable gap in the hills, Selous named it Providential Pass. Emerging on to open, undulating country of grass and scattered trees, the Column halted to raise the flag and establish Fort Victoria.

The Shona people in the region were found living, as they had done for two generations, among inaccessible rocks of the granite kopjes that abound across the plateau. They were friendly enough to the Europeans, as they well might be, and anxious for protection from the dreaded Ndebele, from whose impis a visitation was daily expected. On Jameson's insistence no treaty was entered upon with any Shona chief, and no guarantee of security given. The decision amounted to a tacit recognition of Lobengula's sovereignty in Mashonaland, but the Company could not afford at this stage to put the matter to the test.

Beyond Fort Victoria the Column made faster progress. A hundred miles to the north Fort Charter was set up, and on 12 September, after crossing the Hunyani river, the wagons were outspanned five miles from Mount Hampden and Fort Salisbury was founded. A salute of twenty-one guns boomed out over the veld. The Union Jack, hanging impassively from its tall staff in the dry air, proclaimed to the world that the British flag had this time neither followed nor preceded but marched in step with trade. But the epic spirit of the enterprise could not conceal its harsh reality. In the two clear months before the heavy rains began tents were pitched, a street plan laid out, the construction of pole and mud buildings begun. While traders set up their stores, men hurriedly explored the surrounding country for gold claims and farming land. Hopes of rich gold finds mostly came to nothing, and the severe disillusionment that followed on this discovery did more to threaten the success of the whole enterprise than the deaths from fever and dysentery brought on by the rain season. A number, in their disappointment, packed up and went south. It was not in fact until 1891 that the settlement in Mashonaland was firmly established and that women and children began to come into the country.

Rhodes was concerned not merely to establish a settlement, but to make sure of the boundaries of Company territory. The most urgent threat was from the east. When the Column had reached Fort Charter in September 1890, therefore, Jameson, accompanied by Selous and Sir Archibald Colquhoun, the first administrator designate, had turned off east towards Manicaland, the highlands overlooking Portuguese East Africa. Since 1888 a crisis had been building up between Britain and Portugal with regard to the frontiers of their respective spheres. Referring to their historic treaties with Monomotapa in 1607 and 1629, the Portuguese claimed that both Manicaland and Mashonaland lay within their rightful sphere of influence. They were also making large demands north of the Zambezi which were being vigorously resisted by the Scottish missionaries in the Shire highlands. Salisbury and Rhodes both knew that south of the Zambezi the B.S.A. Company was the only instrument by which the Portuguese could be opposed, but the Prime Minister believed that a reasonable concession here would make easier an agreement in the north, and was not anxious to press the British claim.[3]

The most powerful ruler in Manicaland was Mtasa, whose village was situated on a hilltop not far from present-day Umtali. A hundred miles further south, in the foothills on the Portuguese side, was the Soshangana chief Gungunyana, who had settled in the district south of the Sabi after leaving Swaziland twenty-five years before. This aggressive people, cousins of the Ndebele, used periodically to raid Manicaland as far north as the Vumba hills.

Rhodes wanted to make treaties with both these chiefs. Apart from expectations of alluvial gold, he particularly hoped to obtain for the Chartered Company an outlet to the Indian Ocean, and moreover to complete the encirclement of Kruger's republic within British territory. In August 1890, however, while the Pioneer Column was still forcing its way up the escarpment, Lord Salisbury had reached an agreement with the Portuguese Government which marked the boundary along the Masheke and Sabi rivers, thus placing the highlands between Penhalonga and Chipinga inside Portuguese territory. Rhodes protested vehemently against this decision. 'If you have any regard for the work I am doing', he cabled to London, 'you will show it by now dropping the Anglo-Portuguese agreement.'[4] He need not have worried, for the Portuguese Cortes refused to ratify, while angry Lisbon crowds broke the windows of the British embassy. Renewed negotiations in London produced an interim *modus vivendi* agreement on 14 November 1890 by which the final delimitation of boundaries was left open.[5] Salisbury coldly informed Rhodes that the British Government could make no claim to the highlands unless the Company effectively occupied them, or at least obtained concession treaties from the chiefs of the district.

A sharp struggle for the coveted area followed. Jameson's party reached Mtasa's in September, and on the 14th a treaty was made by which the chief, in exchange for British protection and £100 a year, granted the usual concession of minerals and agreed to a resident, a police force and schools. The Portuguese soon had news of this, and as soon as the Company's party had left, Manoel de Souza, also known as Gouveia, a man who traded in slaves in the coastal district and a Portuguese subsidiary, was despatched to Mtasa's with an armed force. The chief was compelled to disavow the treaty and accept Portuguese sovereignty. De Souza was shortly joined by Colonel d'Andrade of the Mozambique Company with reinforcements. When news of these events reached Fort Salisbury, Major Patrick Forbes, supported later by a party under Captain Fiennes, made their way as rapidly as possible to the scene. On the night of 16 November Mtasa's village was stormed, the

Portuguese leaders arrested, their men disarmed, and the Portuguese flag replaced by the Union Jack. Shortly afterwards, Macequece was also occupied, and Umtali founded as headquarters of the Company's administration.

By these blunt methods Manicaland, or the Eastern District, was secured to the colony in Mashonaland. But though the Portuguese had to acquiesce thus far, further efforts by the Company to gain their keenly sought access to the sea were unsuccessful. In October 1890, while the Manica question was still in the balance, Jameson set off with two companions across the Inyanga highlands and down the Pungwe river. This journey bore many adventures but little profit. Back in Mashonaland at the beginning of 1891, Jameson was despatched on yet another expedition, this time to Gungunyana in Gaza country beyond the Sabi. He managed to obtain a concession treaty, but this and a Company foray towards Beira were to no purpose, for Lord Salisbury was determined to call a halt. The *modus vivendi* agreement of November 1890 was followed by the Anglo-Portuguese Convention of 11 June 1891,[6] and Gazaland was left to the Portuguese.

Lobengula in the meantime was protesting against the activities of the Pioneers in Mashonaland. With the flag raised at Salisbury, and parcels of land being allocated to settlers, the true nature of Rhodes' enterprise was at last revealed. In a final and desperate effort to withdraw from his commitment and to balance the power of the Chartered Company by a rival influence, the king now gave a land concession to the Johannesburg trader Edward Lippert. By this concession Lobengula, styling himself 'King of the Amandebele nation, and of the Makalaka, Mashona and surrounding territories', declared that 'whereas I have granted a concession in respect of . . . rights incidental to mining only . . . and seeing that . . . white people are coming into my kingdom and it is desirable that I should assign land to them . . . and appoint someone to act for me in these respects: I hereby grant to Edward Lippert the sole right . . . to lay out . . . farms and townships (in all territories which) now are, or may hereafter be, occupied by the British South Africa Company.'[7] That Lobengula should have taken such a drastic step only reveals the desperate straits in which he found himself. The move failed in its purpose, however, for Rhodes, by a prior compact with Lippert that John Moffat described as a 'detestable' plan, at once bought the Concession.[8]

By 1891, therefore, Lobengula's policy of keeping the Europeans at arm's length had met with little success. Two advantages alone had he secured. The first was that the group to which he had unwillingly bowed his head was the Chartered Company sanctioned by Queen Victoria, in whom natives of southern Africa, despite many disappointments, still reposed some trust. The second was that the country of the Ndebele themselves as opposed to that of their subject tribes was still inviolate. These facts were little consolation. Influence had been lost, raiding grounds threatened, pride injured. To the rank and file of the tribe it seemed that the trend of events could yet be changed. It was to require the frustrated attempts of a war and a rebellion to show them that what was done could not be undone.

During the early months of 1891 Lobengula faced further and more definite inroads on his authority in Shona country. In April the High Commissioner proclaimed the whole region north of the Transvaal, and between Mozambique and German South-West Africa, to be a British sphere of influence. This was followed by a declaration of jurisdiction over Europeans in the area, under the Foreign Jurisdiction Act of 1890. Finally the Order in Council of 9 May 1891, stating that the territories of the Chartered Company were under the Queen's protection, empowered the High Commissioner to administer justice, raise revenue, and provide for the peace, order and good government 'of all persons within the limits of this order'. The first of such proclamations in June 1891 arranged for Resident Commissioners, police and magistrates. Sir Archibald Colquhoun, formerly of the Indian Civil Service, was appointed Chief Magistrate of Mashonaland in September.

These developments towards the legalization of Rhodes' *fait accompli* Lobengula was powerless to prevent, even had he immediately grasped their implications. He could only protest to Cape Town, through Colenbrander and the Europeans at his capital, that authority in his country was being given to Rhodes without his consent.

The settlers in Mashonaland, having survived through their

first year into their second, were now struggling into their third. On the scattered farms, twenty or thirty miles apart, the first tents and shacks were being replaced by slightly firmer structures. The heaps of gravel at the mines, where they had not been deserted, were a little larger, and the shafts a little deeper. Runners worked on a rudimentary postal service between the two or three main settlements. Where towns were to grow, street plans were being laid out on the grass and among the boulders and anthills. Again people died of sickness, and again more people came to replace them. The Europeans and the Shona into whose country they had come became more accustomed to each other, and the problems that were to arise between them began to show. One of the most important was the labour question. Labour was vital to farmers and miners. What if the Shona refused to work? Then there were quarrels between one headman and another. Should the Company intervene to keep the peace? On two occasions the police had exerted their authority over delinquent Shona chiefs but without legal justification for they were in fact Lobengula's men. Last of all, there was trouble with the Ndebele.

Lobengula had no wish to interfere with the white men. The Shona had, however, long been the prey of his warriors, and their cattle had replenished his herds, the more so since the forming of the Bechuanaland Protectorate had deprived the Ndebele of valuable raiding grounds. Apart from their objections on humanitarian grounds, the European settlers found that whenever a raid impended, it was impossible to find men to work; all had fled. This was particularly true of Fort Victoria, where many newcomers had arrived by 1893, and which, of the larger settlements, was closest to Ndebele territory. A considerable proportion of the local population was in employment there, and formed a bone of contention between Europeans and Ndebele. Repeatedly Lobengula had sent messages to the Administrator, and to the High Commissioner at the Cape, asking, 'To whom do the Mashona belong?' More recently he had been heard to declare that he would fight if the Company would not surrender the Shona in their employment.[9]

In June 1893 the crisis arrived. Some Shona tribesmen cut and stole five hundred yards of wire from the Fort Victoria telegraph, and in retaliation the Company police confiscated a herd of cattle. Lobengula thereupon protested that these cattle were his own, which was probably true, for as proof of their submission Shona tribesmen were often required to look after Ndebele herds. Jameson at Fort Salisbury at once arranged for the return of the cattle, and took steps to punish the thieves in some other way; but Lobengula was meanwhile himself preparing to act against his insubordinate 'subjects'. Early in July he despatched an impi of over three thousand men to ravage the Shona villages west of Fort Victoria. At outlying European farms, Shona servants were butchered, and cattle carried off. Men, women and children fled into Fort Victoria for shelter, where the magistrate refused the demand of the Ndebele indunas that they be surrendered. An uneasy calm settled on the district, while the settlers, alert and at arms, awaited the outcome, and the Ndebele continued to hunt out people for miles around.

Ten days after the trouble had started, Jameson arrived from Salisbury and held an indaba. Provoked by the arrogant manner of the indunas who came to meet him, he told them that they must go back at once into Matabeleland, and must commence moving within an hour, 'or he would drive them'. The indunas, instructed to avoid a clash with the Europeans, decided to comply. Soon the mass of the Ndebele, gathered not far distant, began to move off, and an armed party from Fort Victoria, following two hours later to ensure that they had gone, saw the impi on the hills 'like a black shadow as if the sun had clouded over on that part of the country'.[10] But a few in the rear had been slow to move. Coming up with them a European troop led by a hot-headed ex-police officer, Captain Lendy, opened fire. Most Ndebele escaped but a few were killed.[11]

It has been contended that the deaths caused by this unnecessary action made war inevitable. Lobengula complained that 'the white men seemed to be dragging him into a quarrel', and recalled an impi of six thousand men from across the Zambezi, where a raid on the Lozi had been planned. Strong forces were placed between Bulawayo and Mashonaland. The traders at Bulawayo feared for their lives and Colenbrander wrote that 'but for the King we should all be dead'. In the event, however, hostilities were started by the Company, the final decision being Jameson's responsibility. Jameson had originally hoped to avoid war and to bring about the incorporation of Matabeleland by degrees over the years. He had now come to accept the view that peace and prosperity would never be possible with a militant warrior nation on the border, and he sensed relief as well as anxiety among the rank and file of the settlers that the crisis with the Ndebele, long foreseen, had arrived. This, rather than hopes that the true 'reef' lay in Matabeleland, unquestionably explains Jameson's decision. No doubt such hopes, circulating in London, helped to reconcile anxious shareholders to the war, and to persuade them to double the share capital of the Company. In this sense Rhodes was able to turn the war to his advantage. Since the optimistic second shareholders' meeting the previous year, the value of Chartered shares had fallen from over £3 to about 12s., funds were running short and the Company was relying on subsidies from De Beers and elsewhere. The removal of the Ndebele menace, quite apart from the questions of gold and the easier passage for the railway, would justify the policy of increased capitalization already decided upon. The origins of the war, however, lay in the deteriorating situation in Mashonaland.

As early as August Jameson was making his preparations, recruiting over six hundred men for the enterprise. The contract included the promise of land and cattle as 'loot' after the Ndebele had been defeated. He was still acting on his own initiative. The British Government continued to work for peace and in the same month the Queen wrote through the High Commissioner: 'You can tell the King from me that I have no intention of invading his country.'[12] For his part Lobengula in September returned the current instalment of gold paid according to the Rudd Concession, as well as the rifles and ammunition that he had received—a move calculated to display both his wish to avoid war and his disillusionment with Company policy. But the die was already cast, and Rhodes knew it as well as Jameson. Ndebele envoys sent south to negotiate were held up on false charges. After sending up supplies overland, Rhodes travelled slowly to Mashonaland by sea in order to be out of reach of the High Commissioner, and did not arrive in Fort Salisbury until after the columns had left.

The advancing summer season precipitated war. Jameson realized that the onset of the rains would postpone hopes of coming to grips with the Ndebele for the best part of a year, which could prove fatal to Company and colony together. Incidents were provoked inside the Matabeleland border, and at last in mid October columns moved westwards from Fort Victoria and Fort Salisbury converging at Iron Mine Hill.

Moving south-west along the watershed towards the Matopos, two hundred miles distant, through little-known country, the column was first attacked by a Ndebele force of about five thousand men on the far bank of the Shangani river. The attack was launched at 2.15 a.m. and lasted till dawn. Company fire augmented by machine guns was steady and efficient, while that of the Ndebele was wild and inaccurate, and they were driven off with heavy loss. The commander of the European scouts, climbing a hill soon after dawn, had a panoramic view of the retreating Ndebele, of whom several groups were moving in different directions with swaying shields and assagais glinting in the morning sun. A few days later a second engagement was fought at Imbembezi with similar results, and many Ndebele now took their own lives rather than return defeated.

The news of these disasters caused consternation at Bulawayo. Even now, however, Lobengula insisted that the European traders, of whom two still remained at his kraal, should come to no harm. The impi sent to guard the road against a second column approaching from Bechuanaland was withdrawn, the royal kraal was fired and the magazine exploded, and the king with many followers fled away north towards the Zambezi. Between the Shangani and Gwaai rivers were the grazing grounds of the royal herds, and it is probable that he hoped to settle there. On arriving at the smouldering remains of the village that had been the Ndebele capital since 1872, a Company officer Benjamin Wilson later wrote: 'I was sorry for the King, but for the people of the nation I have not the slightest sympathy. It is a just fate that has overtaken them. They have felt for the first time in their lives what they have been making the surrounding tribes feel for the last fifty years.'[13] Most of his compatriots would have shared this view.

The campaign was not yet ended. Hitherto, though the

European force had required steady nerves, they had had an easy fight against a foe untrained in the use of modern weapons and less well armed though many times their number. But the Ndebele nation was not yet overcome. Many hundreds had survived the battle, thousands had not fought at all. In an attempt to find the king and make a definite peace, Major Forbes set out in his tracks with a lightly equipped force of a hundred and forty-two men, Major Allan Wilson his second in command. It was already October, and the heavy rains had started early. On reaching the Shangani river, Forbes sent Wilson ahead with a patrol to reconnoitre and return by sundown. The last part of the order was not obeyed, for the patrol came up with Lobengula's wagon and hoped to capture the king. It was a rash, and proved a fatal, decision. The following day, Wilson's party found themselves surrounded and outnumbered, and fighting with great gallantry were annihilated to the last man. Meanwhile Forbes himself had been attacked, and later was unable to ford the flooded river.

This was the last event of the war. Lobengula never reached the Zambezi, though two of his impis managed to cross the river and wreak havoc among the Toka on the north side.[14] His efforts to make peace had failed, the message through treachery going astray. The indunas now declared that 'we are tired of war and want to be able to sleep'. They were told that the white men were also tired of strife and wanted to live at peace with the people of the country.

The Company's headquarters in Matabeleland had been established at Bulawayo, where Jameson already, before the war was ended, had been allotting stands for the new township. To the indaba tree therefore, in whose shade Lobengula had used to sit when holding council, and which still stands in the garden of Government House, the indunas came one by one to make their submission. It slowly became known that the king had died, would not be coming back, so that the Company's authority took the place of that of Lobengula. Disputes in the villages were brought to the Resident for his decision. Gradually the country settled down. Many *amaholi* who had been captive in Matabeleland returned eastward. Of the true Ndebele a contemporary witness wrote, 'those who had accompanied Lobengula on his flight have returned and settled on farms allotted by the Company to Europeans, and are now, with the consent of the owners of these farms, hoeing and ploughing'. More ominously he added, 'Others have located themselves in various unallotted lands in the Matopo hills. . . .'[15]

News of the fighting had immediately brought a sharp rise in the price of Chartered Company shares, and £3/4 million of new stock was issued. Critics in London were quick to suggest that the conquest had been deliberately engineered. The Board publicly scouted the idea. What interest had a commercial company in promoting a costly war? Rhodes was closer to the truth when, back in London, he told a shareholder's meeting: 'We either had to have that war or to leave the country.'[16] He now hastened to obtain the Imperial Government's sanction for Company control of the new territory. Sir Henry Loch, High Commissioner at the Cape, would have preferred more direct control from the Colonial Office, but in London Gladstone, premier since 1892, had been replaced by the Liberal Imperialist Lord Rosebery in March 1894, and the new administration supported Rhodes' schemes. The Matabeleland Order in Council of 1894 provided for an Administrator who could issue regulations and for a Court to be presided over by a single judge. Matabeleland was thus placed on the same level as Mashonaland had been since 1891; both were subject to proclamations from the High Commissioner as well as to ordinances issued by the Board of Directors.[17]

A Land Commission appointed in the same year set out two reserves where the Ndebele could hold land in absolute security. One of these was the Gwaai reserve, west of the Gwaai river, which the Ndebele themselves said was good cattle country, but which later proved to be short of water. The other was the Shangani reserve, containing good grazing grounds, some of which Lobengula had formerly kept for his own use, though a portion lay within a tsetse fly belt.[18] Elsewhere, under the Order in Council, Africans could own land on the same terms as Europeans. The distribution of cattle, of which Lobengula had possessed upwards of 200,000, was also left to the Land Commission. Here mistakes were made, for it was never properly understood which cattle had belonged to

Lobengula and which were the private property of individuals. In any case the royal herds were tribal heritage rather than personal to himself. When the Company confiscated a large proportion of them and redistributed the rest, the decision appeared unjust from the African viewpoint.

Discontent over the cattle settlement was made worse by the material disaster of the rinderpest outbreak in 1895. Though the coming of the Europeans was blamed, this sudden epidemic seems to have started among the buffalo herds beyond the Zambezi, possibly as far north as Tanganyika. It swept across the country like a fire over the veld. In Rhodesia and Bechuanaland it was estimated that as many as two million cattle and wild game died in the outbreak. George Pauling, travelling up the line of the railway under construction from Mafeking wrote that 'the journey was a terrible one; at every coach station and frequently along the road there was a stench from the unburied bodies of cattle which had died from the rinderpest'. An effort was made to check the epidemic by shooting infected animals, which aroused deep African resentment.

Most of this resentment was not observed by the settlers, whose confidence had generally been increased by the conquest. The rate of immigration rose, more farms were laid out, more stores were built along the rough wagon roads and at outlying centres such as Headlands and Marandellas, Mazoe, Hartley and Que Que. Beneath the surface, all was far from well. The Ndebele had not lost in a few humiliating months a tradition of national pride that was generations old. While their younger men displayed to the European settlers on occasion an insufferable arrogance, they themselves, young and old, were frequently offered insulting or scornful treatment. The native police, recruited largely from the despised Mashona, often took advantage of their position with rough and abusive behaviour including maltreatment of Ndebele womenfolk. An induna told Selous, 'I have no complaints to make against the white policemen, but the black police, they really give me trouble.'[19] Another grievance concerned the provision of labour. The country had been divided into districts, to each of which a Native Commissioner had been appointed. This officer was required to compel the local headmen to supply miners and farmers with labour, all able-bodied young men being obliged to work for a certain number of months each year on a fixed rate of pay. Sir Richard Martin, later first Resident Commissioner, was to describe this forced labour system as 'synonymous with slavery'.[20]

Thus by the end of 1895 the Ndebele were smouldering with discontent, though their slowly forming intentions were kept a close secret. Meanwhile, Rhodes and Jameson were plotting on their own account elsewhere. The British South Africa Company had yet to live up to its name. Rhodes, having won the north, was anxious to complete his ambition in southern Africa. The Boer republics remained obdurate, but time was on Rhodes' side. Prime Minister of the Cape Colony since 1890, his administration there had been a marked success, and his party had been returned in the recent elections with a renewed majority in which the Cape Dutch vote had bulked large. Kruger's stock by contrast was at last falling in the Transvaal, while the Uitlander population on the Witwatersrand, mainly British, had risen from two to ninety thousand in ten years. But Rhodes, with a diseased heart, and believing, perhaps rightly, that his giant personality alone could effect the reconciliation, felt that time was what could not be spared.

Under cover of great secrecy, plans were laid for an Uitlander rising in Johannesburg, where the mining population, heavily taxed and denied civic rights, talked boldly of overthrowing Kruger's government. Arms were supplied to the Reform Committee leaders, Rhodes sharing the cost with Beit. The strip of territory through Bechuanaland along the Transvaal border was ceded to the Chartered Company, ostensibly for the railway north of Vryburg. Joseph Chamberlain, Colonial Secretary in Salisbury's new administration, who knew what was in the wind, would go to the assistance of the British in Johannesburg provided a rising occurred there first, but Rhodes dared not ask him to countenance a Chartered Company raid. Rhodes however hoped that the force of the *fait accompli* would once again carry him across the fence. By the end of December Jameson was at Pitsani on the Transvaal border with a force of six hundred men consisting of the majority of the Mashonaland Police Force. When the rising 'fizzled out' Rhodes cabled Jameson to stand fast, but in this crisis of fortune his old way of giving his servants *carte blanche* to 'do the best you can as the circumstances arise' turned against him. Jameson, to be free of restraint, cut the telegraph wire to the south and rode across the border on 29 December 1895. Four days later his force surrendered to Kruger's troops at Doornkop.

It was Jameson's act rather than his surrender that brought down Rhodes' South African career in ruins. He resigned from the premiership of the Cape in the full knowledge that all hopes of a federal South Africa under his own or another's leadership were dashed; while in the same moment a new and militant Afrikaner nationalism was born.

North of the Limpopo it was the Doornkop surrender itself that had the most marked effect. It is remarkable that when in October 1895 Jameson had withdrawn all but forty of the Company police, hardly a European voice was raised in protest; but the Ndebele did not fail to note the occurrence. The defeat and capture of the raiding force taught them that the men who had beaten them in 1893 were not invincible. On 20 March, when the rains were just ending, the first murders in the Ndebele rebellion were carried out at Dawson's store. On the 24th, a party of young Ndebele came to Selous' farm to borrow axes. Selous' wife remarked that the murderers would be caught and punished, and received the significant reply: 'How can the white men punish them? Where are the white police? There are none left in the country.'[21]

Within a week the people throughout Matabeleland had risen. Crops had failed, herds been struck down by disease. Nothing would go well till the white man was driven out. Over a hundred European lives were lost in the first onslaught. Farmers and traders from isolated homesteads were brought in to the fortified laager at Bulawayo, where by the beginning of April there were more than fifteen hundred men, women and children. Maurice Clifford wrote, 'This will be a more serious business than the old war', and his prediction was fully justified. For some reason, perhaps in the hope that it would be used as an escape route, the Mangwe road to Bechuanaland was left unguarded, and by this route a relief force under Major Plumer entered the country. Until that time the white population was shut up in the laagers at Bulawayo, Gwelo,

Belingwe and Mangwe, and only three hundred men of the newly formed Bulawayo Field Force were available for active operations in open country. Many fierce actions were fought, in some of which Rhodes himself, having arrived in Bulawayo during the rebellion, took part. Men wrote of the 'utmost fearlessness of the Matabele' and of the 'fanatical and plucky style of their attacks'. But they were poorly organized and ill-equipped, and died in hundreds before the 'mowing guns' of the Europeans. Gradually their units were driven into the Matopo hills, and the fighting was reduced to a barren guerilla struggle.

In July General Carrington informed Rhodes that in order to bring the campaign to a successful conclusion it would be necessary to complete the railway to Bulawayo, and bring up five thousand regular troops the following year. To Rhodes this was unacceptable. The railway could not arrive before November, there was insufficient food to supply Plumer's troops much longer, and if Carrington were right the Company would be in debt for £5 million. Moreover the Shona rising, which had started in June, was causing serious concern. He decided to settle with the Ndebele as was his custom with his opponents, 'on the personal', by talking instead of fighting. The greatest difficulty was in making contact with the rebels, and Rhodes had to wait in an isolated and undefended camp in the foothills for six weeks to send a message through. At length, unarmed and with only three companions, in a clearing near the western spur of the Matopos, he met the Ndebele gathered in a silence heavy with suspicion. One by one the indunas stepped forward and declared peace in their hearts. For five hours on the first day Rhodes talked with them, hearing their grievances, and for days to follow, displaying a patience and sympathy he had not frequently shown towards commerical antagonists. The Ndebele warned that they could and would fight again if necessary, for it was better to die than to live like dogs. The core of their case was that the Shona native police should be disbanded, that their own headmen should exercise some responsibility, and that there should be an undisputed authority to whom they could appeal. While condemning the African attacks on the civilian population, Rhodes admitted that these complaints had substance, and agreed not to employ native police in Matabeleland without the consent of the people. He promised that some of the indunas would be recognized as headmen and, to tide over the immediate crisis, that food would be distributed to the people.

Indeed, though the danger of bloodshed was past, there was widespread hunger. Rhodes ordered up a million bags of grain ·from the south, offering to pay for it himself if the Company would not meet the bill; in the event the Board paid gladly. At some centres food was distributed twice a day to hungry men, women and children, sign of a striking reversal of roles.

Meanwhile away to the east it had steadily dawned upon the Shona, who had only reluctantly submitted to taxation and had questioned Company law-enforcement, that the white new-comers were not traders as the Portuguese had been, but settlers who intended to remain. More deeply-rooted in their own land than the Ndebele, as yet unconquered by force of arms, they produced new leaders, allies rather than rivals of the chiefs, who appealed to the religious traditions of the Rozwi, to the Mwari cult which now embraced the Ndebele as well, and to the solidarity of black men against white men. The revolutionary depth of this movement, and its considerable degree of organization, posed a critical threat to the settlers, most of whose armed men were away in the column relieving Bulawayo. Survivors from Shona raids on outlying farms were brought in to the fortified camps at Headlands, Marandellas and Salisbury. For weeks after the rebellion in Matabeleland was over, the struggle here still dragged on, for there was no authoritative power structure with whom the administration could negotiate. Small communities were subdued singly in the granite outcrops, dynamite driving them from the caves. It was October before the Shona rising was thus extinguished.

Company control over Rhodesia, as its territories had been called since 1895, nearly destroyed as a result of the Raid, was thus in the end more firmly established. On the other hand authorities in London, no longer dazzled by Rhodes' unbroken chain of successes, regarded Company activities as inherently suspect. Efforts by the South Africa Committee to have the Charter rescinded failed in their object; the Foreign Office had already taken East Africa under its wing and the Treasury would not accept the additional burden. Besides, the railway system was still under construction. But Rhodes' hope of including Bechuanaland in his territories faded, and the freedom of action of Rhodesian administrators was curtailed by the presence of a Resident Commissioner after the Order in Council of 1898.

Rhodes himself was practically excluded from Cape politics for three years and was able to give more attention to Rhodesian affairs than would otherwise have been the case. First, in London, he had to face the inquiry into the raid. While his responsibility was admitted, his character was exonerated by Chamberlain, who privately threatened to withdraw the Charter if Rhodes tried to implicate the British Government. In public he defended himself in candid terms. The 'greatest raider in Africa' was President Kruger. Besides, people in England should understand that conditions in Africa were not like those at home. Their ancestors of three centuries before would have understood his actions. If Rhodes thought of Drake, he spoke in the spirit of Hastings; and even now, many of his countrymen applauded. If Gladstone decried this as the age of 'grab and brag', others saw the fallen colossus as the greatest Englishman of their time.

To the shareholders of the Chartered Company, on a visit in 1898, he said: 'I can honestly believe that my two years of trouble have made me a better man. . . . I am determined to go on with my work, the work of forming a railway junction with Egypt and the work of closer union in South Africa.' He still believed federation was possible. 'By federation I mean that the native question, the laws and the railway should be dealt with together.' As for Rhodesia, he was convinced of its future. 'I think that the country will have a great white population and that it will pass to full responsible government. But', he assured them, 'it will have to repay your full expenditure on war, public works and everything connected with its occupation and administration.' This would be possible because 'it is not only a highly mineralized country, but it will be a highly payable country in connection with its minerals.' He was still concerned with Krugerism in South Africa, but 'my North is all right. No human beings could have better prospects.'[22]

Back in Rhodesia he infused new enthusiasm among the struggling pioneers, whose prospects hardly appeared so rosy at close quarters. 'To be in this country is surely a happier thing than the deadly monotony of a Karroo village, or the even deadlier monotony of an English country town. Here at any rate you can share in the creation of a new country, and the civilizing of a new part of the world.' At Bulawayo he entertained on a generous scale and was accessible to all. Settlers came with troubles of all kinds and seldom left without promises of help, promises which Rhodes never failed to keep. He bought two large estates, one of a hundred thousand acres in the Inyanga highlands, the other at Westacres in the Matopos. Here he pursued an interest in farming already developed at the Cape. Trials were made in raising sheep and cattle, and in growing cereals, vegetables and fruit, though without great success. His interest extended to the prospecting companies who year by year sent expeditions across the Zambezi to the Katanga border, to the establishment of administrations in North-Western and North-Eastern Rhodesia, to the extension of the telegraph, and above all to the completion of the railway.

The line of rail has been the greatest single bequest of the Chartered Company to Central Africa. It has been closely bound up with the history of the whole enterprise, for it was Rhodes' offer to build the line which persuaded the British Government to grant the Charter in the first place. Starting north from Mafeking in 1895, George Pauling completed the distance to Bulawayo in two years, work on the last stage being accelerated by the crisis of the rinderpest epidemic and the rebellion. The last four hundred miles had been completed in as many working days, and the first train steamed into the recently beleaguered township on 19 October 1897. The long trek by ox wagon up the missionaries' road was now a thing of the past. Meanwhile in 1892 work had started on the line inland from Beira, across the sweltering coastal plain where men died in hundreds from the fever which had taken such toll of the Portuguese three hundred and fifty years before. The first train arrived in Umtali in 1898 after Rhodes had resited the town. A year later, despite meeting trouble with elephant which used to lift the track and uproot telegraph poles, the line reached Salisbury and in 1902 the connection with Bulawayo was made. Extensions from Salisbury to the Shamvo and

El Dorado mines, from Gwelo to the Falvi mines at Umvuma, and from Bulawayo to the gold mines at Gwanda had been laid down; before long every mine of importance was within twenty miles of a railhead. The construction northwards was delayed by the Boer War, and Rhodes never saw the carriages pass beneath the spray of the Falls as he had planned. He was still intending to complete the line to Cairo, and visited Egypt to make arrangements, but the hope was vain. On a visit to England, he promised to advance £700,000 towards the capital cost of a line along the Muchingas to Lake Tanganyika, but the British Government refused to sanction the scheme. Time has proved George Goldie's prediction to be more accurate, that major communications in Africa would be by sea, with railways running inland from the coast. More success attended the telegraph. In 1898 it was carried from Umtali to Blantyre, and by the end of the following year was at Abercorn. Rhodes saw the Kaiser, and negotiated successfully with the German Government for its extension northwards; but with his death in 1902, by which time Ujiji was in telegraphic contact with the south, construction ceased.

Rhodes' death was felt as a grave blow in Rhodesia. With the current of his energy switched off, just as problems were springing up to beset them, the settlers became acutely aware of their isolation from London, and of the drawbacks of dependence on a remote commercial company for their administration. In fact, however, the event coincided with the passing of an era of militant imperialism of which Rhodes himself had been a leading exponent. Had he lived longer, it is hard to see what more he could have done for 'his North', while his renewed intervention in South African politics could not have eased reconciliation. None the less, he was deeply mourned in Rhodesia, and not only by the white settlers. The Ndebele, despite memories of 1896 and current labour grievances, lined the twenty-mile route from Bulawayo to the Matopos grave, silent in respect for an indisputably great man. This respect was not inconsistent with the remark of an Ndebele induna, who met Francis Thompson at a railway siding two years later: 'Oh Tomosi, how have you treated us, after all your promises, which we believed?'[23]

VI

THE OCCUPATION—
(2) NORTH OF THE ZAMBEZI

Lewanika and the North-West

THE great tract of Africa over which the British South Africa
Company was authorized by royal charter to extend its influence and control was bounded in the north by 'the great lakes
of Central Africa'. The British East Africa Company was
already probing the region of Lake Victoria, and it is clear that
the northern limit referred to was a line roughly from Lake
Mweru past the southern end of Lake Tanganyika to the shores
of Lake Nyasa. On the western side, the four-centuries-old
Portuguese claim to the hinterland of Angola, and the new
Congo state founded by Leopold of Belgium in 1876, presented
the only barriers. The whole vast area between the upper
Zambezi and Lake Nyasa was still, to Europe, open ground.

Both because of distance and transport difficulties beyond
the Zambezi, and because mineral resources were not so confidently believed to exist there as in Mashonaland, concession
hunters did not go often across the Zambezi. Some ventured so
far, and hunters such as George Westbeech had travelled in
Barotse country since the 1880s. A Czech, Dr E. Holub,
journeyed dangerously in Ila country 1884–7, before the
pioneer Methodists reached it; while the French explorer Victor
Giraud, fired by the exploits of Livingstone, traversed the
Bemba plateau and explored the Bangweulu region.

Lewanika's first moves towards connection with a European
authority had nothing to do with trading concessions. The Lozi
had several times suffered from Ndebele raids. The paramount
chief knew that the Mangwato had secured immunity from
such attacks by placing themselves under British protection.
Was such a course open to the Lozi? As early as 1883, Lewanika
sent a message to Khama, inquiring how he got on with the

British, and how, if it was advisable, the protection of the 'Great White Queen' could be obtained. Khama sent a courteous reply, with the gift of a black horse, and recommended the British connection. After 1885, when Lewanika was finally established as chief, he was in close contact with the Paris missionaries, and asked Coillard to write to the Queen for protection; Coillard declined at first, not wishing to interfere in politics, and also because the majority of the indunas was against it.[1] But the progress of the international scramble for territory was making further delay unwise. In 1889 Coillard wrote to Shippard, the Administrator for Bechuanaland, on Lewanika's behalf: 'Lewanika is most anxious to solicit the Protectorate of the British Government.' He went on to add, 'The Zambezian tribes cannot be said to be warlike, but they require to be ruled with a strong hand.'[2] At the time, it was the threat of another Ndebele foray that prompted this inquiry; indeed, fear of the Ndebele throughout influenced Lewanika's policy.

Other considerations were now pressing forward. In 1889 a prospector, Harry Ware, asked Lewanika for permission to look for minerals in his country, and to dig for them when found. This was exactly the situation with which Lobengula had been faced, and the Lozi chief's different response is explained by the different nature of the Lozi people and their way of life. Though accustomed to make raids on their neighbours, particularly the Ila, and though demanding tribute payment from the inhabitants of a wide area to the east of the Barotse plain, the Lozi were not aggressively warlike. They did not live by war. They were an agricultural as well as a pastoral tribe, fished in the Zambezi and pursued many crafts. The possibility of European enterprise, together with a limited enforcement of law and order did not seem to threaten their independence and way of life. The example of Khama was an important though subsidiary factor. Lewanika was a great admirer of the Mangwato chief.

In dealing with Ware, and later with the Chartered Company, the chief also showed remarkable powers as a diplomat. The Lozi kingdom, he pointed out, extended in the north from Lovale country as far as the Katanga, while in the east it included all the tribes as far as the Lenje, including the Ila, and the Tonga and the peoples of the Zambezi valley above the

Victoria Falls. It is doubtful whether the Lozi ever exercised rule over all this area. In much of it their authority, though genuine of a kind, was not such as to justify a claim to sovereignty, as the Arbitration award of 1905 was later to point out. The Ila, for instance, paid tribute from time to time, but the Ila were a confederation of clans and not all clans would pay together; nor was the appointment of any Ila chief in the control of the Lozi paramount. But Lewanika's claim satisfied Ware and those who came after him, as well it might have done. A concession was intended primarily to satisfy not the local chiefs, but the authorities in London and the governments of other European countries. Ware did not quarrel therefore, when he was granted the right to look for minerals, and to mine them when found, for a period of twenty years, through Lewanika's dominions east of the Majili river, north and east of the cattle path from the north end of the Barotse plain to Ila country, and west to the upper Zambezi.[3] The mineral exploitation of a territory very much larger than Ireland was his alone. It was Lewanika's achievement, however, that the arrangement carefully reserved Barotseland proper, the plain and its neighbourhood where the Lozi themselves lived, from mining or other activity by Europeans.

Ware, having obtained the concession, shortly sold it to two other speculators in October 1889, and from them Rhodes bought it a few weeks later on behalf of the newly formed British South Africa Company. It will now be remembered that Rhodes' Company had what Ware and the others had not, a Charter from Queen Victoria giving it authority not only to exploit minerals, but also 'to make treaties, promulgate laws, preserve the peace, maintain a police force, and acquire new concessions'. The next step, therefore, was for Rhodes to send a representative to Barotseland to point out these facts, to offer British protection, and to make a new treaty embodying all these arrangements. Late in 1889, at a time when the Pioneer Column was preparing to set out for Mashonaland, F. E. Lochner, a former officer of the Bechuanaland Police, was appointed to make the journey to Lealui. He crossed the Zambezi at Kazungula in December and met Lewanika at Sesheke in March 1890.

By this time, more trading speculators were on the scent, of whom E. R. Middleton was the most insistent. As at Bulawayo, the object of such men was to sow distrust in the chief's mind, to discredit the Company, and to press their own claims. The French missionaries were on the side of Lochner, and the Company won the day. On 27 June 1890 Lewanika presented Lochner, as the representative of the Queen, with two large elephant tusks. A treaty was signed confirming the Company's possession of mining rights in the area stated, and also guaranteeing that the Company would protect Lewanika and his people from outside interference and attack. A Resident was to be appointed to live in Barotseland and look after these matters. The Company would pay the paramount chief £2,000 a year, and a royalty on any minerals exported under the concession.

The appointment of a Resident in Barotseland was an important clause in the treaty, but no one could be sent immediately. In the meantime, Middleton and Ware set to work. By November 1890 Lewanika, like Lobengula two years previously, was experiencing doubts about the wisdom of what he had done. He sent a letter to the Queen. Why was no Resident appointed? Was the Company indeed representing the Queen? He wished Barotseland to be under the protection of the Queen's Government, not that of commercial enterprise. The High Commissioner's reply came in that a Resident would be sent, and that the Company was, through its charter, acting on the Queen's behalf. A visit was promised from H. H. Johnston, Her Majesty's Commissioner for the Nyasa districts since 1891. Nothing came of this promise, however, for it was impossible for Johnston to leave the Shire highlands for long enough to make the journey, and in 1894 the British Central Africa Protectorate was confined within the limits of present-day Nyasaland. Lt. Col. H. Goold-Adams visited Barotseland in 1896 on behalf of the British Government, but his mission was to inquire into the extent of Lozi territory where it marched with Portuguese Angola; the boundary here was still undrawn. Meanwhile, Lewanika had to wait. Coillard, whose influence was growing during these years, counselled patience. He himself had been invited by Rhodes to act as Resident, but had refused. The question arises therefore, why it was that the representative promised in the Lochner treaty of 1890 did not arrive in Barotseland till 1897.

It was undoubtedly Rhodes' purpose, as it was to his advantage, to send a man as soon as possible. A whole series of events came between him and his design. The years 1891 to 1897 were, as we have seen, loaded with trouble. The early struggles of the Pioneers were aggravated by the Matabele war in 1893, which absorbed all attention. The outbreak of rinderpest in 1895 weakened the colony and disrupted communications with the south. Worst of all, the Jameson Raid in 1895, which not only spelt doom for Rhodes' political aims in South Africa, but nearly lost him Rhodesia as well, so discredited the Company in the eyes of the British Government, that it was forbidden to assume any further responsibilities for the time being. By 1896 Rhodes had been to England, the dust of the Raid was settling down, and arrangements were being made for Hervey, the Resident Magistrate in Salisbury, to proceed to Barotseland as Representative of the Chartered Company. Goold-Adams had informed Lewanika of this at the time of his visit, when there burst on the colony in Mashonaland and Matabeleland the unexpected storm of the rebellions. Again plans were held up, and Hervey himself was killed.

At last in 1897 Robert Coryndon, one of the original twelve whom Rhodes had assembled to form the nucleus of his Pioneer Column, was appointed as Resident in Barotseland.[4] Travelling north from Bechuanaland in the dry season, he arrived at Kazungula in September. For seven years the Lozi had awaited his arrival. The approaching event had assumed great importance in their minds. The first impression created by Coryndon's party on Letia, who met them at Kazungula, was one of disappointment. Where were the soldiers and the staff that would be expected to accompany a representative of the Great Queen among the Lozi? The Europeans, dusty and travel worn after the long, hot journey, short of oxen some of which had been lost to lions and to thirst in the desert, hardly equalled the expectations which had been formed. Coryndon himself was young, being only twenty-seven years of age. He soon earned the respect of the people, however, by his strength and skill as a hunter, and by his personal charm and talent for diplomacy. Lewanika remarked, with cautious optimism, 'He seems a good man'. Coryndon, for his part, set out at once to allay any fears the chief might have. 'You gave a concession to the B.S.A. Company. Afterwards you were afraid that you had sold your country. Do not believe this; you have not sold your country.'[5] Establishing his headquarters at Sesheke, south of the plain, he commenced at once the negotiation of a new agreement. The following year, Arthur Lawley, the Administrator of Matabeleland, came north for a visit, and on 25 June 1898 the settlement was finally made.

Compared with the Rudd Concession and the original Ware concession, this document was long and carefully thought out. The Chartered Company was given the right to prospect, mine and trade, as before, throughout the territory of the Barotse nation, and to do anything necessary for the attainment of these rights, with the restriction already mentioned concerning the Barotse valley and its neighbourhood. A new clause granted the Company 'administrative rights to deal with and adjudicate upon all cases between white men, and between white men and natives, it being clearly understood that all cases between natives shall be left to the King to deal with and dispose of'. The Company also, for the first time, undertook to maintain and endow schools and industrial establishments 'for the education and civilization of the native subjects of the King', and the provision of telegraphic, postal and transport communications. Traditional Lozi rights to game, iron-workings and tree-cutting for the manufacture of canoes were safeguarded. Lewanika, for his part, promised to continue in his endeavours for the suppression of slavery and witchcraft in his country. It was understood that the agreement should be regarded as 'a treaty of alliance between the said Barotse nation and the Government of Her Britannic Majesty Queen Victoria', and the Company undertook 'to protect the King and nation from all outside interference and attack'.[6]

The Barotseland/North-Western Rhodesia Order in Council of 1900 declared North-Western Rhodesia to be a British Protectorate, with the Company's Administrator subject to the High Commissioner at the Cape. A notable inclusion, as the result of Company pressure, was the mineral-rich region between the Kafue and the Katanga. Rights in this area had not been part of the Coryndon Concession, and no treaties with local chiefs had been made.

It is convenient at this stage to go beyond 1900 and describe certain events in Barotseland which followed the signing of the treaty and the issue of the Order in Council. Lewanika was now in increasingly close contact with the Company's administrator, and sought his advice on many points. Goold-Adams in 1896 had formed the opinion that he was 'sober and industrious . . . an intelligent man. . . . He is anxious to get white people to come and teach (arts and trades). . . . He is thoroughly loyal and, in my idea, a man to be made a friend of.'[7] This remarkable change in character of the tyrannical ruler of 1886 was undoubtedly due to the influence of Coillard and the example of Khama. Lewanika's experience of 'civilization' was now further enlarged by a visit to England in 1902 on the occasion of the coronation of Edward VII.

Accompanied by Colonel Harding of the B.S.A. Police he toured the country, and returned profoundly impressed with the hardworking qualities of the English people and an understanding of their hatred of slavery. He determined on his return to end the institution of domestic slavery in Barotseland, and in 1906 an edict was issued to this effect. The number of slaves liberated was about 30,000, many of whom had been his own property. The effect of this measure was moderated by the qualification that every freed slave must do twelve days' free labour on public works for three years to come.

The only other outstanding question to be settled in the North-West after 1900 was the delimitation of the border with Angola. The *modus vivendi* agreement with Portugal in November 1891 had declared that the line should follow the western border of the Barotse kingdom, but neither side could agree on the true extent of Lewanika's sovereignty. The Company on its maps of the time, based on the convention of June 1891, were claiming territory as far as 20° west longitude. Their argument was derived from reports by travellers and administrators, including Selous, Coryndon and Goold-Adams, of the bringing of tribute to Lewanika by tribes scattered widely over this area. Goold-Adams' report of 1896 gave a detailed account of the history and ethnography of North-Western Rhodesia, and in particular described the efforts of the Portuguese to extend their influence into Balovale country immediately adjoining Barotseland to the north.[8] Stating that the Lovale had occupied their present homes at least since the early nineteenth century, he pointed out that, excepting the interval of Kololo rule from 1820–67, the Lovale had customarily paid tribute to the Lozi, and that the present chief Kakenge owed his position to the influence of Lewanika. Nevertheless the Portuguese had established a post across the Zambezi from Kakenge's, and were clearly trying to stake their claim. In 1903 Britain and Portugal agreed that an arbitrator should be appointed to decide what, within the meaning of the treaty of 1891, were the limits of the Barotse kingdom.

The arbitration commission, under the chairmanship of the King of Italy, pointed out that the receipt of tribute could not be regarded as a proof of authority as paramount ruler; 'often a tribe pays tribute to avoid war or to gain goodwill'.[9] The true mark of paramount authority was the appointment or deposition of subordinate chiefs, and the settlement of disputes between them. By these standards a large portion of the Lovale, and a number of other tribes to the west including the Mbunda, had been absolutely independent in 1891. In view of the fluid state of some tribes and the absence of natural frontiers, it was necessary to have recourse to conventional geographical lines, which form a prominent feature of the map of North-Western Rhodesia today.

The Arab War

In the colonizing of Mashonaland, and in the establishment of administrative control in North-Western Rhodesia, the Chartered Company derived its authority from the British Government, but the ideas and the work belonged to Rhodes. With events in Nyasaland, Rhodes was less directly concerned, especially during the initial stages. Here the prime movers were the Scottish missionaries and their trading partners the African Lakes Company, while from 1889 the British Government itself took a leading part.

The first aim in Nyasa country, which all had in mind, was the ending of the slave trade. Until this was achieved, commerce, missionary work and internal order were impossible. Livingstone, who had started the campaign against the East African slave trade, was a missionary and also from 1858 till 1864 the representative of the British Government in the interior of Africa beyond Portuguese coastal territory. This partnership between mission and Government enterprise was a symbol of what was to come. Not that Britain willingly accepted responsibility in the area. It was done step by step, only as it became clear that the country could be pacified, and slaving ended, in no other way.

Since 1842, occasional attempts had been made by the British navy to prevent Arab dhows from shipping slaves off the coast, and for a short time a consul had been appointed in Mozambique to work, through the Portuguese, against the traffic. The Portuguese did not always co-operate, however, and little came of these efforts. Sir John Kirk, who was Consul-General at Zanzibar from 1870, was more successful, managing to persuade Sultan Barghash by 1876 to forbid entirely the transport of slaves in or from his dominions by land and sea. The Sultan made special reference to slaves brought from Nyasa country; with good reason, for as Kirk pointed out in 1877, it was from the districts surrounding the Lake that the greater part of the supply of slaves to Zanzibar and the Mozambique coast was still derived. These decrees of the Sultan were vigorously enforced with British naval support, with the result that the number of slaves exported through Zanzibar each year fell from 20,000 to about a tenth of that amount. This, naturally, damaged the work of slave traders in the interior, but the traffic still continued, some slaves being taken to plantations on the coast, while others were sold in Portuguese ports. Henry O'Neill, British consul at Mozambique since 1879, argued strongly that action on the coast and at sea would always fail.[1] Some means of striking at the root of the slave trade, in the interior, must be found.

In 1883, the British Government made the first move along these lines. A naval officer, Captain Foot, was appointed to be 'Her Majesty's Consul in the territories of the African Kings and Chiefs in the districts adjacent to Lake Nyasa', with the principal object of combating the slave trade. By this time, the Scottish Free Church mission at Livingstonia had been in Nyasaland for eight years, and the mission at Blantyre for five, and the Scottish Churches had long been urging the Foreign Office to send out someone who could exercise authority and look after the Europeans in the area.

Meanwhile the idea that the slave traffic could be driven out by 'legitimate' trade was being put to the test by the African Lakes Company. The Moir brothers were selling a fair amount of their calico, beads and other goods, but at this stage the effect on the tribes most guilty of slaving was small. In 1882 O'Neill, on a journey up to Shire valley, wrote that 'slaves are the chief stock in trade of (the Yao); these they cannot sell to the English. Powder and guns they require in large quantities; these the English do not sell.'[2] The 'Arab' Jumbe, who ruled the country round Kota Kota, argued that if he grew produce instead of capturing and selling slaves, no one would come to buy it.

In 1885, Foot was replaced by A. G. S. Hawes, who built a consulate on the slopes of Zomba mountain. During his first two years in the country, Hawes spent much time touring the highlands south of the lake, doing what he could to persuade the Yao to stop their slave raids, and the Ngoni to cease terrorizing the neighbouring tribes. Chikusi's Ngoni south of the lake were as feared there as were Mbelwa's people on its west shore. Even the Yao were afraid of the Ngoni. Hawes reported that the country between Zomba and Blantyre was empty as the result of their devastation. But his efforts were useless. He could not back his persuasions with force. The chiefs ignored him. The Yao slave-dealing ruler, Matapwiri, who lived close under Mlanje mountain, sent a message that if the English consul should come to visit him, he would be shot. Hawes therefore wrote to England that 'the present deplorable state of affairs' could only be improved by the presence of a few armed steamers on the lake and a small military force at Zomba.[3] Soon afterwards, events took place which greatly strengthened his appeal. In 1887 a violent flare-up in slave raiding and trading developed at the north end of the lake.

For twelve years the decrees of the Sultan of Zanzibar had checked Arab operations in the interior. Since 1885, however, Germany had been laying claim to the territories inland between Zanzibar and Lake Tanganyika. The Sultan's authority had been weakened. His control was confined to a coastal strip. The Arabs inland took advantage of the opportunity thus offered. They were, besides, angry at the incursions made by Europeans, and determined to re-assert themselves.

In this project they were encouraged by the knowledge of the British setback in the Sudan in 1885, when Mohamed Ahmed had established a slave trading Moslem empire on the Upper Nile. The north end of Lake Nyasa was the centre of their renewed activities. For long it had been an important position on the slave route, at which caravans from the Luapula, Southern Tanganyika and the Bemba plateau were despatched to Zanzibar, Kilwa, Ibo or Mozambique. The setting up of a trading post by the African Lakes Company at Karonga attracted a number of 'Arab' half-castes who, having built themselves fortified villages in the district, sold their ivory to the Company and then plundered the local tribes, particularly the Nkonde, for slaves. The most notable of these men were Mlozi, who called himself 'Sultan of Nkonde', Kopa Kopa and Msalema.

The treatment of the Nkonde by the Arabs became increasingly violent. Two of their chiefs were murdered, and in October village after village was devastated, the people slaughtered or taken into captivity. On 27 October a large number of Nkonde were driven into Kambwe lagoon where, unless they dared to come out of the reeds and be shot, they were taken by the crocodiles which infested the water. As their campaign mounted, the Arabs grew unfavourably disposed towards the trading post at Karonga. L. M. Fotheringham, a Company employee and the only European present, took steps to fortify the post, and in November reinforcements arrived, including a solicitor called Alfred Sharpe who, disappointed in an application for a government appointment in Fiji, had come to Africa to hunt big game. There were six Europeans at Karonga when it was attacked on 23 November. A firm defence was maintained, and the attackers withdrew after five days, apparently to obtain further support and supplies. The Europeans took the opportunity, with the help of Nkonde and Mambwe tribesmen, to advance on Mlozi's village, which they burned to the ground. The gloves were now off, and the 'Arab war' had started.

This little war was, in fact, a struggle for power between the Arab and the European traders, for both groups were now claiming the right of paramount authority in the region. It was only the slave hunters at the north end that the English were fighting, however, and not Arabs or Islam in general. Moreover, while the Company and the missions had the practical assistance of the consul at Zomba, they had not, as yet, the official support of the British Government.[4]

After the burning of Mlozi's stockade, there was a lull in hostilities during the early part of 1888, and efforts were made to negotiate with the Arabs, which came to nothing. In April the fighting started again, and armed reinforcements came to Karonga, including Captain F. D. Lugard, D.S.O., who was spending some leave in central Africa. Lugard took the lead in reorganizing the defence of Karonga, where there were now twenty-four Europeans and four hundred Africans. On 15 June a gallant attack was launched on Kopa Kopa's village, but the attempt to storm it failed, and Lugard himself was wounded while trying to climb the stockade. The setback convinced him of the need for artillery, and a seven-pound gun was sent for. The garrison could do nothing but wait. They could not leave. If they went, Lugard wrote, 'the results would be disastrous indeed. Lake Nyasa would be lost to us. . . . God who defends the right, prevent this!' But when the gun at last arrived in January 1889, it proved a disappointment. Lugard again: 'On March 13 I again led my little force against the enemy. . . . Shell after shell crashed into the stockades, now into Msalema's, now into Kopa Kopa's. . . . But no breach in the stockades could be effected for the high velocity of the shells caused them to pass through the poles and burst beyond. . . .'[5]

At this stage, Lugard had to leave to rejoin his regiment. The remainder of the garrison, almost in despair, clung to their post, and desultory fighting dragged on through 1889, both sides growing progressively weaker through sickness and shortage of supplies. The end of hostilities came at length with the arrival at Karonga, in October 1889, of Harry Johnston, the new Consul for Mozambique and the interior.

Sir Harry Johnston and the British Central Africa Protectorate

Johnston was no newcomer to Africa. Since visiting Tunis on a private tour in the Mediterranean ten years previously at the age of twenty-one, he had made the continent, its peoples, flora and fauna the great interest of his life.[1] It had been the time when Britain's commitment in Egypt had aroused heated debates at Westminster, and it was disapproval of Gladstone's negative attitude towards empire that provided him with the raw material of his own version of the imperial idea. Visits to Angola and the Congo in 1882–3, and to Kilimanjaro in 1885, as botanist and student of African languages, increased his awareness of Africa as a region where European exploitation was imminent, and in which Britain in her own interests could not afford to lag behind. Less single-minded than Rhodes, he none the less shared the conviction of most of his countrymen that British colonization would benefit the indigenous peoples far more than German or Portuguese, while his lively mind was genuinely, if naïvely, fired by the prospect of white settlements forming the nuclei of civilization in the dark continent. A profound admirer of Stanley, whom he had met on the Congo in 1883, he was even more a disciple of Livingstone, and throughout his career in East Africa gave his co-operation and encouragement to mission enterprise as the spearhead of British penetration. He was, in fact, prepared to co-operate with any agency including Rhodes then at work for the advancement of British interests and civilization, and for the extinction of the slave trade. During and after his visit to the Kilimanjaro area in 1885, he impressed his views with some effect on Whitehall, made the acquaintance of Anderson and Lister at the Foreign Office, and subsequently obtained an appointment as vice-consul in the Oil Rivers Protectorate.

By the time that Johnston returned on leave in 1888, the political scene throughout Africa had changed vastly. In East Africa the Anglo-German agreement had conferred upon Germany a sphere of influence inland from the Zanzibari coast, though German claims did not yet extend as far as Lake Tanganyika itself. To the south of this region the Nyasa/Tanganyika plateau was still open country, the scene of the conflict between the African Lakes Company and the 'Arab' chiefs, now emancipated from the control of Zanzibar. Meanwhile to the south-east the Portuguese Government was asserting its right of sovereignty over a vast area including Mashonaland, the lower Zambezi, the Shire and Lake Nyasa, and even the country towards Lake Bangweulu if not beyond. Wilder spirits at Lisbon, stimulated by the northward thrust of Rhodes' new British South Africa Company, and basing their claims on the treaties of the sixteenth and seventeenth centuries and on Lacerda's exploit of 1798, were reviving hopes of a *viagem à contra costa* that would provide Portugal with a transcontinental belt of territory from Mozambique to Loanda. Such a project was an impossibility since the International Conference at Berlin had ruled that a government could only uphold such claims if it was able to administer efficiently the territories concerned. The Portuguese hoped none the less to advance their claims inland north and south of the Zambezi and up the Shire valley. Their chief initial advantage was their command of the entrance inland at Quilimane, where all expeditions were compelled to disembark. This advantage was lost with the discovery in 1889 of the Chinde mouth of the Zambezi, by means of which it was possible for boats to sail up river without touching the shore.

Johnston's appointment to Mozambique came therefore at a critical time in the affairs of East Africa. Prior to his departure, two events of considerable importance for the future occurred. Rumours had reached London of Pinto's scientific expedition up the Shire, and Salisbury sent Johnston to Lisbon to discuss mutual policies with the Foreign Minister. Johnston secured an assurance that Portugal abandoned all claim to the interior, including Mashonaland, provided that the coast and the Shire valley were allotted to her sphere. This provisional arrangement satisfied neither Rhodes, who was determined on an outlet to the sea for his Company's territories, nor the Scottish churches, who were adamant against their Nyasa mission stations being placed under Portuguese control. The negotiations were by no means wasted, however, for the ground was cleared for the coming struggle, in which the British Government's hand was strengthened by a petition from the Scottish churches—Scott of Blantyre called it 'the voice of Scotland'—demanding that British protection be extended to the Shire highlands.[2]

The second occurrence was a chance meeting between Johnston and Rhodes for the first time on the eve of the former's departure for Mombasa; Rhodes was in London, busy with negotiations for the charter. In the course of a long conversation, Johnston wrote, 'we settled the immediate course

of events in central Africa'. Rhodes, already envisaging the
extension of his newly formed Company's sphere north to the
Tanganyika plateau, provided Johnston with a cheque for
£2,000 to finance a treaty-making expedition up the shore of
Lake Nyasa and beyond. This surprising arrangement was
accepted by the Foreign Office on the understanding that they
were not committed in advance to handing the administration
of the area over to the Company. It was the commencement of
two decades of somewhat unorthodox co-operation between
the Chartered Company and the British Government in the
establishment of a British administration in the region.

When Johnston at last arrived at Mozambique on 9 July
1889, it was with the knowledge that Major Serpa Pinto's
expedition was already on its way up the Shire valley. Entering
the Zambezi by the Chinde mouth, Johnston made contact
with the African Lakes Company on the lower Shire, and then
proceeded north, coming up with Pinto and his force of 4,000
south of the Ruo confluence. The Portuguese commander was
concerned by the unfriendly attitude of the Makololo chiefs,[3]
headed by Ramukukan's successor Mlauri, north of the Ruo.
The Makololo were stiffened in their resistance to the Portuguese by the presence of the Moir brothers and the African
Lakes Company, and supplied with Union Jacks hastily
manufactured by the ladies of the Blantyre mission. Despite
the Portuguese insistence on the purely scientific nature of the
expedition, Johnston firmly warned them not to enter the
highlands. Pinto therefore halted at the confluence. Johnston
proceeded north on his treaty-making expedition, leaving
Buchanan of the African Lakes Company as acting consul at
Zomba. A few weeks later small Portuguese forces twice
crossed the Ruo, whereupon Buchanan according to instructions declared a formal British protectorate over Yao and
Makololo country.[4]

By this time, however, the mounting Portuguese pressure
had sparked off sharp reaction in London. Early in January an
ultimatum was sent to Lisbon, threatening that if activities
across the Ruo were commenced the island of Mozambique
would be occupied by a British naval force. Before this determined front the Portuguese gave way. Their local forces were
ordered to respect the Ruo as the limit of Portuguese territory

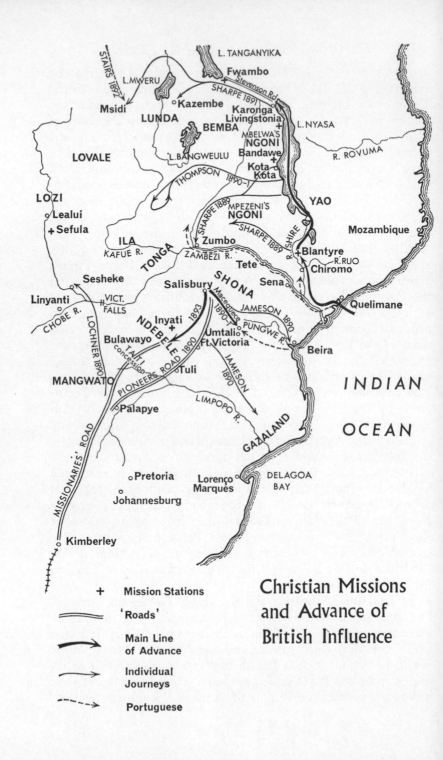

STAIRS 1892
L. TANGANYIKA
L.MWERU
Fwambo
Stevenson Rd.
SHARPE 1891
Msidi
Kazembe
Karonga
LUNDA
Livingstonia
L. NYASA
BEMBA
MBELWA'S
NGONI
L.BANGWEULU
Bandawe
R. ROVUMA
THOMPSON 1890-1
Kota-
Kota
LOZI
SHARPE 1889
MPEZENI'S
YAO
Lealui
NGONI
Sefula
SHARPE 1889
Mozambique
ILA
Zumbo
R.SHIRE
KAFUE R.
ZAMBEZI R.
+ Blantyre
TONGA
Tete
R.RUO
Sesheke
Sena
Chiromo
SHONA
Linyanti
VICT.
Salisbury
FALLS
Macequece
Quelimane
CHOBE R.
1893
JAMESON 1890
LOCHNER 1890
Inyati
PUNGWE R.
NDEBELE
Umtali
Bulawayo
1890
Ft.Victoria
Beira
TATI
concession
Tuli
JAMESON
PIONEERS' ROAD
MANGWATO
1890
LIMPOPO R.
INDIAN
Palapye
GAZALAND
OCEAN
MISSIONARIES' ROAD
Pretoria
Lorenço
DELAGOA
Johannesburg
Marques
BAY
Kimberley

+   Mission Stations

         'Roads'

         Main Line   Christian Missions
         of Advance   and Advance of
                            British Influence
         Individual
         Journeys

         Portuguese

in the district, an arrangement which was repeated in the Anglo-Portuguese agreement of 20 August 1890. Though this was not ratified by the Cortes, its details with minor modifications were finally confirmed in the Convention of 11 June 1891.[5]

In the meantime Johnston had proceeded on his journey north. His object, somewhat ill-defined, was to secure, at this critical juncture of European imperialism, as much as possible of the Nyasa/Tanganyika plateau for Britain. In fact he had a fourfold task. First, to make treaties in the Shire highlands that would ensure beyond possible doubt the coming British claim to a protectorate and that would precede the establishment of order among the Yao and Ngoni tribes. Second, to extend the British liaison among the chiefs in the Luangwa valley and along the escarpment—this in co-ordination with Rhodes, making sure of the northward communications of the Chartered Company. Third, to assert British authority over the slave-trading 'Arab' empire at the north end of Lake Nyasa. Fourth and last, he hoped to make treaties along the line of the Stevenson road, thus gaining the Tanganyika plateau, at present in dispute between Britain and Germany, for the British sphere of influence.

During August 1889, Johnston was at work along the upper Shire and the highlands, making treaties with the Makololo and Yao chiefs. During September he worked his way through Cewa villages, to reach Jumbe's 'Arab' town at Kota Kota. Jumbe, who had at one time combined participation in the slave traffic with a lucrative trade in ivory, and had been supporting the Arabs at Karonga in the war against the Lakes Company, had recently been more friendly towards the British. Johnston's persuasive diplomacy, warning him of Portuguese pressure in the south and German in the north, secured a treaty by which Jumbe surrendered political control of his country to the Queen's representative,[6] an achievement which paved the way towards a settlement with Mlozi at the north end. Thither the consul now proceeded, making further treaties with the Tonga chiefs in the neighbourhood of the Bandawe mission on the way.[7] At Karonga the desultory struggle of two years' standing had reached a stalemate, and Johnston, arriving there in October, at the risk of his life visited the Arab leaders in their stockade and brought about a truce agreement. The molestation of the local people was to cease, and disputes with the

Lakes Company were to be settled through the consul himself or his representative. Although outright victory had not been achieved, 'the Arabs', wrote Johnston, 'have had a most severe lesson . . . and I do not think they will attempt to tackle us again; at any rate, not for several years'.[8]

Johnston indeed regarded the Bemba and Ngoni as the main threat to peace, and had formed a rather over-optimistic opinion of the local 'Arab' chiefs. This view was strengthened by the friendly reception he received from those in the Tanganyika/Mweru area, which he reached in December after crossing the Tanganyika plateau. He was concluding further treaties, and had made the acquaintance of the London Society missionaries at Fwambo, when news of the Portuguese moves on the Shire brought him hastening back to Mozambique in January 1890.

During the following year British influence, still a combined operation between the British Government and the Chartered Company, penetrated the wide stretch of country between the Shire and the Katanga that had earlier been crossed at various times by Livingstone and a few Portuguese pioneers. Shortly after entering the Shire highlands in August 1889, Johnston had come by chance across Alfred Sharpe who, having taken part in the fighting at Karonga, was pursuing his big-game hunting. At once impressed with Sharpe's character, Johnston engaged him as a temporary vice-consul with instructions to travel westwards to the lower Luangwa and negotiate with the chiefs in that region. The commission was willingly accepted. After a preliminary expedition that season, Sharpe set out in March 1890, his carriers dispirited by the prolonged rains and fearing for their lives in Ngoni country. On reaching Mpezeni's village at the end of March, he found the chief—the son of the Ngoni leader who had settled in the district about twenty years before —friendly but unco-operative. 'Treaties he would not touch, nor the flag.' Mpezeni appeared to think himself the most powerful monarch in the world, except possibly Mbelwa. 'The suggestion', wrote Sharpe, 'that it would be a good thing for him to have (in case of further war) so powerful a friend as the Queen, created great amusement.'[9] The only satisfaction to be gained from this rebuff was that the Portuguese had met with a similar refusal. The rest of the journey, which took Sharpe through Nsenga and Cewa country, was hardly more successful, for the inhabitants lived in terror of the Portuguese half-caste 'prazo' owners in the district of Zumbo. Matakenya was the most notorious of these men, who by their activities had stripped the country of most of its population. Only two headmen dared to sign, and on reaching his furthest point Sharpe, despairing of any more valid achievement, hoisted the flag, fired a salute and declared a protectorate west of the Luangwa which needless to say was without authority and of no effect.

After returning to Lake Nyasa, Sharpe set out again early in July and passing through Karonga, made his way across the Nyasa/Tanganyika plateau visited by Johnston the year before. His object now was to secure the Luapula valley and the Katanga, already known to be rich in copper, regardless of the terms of the Berlin treaty which had provisionally allotted it to the Congo sphere. The Lunda capital was reached at the end of September. Kazembe, unlike Mpezeni, made no difficulty, received the British flag, adopted British protection, and agreed to grant mineral concessions to the Chartered Company, whom Sharpe was representing through Johnston's agreement with Rhodes. Kazembe's power, however, only extended over the country east of the Luapula. The principal chief in Garanganze, the Katanga area to the south-west of the river, was Msidi, a slave trader with some Arab blood, among whose subjects were included those Shila whom the Lunda had found on the Luapula when they arrived there in the eighteenth century.[10] As Lacerda had discovered, they and Kazembe's Lunda were rivals of long standing. Kazembe now refused permission for Sharpe to cross the river. After some delay, the party made a detour round the north end of Lake Mweru, and at last reached Msidi's in November. In the meantime Arnot, the missionary, who had advised Msidi to make no treaty without his advice, had left the country. The chief, a dour tyrant whom the local missionaries treated with considerable respect, was obdurate, and Sharpe had no choice but to return by the way he had come.[11]

In the meantime, ignorant of Johnston's engagement of Sharpe, Rhodes had despatched Joseph Thomson, the African explorer, to the same destination. Rhodes, beset by the urgent need to exploit to the full the opportunity provided by the indefinite terms of the charter concerning the northern limits of his territory, had already sent Frank Lochner to Lealui, and was particularly anxious about the fate of the rich Katanga region. Thomson met Sharpe in Nyasaland, and it was agreed that he should proceed by a more southerly route. Travelling west from Kota Kota during the dry season of 1890, Thomson crossed the Luangwa, passed south of Lake Bangweulu, and reached the upper Kafue. Here he became too ill to go further, and had to turn back without having visited Msidi. He had, none the less, covered a great distance over country never before seen by a European, including much of the present Central Province of Zambia. In the course of his journey he had secured the 'signatures' of a number of chiefs to the treaty forms with which he had been supplied.

It has since been remarked that the wording of these and other such documents was absurd, and that many of the 'chiefs' who signed them were in fact not true chiefs and had no authority to do so. Since no missionaries were present in this area as in Matabeleland and Barotseland to interpret and explain the meaning of the agreements, they can hardly be regarded as legally valid. At the time, however, they constituted a sufficiently strong claim to the extension of the Company's influence in the region against other competitors, which was the purpose for which they were designed.

During the dry season of 1890, therefore, the Katanga question was still unsettled. The work of Johnston and Sharpe on the Tanganyika plateau and the Luapula, however, now bore fruit. At the time of Johnston's journey late in 1889, Lord Salisbury had been concerned lest this intrusion into a disputed sphere should antagonize the German Government, laying claim to the Tanganyika area since the agreement of 1886. Britain had no wish to make trouble with Germany since colonial competition with France in Africa and with Russia in Asia had left her isolated. But events in Uganda, where the activities of the Imperial British East Africa Company in competition with German interests had created for Britain the opportunity of controlling the headwaters of the Nile, had meanwhile made imperative the conclusion of a fresh agreement.[12] The new German administration following Bismarck's fall from office was favourable to a détente with Britain, and a general convention covering the boundaries of the two countries' colonial territories was signed on 1 July 1890.[13] The north end of Lake Nyasa beyond the Songwe river was surrendered to Germany, but most of the Nyasa/Tanganyika plateau was secured to Britain, the boundary running a short distance to the north of the Stevenson road.

This treaty finally put an end to the hopes of an all-British route to Cairo. Rhodes, who never fully realized that Britain's affairs in Africa were set against a background of European politics, was indignant. Salisbury however considered that in establishing protectorates in Uganda and over the Shire highlands, Britain had discharged her share of the responsibility for subduing the slave trade, and scorned the 'curious idea' that there was some special advantage in handling a stretch of territory extending all the way from Cape Town to the sources of the Nile.[14]

As yet, no treaties had been concluded with three of the most powerful chiefs west of Lake Nyasa—Msidi, Mpezeni and Chitimukulu. The Katanga fell to King Leopold's territory of the Congo the following year, 1891, when a Belgian expedition led by Captain Stairs, an Englishman, came to Msidi's. The outcome of this expedition was less peaceful than Sharpe's, for in a scuffle at the chief's enclosure Stairs shot Msidi dead and at once ran up the Belgian flag. The fate may have been well-deserved, but most of the Katanga was lost to the Chartered Company and Britain.[15] When in 1893–4 the whole country between Lake Nyasa and the Kafue was formally declared a British Protectorate, the Bemba and Mpezeni's Ngoni were still nominally independent. It was to be only a matter of time before they were absorbed.

By 1891 the African Lakes Company, the Scottish missions and the B.S.A. Company, under the general supervision of the British Government through Her Majesty's Consul, were asserting their influence over most of the area. None the less, their power of control was small. Slave trading was still being carried on. Ngoni raids were still commonplace. Traders and concession hunters, often men of ill repute, were entering Nyasa country and trying to buy up land. The need to establish a firm administration was clear, but the B.S.A. Company was fully occupied with its colony in Mashonaland, while the British Government was, as always, unwilling to shoulder the extra responsibility and expense. Rhodes therefore entered into an agreement with the African Lakes Company in 1890 to pay the latter an annual subsidy of £9,000 for the purpose of maintaining law and order and protecting mission stations.[16] For eighteen months the Lakes Company drew the subsidy, but did little to justify it. Johnston was impatient. He considered the Company 'entirely unfitted to be entrusted with governing powers', a true estimate which was increasingly plain to all. In February 1891, therefore, a new agreement was arrived at between the Chartered Company and the Imperial Government, by which the former retained the right of commercial and mineral development in the area west of Lake Nyasa, and would pay £10,000 a year to maintain a police force which the Government, not the Lakes Company, would provide. The Government would appoint a Commissioner for the area, who would be independent of Chartered Company control.

On 14 February 1891 Johnston, who had been on leave in England since his exploits of the previous year, was appointed to this post as 'Her Majesty's Commissioner and Consul-General to the territories under British influence to the north of the Zambezi'. While the country west of the Nyasa watershed was to fall within the B.S.A. Company's charter, the country to the east was to be controlled directly by the Foreign Office. In May came the official statement that 'by virtue of agreements with the native chiefs ... the Nyasaland Districts are under the Protectorate of Her Majesty the Queen'. A short time later the Nyasaland Districts were renamed the 'British Central Africa Protectorate'.

Protracted negotiations continued between the Chartered Company and the African Lakes Company, at the end of which in 1893 the affairs of the latter were wound up. Its land concessions, principally to the north of Lake Nyasa, were transferred to the Chartered Company, while its trading activities passed to the new African Lakes Corporation.

Johnston arrived on the Shire to take up his new appointment in July 1891. It was to find that, apart from intermittent fighting by the Ngoni, the Yao chiefs were intensifying their violent and bloody slave raiding, which Vice-Consul Buchanan had been unable to prevent. Johnston now had at his disposal a small force of under 200 men, including seventy-one Indians,

mostly Sikhs, commanded by Captain Maguire. The Commissioner at once took the initiative, attacking Chikumba on
the slopes of Mlanje mountain, subduing Mponda at the south
end of Lake Nyasa where Fort Johnston was set up, and driving
Makanjira, the principal slave raider, back from the eastern
shore of the lake. Johnston himself frequently took part in the
fighting. He invariably wore a straw hat and carried a white
umbrella, seeming to fear sunstroke more than bullets. 'Native
troops', stated a contemporary account, 'followed this standard
up to and over stockades belching with gunfire.'[17] Zarafi,
Liwonde and other Yao chiefs were compelled to sign treaties
ceding sovereign rights to the Queen, and the extent of Crown
land was enlarged over a considerable area, including the
upper part of Mlanje mountain.

In December 1891 affairs took a turn for the worse when,
during a renewed assault on Makanjira, Maguire was killed.
Sharpe and Buchanan were on leave in Britain, and it was a
difficult time for Johnston; but in this crisis he obtained a
further £10,000 from Rhodes with which the following year
he was able to strengthen his puny force. Two gunboats for the
lake were provided by the Admiralty, and late in 1893 a third
campaign against Makanjira forced the latter to take refuge
in Portuguese territory. Fort Maguire was established on the
lake shore near the Yao chief's former headquarters. But
pacification was not even yet complete. During the next season
Makanjira, supported by Zarafi, Kawinga and Matapwiri,
summoned up a last effort to drive the British out of the Shire
highlands. The attempt failed. The Yao lacked co-ordination,
and had moreover now aroused the enmity of the Portuguese
across the border. The forts constructed by Johnston, which now
included Forts Lister, Anderson and Liwonde, though no more
than rectangular earthworks two hundred yards square with a
watchtower for surveying the surrounding country, buttressed
the British force. In September 1895, Matapwiri surrendered
and two months later Makanjira's villages south-east of the lake
were destroyed, many slaves being set free and the chief himself
being driven across the border, this time not to return. By 1896
the Yao chiefs had been finally subdued, the Ngoni had been
pacified, and order had come at last to the Shire highlands.[18]

In the north, the task of establishing British authority was not yet completed. The Germans in East Africa, according to the terms of the Brussels agreement of 1890, were endeavouring to suppress the slave trade, but were on the other hand turning a blind eye towards, and even encouraging, the import of weapons and gunpowder. In 1892 they launched the *Hermann von Wissman* for use against slaving on the north-east corner of the lake, but before long it was shipping powder across. The slave traders at the north end, being thus kept supplied, were able to continue their activities, and Johnston, fully occupied in the south, was unable to prevent them. Many slaves still came from the Luapula and Bangweulu regions, supplied by the Lunda and the Bemba. A fortified post established at Deep Bay was of small effect. By 1895 the attitude of the 'Arabs', and of Mlozi in particular, was hostile and offensive in the extreme. Johnston decided to act. Sailing swiftly to Karonga with an armed force at the end of November, he took the 'Arabs' by surprise. They and their supporters were driven from their villages, and Mlozi's was surrounded. After a fierce struggle the defenders were overcome and the chief summarily tried and put to death.[19]

This exploit all but completed Johnston's services to Nyasaland. A man of small physique, he was tired out by the constant strain of the past six years, and suffered from blackwater fever. At the end of the year he retired to England, his place in the Protectorate being taken by Alfred Sharpe[20]. He had, however, laid the foundations of British policy for many years to come— first by establishing order, putting an end to the slave trade and constructing the framework of an administrative system; second by encouraging not only European immigrants but also Indian traders, who would perform a vital service to the country as a connecting link, as he saw it, between the white and black communities; third, by inaugurating a land policy based on Certificates of Claim. It was an achievement which was not matched by any other administrator during that pioneer decade in Central Africa.

The Pacification of the North-East

According to the agreement of 1891, the Chartered Company was providing the money for the policing and administration of British Central Africa, except for the salaries of the Commissioner and his deputy who were Imperial appointments, while itself controlling the mineral rights of the area. This arrangement did not work very smoothly, and led to bitter recriminations between Johnston and Rhodes. The main purpose of the British Government in Nyasa country was the suppression of the slave trade; Rhodes had commercial development and the extension of the Cape to Cairo communications chiefly in mind. So it came about, as we have seen, that in 1894 Nyasaland, according to its present boundaries, was separated from the rest of British Central Africa and controlled directly from the Foreign Office. The remainder of the former territory was placed under the administration of the Chartered Company. In 1895 Major Forbes, who had commanded the Salisbury column and the Shangani column in 1893, and had taken part in the Manicaland expedition, was appointed to be the Company's Administrator in its territories north of the Zambezi. These included the whole region from Barotseland to the Nyasa border.

For the first four years Forbes' headquarters were outside his own territory at Zomba, while from 1897 Robert Coryndon, at Lealui, nominally his subordinate, was discharging the responsibilities of Resident in North-Western Rhodesia. The hand of the Company's administration was still hardly felt over the huge area between the Zambezi and the Tanganyika plateau, which contained three of the most powerful Central African tribes—Mpezeni's Ngoni, the Bemba, and the Luapula Lunda—all still requiring to be incorporated and subdued.

It will be remembered that when Sharpe visited Mpezeni's in 1890, the Ngoni chief had refused to accept the flag or to make any agreement. Ignoring this determined show of independence, the Anglo-Portuguese Convention of 11 June 1891[1] marked the boundary between the Portuguese and British spheres of influence and placed almost the whole of Mpezeni's country inside the British sphere. According to the 1885 Berlin Convention, such a claim to territory must be supported by valid treaties and followed up by effective administration, but for the time being Rhodes and Johnston were fully engaged elsewhere Thus although the ultimate outcome was hardly in doubt, the method by which the Ngoni and Cewa should be politically

incorporated in British territory was still uncertain. The
B.S.A. Company meanwhile, in default of a concession treaty,
could not lay claim to the economic resources of the area.
Some anxiety was therefore aroused by the activities of Karl
Wiese, a trader of German birth who had been living among
the Ngoni and neighbouring tribes since 1885. Though free-
lance, Wiese had sold slaves in Portuguese territory and
obtained certain mining rights from the authorities at Mozambique. He now in June 1891 informed Johnston of concessions
obtained from various chiefs in the Nyasa/Zambezi watershed,
including one for exclusive mineral, timber and railway rights
from Mpezeni himself, dated April 1891.[2] Wiese requested a
Certificate of Claim under Johnston's recently inaugurated
system. This Johnston refused, his grounds being that Wiese was
objectionable as a slave dealer, and that Mpezeni had not
himself signed the document. Moreover he argued now and
subsequently, though with flimsy justification, that Mpezeni's
people, being armed intruders of recent origin, lacked true
territorial or other rights in the area. Wiese left for Europe to
form the Mozambique Company and to plead at the Foreign
Office for recognition, but was referred back to Blantyre. In
September 1893 during his continued absence, Johnston granted
a Certificate of Claim to the B.S.A. Company, basing it on the
treaties of Sharpe and Stevenson with certain Cewa chiefs. The
validity of these treaties was at least as dubious as that of
Wiese's, but the Foreign Office supported Johnston. Fear that
the German trader might seek support from Berlin hastened
the agreement of 1894 by which the territory west of the Nyasa
districts was placed under the B.S.A. Company's administrative
control. The agreement stipulated that Wiese's claim should
not be prejudiced. Rhodes' action now compared closely with
his policy towards Lippert in Mashonaland and Ware in
Barotseland. Coming to terms with Wiese and the Mozambique
Company, he secured the formation of a new Company, the
North Charterland Exploration Company, in which the B.S.A.
Company had an interest. The whole of Mpezeni's country was
placed in the territory of the North Charterland Concession.[3]

   In 1896 the pioneer party of European prospectors arrived in
Ngoni territory. A small administrative post was set up at
Cinunda's, some distance from the site of the present Fort

Jameson and thirty miles north of Mpezeni's village at Loan-gweni. Prospectors were encouraged to visit the district, a reward of £10,000 having been offered for the discovery of the first payable goldfield, and together with local traders formed a small community just outside the Ngoni capital. Wiese, now back in Africa, had his camp nearby, and exerted considerable influence over the chief, with whom he had now been associated for several years. Mpezeni however was by this time an old man of between sixty-five and seventy years of age, and his hold on the younger generation was growing weaker. Though he continued to maintain the friendly, independent attitude towards Europeans that Sharpe had found in 1890, the younger leaders were hostile, particularly the chief's son Nsingu, who had twice recently been insulted by North Charterland officials. The presence of a slowly growing community of white men in the heart of the country was now arousing general fear and dislike. The situation bore a close similarity to that in Matabeleland ten years before. But the Ngoni, unlike the Ndebele, the Lozi, their cousins under Mbelwa, and even lately the Bemba, had no missionaries resident among them to interpret, to advise, to set an example in goodwill and allay misunderstanding. On the other hand, far more than the Ndebele, they had lost their continuity of blood and tradition. Many members of the tribe did not speak the Ngoni language, and though the tribal organization remained its discipline had deteriorated.

Towards the end of 1897, Ngoni military activity became threatening. In December two Europeans coming up from Tete were killed, and by the New Year Wiese and his companions were more or less surrounded. An urgent message was sent to Cinunda's asking for assistance. The North Charterland police there were too few to cope with a crisis of this magnitude, and the appeal was relayed to Blantyre. The Acting Administrator for Northern Rhodesia at Zomba accepted an offer of help from Captain Manning, commanding the British Central Africa Rifles, and a column of 650 men left Blantyre on 2 January 1898. By the 16th they were in Mpezeni's country, and two days later met and fought with the Ngoni for the first time. It was believed that Ngoni impis at full strength could total 10,000 fighting men, but partly because it was the season of the first fruits festival they could only muster half this number; even these used not to attack together, for each regiment would take its turn in a spirit of competition. By the 19th Captain Brake with one company had reached Loangweni (Fort Young) and relieved the beleaguered Europeans.

On the following day a large number of Ngoni attacked the British force, but in a short while were driven off. Brake recorded that 'although the Ngoni showed considerable courage, frequently advancing to within fifty yards of our men, they could not face the volleys. Guns amongst them were rare, and their fire is most inaccurate, and in no case did they endeavour to charge home.'[4] Brake's company now advanced into the neighbouring hills, into which most of the Ngoni led by Nsingu had fled, leaving Mpezeni with a few supporters in his kraal. A number of villages, including Nsingu's, were burned. Mpezeni refused to negotiate, and also took refuge in the hills. There were several skirmishes before he and his son were captured and the tribe finally subdued. Nsingu was tried 'for murder, instigating to murder, and raiding in British territory', and shot in the presence of the assembled headmen. Twelve thousand cattle, nearly a third of the tribal herds, were confiscated. Mpezeni was moved to Fort Manning and held in custody. He was allowed to return a year later, but died in October 1900.

Although this war has sometimes been called the Ngoni 'rebellion', the Ngoni themselves can hardly have seen it in that light. They had never accepted the sovereignty of the Company or the Queen, and had entered into no agreement with a European, unless Wiese's doubtful trading concession be regarded as valid. Up till this time no definite move had been made towards their subjugation. The British attitude was expressed in Johnston's convenient opinion that Mpezeni was an alien invader, and that his refusal to fall into line could be ignored until an opportunity occurred for reducing him to submission.[5] Wiese's appeal for help had created that opportunity. The episode provides interesting contrasts with events in Matabeleland and illustrates the wisdom of Lobengula in withholding his own recruits. Johnston's outlook was coloured by his own experience of fighting, often with Chikusi's Ngoni, in the Shire highlands. Missionary influence averted war with Mbelwa. War with Mpezeni was only made inevitable by the mistaken belief that his country was rich in gold deposits. No such hopes impelled traders to visit Chitimukulu's country north of the Luangwa valley. The Bemba plateau in 1896 was still a closed territory into which a white man had scarcely ventured since Livingstone's day, apart from the Roman Catholic missionaries. Their exploits have been referred to earlier, together with the founding of Chilubula station near Mwamba's village. The White Fathers derived a small amount of moral support from the presence of B.S.A. Company administrative outposts on the borders of Lubemba at Abercorn and Fife.

On transferring Hugh Marshall from Chiromo to Abercorn in 1893, Johnston had told him that 'this seems to be a suitable spot for checking the slave caravan routes to the east coast, and for defending the European settlements at the south end of Tanganyika against the raids of the Awemba. . . . It would be a very good thing if you could enter into friendly relations with the Awemba chiefs. . . . They are a fierce and an intractable people, however, and you will need to be cautious in your first dealings with them.'[6] Marshall, a good, steady servant of the Company, built an impregnable stockade at Abercorn of poles tightly wedged together, ten feet high, with a look-out platform over the main gate, and to this sanctuary came many refugees from among the neighbouring tribes including the Bemba themselves. The Bemba were going through one of the most troubled periods in their history, when the death of a chief was the signal for wholesale carnage, and the population was in a state of uneasiness that could quickly turn to terror on account of slave-hunting raids.[7] Their villages, stockaded and surrounded by a ditch as much as eight feet deep, with huts crowded inside, were in a perpetual state of defence against possible visits from Arab caravans.

The overthrow of Mlozi at Karonga in December 1895 had dislodged the 'Arabs' from their position at the north end of Lake Nyasa, but had not destroyed their power altogether. A few of their leaders, notably Kopa Kopa and Nasoro bin Suleiman, escaped further inland to the west with their own armed escorts. There had of course been Muslim chiefs in the area for a long time. Forbes wrote that 'the people of the Mweru district appear to have sustained the first Arab invasion about the year 1865, when the Watabwa were raided with overwhelming force and in a few years completely broken up. The Chishinga, Lunda and Ushi alone appeared to have been able to withstand . . . Arab attacks.' Some 'Arab' chiefs, desiring to be free from the growing influence of the Germans in the north-east and the British in the east, now conceived the idea of a Muslim kingdom in the Luapula/Katanga region. Others, in alliance with groups of Bemba, attempted to continue the old traffic in slaves, preying on the weaker tribes around from new headquarters.

Of these new centres one of the most important was in Senga country near the upper reaches of the Luangwa river, little over a hundred miles from Lake Nyasa, but separated from the lake shore by the highland ranges of the Nyika plateau. From here, slave caravans had to cross the Stevenson road and the border into German East Africa, and make their way down to the coast keeping well to the north of the lake. In order to check this traffic, Forbes set up a new sub-station at Inyala between Fife and Karonga on the B.C.A./N.E.R. border in 1896, and to the south, near to present-day Isoka, a fortified post was built at Mirongo. In September 1897 Robert Young was travelling in the Mirongo locality when he received a call for help from a friendly local chief, Chiwale, who expected an attack by Senga 'Arabs' together with numbers of Bemba tribesmen. Young took the fifteen native police who were with him to Chiwale's and being attacked soon afterwards, defended the village for five days against determined rushes from 'Arabs' and Bemba. He himself built a rough platform in a tree, from which vantage point he was able to pick off a number of the attackers. Soon after the raiders had made off reinforcements from Fife arrived under William McKinnon, a capable man though with wild ideas, and the combined force advanced into the neighbouring country, burning villages and freeing slaves. Young wrote of the action: 'This has had the most pacifying effect on the district. The people had thought we were afraid of the Arabs. If ever people were released from bondage it is the Senga, who were absolute slaves of the Arabs, having to grow grain for them, kill elephants, etc.'[8]

Muslim influence in the eastern part of the Bemba plateau was now almost entirely destroyed, while to the north the Boma at Abercorn was noticeably restricting their freedom of action. The Bemba were becoming increasingly hemmed into their own territory. They were still, at this time, adamantly hostile to any Europeans visiting their country, and the next task, Forbes believed, was to break their power. The task was made easier by the fact that, in order to obtain slaves, the more powerful among them began to raid villages belonging to their own tribe. This led to rivalry between the larger groups, and in particular between Mwamba and Chitimukulu. Though Chiti was the paramount, Mwamba had for a long time had more or less independent status. In 1897, Chitimukulu was appealing to Young for his assistance in this probable conflict, and Young sent his deputation on to McKinnon at Fife. After the incident at Chiwale's, Mwamba, whose clansmen had helped in the attack on Chiwale, followed suit by asking the Company's support against Chitimukulu.

In this way, disunity was the downfall of Bemba. Company intervention in the affairs of the tribe was inevitable. The course of events was unexpectedly modified, however, by the death of Mwamba in October 1898. The succession was disputed, and Ponde, a nephew of Mwamba and a man of forceful personality, claimed the chieftainship. McKinnon did not like the look of Ponde, however, and Young wrote that his claim seemed to have no justification; though it is probable that their understanding of Bemba custom was at fault. Marching from Mirongo, the Company police turned Ponde out of Mwamba's village, and constructed a fortified post at Kasama, then a few miles from its present position. Young was left in control there, while McKinnon returned to his station at Fife. Ponde, however, refused to acknowledge himself beaten, and coming back to the district, proceeded to build a fortified village on some high ground naturally defended by rocks. Young wisely considered that his own small force was insufficient to attack the place with success, and asked McKinnon to send reinforcements. Charging the village just before dawn in 1898, the police took the Bemba by surprise. Hardly any resistance was offered. Ponde and some of his followers escaped and there was no loss of life.[9]

Meanwhile, the Company's officers in the Mweru-Luapula area were having trouble with the 'Arabs', who were still at large

in those parts. Andrew Law, the Assistant Collector at Kalungwisi, had approached Mporokoso's village in 1898 in the hope
of recruiting labour for the construction of the telegraph line,
then moving up the shore of Lake Nyasa. He had received a
hot welcome and been driven off. It appeared that Nasoro,
the slave dealer from Karonga, had established himself with
Chief Mporokoso. In April 1899 therefore, Harrington, who
was then at Abercorn as Assistant Collector for the Luapula-
Mweru district, raised a force of a hundred native police with
three other Europeans, and marched south. The village was
found to be strongly stockaded, and there was a full day of
preliminary firing before the assault was launched. Most of the
resistance came from the 'Arabs' rather than from Mporokoso's
people themselves. The village was soon captured and though
Nasoro escaped, he gave himself up to Harrington a few weeks
later.

The fourth and last big 'military' operation in this part of
North-Eastern Rhodesia concerned Kazembe's Lunda on the
Luapula. This area was the last refuge of the 'Arab' traders.
The Luapula chiefs were much under their influence, and the
Company's stations on Lake Mweru had not been sufficiently
strong to prevent them from doing as they wished. In October
1899 Alfred Sharpe, who had been made Commissioner of the
Nyasaland Protectorate, marched on Kalungwisi himself with
two companies of the British Central Africa Rifles, making the
journey from Blantyre in two months. There was no fighting.
When the column approached the Lunda capital the 'Arabs'
fled. After declaring that he would not discuss matters at all but
would fight rather than acknowledge European authority,
Kazembe went with them, but early in the following year he
returned, and was reinstated as chief. This show of strength had
a marked effect. Codrington, in his report to the Company in
1900, wrote that at last 'the power and influence of the Arabs,
who defied Lugard at Karonga in 1887, who blocked the Nyasa-
Tanganyika road till defeated by Sir H. Johnston in 1895, and
who were broken up and dispersed by B.S.A. Company officials
in Senga country, have dwindled to absolute insignificance.
. . . Not more than three of the Arab chiefs . . . remain in the
country; they have been deserted by their followers . . . and
are on quite friendly terms with the Administration.'[10]

VII

THE FIRST YEARS OF
OCCUPATION

Mining and Land Settlement

'BEFORE many years are over,' the Duke of Fife predicted in 1893 before a London meeting of the B.S.A. Company shareholders, 'thousands of our countrymen, who are too crowded here, will take advantage of the enormous space, the healthful climate and the immense resources which this territory offers to those who will go in and possess the land.'[1] He was greeted with enthusiastic applause. The words, as well as the aspirations, were akin to those of Rhodes himself, who frequently boasted of the quantity of land and minerals that his Company 'possessed'. By 1900 it still appeared as if such optimism could not be exaggerated. The tide of imperialism still flowed strong in Britain, where the Rhodesias were regarded as perhaps the greatest of Chamberlain's 'undeveloped estates', and the prolonged series of trade depressions that accompanied the collapse of agriculture in the last years of the century encouraged many of the more enterprising to emigrate abroad. Moreover the difficulties brought upon the pioneer settlements by the rebellions followed by the Boer war, and the incomplete state of the railway line, all helped to obscure the sobering magnitude of the real obstacles in the way of development. The truth did not in fact emerge until after Rhodes' death in 1902.

By this time however Rhodesians were beginning to grasp the fact that, south of the Zambezi at least, there was no great single source of mineral wealth. The dramatic story of the Californian, Canadian, Australian and South African gold strikes was not after all here to be repeated. Gold was found, chiefly around ancient workings, but it was scattered across the country in small deposits and not, as along the Witwatersrand, in one rich reef; by 1898 over 160,000 claims had been registered. It could be most profitably worked by units carrying limited overheads. In 1903 the law requiring that, in Southern Rhodesia, only enterprises in which the B.S.A. Company had an interest could perform mining operations, was relaxed, so that individual prospectors could work their own private claims. These 'small workers' effected a revolution in Southern Rhodesian gold mining that was assisted by the Company's revision of its royalties policy.[2] Between 1904 and 1906 output, which had been climbing slowly for a decade, doubled to 551,895 ozs. Meanwhile other mineral deposits had been found of which, apart from the huge coal field at Wankie, asbestos was to prove the most important. The production of fibre at Shabani began in 1908; Southern Rhodesia was in time to become the third largest producer in the world. Chrome and zinc were also being produced before the war.

North of the Zambezi, the existence of copper deposits in the Katanga region had been known for years. Accounts in early Portuguese records were confirmed by the reports of nineteenth-century explorers; in 1868 Livingstone, for example, had met a large slave caravan travelling east from the Katanga whose loads contained, according to his estimate, a total of five tons of smelted copper. The sulphide ore, the 'green stones' described by the Pombeiros, was widely employed for medicinal purposes. The metal itself was used for making implements, and latterly for manufacturing bullets. Ornamental rings worn upon ankles and arms were often of copper. Over the centuries a great deal of the metal must have been produced, the tribes concerned guarding jealously the craft of smelting and the location of the ore deposits.[3] In the Europe of the nineties, when electric light was replacing gas, and electric trams were competing with horsedrawn cabs, the demand for copper was surging upward and put a new zest into the search for African minerals.

The prospecting that was now in progress was not carried out by the British South Africa Company itself but by subsidiaries. Of these one of the first was the Zambezi Exploring Company formed in 1891 by Robert Williams, a friend of Rhodes. Convinced that the Congo-Zambezi watershed was rich in minerals, Williams obtained a concession over an area of two thousand square miles round the source of the Kafue, and in 1899 also received permission from King Leopold to prospect in the Congo territory of Katanga. In that year George Grey, employed by Williams, made the first serious search, leading to the discovery of the fabulous deposits in the Katanga that were to become the 'Star of the Congo' Mine. In the same year Edmund Davis' Northern Copper Company, later the Rhodesia Copper Company, made discoveries in the bend of the Kafue that were to become the mines known as Sable Antelope and Silver King. These early proved disappointing and were later abandoned. In 1902, however, the Company's engineer, T. G. Davey, returning from a visit to Silver King, made a far more important discovery in Lenje country. An outcrop of rocks close by his path was found to contain rich samples of sulphide of lead. Subsequent investigations revealed deposits of this and other ores large enough to determine without any further doubt the course of the railway beyond the Falls. Mining operations began in 1904. Owing to the similarity of the geological configuration with that at Broken Hill in New South Wales, the mine was given the same name.

Linked with Davis' enterprise was the Bechuanaland Exploration Company, which sent William Collier into Lamba country in 1902.[4] Collier's first find was of a deposit of ore near Ndola's village, which he pegged and named 'Bwana Mkubwa' after the local Lamba nickname for Moffat Jones, then Native Commissioner in the district. Further north-west, near Kapopo where the administration's Boma then was, the people were using malachite ore. Despite their unwillingness to reveal its source, Collier with the aid of a local guide discovered a rich strain of copper ore and named the site after a roan antelope that he had just shot nearby. A few days later he came upon the Chambeshi deposit, which had already been seen but inaccurately marked by George Grey.

The ore deposits at Nkana and Mufulira were not found till later; Moffat Thompson pegged Nkana in 1910 and sold his claim for £100. But by 1902 the possibilities in Lamba country, later to become the 'copper belt', conveniently regarded as falling within the scope of Lewanika's concession in 1890, were beyond doubt, and the way forward for the railway was clear. Apart from the Kafue escarpment and the river crossing, there were no outstanding obstacles to be overcome. The 281 miles between Kalomo and Broken Hill were covered in 277 working days, and near Pemba in one day six miles of plate-laying were completed.[5] Until this time the Tonga plateau and the fringes of Ila country had not often been visited by Europeans since Livingstone's journey in 1855. The only wagon trail beyond the Zambezi ran from Kazungula north to the Methodist station at Nkala River, two hundred miles upstream from the new Kafue bridge. The railway would have followed the route of this wagon trail but for the discovery of ore at Broken Hill.

The variety of mineral deposits made up in some degree for the failure to discover an 'El Dorado' such as Kimberley or the Rand. Minerals had the advantage that as long as prices remained steady they were a reliable target for investment, and not the prey of disease and drought that periodically beset the farmer. None the less it was plain to the Company Directors visiting central Africa in 1907 that the economy ought to be more balanced. In any case the growth of the mining industry after 1904 was creating a demand for farm produce that could no longer satisfactorily be met from the south with the high freight costs involved, despite the 1903 customs agreement with the South African colonies permitting the free import of foodstuffs.

It was decided to encourage agriculture with the combined objects of allowing an increase of self-sufficiency, of reducing the cost of living, and of attracting a different type of settler. Much early 'farming' had consisted simply of cutting timbers for fuel and for mine pit props. In 1908 a Department of Agriculture was created to assist and advise farmers and to carry out research. A Land Settlement Department was established, together with a Land Bank which would grant loans for farm development. Experiments were made with cotton and tobacco. Maize farming expanded on the red soils of Mashonaland, while in Matabeleland extensive cattle ranching was carried on.

Great efforts were made to advertise Rhodesia, not simply as a prospector's hope, but as a land where British people accustomed to a temperate environment could make their homes. The great expanse of the undulating grasslands, the ruggedly handsome horizons of the eastern hills, the equable temperatures and the brilliant sun, the sheer opportunity of a new and exciting land, these things appealed to the inhabitants of crowded industrial towns and also to farmers in a country-side facing ruin from the competition of cheap imported grain from the Canadian prairies. Lord Winchester, back in London after the 1907 tour, thus had an interested audience when he spoke of 'vast spaces of a smiling country waiting, waiting, waiting for somebody to come and plough and develop them', and added, blandly, 'it is ripe for cultivation; but there is no population'.[6]

At the beginning only the healthiest, which were the highest, districts of the plateau had been the targets of settlement. Throughout Rhodesia, Zambia and Malawi the largest areas of land above 4,000 feet are in Rhodesia which, being known to be richest in gold, and also being easily accessible from the south, attracted far more immigrants than did the territories north of the Zambezi.

The acquisition of land, and the title by which it was held, varied between one territory and another. Since this was a matter in which the interests of European and African at this early stage were most clearly in conflict, and since it was one concerning which disputes were to occur in later years, it is convenient to examine the issues more closely.

In Southern Rhodesia the standard area for a farm was 1,500 morgen or 3,000 acres. It will be recalled that each member of the Pioneer Column to Mashonaland was promised 3,000 acres of land and that Jameson by the Victoria Agreement of 1893 made a similar guarantee to each man who rode in the Victoria and Salisbury columns. At other times land was sold at ninepence an acre with an annual ground rent of three pounds for every 3,000 acres; the maximum single grant was 6,000 acres. The cost of survey was to be met by the settler and there were reservations concerning mineral rights and the construction of roads and railways. The low price of land is remarkable, but the Company was anxious to attract immigrants as well as to raise revenue from land sales. Besides, the lie of the land as well as memories of the African risings encouraged a certain degree of concentration. Most Southern Rhodesian farms were situated on the high backbone ridge of the country and in the Eastern Highlands, at an altitude of over 4,000 feet. None the less Land Companies managed to evade the restriction and by 1900 had bought large blocks, totalling 10,000 square miles, for resale. In that year a Land Occupation Ordinance compelled occupation and use of farms alienated, or the payment of a tax in lieu.[7] By 1923, thirty million acres were occupied by Europeans, ten million acres of Native Reserves had been surveyed and fifty million acres remained.

It is difficult to find a firm legal basis for these alienations apart from the *de facto* right of conquest. The Company's initial viewpoint was expressed in the annual report for 1892: 'The Directors were advised that under the clauses of the Rudd Concession the Company might grant occupation rights over vacant lands, which would be good as against any other white claimant though they did not enable them to effect a permanent land settlement, as it was clear that under this concession the land could not be completely dealt with without the joint consent of Lobengula and the grantees.'[8] The subsequent purchase of the Lippert Concession invested the Company 'with full power to deal with the land throughout Lobengula's dominions, subject of course to a full recognition of and respect for native rights'. The 1890 settlers would probably have been surprised to be told that their land granted freehold was not part of a 'permanent settlement'; any legal questions were nullified however by the conquest of the Ndebele in 1893. In 1920 the Imperial Government was to state its opinion that both in obtaining the Lippert Concession and in making the conquest the Company, through the Charter, had been acting as its agent, and that the land was ultimately vested in the Crown.

It was one of the major consequences of initial rule by a commercial company, which needed urgently to cover its costs, that so much of the land in Southern Rhodesia, and the best of it, was alienated to Europeans, or made available for this purpose. The forebodings of the South Africa Committee in 1889 and the subsequent protests of the Aborigines Protection Society were being justified by events. Criticism did not only arise in England. The Resident Commissioner in Salisbury wrote in 1901 that 'it would be unfair to allow errors which unfortunately occurred in the distribution of land grants in this territory to be repeated (in Northern Rhodesia).'[9]

It should not be supposed that there was a general displacement of native occupants. In Southern Rhodesia, a territory larger in area than the whole of the British Isles, there lived in 1890 an indigenous population of perhaps 500,000 Africans. To European eyes much of the land was practically or completely empty. If a small native settlement should be found on a farm of three thousand acres, it could remain without hindrance to the new occupant. Indeed, the original inhabitants were generally encouraged to live on as 'squatters', since they provided a welcome source of labour. Africans who preferred not to work for the European farmer were, as in Nyasaland, charged rent at the rate of £1 per head per annum. This, with the alternative of eviction, was an early source of African resentment. Not until after 1920, however, was a general move made to shift these 'squatter' kraals away from European land.

In allocating land between native reserves and areas available for European occupation, two sets of values were applied. For the Europeans it was essential to provide the maximum opportunity, which was the life spirit of the enterprise. Towards the African people the Land Commissions were moved by the wish to protect. As the country stood in 1898, land anywhere could be alienated to a European—or to an African on the same conditions. Manifestly the African could not compete in capital or techniques. The purpose of demarcating the reserves, therefore, was to ensure that the African would not be 'bought out', but would always be sure of land. How much should be reserved?

In 1895 the Gwaai and Shangani Reserves had been set aside for the Ndebele, but it was never supposed that these areas, covering two and a half million acres of land which varied greatly in quality, should accommodate the whole Ndebele population, let alone the Mashona as well. The Southern Rhodesia Order in Council of 1898 commanded that the Company's administration 'shall from time to time assign to the native inhabitants of Southern Rhodesia land sufficient for their occupation, whether as tribes or portions of tribes, and suitable for their agricultural and pastoral requirements, including in all cases a fair and equitable proportion of springs and permanent water'. By the following year reserves in Matabeleland had been planned, and surveyors were at work in Mashonaland. In an Order in Council of 1902, native reserves were created which covered altogether twenty-five and a half million acres—about twenty-one per cent. of the area of the colony. These reserves were revised by a Commission appointed in 1915 under the chairmanship of R. T. Coryndon, and according to its recommendations the final and more exactly surveyed reserves were laid down by Order in Council in 1920. These were slightly smaller in total area than those of 1902, amounting to twenty-one million acres, but were improved in quality and situation in some places.

The 1915 Commission estimated the African population as 732,153, of whom 405,326 were living in existing reserves.[10] It assumed that the Africans' capacity for getting the best out of the soil would grow at the same rate as the population, so that 'an allocation of land which is more than sufficient for them today will also be sufficient for their needs in fifty years' time.' In a number of paragraphs the ambiguity caused by the application of the two sets of values—protection for the African, opportunity for the European—came to the surface. Declaring, for instance, that the absence of any conflict of interests between white and black on the land question was 'partly due to a natural genius (on the part of the British) for native administration', it went on to add that 'the natives have, of course, no united policy and are, as a people, almost inarticulate'. Again, 'it must be borne in mind that the great bulk of the country occupied by the natives is of their own choosing'; yet we are told 'in certain districts . . . white settlement has driven the indigenous inhabitants further afield. . . . As a rule the country to which (they) are retiring . . . was selected for them by Native Commissioners in the early years as being suitable land which they had chosen and settled upon.' In considering the type of soil on which Africans should be settled, the Commission noted that the Ndebele liked dark earth, 'a preference which they probably brought with them in their comparatively recent pilgrimage from the more granitic countries of their origin.' The Shona preferred light, sandy soil. But these preferences were not considered to be permanent—they would change as farming methods and crops changed. The Commission believed that they had 'erred if anything on the side of generosity to the people who lived in this country for generations before the white man came'. None the less, while four-fifths of the land alienated to Europeans at that time were within twenty-five miles of a railway, only one-third of the native reserves were so placed. A large proportion of European land was, of course, on high ground. The Southern Rhodesian Minister of Native Affairs told Parliament in June 1950 that only eighteen of the twenty-one million acres of reserves were suitable for agriculture, either crops or cattle, and that a large percentage of that was even then waterless, or subject to tsetse fly.[11]

A rather different picture was presented by North-Western Rhodesia. Although, under the Concession granted by Lewanika, the Chartered Company gained only trading and mineral rights, it was stated that it could 'make grants of land for farming purposes in any portion of the Batoka or Mashukulumbwe country to white men approved by the King, the Company undertaking that the native lands, villages, cattle posts, gardens and fountains shall be in no way interfered with'. In 1904, in response to Coryndon's further request for authority to 'issue land all over your territory to whomever I consider to be a good farmer or settler', Lewanika, while reserving central Barotseland as always, replied: 'I and my people agree that you shall give some lands.'[12] The Lozi sovereignty over land so far east was later to be called in question, but for the present this concurrence was sufficient. By 1904 the railway had reached Kalomo, and the line it was to follow as far as Broken Hill at least was practically decided upon. The wagon route from Kazungula north to Nkala Mission and the copper claims in the bend of the Kafue was falling into disuse. The track across the Zambezi at Walker's Drift, above the Kariba Gorge, was seldom employed. The highway to the north was instead to follow the plateau escarpment north-east from the Victoria Falls through Tonga and Soli and Lenje country seldom traversed before, and it was here that farms were allocated to the first settlers coming in.

There was little question of dispossessing African peasants, for the land was sparsely inhabited—so much so that before long there was an acute shortage of labour in the area. The few occupants that were encountered were compensated at the rate of £1 to £2 per hut and ten shillings per acre of garden[13]; the land on the seemingly endless plateau was so plentiful, that it is doubtful whether hardship was experienced. When considering the question of dispossession of African villagers from their land, and replacement on a similar piece of land elsewhere, it must be remembered that by their system of agriculture, universal then and still common today, villages were shifted to a new site for the cultivation of new fields at intervals of five to seven years. Besides, not only was the land in Northern Rhodesia even more thinly occupied than in the south; white immigration was at a far slower rate. By 1911, including the North-East, there were still only 159 holdings in the territory. About a hundred of these, many of them owned by Afrikaners from the Transvaal, were along the line of rail between Kolomo and Broken Hill—the fertile plateau astride the Kafue river, which was to become known as 'the Maize Belt' of Northern Rhodesia. Most early farming here consisted of cattle ranching. The Administration encouraged this settlement, both as a source of immediate revenue, and because a local food supply was needed for the future mining population at Broken Hill and perhaps further north.

North-Eastern Rhodesia was less attractive to the prospective farmer, because of its inaccessibility and the prevalence of tsetse fly. Hopes that Rhodes' Cape to Cairo railway from the Kafue along the Muchingas to Lake Tanganyika would be completed, encouraged a number of settlers to acquire land at Abercorn, where the fine scenery and altitude of 5,500 feet make pleasant conditions. But the railway never came, and the number was reduced to the indomitable few. Fort Jameson, only 100 miles from lakeside Kotakota on the water route, prospered by comparison. Here the land was in the gift of the North Charterland Exploration Company, apart from the duty of the Administration under the 1899 Order in Council to create a Native Reserve for the sole use and occupation of the Ngoni. Already by 1900, only a year after the suppression of the Ngoni rising, Fort Jameson, Codrington's new headquarters on the site of Mpezeni's old capital, was described as 'a splendid station with twenty brick houses'.[14] The fact of conquest introduced a different element into the European attitude towards Ngoni interests, when land was alienated to settlers, from that prevailing over most of Northern Rhodesia.

In relation to the granting of land, North-Eastern Rhodesia

was not, as was North-Western Rhodesia, covered by the Barotse concessions. Nor were the treaties with the North-Eastern chiefs obtained by Sharpe and Thomson in the 1890s sufficient title to land ownership. These treaties were, as we have seen, moves in the general scramble for African territory played according to the rules laid down at Berlin in 1885, and had an international rather than a local significance. Mpezeni's country might be regarded as having been annexed by force in 1898. In the case of Abercorn and the British Central Africa Protectorate, on the other hand, though force was used to suppress the slave trade and quell disorders, the country was never supposed to have been taken by conquest; rather, it had been occupied in order to liberate and protect the indigenous inhabitants. In the early 1890s, however, traders were entering the country and acquiring land in the Shire highlands, generally without reference to authority but by direct negotiation with chiefs. In May 1891, for example, Kapeni, a Yao chief, sold to Steblecki, a Pole and Lamagna, an Italian, a large tract of 'lands, woods, rivers, minerals etc. as described . . . in exchange for thirty-one pieces of calico, eight kegs of powder, eight tin caps, two elephant guns, one piece of blue calico and one of print, fourteen handkerchiefs, eighty-four pounds of brass wire, an iron kettle, two blankets and a scarf.'[15] This transaction was witnessed by David Buchanan, the British vice-consul, and when examined subsequently by Johnston was declared valid. The introduction of traders, so long as they were of reasonably good character, was officially encouraged for the good of the country. Both Johnston and Sharpe after him strongly favoured the immigration of Indian traders, to act as middlemen between the European planters and the native population. Not all early European immigrants were *bona fide* settlers, however, and for this and other reasons Johnston instituted in 1894 Certificates of Claim, papers which certified that the individual concerned was justified in his title to his land since no other claimant had come forward.[16] Certificates of Claim were also granted to the B.S.A. Company and others for estates in Abercorn, which at that time was still included in the British Central Africa Protectorate, and to the B.S.A. Company for its large tract of territory at the north end of the lake. Thereafter, purchases of land were strictly regulated by the Commissioner, and payments were made to the Crown. A number of disputes arose after 1900 about Certificates of Claim, and there was discussion in the High Court at Zomba and in the Appeals Court at Zanzibar concerning the right of the Government to make grants of land in a Protectorate at all. An opinion was advanced that it was 'alien to the idea of a Protectorate that the Crown should by any process immediately acquire the property in all lands. . . . Yet if it does not, whence comes the idea of Crown Lands in a Protectorate?' Chief Justice Nunan declared in 1905 that 'Nyasaland was a Protectorate in which, unlike Nigeria or Zanzibar, there had been an utter absence of settled government, civilization, or established native laws' when the Protectorate was proclaimed in 1891. 'In consequence, the Administration assumed full power to deal with all lands and has sold and leased them on its own authority since that date.' He also said that 'absolute ownership of land is impossible here as well as in England, and lands held by Certificate of Claim as well as other lands in the Protectorate are held of the Crown. . . . Title to land in this country depends upon the grant from the Crown and not upon any agreements with Native Chiefs.'[17]

Land agreements with native chiefs could hardly be valid in any case, unless the chief were educated or had special advice, for the two parties would have quite different conceptions of the meaning of land ownership. African custom nowhere admitted of individual title to land. An individual peasant could hoe a certain piece of ground, or graze his animals in a certain area, with the chief's approval expressed through the headman; but he had no property in the land and did not even pay rent for its use. The land belonged to the tribe, on whose behalf the chief was trustee; but 'the tribe' in this context means not merely the present generation, but ancestors past and generations to come. Future members of the tribe might need to move, or to expand their boundaries; land unoccupied might therefore be required at some future date and so was part of the heritage of the people. Land was thought of in terms of use rather than of property ownership. Yet from time immemorial the Bantu had experienced schism and movement and conquest; many tribes had only recently come to occupy their existing homes. All acknowledged the ability of a stronger group to acquire rights in land. The European Governments were now in the position of such groups, but of a new kind, more powerful, more benevolent and more remote. In all three territories, therefore, the rights in land were from the outset vested ultimately in the Crown. This did not mean that the tribes were totally dispossessed, but that the Crown (in the case of Rhodesia through its agent the Chartered Company) exercised the right to allocate land to European settlers or to whomever it wished, bearing in mind the future development of the country, the interests of the native peoples, and the aspirations of the European. Only in Southern Rhodesia, more than the other two territories a conquered country, were European interests in land and elsewhere given a dominant place in the early years.

The distribution of land grants was closely bound up with the line of the railway. In Southern Rhodesia this was determined by the structure of the country, whose healthy uplands combined with mineral deposits to attract both settlement and railway together. North of the Zambezi the railway was itself the reason for land settlement, and it was only by chance that its route lay through the fertile Tonga plateau, later to become the 'maize belt' of the territory. As originally planned the line was to cross the Zambezi near Chirundu and proceed northwards along the Muchingas to Lake Tanganyika. The discovery of coal at Wankie, ninety miles south of the Victoria Falls, together with the probable value of the Falls as a tourist attraction, had deflected the route westward; the lead and zinc deposits at Broken Hill had decided the matter. Construction had been held up during the Boer War, but in 1903 the coalfields were reached, and in 1904 the chasm below the falls was spanned, despite the scepticism of Toka tribesmen who came to watch the progress on the bridge.

Throughout Central Africa the railway, tenuous though it was, accelerated change. Over the wide bushveld, green and fresh in summer, dry, dusty and sunbleached in the winter season, the long brown trains, with their black grimy engines spouting out smoke into the blue African sky, rattled and rumbled their way between granite kopjes, across great rivers, among the grasses and the endless trees. The bellow of an accelerating locomotive, the sad wail of the steam signal, sounds like these wandered across the plateau, startling men, beasts and birds accustomed hitherto to the clap of thunder or the trumpeting of the elephant herd as the greatest breakers of the silence of the veld. Freight wagons loaded with coal, corrugated iron, steam pumps and mining tackle, blankets and hardware, sugar and grain, wound their way up the long escarpments and over the enormous plains. At the sidings, placed every ten miles along the line, a few of which in time grew to be railhead townships, were clustered a few railway workers' huts, and sometimes a store where all manner of goods were sold, permeating slowly to the ultimate limits of the country.

Administration

Southern Rhodesia obtained a measure of representative government in 1898. The high rate of immigration had slackened off after the rebellions, but in that year there were already over five thousand Europeans in the colony. The Southern Rhodesia Order in Council combined Matabeleland and Mashonaland under one administration with its headquarters at Salisbury.[1] A Legislative Council was established, over which the Administrator was to preside, consisting of five members appointed by the Company and four elected. The minimum electoral qualifications were the ability to complete the application form, and the occupation of a house valued at £75 or the receipt of an income of fifty pounds a year. Rhodes said of this provision: 'Everyone has the vote who is educated and not a loafer.' There was in fact no attempt to exclude Africans on grounds of race, but the property qualifications excluded them in practice. In 1912 these were to be doubled, and could always be increased further if Africans approached them in any number.[2]

Rhodes also said of the Order in Council that it was 'the first step in the direction of self-government'. This was true, but equally significant was the placing of the Company's administration more closely under the surveillance of the Imperial Government. As a consequence of Jameson's raid on the Transvaal, a Commandant-General was appointed over the British South Africa Police, while a Resident Commissioner was to represent the Queen in Salisbury and to inform the Colonial Secretary through the High Commissioner at the Cape. He was particularly instructed to discern any law which might discriminate against Africans, and whose enactment was to be reserved against the consent of the Secretary of State. This precaution was brought into play several times during the remaining years of Company rule, notably in 1901 when it was attempted to double the African poll tax. Thus, restraint over the white settlers came to be exercised less by the Company and more by the Crown.

But the Crown was never to obtain a firm hold on the conduct of affairs south of the Limpopo. On the one hand, progress towards responsible government was steady. Rhodes had promised that the Company would part with the control of administration in due course, and after his death in 1902 the settlers, conscious of neglect, demanded this control more insistently. In 1903, then in 1911 and 1913, the proportion of elected members in the Legislative Council was increased until by the time the world war commenced there were twelve elected members in a council of eighteen. On the other hand, imperialism no longer kindled the same enthusiasm in Britain. The South African war, with its international repercussions and its cost in blood and treasure, had sternly demonstrated that Britain was alone in a dangerous world and should beware of her commitments. The Orange Free State in 1907 and the Transvaal in 1908 were given responsible government, and two years later the four colonies merged in the Union of South Africa as an independent dominion of the British Crown. Its constitution provided for the incorporation of Rhodesia, south of the Zambezi at least, at any time. Even before the war the trend both in London and Africa was towards the cutting of the Imperial tie.

The first years of the century were hard ones for all in Rhodesia, European and African. The latter were undergoing the initial stages of a revolution that had been thrust upon them and about which more has to be said. The white colonists faced their own problems. The Boer War cut off supplies from the south for many months and disrupted trade. Even when it was over, an acute labour shortage made it impossible for mines and farms to pay their way. The railway, especially north of Bulawayo, was running at a loss, and high freight charges inflated the cost of living. After 1902 little personal contact remained between Rhodesians and the Company's directors in London. Settlers felt increasingly that their interests were being ignored, possibly subordinated to commercial objectives, and that no definite policy existed.[3] Many fundamental white Rhodesian attitudes towards nagging indifference from London on the one hand and towards a supposedly shiftless African population on the other, can be traced back to the years between 1900 and 1905.

Rhodes' much publicized 'North' appeared to be drifting into a backwater, when Lord Selborne, High Commissioner for South Africa, toured the country in 1906. He reported favourably, having found even beyond the Zambezi 'everywhere the traces of a civilized administration in existence'. He also observed a certain despondency among the European population and the Company decided to send out a commission to see for themselves. Jameson described the visit which followed in 1907 as 'an avalanche of directors'; every aspect of the colonists' existence was thoroughly investigated. Back in London Henry Birchenough spoke of 'a feeling of unhappiness, of loneliness if you like'. There were complaints that the legislative council was a farce. 'The mines are interfered with by the farms and we cannot mine. The farms are interfered with by the mines and we cannot farm; and when there is nothing but the land and what is underneath it, what are we to do?' The administration was accused of appropriating revenue for the Company's commercial purposes. There was even talk of the need to replace the present administration with Crown Colony rule.[4]

The directors decided to 'get a move on' in Rhodesia. Though even now no dividend had been paid they persuaded shareholders to accept an increase in the Company's share capital by a further three million one pound shares to nine million. Great efforts were made to encourage emigration to Rhodesia and the development of farming there. Work on the railway from Broken Hill to the Katanga border was pressed forward in the hope, that was soon justified, that the line north of Bulawayo would pay its way and cease to be a perpetual drain on Company resources. It was agreed that in future administrative and commercial revenue and expenditure should be clearly distinguished. The lines of future policy were declared—an elected majority in the Legislative Council, the reduction of the Civil Service, better schools and medical facilities. Public economy was harder to effect; the typewriter was coming into use, more records were being kept, and the administrative system was expanding. But after 1908 the railways began to make a profit, and revenue balanced expenditure for the first time.

North of the Zambezi, affairs progressed more slowly. The country had not been pacified nor administration properly begun until the rebellions in Southern Rhodesia were over. Since 1895 Major Forbes had in theory been responsible for the area extending from the border of the British Central Africa Protectorate in the east to the limits of Barotseland in the west. No European had ventured into much of this territory. Most of it was entirely unmapped, much of the borderline was undefined or in dispute. In the north-east, fighting and slaving were still carried on, and throughout the country the Company's influence only began to be exerted in 1897, the year of Coryndon's arrival in Lealui and of Robert Young's first open conflict with the Arabs and Bemba in Senga country.

In that same year, the Foreign Office in London gave its approval for the name of 'Northern Rhodesia' for the British South Africa Company's territories north of the Zambezi, and that of Rhodesia for the whole of the territories north and south of that river. Although Southern Rhodesia was not mentioned in the despatch, the name 'Rhodesia' had in practice been used there since May 1895. Meanwhile, the British Central Africa Protectorate, though now confined to the districts immediately adjoining the lake to the west and south, still continued to be so called until it was renamed the Nyasaland Protectorate in 1907.

The Company's territory north of the Zambezi extended over nearly a thousand miles from east to west. Some of its borders were formed of natural boundaries, such as the Luapula river, the Nyasa-Tanganyika plateau and the Congo-Zambezi watershed. Elsewhere they were arbitrarily or incompletely drawn. In some places the delineation of the tribes had been wholly ignored, and in these instances, different parts of the same tribe would find themselves under the administration of different governments. From the point of view of communications the North-East and the North-West were entirely separate. While the North-East was approached by the rivers Zambezi and Shire, the route to the North-West lay through and to the west of Bulawayo. Means for direct and regular communication between the eastern and western sections did not exist, and in 1899 and 1900 Orders in Council were issued for the separate administration of North-Eastern and North-Western Rhodesia.

Only a handful of Europeans was scattered across the huge area, of whom few or none had permanent interests there. Apart from the Company's employees there were only travelling prospectors, one or two traders, and a few isolated missionaries. The total number of white men in Northern Rhodesia in 1898 cannot have exceeded a hundred. The North-Eastern Rhodesia Order in Council of 1900 provided simply for the appointment of an Administrator, whose task was to maintain law and order through Native Commissioners and a local police force, exercise authority over the Europeans who should come into the country, and control the development of communications and wealth. A High Court was created to dispense justice according to English law, though native law was to be applied to civil cases between Africans 'unless contrary to natural justice'. The first Administrator was Robert Codrington, who did much to lay the foundations of the territory's public service.[5]

The North-Western Rhodesia Order in Council of the previous year (1899) had not gone quite so far. The whole of North-Western Rhodesia was regarded as having been subject to Lewanika, and was covered by the treaties that had been signed with the Lozi Paramount. At first, therefore, the Administrator did not have such power to settle disputes between Africans as was given to his counterpart in the North-East; but after 1905 with Lewanika's consent the two systems were brought into line, and a High Court of North-Western Rhodesia was set up in 1906. Meanwhile the territory, as in the North-East, had been divided into administrative districts, to which Native Commissioners were appointed. In 1905 the Barotse border with Angola was defined by arbitration.

In 1911, two years after the railway had reached the Congo

Border, the two northern territories were combined, and the administrative system throughout Northern Rhodesia, apart from special reservations for Barotseland, was made the same. The Northern Rhodesia Order in Council of that year provided for an Administrator for the whole territory, to be appointed by the Company subject to the approval of the Secretary of State. A High Court of Northern Rhodesia was set up. There was still no Council; the Europeans in the territory did not yet number a thousand. As in Southern Rhodesia there was to be a Resident Commissioner to represent the British Government; in fact the same man did duty for the northern and southern territories. The first Administrator of Northern Rhodesia was Sir Lawrence Wallace, who had earlier succeeded Codrington in North-Eastern Rhodesia. His headquarters were at Livingstone, which was to remain the capital of the territory until 1933.

In Nyasaland the situation was a compound of the positions in Northern and Southern Rhodesia. The similarity to Northern Rhodesia lay in the fact that the tribes had in the main been liberated from slave raiders, and the attitude of the Imperial Government was that of a 'protecting' power. Much of the country, besides, was not really suitable for European settlement. There was no overall claim on the land by any commercial company, and the long-term interests of the native population were predominant from the outset. On the other hand, the Protectorate compared closely with Southern Rhodesia in that the Shire highlands had long been regarded as an area suitable for white settlement, and by 1900 these healthy uplands around Blantyre contained a European population of over 300. This was small compared with Southern Rhodesia's 6,000, but the area available was more confined, and in fact many of Southern Rhodesia's early problems were repeated in miniature on the Shire highlands.

The chief factor which distinguished the Protectorate from the two Rhodesias was that it came directly under the authority of the Imperial Government. Rhodes' £10,000 subsidy was paid by the B.S.A. Company down to 1911, during which time the Protectorate's armed force was available for the maintenance of order in North-Eastern Rhodesia in an emergency; beyond this there was no link between the administrations. This at first had little practical significance. The Commissioner's reports during the early years differed little in nature from those of the Chartered Company's Administrators in Rhodesia. But as time passed and the European population of Southern Rhodesia increased and approached self-government, the gulf separating Nyasaland, with its social structure and political outlook, from Rhodesia widened. The European population in the Shire highlands did not increase in proportion, and never gained the authority in the affairs of the Protectorate which was early obtained in the south. Lacking direct contact with South Africa, approached always by sea direct from the United Kingdom, the 'imperial' tradition continued unimpeded and unbroken.

When the Nyasa districts were declared a British Protectorate in 1891, Johnston had been appointed Commissioner according to the Africa (Acquisition of Lands) Order in Council of that year, with authority to create administrative districts and to appoint officers to reside in them. By the time that Alfred Sharpe replaced him in 1897, the country had been divided into thirteen such districts, nine of them concentrated in the Shire area south of the Lake. Though early falling behind Southern Rhodesia in political advance, the Protectorate was in this respect well abreast of Northern Rhodesia. Its constitution was more clearly defined in the British Central Africa Order in Council of 1902, which empowered the Commissioner to appoint heads of departments and to make ordinances, and which set up a High Court with full jurisdiction to exercise English law. All mines and mineral rights were to vest in the Commissioner as the representative of Her Majesty, and the meaning of Crown Lands was defined. Under this Order, the position of the Protectorate differed little from that of North-Eastern and North-Western Rhodesia, with the Crown in the place of the Chartered Company. In 1907, however, there was a step forward in the Nyasaland Order in Council, which not only gave the Protectorate its present name and altered the Commissioner's title to that of Governor, but provided for an Executive and a Legislative Council. The latter was to consist of at least two members nominated by the Governor to represent the local European population, a development which aroused some chagrin among the yet unrepresented North-Western Rhodesian settlers.

At this time a serious obstacle facing miners and farmers, railway builders and those in need of carriers for transport, and threatening the economic prospects of the new territories, was the shortage of labour. A clause in the 1897 Native Regulations for Southern Rhodesia had made it compulsory for chiefs to provide labour for public works if required to do so, and though this was cancelled on the insistence of the Secretary of State the following year, it remained one of the duties of District Commissioners to aid in supplying labour for the mines'.[6] This dual role of labour agent and Government official was a difficult one, another of the consequences of the ambiguity inherent in administration by a commercial company. In 1899 Labour Bureaux were established by the Southern Rhodesian Chamber of Mines to carry out recruiting. They did not have the desired effect. Only a fraction of the adult male population of the Ndebele went out to work. The remainder, wrote Taylor, the Chief Native Commissioner, spent their time 'in unprofitable idleness ... or become a dangerous element in the community to be reckoned with ... the more so when enjoying a comparative independence never experienced by them in the time of Lobengula. ... There is but one course open, namely to educate (the native) to work for a better livelihood.'[7] In 1900 Sir William Milton wrote that 'Native Commissioners in the course of their tours of inspection constantly bring before the chiefs and people the advantages of obtaining money by labour in order to pay taxes and acquire stock'.[8]

It was of little avail. The idea of working voluntarily for a money wage was quite new to the Ndebele, accustomed to a traditional division of labour within the family whereby women and slaves toiled in the field; the duty of men was to herd and hunt and fight. This was an attitude common to the great warrior tribes including Bemba and Ngoni. The Shona, though less proud, were agriculturists and tended to leave employment with the onset of the rains. Labour, declared the Chief Native Commissioner for Mashonaland in 1903, was 'never forthcoming' from October to December.[9] Moreover the Shona were 'distinctly averse to underground work', preferring road and railway work and woodcutting.

The explanation was not all on the side of the Africans. There were employers who would withhold their pay in order to persuade labourers to remain, and other bad masters. A missionary commented that 'a proud and hitherto unconquered Matabele cannot be turned, in a year, into a useful servant by kicks and blows, by cursing him for not understanding an order given in English, nor by being too kind to him'. Good employers became known, and could find labour more easily, but the problem was an acute one for years. Many favoured an authoritarian solution. 'I have never shared the objection', wrote Sir William Milton in 1900, 'which is so strongly felt at home, to a well-regulated system of state compulsion. . . . The black man is inclined, much more than the white, to do nothing at all.'[10] Anything remotely like forced labour, however, was anathema to the British Government, particularly now at a time when the working class trade union movement was becoming a force in the land. Foiled in this approach, the Chamber of Mines passed a resolution in 1900 calling for the importation of Asiatic labour. Rhodes cabled to Salisbury: 'I am opposed to Chinese labour as undesirable. We ought to exhaust every other means.' The suggestion appeared again two or three times during the next few years, till it was extinguished by the storm over Chinese labour on the Rand.

The 'other means' included an attempt in 1901 to double the recently inaugurated poll tax to two pounds per head. The Secretary of State disallowed this ordinance. More successful was the establishment of the Southern Rhodesia Native Labour Bureau in 1903, which sent recruiting agents across the Zambezi, particularly to North-Western Rhodesia, and set up rest houses with supplies of food for men on their way to find work. The labour traffic from the north-east was regulated at Feira. The Bureau recorded nearly 7,000 Africans passing through from north to south during the winter months 1903/4, over 6,000 of them from the British Central Africa Protectorate.[11]

The exodus was causing settlers in the Shire highlands to experience their own dearth of labour. This was surprising in view of the small white population. Of the 164 in the territory in 1900, seventy-one (less than half) were traders and planters. Yet the Blantyre Chamber of Commerce had to petition for legislation against Africans leaving the Protectorate to seek work elsewhere. The authorities did not at once respond, but labour bureaux were set up to recruit labour for carriers, road-making and plantation work. 'The administration', wrote Sharpe in 1901, 'has taken a more active part in the endeavour to secure a good supply of local native labour for employers than is perhaps general in protectorates or colonies. Cheap labour has become a matter of vital necessity.'[12] When work began on the railway from Chiromo the local shortage was still acute. It was now becoming a social problem in the villages themselves. In 1909 'hardly an able bodied man could be found in Tonga country—only old men, women and children, all the young men having left for South Africa'.[13] The Employment of Natives Ordinance of that year sought to control the outward flow by requiring every African leaving the territory to obtain a pass from his District Officer. This rule was easily evaded, and an official ban upon recruitment of labour by external agents was hardly more effective.

The migrant labour system influenced the working conditions in Nyasaland itself. Standards were higher in the more mature industrial society of the Witwatersrand, and this led to a demand for proper food and housing and medical care for employees—amenities conspicuously lacking in early days. The Native Labour regulations in 1903 provided for a minimum wage and daily ration, the issue of a blanket in the cold season, and the payment of the fare home on completion of contract. The supply of food was especially needed, as without it many labourers would leave work during the early rains to cultivate their village gardens. In 1905 the Commissioner was able to report encouragingly on 'the increased willingness of the native workman to engage on longer periods of work'.[14] By 1912, when the railway from Chiromo to Blantyre was completed and in operation, there was plenty of labour for the Shire highland planters. But thousands continued to depart annually to Southern Rhodesia and the Union, where they earned a reputation for steady and reliable work.

During the days of labour scarcity, which was most severely felt in Southern Rhodesia, but which was common to all three territories, the accepted remedy came to be the hut tax, which was first imposed in Southern Rhodesia in 1898, in North-Eastern Rhodesia in 1900, and in North-Western Rhodesia in

1904. The tax served the double purpose of encouraging men to work, and of contributing to the revenue.

In the Shire highlands, Johnston had been levying tax as early as 1892, with the exception of 'a few recalcitrant chiefs who . . . not unnaturally declined to contribute towards the suppression of the slave trade'.[15] This tax, amounting to three shillings per hut, was raised according to treaty with the chiefs concerned, and the possibility of increasing the amount to six shillings later was written into the agreement. This amounted, wrote Johnston, to a transference of sovereign rights to Her Majesty, in return for which (i.e. for the signing of treaties) considerable presents and payments were given. Thereafter there was to be no direct subsidy to the chiefs, but they were to receive ten per cent. of the tax collected from their areas. Collectors, as in North-Eastern Rhodesia, were appointed to administer districts. Johnston instructed H. C. Marshall on his posting as Collector of Revenue at Chiromo in 1891 as follows: 'You will divide the whole of your district into sub-districts, perhaps twelve or more, representing the chief centres of population. In each of these you will select the ruling chief . . . and will look to him to rightly assess the number of tax-payers, and collect and transmit the taxes to your administrative centre. . . . Of every elephant killed in the country, one tusk must be given to the Government, and consequently sent in to you. The purchase and sale of ardent spirits by or to natives is absolutely forbidden.'[16] Taxes could be paid in money, or in ivory, gold, copper, limestone, salt, oil-seeds, cotton, coffee or livestock, the value of each of these being assessed. An ox for example was worth fifteen shillings, a sheep four shillings, a fowl threepence. In ten years, these prices were to be quadrupled. The general imposition of tax followed the extension of British authority throughout the Protectorate after 1897, and by 1901 the rate was being increased to six shillings in areas near 'settled' districts, particularly in the Shire highlands, where there were coffee and other plantations.

Wages were higher in Southern Rhodesia, averaging thirty shillings and sometimes a good deal more, against an average fifteen shillings north of the Zambezi, so the tax was heavier, amounting to ten shillings for each hut. In 1901 this rate was increased to a pound and made payable by every adult man instead of by huts, and the amount of labour necessary to be worked in order to obtain remission was raised to four months. From the beginning, however, payment seems to have been generally accepted and understood, and to have been made with a willingness that contrasted sharply with the disinclination to work. In 1898 Lawley reported from Matabeleland that 'the total amount collected was £20,849, and in hardly a single case was any attempt made to evade it', while next year the Chief Native Commissioner in Mashonaland wrote 'the natives continue to pay the tax cheerfully'.[17]

In North-Eastern Rhodesia the story was the same. Codrington's annual report in 1902 stated that 'the imposition of hut tax, which took place in 1901, was well-received.' . . . 'Its imposition seems to have been anticipated. . . . They have willingly paid, knowing that they will be protected, whereas in the old days they had to pay taxes to chiefs in work and kind, though in many cases the chiefs were unable to protect them.'[18] Harrington, the Assistant Collector in the Mweru-Luapula District, wrote this account in 1898: 'As the hut tax was shortly to be introduced . . . I had to travel about the district explaining the tax to them and taking a census. The method was to travel with tents and porters to each chief's village, and that particular chief would then accompany me to all his other villages, and at that time we wrote down, as liable for tax, the able bodied young men. Much amusement was caused in some of the villages, because upon our arrival the only persons to be seen were women and girls. On being asked where all the men were, they would shout out, "There are no men." To which I would reply, "What about these babies?" This caused much laughter, and when I suggested they should go and fetch their husbands whom I knew to be hiding in the bush not far away, they did so. We lined up the men and asked how many huts they had, and as I explained to them that three shillings would have to be paid on each hut, nearly all of them declared to have only one hut.'[19] He added that he received great assistance from the chiefs, and was surprised at the hold most of them had over their people.

One result of the new security felt by the people, was that they were no longer bound to combine together in large villages for defence. In Southern Rhodesia the size of villages was fairly strictly controlled, but in the north the bigger villages were splitting up in many areas, particularly the North-East, and small settlements were spreading out into the surrounding country. This lessened the risk of famine and checked the spread of disease, but the authority of chiefs and headmen was diminished, control was more difficult, and among weaker tribes, especially in the wide tract around Lake Bangweulu, taxes were harder to collect.

North of the Zambezi, the peace of the country was established and maintained by a very small number of men. Codrington's team in the North-East was closely akin to that of the British Central Africa Protectorate, of sterling quality carefully chosen from a generation strongly imbued with the spirit of empire. So too in the North-West, though here Company officers had more often seen service in Southern Rhodesia, and were frequently drawn from the Cape rather than from England.

Their police forces also were strictly limited in size. In North-Eastern Rhodesia, the Company had employed an unofficial force of its own, including a number of Yao and Makwa from Nyasa country, who had fought with Bell, McKinnon and Young against the slave traders. After 1900 these were given official status under the Order in Council, and were called the North-Eastern Rhodesia Constabulary, though the British Central Africa Protectorate Government continued to be militarily responsible down to 1911.[20] In the North-West, on the other hand, there had been no native police up to this time. A small detachment of British South Africa Police, Europeans, had been posted at Kalomo, but in 1900 these were withdrawn. Coryndon, for reasons both of health and economy, believed that 'in a country where the white population is not large, and where the administrative machinery has been well established . . . (well-officered native police) would be reliable, well-disciplined and efficient'.[21] Lewanika was afraid that a police force would weaken his authority, but finally agreed, and later sent twenty recruits. Angoni were also recruited, and came to form the backbone of the new force. A proposal to employ Sikhs was not pursued, for the African N.C.O.s proved their worth. The new unit was named the Barotse Native Police, and was first commanded by Colonel Harding, who travelled widely in the North-West during the early years of the century. Fears that these police might have the same disturbing effect on the Lozi as the native police had had in Matabeleland after the war were not realized. The force was effective in twice suppressing disorders among the Ila, and patrolling the Barotse border. In 1911, when the two territories combined into Northern Rhodesia, the N.E.R. Constabulary and the Barotse Native Police joined to form the Northern Rhodesia Police.

In the British Central Africa Protectorate, the arm of Government was supported by the military unit called the British Central Africa Rifles, formed by Johnston to fight the slave traders. Consisting of European officers, Sikh N.C.O.s, and chiefly Ngoni and Yao soldiers, this force in 1902 became part of the King's African Rifles, of which it formed the B.C.A. Battalion. After 1902 it was frequently serving abroad in other parts of Africa and did not generally perform police duties in the Protectorate. This work was carried out by 'district police', or boma messengers, who were appointed and controlled on a district basis by administrative officers.

The organization was again different in Southern Rhodesia. The British South Africa Police, descended from the force which had accompanied the Pioneer Column in 1890, was a quasi-military body. Its officers and men preferred to be regarded as a military organization rather than as civil police, and indeed civil police duties were in many ways more easily carried out by Africans. In 1900 the Mashonaland Police, posted around the district headquarters, numbered 381, but true to Rhodes' promise no native police had been posted in Matabeleland. However, in the interests of both economy and convenience, after discussion with the indunas, a native police force for Matabeleland, recruited principally from the Ndebele themselves, was started in 1901.[22]

The administrative officers in the districts north of the Zambezi, counterparts of the Native Commissioners of Southern Rhodesia, were at first sometimes known as Collectors, sometimes Native Commissioners, but within a few years generally as District Commissioners. The first duty of one of these officers when appointed was to travel round his district, learning the language and customs of the people, recording the numbers of villages and their inhabitants and the area of cultivated ground, noting the existence of tsetse fly, and mapping the country. He had to keep account of any white men in the district and prevent friction between them and the native people; and among the natives themselves, to keep in touch with the chiefs, settle disputes, keep accounts.[23] During the years immediately after 1900, the Native Commissioners north of the Zambezi were making carriers' paths through the bush, such as that from Tete to Fort Jameson. The work as a rule merely involved the widening of existing footpaths; these tracks became not only the means of communication between Bomas, but also internal transport routes.

Even before 1900, a number of the more important bomas had been established. The British Central Africa Protectorate had been divided into fourteen districts, North-Eastern Rhodesia into seventeen, the North-West into five. In Nyasa country and along the road to Tanganyika, the names of several 'forts' testify to the wars on the slave trade, and on warrior tribes, now ended. Fort Jameson, Fort Lister and Fort Macguire, Fort Rosebery and Fort Hill were, by 1900, no longer stockaded military posts, but were being used as the headquarters of the District Commissioners going about their peaceful purposes. A station was set up at Kasama in 1898, at Serenje in 1900, at Johnston Falls in 1901 and at Feira in 1902. In Barotseland residents were stationed at Lealui, Sesheke and Nalolo and at the Falls, and in preparation for the Barotse native tax in 1904, Coryndon opened new bomas at Kafue, Mazabuka, Nkala and Kasempa. Some of these stations were later moved from their original sites to more suitable or more healthy positions. Finding Lealui unhealthy, Coryndon in 1899 transferred his headquarters to Kalomo. Worthington, his senior Native Commissioner, wrote: 'Kalomo was chosen because Dr Livingstone mentioned it in one of his books.'[24] In 1907 when Robert Codrington succeeded Coryndon, he moved the capital to Livingstone and buying the hotel there turned it into the Government residence. Codrington's place was taken by Lawrence Wallace in the North-East where Government headquarters had, since 1900, been at Fort Jameson.

Effective administration depended upon adequate communications. The railway and the telegraph did not of course reach more than a fraction of the country. Contact between most areas was maintained by a rudimentary postal service whose efficiency has received high praise, and was sufficiently developed by 1900 for Southern Rhodesia to join the International Postal Union. A mail coach service run by the Zeederburg brothers operated in parts of Southern Rhodesia, and for a time as far as Kalomo in Northern Rhodesia till the railway reached it in 1902, though here the conveyance was a simple ox cart. Thefts and hold-ups were rare, but as the coaches were generally pulled by pack mules rather than by horses, passengers had to endure slow and tedious journeys, especially uncomfortable in the rainy season. Mules were preferred because of the prevalence of horse-sickness. Immunized horses were obtainable at a cost. In 1900 Harding wrote from Kalomo to B.S.A. Police headquarters: 'It is a mistake to send other than salted horses as one goes to the trouble and expense of getting them here and ninety per cent. die within the first month, whilst with a salted horse the expense of transport is no more, and eighty per cent. survive the ravages of the country.'[25]

The postal system rested, above all, on the African 'runner'. A regular service was being operated in Southern Rhodesia after the Matabele war. In 1897, when the Resident Commissioner took up his duties in Barotseland, a service to the upper Zambezi was started, using Tswana runners taking three weeks from Francistown to Kazungula, and Lozi north from there. Two years later plans were being made for a service to North-Eastern Rhodesia. In 1899 the Postmaster General wrote that 'efforts have been made to establish an overland weekly mail service between Southern and North-Eastern Rhodesia by native runners, but owing to an outbreak of smallpox and other disturbing causes, it has not yet been possible to inaugurate the service. The mails to and from North-Western Rhodesia have continued to be conveyed with fair regularity, notwithstanding the immense and lonely tract of country covered and the malarial attacks to which these boys are subject.'[26] The following year this service was opened, and by 1905 there were three hundred runners employed in North-Eastern Rhodesia alone. They travelled on foot across great stretches of wild country, clad in the uniform of scarlet calico that came to be well known, bearing the letters in a cleft stick if there were few, or else in a canvas bag, which might weigh up to eighty pounds. It was unusual, even when attacked by lions, for the runners to risk their mail bags. In general they were absolutely reliable, and incidentally were treated with great respect by the African population. Pearce, Acting Commissioner in Nyasaland, wrote that 'the extraordinary honesty of the natives is one of the features which makes it possible to possess the efficient postal service we have'.

The system at Luwingu, described by the District Commissioner there in 1930, was typical of an outstation's postal arrangements for many years: 'There are four runners employed at Luwingu; the men travel alternate weeks—two at a time. They leave Kasama on Wednesday afternoon and arrive at Luwingu on Saturday morning (then return to Kasama by Tuesday afternoon). The route by which they have to travel is 210 miles, out and return, in six days, an average of thirty-five miles a day, with a heavy load on rough and dangerous paths. They then rest for one week.'[27] Although motor transport began to carry mail after 1927 both north and south of the Zambezi, though not yet in Nyasaland, the road still did not reach outlying districts, and postal runners were being used right up to 1939.

Once the railway to the Congo border had been completed by 1909, however, a letter from Cape Town could reach almost any part of Rhodesia and Nyasaland within a fortnight, while the time from England was nine or ten weeks. Needless to say this network of communications greatly facilitated government and administration, particularly in the northern territories.

In the matter of law and administration, the chief differences between north and south were that in Southern Rhodesia the law was Roman-Dutch, after the law of South Africa, it having been Rhodes' early expectation that the colony would in due course federate with the south, while in Northern Rhodesia English law was upheld. The Chartered Company had wanted the same law to run in both territories, but in drawing up the Orders in Council the Secretary of State had insisted on English law, which also prevailed in the British Central Africa Protectorate. In administering law among the African people, too, there were differences—at first merely of emphasis, but later hardening into divergent policies. Commenting on the Southern Rhodesia Native Regulations of 1897, the Secretary of the B.S.A. Company pointed out that they were based on the regulations in Natal, but 'whereas in Natal law chiefs are given power to try and settle certain cases, it has not been deemed advisable to apply the same rule here'.[28] All criminal cases and most disputes had to be brought to the Native Commissioner for judgement. In practice this did not always happen, but as administrative authority in time grew stronger and more extensive, the power of the chiefs tended not to increase but to be diminished. The native affairs department, being only a department of a government in which other matters bulked more largely, and being in part at least recruited from the local European population, lacked the responsibility and independent interest held by the administrative arm in the north and in other British colonies. Without such responsibility, the devolution of further authority on tribal chiefs was less likely to be accomplished.[29]

In Northern Rhodesia from the beginning there was a greater willingness to let matters take their traditional course 'except where repugnant to justice and humanity'. Harrington, in the Luapula district in 1899 (before the Order in Council) described how he frequently sat with a chief while he was settling disputes, and also illustrated the *ad hoc* methods by which officers were expected to deal with their problems. 'Some decisions which the chief gave were quite contrary to what I would have given myself, but they seemed to give great satisfaction to all the people. However, serious crime such as murder, about which the natives did not seem to think very much, and decisions about the ownership of land, were settled by me personally with the assistance of a chief.'[30] After 1900 the powers of Native Commissioners were more clearly defined. Provision was made for magistrates, but magistrate and administrative officer, if the latter had passed the law examination, were usually the same person. In the nothern territories it continued so, but in Southern Rhodesia the civil magistrate in due course became distinct from and superior to the Native Commissioner. The authority of chiefs was usually confined to the settlement of civil disputes; in criminal cases owing to their use of the ordeal and of harsh punishment, decisions were made by Company officers with native assessors in attendance.

In Nyasaland Johnston had at first tried to avoid interfering with the authority of the chiefs provided that cruel methods were abandoned, but let it be understood that there was an appeal from the chief's decision to the nearest magistrate.

'Except in the case of the Yao, the chiefs govern their people kindly and leniently, though among the Ngoni there is horrible use of the poison ordeal.'[31] The Order in Council of 1902 made judicial provisions similar to those in North-Eastern and North-Western Rhodesia. But the greater concentration of population in Nyasaland made possible an earlier trend towards the devolution of authority. The District Administration (Natives) Ordinance of 1912 set up councils of local headmen under the chairmanship of the District Officer. Judicial authority was not affected at first, but it was intended to confer upon headmen 'the power to hear and determine petty cases' in due course.[32]

The obstacle to wise dispensation of justice by Africans was their universal belief that their lives were ordered and actions impelled by unseen spirits and that misfortune never occurred save through the will of another human being endowed with supernatural power. Such beliefs were not peculiar to Africa and trial by ordeal had been condemned by the Christian Church in Europe as recently as the Lateran Council in 1215. The tradition was early recognized as one of the most serious obstacles to African advance, as well as to just administration. 'As for the "poison ordeal",' wrote Sharpe in 1905, 'this is a crime which exists throughout Africa. Many cases come before our District Magistrates.'[33] Special legislation had become necessary. The Protectorate's Criminal Offences Ordinance of that year created a prison sentence of two years for any person unlawfully administering *mwavi* or any other poison for the purpose of trial by ordeal. A second offence was to be regarded as murder. In Southern Rhodesia, under a law of 1898, the penalty for a similar offence was a fine of £100 or thirty-six lashes. Witchfinding and witchcraft came to be less openly practised, and were slowly reduced, though there were outbreaks from time to time over the next half century particularly in the Lunda-related parts of Northern Rhodesia and in Nyasaland. For long Africans regarded the punishment of witchfinders as interference in their one means of bringing a culprit to justice.

Over most of the wide territories the greatest change brought by the administration was the coming of peace and security from slave raids and war. Ordinary life in the sparsely scattered villages went on much as it had done for centuries, sometimes returned to a more civilized existence. 'Among the Bemba', stated the Company's report of 1900, 'people are reverting to their former habits (i.e. prior to the slave trade) of peaceable agriculture. The manufacture of bark cloth has been brought to a great perfection; it is a really durable and handsome article, elaborately stitched and dyed.' It should not be forgotten that at mission stations European influence had already been at work for years; but their efforts were much enhanced by administrative authority. At Fort Jameson Africans 'have adapted themselves in the most remarkable manner to the altered conditions of existence, and are now being trained as carpenters, sawyers, bricklayers and mail carriers, and perform their various duties with intelligence and conscientiousness. . . . The patient and thorough work of officials in the more outlying districts has borne fruit in many ways.'[34]

The African Submission

Around the turn of the century, with an almost dramatic suddenness, the African communities which for centuries had held the centre of the stage receded into the background. It was possible for the high-powered commission touring Rhodesia only a decade after the rebellions had jeopardized the very existence of white settlement to give lengthy accounts of their experiences without any mention of the African population, except in connection with the shortage of labour for the mines. Outside detailed local reports the different tribal nomenclatures seldom found place, being replaced by the all-inclusive term of 'native'. Tribal politics, with rare exceptions, no longer had significance. Inter-tribal disputes were no longer permitted to exist. Tribal distinctions did not disappear, but faded perceptibly as the different groups became more and more closely integrated with the wider society. The African sovereign state, as J. A. Barnes has said of the Ngoni, was in time to become 'more and more like a rural district council in a backward area'.[1]

This is more easily understood if we bear in mind the relatively small size of the African community, smaller then than today. Even the largest tribes such as Cewa and Bemba numbered little more than three hundred thousand all told.[2] Northern Rhodesia's population in 1900 of less than a million included over thirty distinct tribal groups scattered over an area twice as large as the British Isles. These groups were socially exclusive and self-contained, differing sometimes to a marked degree in custom and language, and intermarriage rarely took place except as a result of conquest. The African was therefore born into a very small world, a patriarchal society through the length and breadth of which he knew and was known. It was an autonomous society as well as a complete one; it was its completeness as well as its autonomy that was now taken away.

The very rapidity of the transformation helps to explain the silence of the years that followed, as though a shock had numbed the senses of the social organism. In some respects life was hardly changed; in others it changed more profoundly than ever before. To submit to alien authority was nothing new in African experience. But whereas in the past captives taken by the Ngoni had been rapidly indoctrinated and themselves become proud Ngoni, the Ngoni now complained that, although captured by Europeans they were not able, even if allowed, to become Europeans.[3] The Shona, by contrast, were accustomed to Ndebele raids, but the raiders would go away and leave them after it was over; their new rulers would never go away. That they should neither depart nor assimilate provided a new, perhaps a humiliating experience. The laws now imposed were of course different, and so too was the acceptance of what was reasonable, what was to be expected, and what was not to be tolerated. Above all the tax, the most comprehensible, was yet the most revolutionary of all the new features of life instituted by new administrations. It compelled men to work when they might have hunted, to travel far while they might have stayed at home; by it they acknowledged a new authority, higher than the chief; and by it they became equal with men of all tribes. Ngoni and Tonga, Bemba and Lovale, Ndebele and Shona, all were compelled to submit to this common obligation that placed all men, high and low, weak and strong, in a common predicament.

To the tax itself the reaction appeared, as we have seen, to be nowhere unfavourable. It is even possible that its incidence served to make more acceptable the coming of change by presenting the individual with an incontestable recognition of his place in the new order; also, perhaps, by providing him with an objective whose realization called for effort and ingenuity that might otherwise lie waste. In doing so it carried tremendous consequences for the indigenous society, by bringing the African into contact with the money economy; though it did not at once make him a part of it. The possibility of growing wealthier than one's neighbour, by harder work or by more skilful manipulation of exchange, hitherto almost a stranger to African society, made its appearance. A new and significant phrase, *kuchita gain* (to trade at profit) entered at least one Bantu vocabulary and thereby marked the commencement of a slow revolution in a people's thinking and entire way of life.[4]

The advent of money altered tradition in more specific ways. Obligations between individuals had been discharged, and differences in social grade recognized and honoured, by gifts and dues in kind. These requirements imposed restrictions on the individual and, in a society where all men in the material sense were relatively equal, helped to govern his way of life. Among cattle-owning and patrilineal people such as Ndebele or Ngoni, the marriage of a son was confirmed through the presentation by his parents of cattle to the parents of the bride. Not only was *lobola* or bridewealth an earnest of the serious intentions of the bridegroom and his family; it also helped to cement the union from the other side, and to stabilize the marriage at least until the first child was born. The gradual substitution of a cash *lobola* provided less security. The amount was more liable to reduction, the man was less dependent on his parents, and the custom of repayment on dissolution tended to lapse. The transaction began to assume the appearance of a superficial formality, which combined with other factors, helped to break down the stability of family life. At the same time it tended to accentuate rather than to regularize the differences in wealth and social grade that found a controlled existence in indigenous African society.[5]

Contact with the money economy combined with other influences including secular education and Christian teaching to emphasize individualism in the place of the communal basis of society. Traditionally co-operation had been an important characteristic in most social activities—in producing food, brewing beer, constructing a hut. The social unit of the village was often no more than an extended family, all its members mutually interdependent, supported by a hierarchy leading through the village headman and the subordinate chief to the paramount in his capital seldom more than a few days distant. Status was measured in terms of dependants. Men hoped to gather their children about them as they grew old, and to build up new villages so that their names would be remembered. In the new society, status was measured by material wealth, derived from a man's ability and hard work in competition with his neighbour. Such criteria were for more than a generation quite strange to the African. His hard work was done during seasonal bursts of activity on communal projects; hence his reluctance to work continuously to a regular schedule on mine or farm. Moreover, the deep-seated belief that the fertility of his cattle and the productivity of his gardens were subject not to natural laws but to supernatural influences was a further discouragement from individual exertion. To the early settlers from late nineteenth-century Britain, reared on *laisser faire* individualism, and Darwinian theories of the survival of the fittest, with belief in the value of self-help, thrift and hard work ingrained in their minds, the African outlook was not only incomprehensible but profoundly irritating.

Equally opposed to the late Victorian way of thinking were African ideas of marriage. Among most tribes polygyny was customary, especially for men of rank who could afford to keep more than one household. The status engendered by the number of a man's dependants was one of the social reasons accounting for this. In conjunction with *lobola* however it appeared to contemporary European eyes as a debasement of the married estate. The African, it was supposed, had no proper understanding of family life; though in fact in Bantu custom family bonds were extremely powerful and compulsive. Consequently for the first generation of European rule the African communities were finding that not only was the whole justification for their existence as separate units taken away, but the basic tenets underlying their traditional economic activity and marriage custom were being undermined. While security was a boon, they would accept this; but when insecurity was forgotten a generation later, a more positive reaction could be expected. As many thousands of individuals emigrated annually to the centres of European employment, they were subjected to countless influences both from association with men of other tribes and from subordination to white law and custom. These began to interrupt the rhythm of tribal life, and in time must break that rhythm altogether. The tribe and its ethos were an integral whole. The decay in one part must lead, if alien cultural influences continued, to the destruction of all.

At this time, anthropological studies had not been made. To the general run of the settler population the African was self-evidently lower down on Darwin's scale of evolution, not long 'out of the trees'; his inferiority as a rational species being confirmed by the fact that he had never invented the wheel. The delicate and complex question of cultural change was seen as an over-simplified problem of 'civilizing the native', a process that even by those who were prepared to make the very real effort of imagination required, was expected to take several hundred years. The pre-war generation, content with the inevitable march of progress, was with rare exceptions satisfied with this convenient hypothesis. It was only later realized that the existing culture might petrify with dangerous consequences before it could adapt to the alien way of life.

The Christian missions had their part to play in transmitting this impact. Their influence was all the greater since with their widely scattered stations they were in close contact with the tribal system at its source. To begin with, the central mission stations had gathered the remnants of the slave trade. As the years passed it was found that except in Nyasaland where the population was more concentrated, the people could only be reached effectively by building outstations and by touring the villages. The great instrument of mission influence was the school, education being almost entirely run by the churches in all three territories down to the Second World War. For the first two decades of the century, during which missionary activity increased rapidly, instruction was mainly in literacy with a bias towards evangelism. Enormous labour was expended on devising grammars and literary courses in many languages, and in translating the scriptures. The Roman Catholics taught their older students practical arts in order to maintain their homesteads. The Scottish churches alone stood out for a balance of 'industrial' education for its own sake; the concentration of population again helped them here.

Mission teaching was only one of the many forces undermining the basis of the old order, but for various reasons bore the main brunt of criticism from those who preferred to believe that 'the native' could continue peacefully unchanging in his reserve, cut off from the world. This criticism could hardly be upheld in any case. It is more accurate to hold that 'Christianity had not so much to drive out the old gods, which were already doomed, as to temper, by industrial and religious education, a social and economic revolution . . . which threatened to be physically and morally overwhelming.'[6] Yet even this was beyond the resources of the churches in the early years, and challenges them even today. The charge that schools were inadequately staffed and supervised, widely made and not only at the time of the Chilembwe rising, carried much justification. What weakened mission influence still further was disunity. Half a dozen societies had dominated the pioneer period; by 1920 there were over twenty denominations operating in Northern Rhodesia alone. The variety of teaching, to give only one instance, on the fulfilment of customary obligations in addition to the Christian marriage rites was confusing to the African mind.[7] It was not surprising that Africans in the first years of the occupation, their political systems destroyed or modified, but admitted in theory on equal terms to the European religious system, should seek their direction forward through their own 'Ethiopian' religious sects.

Ethiopianism had a history of its own in South Africa dating back to the 1890s when many Africans, reacting against colour prejudice in religious observance, had set up churches of their own. The first 'African church' in Central Africa was founded by a man who had had experience of the intense race prejudice prevailing in the United States at the end of the last century. Its brief career culminated in an insurrection which is of interest since it casts light on the attitude of Africans in one part of the country during the first generation of European rule.[8]

John Chilembwe, a Yao convert, had been the protégé of Joseph Booth, a free-lance missionary who had come to Nyasaland in the late nineties. Booth had sent him to study at a seminary in the United States. On returning to Africa in 1900,

Chilembwe parted company with Booth and founded his own Providence Industrial Mission, which built churches and acquired a considerable following in the Blantyre district prior to the war. A number of circumstances combined to create a level of discontent which Chilembwe was able to exploit. Pressure of population was growing on the Shire highlands. A drought in 1912 led to famine prices the following year, maintained into 1914 by war requisitions. Recruitment for military work dislocated the labour force more than usual. The increased hut tax of 1912 from six to eight shillings had come at an unfortunate time, while the District Administration (Natives) Ordinance interfered with traditional authority and appeared to enhance the direct rule of the European administration. Meanwhile, on a more local scale, resentment was aroused against A. L. Bruce's Estates. The safeguards for 'squatters' in the 1904 Land Ordinance were difficult to apply, and Bruce in particular paid them scant attention. To this friction between landlord and tenant was added religious and race recriminations when the estate manager commenced a vendetta against the Providence Industrial Mission and a number of Chilembwe's churches were burned down.

The rising began with an attack on the Magomero estate north of Mlanje mountain on 23 January 1915, when three European estate officers were killed, and lasted for two weeks, by which time the Administration's forces, depleted owing to the campaign on the northern border, brought the movement to an end. Chilembwe was shot while escaping; most other leaders were executed or sentenced to imprisonment. The incident was remarkable for the restraint shown by the African insurgents in their treatment of the European women and children. Chilembwe had preached the establishment of an African state. The rising is more properly seen as a gesture of protest against the disregard of African values, particularly evident during the early months of a new and quite foreign war; while it also expressed the frustration of capable Africans whose outlets for the exercise of leadership under the old system had been stopped. It could not have taken place had its leaders not had experience of the wider world abroad. The resentment which Chilembwe was able to kindle, on the other hand, had much of its origin in local circumstances. The increase of the population in other parts existed no doubt, but African emotions nowhere attained the intensity and coherence displayed in the Shire highlands.

Contemporary reaction was superficial. The leading part played by educated Africans did not pass unnoticed, but the Governor's comment was merely that 'the effect of the episode has been to shatter some of our beliefs in the efficiency of past efforts at Christianizing and civilizing the native population'.[9] Laws with greater insight blamed the slowness in encouraging African leadership and exercise of responsibility in the missions.

If the rising displayed the angry discontent of those who no longer had a tribe to give them effective voice, its religious manifestations had a comparable significance. In African tradition, political and spiritual power were closely linked. Spiritual association with the land could be broken when political power over it was lost, and a defeated chief, even a paramount, could lose his ritual authority.[10] In the Shire highlands, owing to a generation of conflict and the influx of alien groups, the tribal structure had collapsed. None the less, it was through theological and spiritual activities that Africans sought to recover some political expression. In this sense Chilembwe's revolt was not an isolated occurrence, though the quality of its leader set it apart in the clarity of its aim and the competence of its organization. In searching for a new lead, a bewildered generation was to find particular appeal in the prophet movements of the twenties, which were not confined to Central Africa.

Notable among these were the Jehovah's Witnesses, preaching that all human governments were doomed to destruction, the existing administrations among them.[11] The movement had already been active in Nyasaland before the war, brought there from Johannesburg by Elliot Kamwana, another protégé of Joseph Booth. Known widely as the Watchtower, it was proscribed in Nyasaland and North-Eastern Rhodesia during the war, but various associated groups reappeared after 1920. They were generally treated with a policy of toleration. Tomo Nyirenda's 'Mwanalesa' movement was not truly Watchtower nor even political. Directed at witch-finding for personal ends, it achieved brief notoriety for its murders in North-Eastern Rhodesia during 1925–6, and ended in the execution of its leaders. The Jehovah's Witnesses do not appear to have been actively subversive, but managed to become scapegoats for minor outbreaks of violence, including the later Copperbelt disturbances of 1935.

The Great War

Yet another impact upon the African consciousness during the first generation of European rule was the East African campaign of the Great War. Indeed the largest significance of the campaign, which was militarily of minor importance, can be seen in terms of this impact, of which a closer study has yet to be made. In addition, the four years of hostilities influenced the rate and direction of the economic and political development of all three Central African territories. An expected acceleration was postponed for a decade when events in Europe, their consequences reaching out all over the world, intervened.

The East African campaign was not altogether disconnected from the mainsprings of the conflict, which derived in great measure from the spectacular movement since the last years of the nineteenth century towards the imperial expansion of Europe. Germany's anxiety to catch up on the lead of the maritime powers had already resulted in her control of South-West Africa, East Africa, part of Togoland and the Cameroons. A powerful navy had been built, and great efforts were planned to displace Britain and France from their position as the leading imperial powers. Of this, German support for Kruger between 1895 and 1899, intervention in Morocco in 1905 and 1911, and activities in the Middle East, the Far East and the Pacific were clear indications.

In Central Africa, Germany's ambition had been chiefly that of preventing the spread of British influence northwards. Rhodes' scheme for an 'all-red route' from the Cape to Cairo were countered by German plans to link together their possessions in East and South-West Africa. Such a link would include control of the rich mineral deposits in the Katanga region. In 1912 Robert Williams, when negotiating a concession from the Portuguese to build the Bengwella railway through Angola, found the Germans competing against him. He said after the war that he had had exceptional opportunities for watching Germany's 'persistent subterranean attempts to secure a sphere of influence right across Central Africa by which she could for ever block this country (Britain) from building a railway between our northern and southern African possessions'.[1] However true these fears may or may not have been at the time, there is little doubt that, had Germany gained a major victory, parts of North-Western and North-Eastern Rhodesia and of the southern Belgian Congo, would have been taken.

In the event, Germany lost the fight in Africa as well as in Europe. Her first setback came when Botha and Smuts brought the newly independent Union into the war on the side of Britain. As a result, the German forces in South-West Africa were unable to march north, and were in fact overcome by the South Africans, in conjunction with Rhodesian elements, by the end of 1915. Smuts was thereafter able to concentrate his forces in East Africa, where the Germans had the disadvantage of having to fight on two fronts, facing Northern Rhodesia and Nyasaland in the south and being attacked from Uganda and Kenya in the north.

Britain having declared war on Germany on 4 August 1914, emergency plans for the defence of the Central African borders which faced German territory were quickly made. The Germans had, in 1890, been given access to the Zambezi by the cession of the Caprivi strip, and a fort had been established at Schuckmannsburg across the river three miles from Sesheke. A week after war began, a detachment of B.S.A. Police was sent to join the Northern Rhodesia Police in patrolling both banks of the Zambezi above the Victoria Falls. The precaution was a sensible one, but there was in fact no danger, for there were no German forces in support for hundreds of miles across hot, sandy country. On 21 September Schuckmannsburg was captured without a shot being fired, and a unit of the Northern Rhodesia Police was left in control.

Meanwhile recruitment was in progress in Southern Rhodesia, and in October the 1st Rhodesia Regiment was formed with a strength of five hundred Europeans. This force was sent to fight the Germans in South-West Africa, where it was actively engaged for eighteen months. In 1916, when the campaign was over, the regiment was disbanded, and its members went to take part in the East African campaign, while others joined the South African army or went individually to Europe, as other Southern Rhodesians had done at the outbreak of war.

In Northern Rhodesia the Rifle Association was converted into a volunteer military force, the Northern Rhodesia Rifles, into which every available able-bodied man in the small white population enrolled. At the same time, the Northern Rhodesia Police was placed on a full military footing. All police were withdrawn from outstation bomas and these, combined with new African recruits, were drilled into a fighting force.[2] Meanwhile, to take their place in the administration, boma 'messengers' were trained; these continued their duties after the war, and have done so ever since. In December 1914 these two units, the Northern Rhodesia Rifles and the Northern Rhodesia Police, were formed into a mobile column and sent with all speed to the Tanganyika border.

The Germans had a strong military post at Bismarcksburg on Lake Tanganyika, and already in September had attacked Abercorn thirty miles to the south, which was held by the District Commissioner and a handful of police. A request was sent urgently to Kasama for reinforcements, and a hundred police who had just arrived from Livingstone marched the ninety-two miles in seventy-two hours, arriving just in time to repulse a fresh enemy attack. Belgian African troops also arrived in September from Katanga, and Abercorn was for the time being made secure. The border from Lake Tanganyika to Lake Nyasa was however too long to be adequately guarded by these small forces, and the arrival of the column from the south was anxiously awaited. German patrols were active, and the telephone wire which ran along the Stevenson road was constantly being cut.

The column, led by Major Boyd Cunningham and Major Gordon, arrived at Abercorn in December, having marched rapidly from the railhead at Sakania on the Congo border, a notable feat in the heavy rains. Thence a detachment continued to the advance post on the Saisi stream forty miles further east. These events greatly strengthened the defence of the north-east where skirmishing went on throughout the rainy season.

In Nyasaland also fighting had taken place. The Government's armed forces in the Protectorate, which Johnston had

organized to quell the Arab slave trade, and which had inter-
vened in North-Eastern Rhodesia against Mpezeni and
Kazembe in 1898–99, had then been known as the British
Central Africa Rifles. In 1902 the forces of the four protectorates under the Foreign Office—the B.C.A. Protectorate, Kenya,
Uganda and Somaliland—were combined into a new unit, the
King's African Rifles, of which the troops in the B.C.A. Protectorate formed the 1st (Central Africa) Battalion. At the time
that war broke out, more than half the battalion was away in
Jubaland on the Upper Nile. At once all leave was cancelled,
and more African recruits enrolled. A number of European
civilians formed the new Nyasaland Volunteer Reserve, which
with the units of the 1st K.A.R. was organized for the time being
into the Nyasaland Field Force.

The British in Nyasaland were informed of the declaration
of war sooner than the Germans across the border, and were
quick to make use of this advantage. The only German vessel
on the lake was the *Hermann von Wissmann*, at that time
beached for repairs at the harbour of Alt Langenburg. Relations between her commander and the British had always been
cordial, and the appearance of the gunboat *Gwendolen*, firing
warning shots, on the morning of 13 August was entirely unexpected. The German officers and crew were captured, and
the engines of the *Von Wissmann* put out of action. Later an
attempt was made to repair it, but during an amphibious attack
on Sphinxhaven in March 1915 the garrison was overcome
and the boat finally disabled.

Across the lake at Karonga troops were already being dis-
embarked, having been brought up from the south by the other
six British vessels on the lake, of which two belonged to the
Administration, two to the African Lakes Corporation, and two
to the U.M.C.A. The Germans had crossed the Songwe on 20
August, and occupied Kapora three miles inside British territory. In the meantime the troops were hard at work on the
defences of Karonga, and by 7 September these were complete.
The following day a German force was reported to be advancing
south, and in fact by-passed a unit of K.A.R. sent out to inter-
cept them. On the 9th, Karonga was attacked, but the enemy
was beaten off. Withdrawing to the north, they were met by
the K.A.R. force which had come round in their rear, and were

severely mauled before they could cross the border, losing seven European and fifty-one African dead, and several captured. Among the British, five Europeans and eight Africans lost their lives, and about fifty were wounded. This was the first serious engagement of the war on the Nyasaland/North-Eastern Rhodesia border.[3]

By the beginning of the dry season of 1915, the north-eastern border was being firmly defended. There was, however, no question yet of advancing into German territory. The campaign in South-West Africa was still engaging Smuts' army. A large proportion of the K.A.R. was still committed to the defence of the Uganda railway in the north. Thirdly, the Germans still had control of Lake Tanganyika itself. Until at least two of these factors were altered, there could be little change in strategy. Meanwhile there was some hard fighting on the border during 1915.

The Germans were the stronger in numbers at this stage, and as they were more often the attacking force, they suffered heavier casualties. Of the small but hard-fought engagements of this season, that at Saisi is the best known.[4] At this fortified post on a rocky knoll overlooking the bridge by which the Stevenson road crossed the Saisi stream, a redoubtable Irishman, Captain O'Sullevan, was in command of a force of forty Europeans and 450 Africans. In July, after a preliminary skirmish, an enemy force numbering two thousand men equipped with twelve-pounder guns and machine guns surrounded the stockaded fort. Shelling began and continued intermittently for nine days during which the shortage of water became acute. O'Sullevan refused to surrender but could hardly have held out much longer when the enemy, having expended their ammunition, retired. This determined defence did more than prevent the Germans from entering Rhodesian territory. The High Commissioner for South Africa had recorded a short while earlier that the tactics of passive defence were having 'a demoralizing effect on our troops and the opposite effect on the enemy's morale'. Not only British but allied (Belgian) prestige was now enhanced among the Africans, whose sympathies the Germans had made great efforts to detach.

If Saisi was the turning point in the campaign on the border, the offensive nature of the new phase commenced with water-borne operations on Lake Tanganyika. In June 1915 two motor vessels, *Mimi* and *Toutou*, each armed with a three-pounder gun and a machine gun and crewed by naval seamen, were despatched with utmost secrecy from England to Cape Town. After being taken in parts by train as far as the Katanga border, the two boats made an epic journey transported by tractors and oxen to the Lualaba river and thence by railway to the west shore of Lake Tanganyika, reached in October. Assembly of the boats and the construction of a harbour took some weeks. The boats were launched two days before Christmas, and on Boxing Day the German armed steamboat *Kingani* was captured and converted to British use. 'It was', comments the official history with some pride, 'the first German warship (in any theatre of war) to be brought in as a prize and transferred to the Royal Navy.' Early in 1916 another German craft was sunk while two others were driven ashore. The last enemy vessel on the lake was scuttled in July.

The command of the lake thus obtained made an advance northwards by land forces possible. The arrival of Smuts and his troops from South-West Africa where the campaign was being successfully concluded, was now awaited. In the meantime fighting at the border posts continued sporadically. General Northey had taken command of the combined forces on the Rhodesia/Nyasaland frontier in November 1915. One of his concerns was the supply of African recruits, which was dwindling as a large proportion of the available African manpower was already employed; there was, besides, better money to be earned elsewhere. It was particularly hard to obtain recruits from the Bemba and Ngoni, who were among the most highly valued of the fighting men. Recruiting now went on among the Lozi and Ila in the north-west, and the pay of the ordinary troops was raised. After April 1916 the number of African troops, which experience had shown to be vital to eventual success, was steadily increasing.

Early in the dry season of 1916, a general offensive began. Smuts' army was now pressing on the enemy commanded by General Wahle in the north. On 5 May an advance into German territory by a force including five companies of Northern Rhodesian Police as well as Southern Rhodesian units began from the south. For the eighteen months that followed, there was continuous campaigning in German East Africa, the Germans being steadily hemmed in and driven eastwards. The German commanders for the most part cleverly avoided decisive action, and most of the fighting consisted of scraps in pursuit of an elusive enemy. Northey's forces had some support from the local Africans, particularly the Hehe around Iringa, who remembered the German suppression of the Maji Maji rebellion in 1906. The country was very rough on the troops, who had to march and manhandle artillery and supplies through thick bush, across marshes and streams, over hill ranges and along narrow ravines. It was a war of forced marches in the long cool-shadowed hours that surrounded the African dawn, and of actions fought by tattered, hungry men in the heat and dust of the dry season and the steamy mud of the rains. 'Neither before nor since', says the official record, 'has the K.A.R. been faced with a campaign at once so prolonged, arduous and stubborn as that of the First World War.'[5]

The last months of 1917 saw the heaviest fighting. By November the German force had been driven round the north end of Lake Nyasa and south as far as the Rovuma. There a large quantity of supplies was captured and troops taken prisoner, and the remainder, a band of fifteen hundred led by Von Lettow Vorbeck, with as many carriers, escaped across the Rovuma into Portuguese East Africa. The campaign was virtually over.

Little action was taken during the rains of 1917–18, but in June 1918 units of the Northern Rhodesia Police and the K.A.R. set out in pursuit of Von Lettow. The Germans moved back to the north along Nyasa's east shore. There was an action at Fusi in October followed by another at Fife beyond the north end. From Fife Von Lettow moved south west to Kasama. The boma there was undefended, for the Northern Rhodesia Police, believing the Germans were heading for Katanga, had moved west to reinforce Abercorn. The District Commissioner at Kasama had news of the enemy approach the day before their arrival on 9 November, and sending the European women and children south to Mpika, withdrew his own police as far as the rubber factory at the Chambeshi pontoon. Arriving at Kasama Von Lettow blew up the Government Offices, and on the 12th made his way along the road south towards the Chambeshi.

On the morning of the 13th he was established on the north bank, and commenced firing with Lewis guns at the factory buildings.

It is believed that these were the last shots fired in the Great War. News of the armistice had been received in Livingstone on the 11th, but owing to a fault in the telegraph did not reach the Chambeshi till two days later. The District Commissioner immediately informed Von Lettow that hostilities had ceased in Europe, where his government had capitulated, and the German commander agreed to surrender. His formal submission was received by General Edwards of the K.A.R. at Abercorn on 18 November.

The importance of the East and South-West African campaigns need not be exaggerated. While the war in Europe had been the most terrible cataclysm that had befallen the Western world, the African affair was by contrast a sideshow. It has been described, however, and the description is worth noting, as 'a hard clean fight, without ill-feeling on either side, and with no legacy of bitterness to mar the years ahead'. It is perhaps significant that similar remarks were later made of the North African campaign in the Second World War. The East African fighting in 1914–18 was of smaller military importance. Even had British territories in East and Central Africa been overrun, the outcome would have been the same, as Germany's surrender was unconditional. The peace brought no changes in the territorial boundaries. Germany's colonies, however, were taken away from her and entrusted to the League of Nations as 'mandated territories'. South-West Africa was to be administered by the Union Government, and German East Africa, now to be called the Tanganyika Territory, by Great Britain.

It is ironical that violent conflict should have been brought to the African continent by those European Governments that thirty years before had imposed their administrations in the name of peace and order. The official record referred in extravagant terms to the Africans' 'wholehearted loyalty and affection for the white leaders whom he has come to know and trust, and to his even deeper and more devoted loyalty to the sovereign and empire he serves'. A glimpse of the other side of the picture appeared in the *Nyasaland Times* after the Karonga fighting. 'The poor Africans', wrote John Chilembwe, 'who have nothing to own in this present world, who in death leave only a long line of widows and orphans in bitter want and dire distress, are invited to die for a cause which is not theirs.'⁶ Chilembwe had lived abroad, seen the wider world, and gained a perspective denied to most of his fellow countrymen; and this was only one among several reasons for the heartburning that prompted him to lead the January uprising. None the less, it is likely that the campaign made at least as great an impact on the African consciousness as on that of Europeans, for whom it was part of a greater whole; certainly it appeared in a different light. The white man's government, as opposed to individuals, was no longer seen as infallible, having descended to warfare of a kind that its first consuls had condemned among the tribes. Africans, sometimes with considerable reluctance, had been persuaded to fire on a European enemy; what was for many a taboo, had been broken.⁷

For the most part, however, troops and carriers engaged in the conflict displayed the courage, tenacity and fighting qualities with which they were widely credited by their European commanders. This is not to be explained by the desire for money reward, nor even by the fighting traditions of some of the tribes. These motives existed no doubt, but there was also a wish to serve the new chief, to earn a place in the new community, which was not always so wisely cultivated, nor so easily entertained, in the years of peace that followed.

VIII

THREE TERRITORIES

The Passing of Company Rule

IN 1915 the Company's charter, which had been granted for twenty-five years, expired and was replaced by a supplemental charter. Into this a new clause was written providing that 'if at any time after 29 October, 1915, the Legislative Council of Southern Rhodesia shall, by an absolute majority, . . pass a resolution praying the Crown to establish in Southern Rhodesia the form of government known as Responsible Government, and shall support such Resolution with evidence showing that the condition of the territory financially and in other respects is such as to justify the establishment of such government,' steps would be taken accordingly. In 1917 a Responsible Government Association was formed under the leadership of Charles Coghlan, a Salisbury barrister, which quickly assumed the character of a political party.

Among the European population, there was general agreement that the Company's rule should come to a close. A chartered company has a divided loyalty, to its shareholders as well as to the settlers within its territories. It was true that, even then, thirty years after it was founded, the Company had paid no dividend to those who had invested their money in Rhodes' imperial dream. At a Company meeting in March 1923 an old and disgruntled shareholder expressed the general view when he said, 'Many years ago an old friend told me: "You buy Chartereds; there is only one Chartered and there will never be another. You will get £100 each for them." Well, I have had them long enough . . . and have never had one halfpenny yet in the way of return from them. . . . This is not a philanthropic institution, but a commercial undertaking.'[1] The Company had, in fact, tried to strike a balance between the considerations of commerce and the imperial ideal. Referring to the intentions of the 'great Founder', the Administrator told the same meeting that 'the administration of Rhodesia has not been a profitable business for you, but it has enabled you to do good work'. On the other hand it was inevitable that thoughts of profit should rank largely in its design. The link between the railway and the mines may be taken for an example. The Company had a monopoly of railway construction, and had formed subsidiary companies to build them. Its connection with the mines was similar. Discontent was felt among many settlers that the mines had benefited to a greater extent than farming and other interests, which bore less direct profit to the Company. It was not felt with any confidence that the welfare of the population as a whole was always the first consideration when a decision had to be made.

For its own part, the Company was not reluctant to relinquish administrative responsibility. The governing of the two Rhodesias caused a regular deficit in its accounts, which absorbed all of whatever profits were made elsewhere. There was no doubt in Company circles at London Wall that the time was coming when its activities must be confined to commerce, industry and finance. Indeed most were anxious that it should do so. The question to be settled was whether the young colony should be handed over to the Imperial Government, which would grant responsible government at once, or to the Union of South Africa, formed in 1910, in whose constitution there existed a clause providing for the absorption of Southern Rhodesia at any time. There was no reference in this clause to the consent of the Rhodesians. The consequent feeling of insecurity was a large source of the demand for responsible government. The Company strongly favoured the South African solution, and were supported by their shareholders in London. It was, after all, the destiny which Rhodes had always intended for 'his North.' The Union at that time, whose government was led by General Smuts, was anxious that Southern Rhodesia should join it, and was prepared to offer generous terms—far more generous than the Company could hope to obtain from the British Government, which was struggling with its post-war problems.

It was soon evident that the Company did not see eye to eye with the Rhodesians, who in any case formed half the number of the shareholders. The Responsible Government Party won the 1920 elections, and in that year a majority in the Legislative Council, including all the elected members and one official, voted for a resolution in favour of Responsible Government. 'Liberty in rags,' declared Sir Charles Coghlan, 'is better than well-fed tutelage. .... We have souls to be saved as well as bodies to be kicked.'[2] According to the 1915 Charter the Imperial Government was bound to take note of this decision. The following year a Commission was appointed by the Colonial Secretary, then Winston Churchill. Under the chairmanship of Lord Buxton, who had had considerable experience of Rhodesia, it recommended that a scheme for responsible government should be prepared forthwith, and that the alternatives of such a scheme or of the merging of the colony with the Union should be decided by referendum as soon as possible.

Although the issue appeared to be clear cut, each choice had many implications. Most Rhodesians owned a common political creed compounded of a desire for self-government, a dislike of Crown Colony status, and a feeling that Union with the south would mean loss of individuality. On the other hand, many doubted whether the colony of 33,000 Europeans and 770,000 Africans, the latter still living a primitive though peaceful existence, could stand on its own financial feet. Though all the time seeking better services, the settlers were unwilling to pay higher taxes, and the administrative deficit had always been met by the Company. Now the Company was going, and the winning of responsible government seemed likely to be at the cost of a disadvantageous bargain with the United Kingdom Government. South Africa was offering to take over the unalienated land and the Rhodesia Railways system, and to pay the Company in compensation the sum of £6,836,500. This arrangement appeared favourable to the Directors; it offered security for Southern Rhodesia and indemnity for themselves. There was no chance of such favourable terms from the Imperial government, 'which', said Malcolm at a shareholders' meeting in 1922, 'is confoundedly hard up'. It was the time of the Geddes Axe. At first the British Government was even demanding that the Company should pay the costs that had fallen on the home country for the defence of Central Africa during the war, estimated at £1½ million, a demand that caused bitter resentment in Rhodesia and was eventually dropped.

Two other outstanding differences remained. The first was the question whether the Imperial Government should pay the Company a lump sum to cover the cost of administrative deficits over the thirty years of Company rule, a sum which the Company estimated at upwards of £8 millions. There were references, such as that in a motion put in a Company meeting in 1923, protesting against the Crown's 'callous disregard of our Company's services to the Empire, doing the Government's work for over thirty years, and making a colony'.[3] The British Government took a more qualified view. None the less, a Commission under the Chairmanship of Lord Cave, appointed in 1918 to examine the Company's case and the extent of their claim, published its estimate of £4 millions owing to the Company when its administrative responsibilities should be handed over.

This was much less than the Company hoped for, but would have been more acceptable had there been a favourable settlement of the second outstanding issue, the thorny question of the unalienated lands. Vast tracts of land had not been allocated to any titled occupant, while still lying outside the scheduled reserves. The Company claimed that this land was its own property, the legal title resting on the Lippert Concession of 1890. The Company's case appeared a strong one, for had it not from the beginning made grants of land to occupiers? The Imperial Government pointed out, however, that though the Lippert Concession may have had some value in helping to explain how and why the Crown came to confer the administration of Southern Rhodesia upon the Company, as a title deed to the unalienated lands, many of which were the Crown's by virtue of the conquest of 1893, it was valueless. In this respect the Concession was, of course, a legal fiction. The opinion of the Imperial Government in any case was that throughout the Company was acting as its agent. While the Company held the land, it was entitled to use the revenue from it towards the cost of administration. Whenever the Company should hand over the administration of the Colony, the Imperial Government would make up the balance of the debt, but would not pay for the unalienated land.[4]

The African people, who had been in undisputed occupation of the whole territory little more than a generation earlier, were not heard, though the theory that they were in fact the rightful owners of the unalienated lands was put forward by the Aborigines Protection Society.

All this tedious negotiation aroused considerable discontent among the European population of Southern Rhodesia. Apart from the fact that many believed the land in any case rightly belonged to the taxpayers of the colony, the settlement of the issue had been dragging on for several years. Complaints were made of 'cat and mouse' treatment, of the procrastination of London Wall, and of the secrecy with which the Company conducted its affairs in contrast with the openness of Rhodesian political discussion.

Behind these issues, which were beaten out in stately committee rooms in far away London, the Rhodesians were preparing for the referendum, which would decide whether the colony would be merged with the Union or pursue its own course. Intense interest was aroused in the public debate, meetings were held throughout the colony, some of them addressed by Smuts himself. Posters and propaganda helped to raise the political temperature to fever heat, matched only by the early summer season, which was building up to the worst drought experienced for many years. On 27 October 1923 polling was held. The count revealed 8,774 votes for responsible government against 5,999 for union with the south. The fact that two-fifths of the voters favoured the latter course was due to the considerable proportion of South Africans in the country, and also to the success attending Smuts' party in consolidating Anglo-Dutch unity in the Union. The margin in favour of responsible government, however, was clear and emphatic.

The negotiations in London were in the meantime being pursued, and the final settlement was embodied in the Devonshire Agreement of September 1923.[5] The Imperial Government paid to the British South Africa Company the sum of £3,750,000, which purported to cover the administrative deficits during Company rule, and the cost of public works and buildings which now became Crown property. The Company agreed to forgo all rights and interests in the lands in Southern and Northern Rhodesia, except for its own estates, farms and ranches. Mineral rights throughout the Rhodesias, on the other hand, were to be retained by the Company, and there was a special clause protecting the Rhodesia Railways. A new constitution embodying responsible government was to be drafted, while administrative obligations in Northern Rhodesia were to be assumed by the Crown. This last clause lifted a great burden from the Company's shoulders, for though the subsidy of £850 to Lewanika was still to be a Company responsibility, the costs of which it was relieved had been averaging £100,000 a year.

The new constitution for Southern Rhodesia came into force on 1 October 1923, immediately after the colony had been annexed to the Crown by Order in Council.[6] It provided for a Governor to represent the King in Southern Rhodesia, and for a single house of Parliament to consist of thirty members. There were to be fifteen electoral districts, each sending two representatives to Parliament. Provision was made for a second chamber to be added later on. The franchise, as before, was open to British subjects of any race having an income of over two hundred pounds. Elections were to be held at least every five years, and the prime minister, chosen from the strongest party returned at the polls, was to govern with the aid of a cabinet of six members. Parliament had control over all the territory's affairs except those concerning mining royalties, and laws affecting Africans. Differential legislation 'whereby natives may be subjected to disabilities to which persons of European descent are not also subjected' required the assent of the Secretary of State before it could become law.

The existing administration continued in office for a few months while preparations for the first general election were made. The principal contestants were the Rhodesia Party, a continuation under a new name of the old Responsible Government Party, led by the redoubtable Sir Charles Coghlan; while his opponents were the Independents, mainly consisting of those who had favoured union in the referendum. Now that the question of the colony's future was settled, no great issue divided these parties, but Coghlan stumped the country proclaiming the danger of a small majority and a coalition, and calling for a decisive verdict in favour of his party. The result of the election was an overwhelming victory for the Rhodesia

Party, which gained twenty-six seats against the Independents' four. The Rhodesian Labour Party, a group inspired and controlled by the Rhodesia Railway Workers' Union, failed to win a seat. It was significant of the way the colony was developing, that farming interests were more strongly represented in the new Parliament than those of the mining companies.[7]

Meanwhile the small European community in Northern Rhodesia had acquired a character and outlook of its own by 1924. An influential channel for opinion was the *Livingstone Mail*, started by a Livingstone chemist, Leopold Moore, in 1906. Expounding loyalty to Crown and Empire, it constantly attacked B.S.A. Company rule.[8] In 1911, when the whole territory was combined under one administrator, the Kafue farmers petitioned the High Commissioner for an Advisory Council, which had been provided for in the Order in Council. Two years later the North-Western Rhodesia Farmers' Association began to agitate for a full Legislative Council with unofficial membership. The outbreak of war shelved the question, but in 1918 an Advisory Council consisting of five elected members was established. It had no legislative powers but provided an official outlet for voicing settler opinion. The principal complaints brought forward were the diversion of African labour to Southern Rhodesia, the inadequate veterinary services and the Company's restrictive land distribution policy. Railway development was disappointing; the Company would not spend enough money, had not encouraged immigration and prospecting.[9] The company's response, that it had had first to develop Southern Rhodesia, and that in any case the opening up of the North must be carried out cautiously because of different relations with the native population, was small consolation.

Responsible government was out of the question for a white population of 3,600 in 1921 among close on a million Africans. Most of the Europeans were concentrated along the railway strip, apart from 250 at Fort Jameson and a handful at Abercorn, and the few scattered missionaries and administrative officers. The territory, besides, was far from self-supporting. The revenue of £224,270 in 1920, for example, had fallen short of expenditure by £147,728. Most settlers, realizing the impossibility of self-rule at this stage from all points of view, would be content with Crown Colony status. There was strong pressure, however, that this should include representation on the legislature. In 1920 an attempt to raise income tax had been met with vociferous protest, and a petition was sent to the Secretary of State praying that in future any new taxation and any new law should have the prior approval of the Advisory Council.

Negligible support was found for amalgamation with the south, apart from a few farmers who would be glad of the service of Southern Rhodesian experts. Most Northern Rhodesians, particularly in the Civil Service, were keenly British in sentiment. At a time when there was talk of Southern Rhodesia joining hands with the Union, they wanted to keep their own traditions, and feared anything that would draw them towards the south. For different reasons described later, most Southern Rhodesians were also opposed to amalgamation, and the proposal was never seriously entertained at this time.

The Buxton Report of 1921, which advised a solution of the Southern Rhodesian issue by referendum, also reported on the Northern Rhodesian problem. Pressing the Company to establish a Legislative Council, it recommended an inquiry into settler opinion, for various ideas, besides Crown Colony status, were in the air, including the partition scheme, whereby North-Eastern Rhodesia would form a separate protectorate, and the railway belt would amalgamate with the south, or else receive self-government on its own. The report also emphasized the different approach to the land question. 'In Northern Rhodesia there was no conquest and no consequent settlement; but only a series of agreements and instruments made in wholly different circumstances from those which prevailed in Southern Rhodesia. . . . It is possible indeed that a claim might be put forward that the unalienated lands . . . belong . . . to the natives.'[10]

The Devonshire Agreement of September 1923 determined Northern Rhodesia's future as a Crown Colony. On 10 April 1924 the Imperial Government was to take over its administration, and also 'full and entire control of the lands throughout North-Western and North-Eastern Rhodesia, to be administered as it thinks best in the interest of the native population and in the public interest generally.' The B.S.A. Company was to retain mineral rights, and its freehold estates in North-Eastern Rhodesia. There was to be special protection for the railway companies, in view of their heavy investment. The last two clauses were written into the new Constitution, which was brought into force by the Northern Rhodesia Order in Council of 1924. This provided for a Governor and an Executive Council nominated by the Crown. There was to be, for the first time, a Legislative Council, set up by separate Order, containing nine nominated and five elected members under the Chairmanship of the Governor. Ordinances were to 'respect native laws and customs, except where incompatible with the due exercise of His Majesty's power and jurisdiction'. There was to be no discriminatory legislation on grounds of race, apart from laws relating to arms, ammunition and liquor. The perennial clause reserving Barotseland was included, and it was stated that throughout the country 'a native may acquire ... land on the same conditions as a person who is not a native'.

Divergent Policies in the Rhodesias

Southern Rhodesia in the late twenties, wrote Professor Clay in 1929, was 'in the position of a firm with heavy overhead expenses and inadequate turnover'[1]. He was referring to the high cost of living, which derived from two factors—the expense of providing the amenities of civilization over a large area for a small population, and the high wages—between two and two and a half times their London equivalents—earned by skilled and semi-skilled European labour and which resulted from its scarcity. In both cases the only ultimate remedy was to increase the 'turnover', which in this case meant to secure an increase in white population. The number of settlers had risen in six years from 36,000 to 51,000 and was increasing at the rate of eight per cent. per annum, an exceptionally high rate for any country of European settlement, but the figures were still low in absolute terms. The Europeanization of the African population was seen to be equivalent economically to the immigration of more Europeans, but was then regarded as a very long term possibility indeed. To the cursory glance, wrote the Chief Native Commissioner that year, African development was 'stationary', while 'the passive strength of immemorial custom still opposes itself to the active and not always well-directed attacks of modern thought'.[2]

The economy still rested almost entirely on primary products for export, and the principal economic activities of
Southern Rhodesia in 1930 still consisted of mining, agriculture
and railway operation. It had long become clear that the extent
of the resources which had drawn white immigrants had been
over-estimated. Chrome, zinc and asbestos production were
still mounting, but gold mining had nearly reached its maximum level. Farmers, particularly in Mashonaland, had directed
their efforts at tobacco growing, encouraged by Imperial preference since 1919; though alternate years of flood and drought
had hit pioneer growers in the early twenties. A recovery in
1926 brought new expansion in tobacco acreage, but the market was flooded and the Union amended its customs agreement
to exclude Rhodesian scrap tobacco. Again many settlers were
ruined by the fall in prices, which was to be perpetuated by the
world depression in 1931. Partly because of this uncertainty the
agricultural front was broadening. Assisted by the Empire
Cotton Growing Corporation, the Government set up a cotton
breeding station at Gatooma in 1926, and cotton planting
spread slowly among both European and African farmers. The
increasing white population created a demand for dairy and
other local farm produce, and market gardening, even the
growing and milling of wheat, were making it possible to
supply the townships with home-grown food.

The railways employed the largest number of men, white and
black, of any single industry.[3] Their efficient working was still
the key to the colony's economic stability, and the high transport rates were still a principal cause of high price levels. The
Devonshire Agreement of 1923 had retained B.S.A. Company
ownership of the railways system, but the arrangement caused
dissatisfaction since it was felt that the Company was even now
growing rich at the colony's expense. In fact, the earnings of
the railway were still meagre; moreover a large proportion of
them came from outside the country, depending on traffic
through Cape Town, Beira and the Katanga. The cost of buying the whole system, amounting to some £3 millions, would be
prohibitive. The Railways Act of 1926, a compromise measure
not unlike that in Britain in 1921, set up a statutory commission,
consisting of representatives from Northern Rhodesia, Southern
Rhodesia and Bechuanaland, to regulate fares and control the

issue of dividends and the level of the reserves. None the less, high charges continued, and efforts to keep down costs brought the first serious industrial trouble in 1929.

None of these growing pains was grave enough to upset the even tenor of settler politics. When Sir Charles Coghlan died in 1926 the premiership passed without dispute to the former Minister for Mines, Howard Unwin Moffat, who had been born at Inyati when Lobengula was still king. Moffat was a straightforward man of high integrity, but lacked the forcefulness required of leadership in a crisis. The Government rode the 1928 election with ease, but by 1930 its popularity was declining, and the following year the storm of the trade depression broke upon it. The measures taken to protect the economy aroused public resentment. Protective legislation—the Maize Control Act which fixed the market price of grain, the purchase of mineral rights from the B.S.A. Company for £2 millions when many thought they should have been transferred without payment, even the Land Apportionment Act—brought vigorous criticism especially from the right wing. In 1933 Moffat resigned in favour of his deputy, George Mitchell, who at once prepared to dissolve the House of Assembly.

Meanwhile the Independents, who had formed the core of the parliamentary opposition, combined with dissatisfied Rhodesia Party members to make the Reform Party under the leadership of Dr Godfrey Huggins, an erstwhile follower of Coghlan. Huggins had settled in Southern Rhodesia before the war and had rapidly become one of its leading doctors, widely known and respected. A shrewd and vigorous politician, he had criticized Moffat's handling of the economic crisis, and had left the Rhodesia Party in 1931. In the general election that now took place in October 1933 he led his new group to a narrow victory over the Rhodesia and Labour Parties. A fresh railways bill, by its apparent generosity to the companies, aroused sharp criticism, in which a number of Reform Party men joined. Huggins without hesitation broke up the Reform Party, and taking his own adherents back into the Rhodesia Party camp, formed a new United Party.[4] The chief lesson drawn from this political turbulence was that men mattered more than measures in Rhodesian politics. The election following the inevitable dissolution in November 1934 gave the United Party an overwhelming victory with twenty-four seats in the legislature. A new stage now commenced in the colony's development. The country was led by an able and determined Prime Minister of the younger school, and the remnants of the old 'Company men' were, as in Northern Rhodesia, fast disappearing from the administrative scene. Recovery from the trade depression was beginning, particularly in the tobacco industry, which was greatly assisted by the formation of the Tobacco Marketing Board in 1936. Motor traffic was increasing. The old tracks no longer served the heavy burden, and many miles of thin tar strips were laid down. Money from the Beit Trust financed a bridge-building programme which included before 1939 the completion of the Beit Bridge at Messina over the Limpopo linking the Rhodesias by road with the Union, the stately Birchenough Bridge across the Sabi, and the Otto Beit Bridge at Chirundu on the Zambezi, bringing the new Northern Rhodesian capital within two days' drive of Salisbury. In 1931 the Rhodesian Aviation Company was formed, soon to become the Rhodesia and Nyasaland Airways. A self-confident spirit of independence was abroad, reflected on the one hand in the ending of the customs agreement with the Union in 1935, and on the other in talk of the formation of a 'larger economic unit' in Central Africa that would have its own rail links with the coast. Indeed it was Huggins' express aim to intensify white immigration, widen the sector of secondary industry, and wrest from the Imperial Government as much further independence as was possible short of dominion status.

The foundation of the United Party's power in the colony was the policy of the 'double pyramid' or of parallel development for the European and African races. The principle was that each race should develop in its own sphere. Apart from the absence of religious overtones, the 'double pyramid' differed from the 'apartheid' of the South African Nationalists in that ultimately the two pyramids should meet at the top; that is, at the level of national government. Such a time was generally supposed to be generations ahead. In the meantime the two societies should not be allowed to mingle, except in a master-servant relationship. 'The Europeans in the country', declared Huggins in 1938, 'can be likened to an island in a sea of black, with the artisan and the tradesman forming the shores and the professional class the highlands in the centre. Is the native to be allowed to erode the shores and gradually attack the highlands? To permit this would mean that the leaven of civilization would be removed from the country, and the black man would revert to a barbarism worse than before. . . . . While there is still time, the country should be divided into white and black areas. In the black areas, natives should be allowed to rise to any position they are capable of and should be protected from white competition. Every step of the industrial and social pyramid must be open to him, excepting only—and always— the very top. In the white areas the native should be welcomed, but on the understanding that he merely assists and does not compete with the white man.'[5]

This policy found expression in the twin pillars of legislation, the Land Apportionment Act, which aroused resentment among some white farmers but satisfied the ordinary European citizens of the growing townships, and the Industrial Conciliation Act, 1934, which was a concession to the fears of the European artisan. The Native Registration Act of 1936 and Native Passes Act of 1937 completed the edifice by providing the Government with controls to enforce the segregation of the races. This legislation was the response of the European minority to its first awareness of an African challenge; this had been aroused less by African development, still hardly observable, than by the insecurity of the depression during which many had been compelled to resort to unskilled work on the roads and other government construction jobs. The African could return to his village; not so the European settler, who now sought to guarantee his own security through elaborate safeguards not only for land and work, but also for social and political privileges which would preserve, even for ever, his political and economic predominance.

The Industrial Conciliation Act of 1934, modelled on South African legislation, provided for the regulation and registration of trade unions and set up an Industrial Conciliation Board for the settlement of disputes. African workers however were entirely deprived of the benefits of the Act. Not only was the 'native' not covered by the term 'employee', but it was explicitly stated that Africans could not be employed at wage rates other than those specified in an agreement under the

Act. These clauses were repeated in the 1945 amendment, and effectively prevented Africans from forming Trade Unions till 1959. More than that, Africans were excluded from competition in white areas of employment.

In doing so, this Act was the complement of the Land Apportionment Act of 1931. The latter was not altogether a product of the economic crisis—the partitioning of the land between the two races was being considered before the trade depression of 1930 developed. Native reserves had been created in 1915. Outside the reserves the 1898 constitution still applied, whereby 'a native may acquire land on the same conditions as a person who is not a native'. Few could avail themselves of this opportunity. By 1926 only 45,000 acres of alienable land had been acquired by Africans against 31,000,000 by Europeans. Official concern about this disparity, as well as a growing segregationist public opinion in the towns, accounted for the appointment of the Southern Rhodesia Lands Commission under Sir William Morris Carter in 1926. Its report revealed that the alienable land outside the reserves was rapidly passing to European ownership while the reserves could not hold the growing population for long. The future of 'the natives' in Southern Rhodesia was mainly agricultural and pastoral, and though growing numbers would move into urban areas they should not be allowed to take up permanent residence there. 'Until the native has advanced very much further on the paths of civilization, it is better that the points of contact in this respect (landholding) should be reduced'.[6]

The Land Apportionment Act of 1931 set out to achieve this by forbidding Africans to obtain permanent rights in European areas. The corollary was to secure enough African land to contain the growing population. The amount was a thorny problem of ethics as well as of economics. 'It is a misconception', declared Lord Buxton, defending the Rhodesian Government in the House of Lords, 'to regard the question of land in Southern Rhodesia as one of mathematical division per head of population. The best way to deal with it is to act sympathetically and generously towards the native population by considering what is the fullest amount of land they require now and in the future.'[7] This way of thinking was as old as white settlement, as was the argument that Europeans were most fitted to till large acreages which indeed they were. What Africans required 'now and in the future' was a question to which a variety of answers might be given, depending on the type of soil, the crop cultivated and the methods used, the local rainfall, the increase in population density and the rate of urbanization. The European administration was once again acting in its own cause, for the Africans could not be consulted.

A new class of land was created called the Native Purchase Area—usually just the 'Native Area'—which was outside the Native Reserve but none the less closed to European occupation. Here an African could buy land on individual tenure at a price he was more able to pay; it was hoped that a class of non-tribal peasant farmers carrying out improved agricultural methods would thereby be developed. On the other hand, as Africans were now excluded from the European area, the total amount of land available to them was greatly reduced. The four main areas were distributed as follows: Native Reserves, 21 million acres; Native Purchase Area, 7½ million; European Area, 49 million; Unassigned Area (which might be allocated to the Native or the European Area), 17¾ million. This situation was to continue for thirty years with minor alterations, of which the most notable were the amendments of 1941 and 1950 creating a Special Native Area, ultimately from Unassigned Land, to provide communal land for people resettled on being moved from their 'squatter' villages on European farms.

Land apportionment was not officially regarded as a permanent policy. It was defended on grounds of encouragement of white immigration, the scientific cultivation of the soil, and protection of Africans from competition in land. It is true that large areas were preserved from erosion; but the interests of one race were placed before those of the community as a whole. The division of land and people occurred just when healthy urban growth was becoming necessary and when the virtual interdependence of white and black labour could confidently be expected to increase.[8] Europeans, however, saw the Act as liberal compared with land distribution in the Union; while African criticism of the land settlement was not observed by the Bledisloe Commission in 1939, and did not in fact develop till after the war.

During negotiations with the Dominions office between 1934

and 1936, Huggins claimed that 'in view of the record of this colony in the matter of native administration, the necessity for some of the detailed safeguards which were thought desirable in 1923 no longer exists'.[9] The supervision of native policy together with some restraints in financial autonomy by the High Commissioner for South Africa were now removed, and henceforth the Government in Salisbury dealt directly with London.

At this stage we must turn to the progress of events beyond the Zambezi. There the new Crown Colony of Northern Rhodesia with its diminutive white population had commenced its career in an atmosphere of cheerful optimism. Till 1924 mining progress had been slow, capital harder to find than in the south. After that date the B.S.A. Company, having relinquished its political responsibilities, revised its concession policy, confining itself to powerful organizations able to comply with new minimum expenditure clauses. Prospecting now began in earnest. A vast aerial survey was carried out, leading to the discovery near the Katanga border of rich sulphide ores a hundred feet below the surface. Hitherto Rhodesian oxide ores had averaged scarcely a third of the copper content of Congo ores; sulphide ore, besides, was cheaper to work. These events coincided with a sharp rise in the demand from Europe and America, associated chiefly with the new motor car industry. Copper enterprises merged into two powerful groups in 1929.[10] The Rhodesia Anglo American Corporation, financed mainly in Britain and South Africa, controlled Nkana, Bwana Mkubwa and the as yet unworked deposits at Nchanga. The Rhodesia Selection Trust, with strong American backing, controlled Roan Antelope and Mufulira, where work was shortly to begin. World prices soared, forced up by a huge American combine; capital flowed into the Copperbelt, production expanded. The size of the African labour force leapt from 8,000 in 1927 to 23,000 in 1930. The colony's revenue balanced expenditure for the first time.

A classic pattern of over-production was followed by the inevitable slump in prices in November 1931. The collapse of the copper boom merged with the world trade depression to create an acutely difficult situation in all three Central African territories, but the Copperbelt especially suffered. Its African population fell from 32,000 to 9,300 in eighteen months; likewise its European from 3,600 to 1,200. Imports dwindled. Railway profits, from which governments derived considerable tax revenue, fell away. Northern Rhodesia especially was burdened with the cost of repatriating European destitutes, and found it necessary to reduce Civil Service salaries. Other employers did likewise, and many Africans found their by now accustomed source of income suddenly dried up. All three territories followed the home government in abandoning the gold standard, a move resulting in dislocation of already worsening trade with South Africa, who held to gold with grim determination.

Despite these setbacks Northern Rhodesia gained more than lost from the trade depression. Housing had not kept pace with population in the urban centres; African compounds were unsatisfactory and much European accommodation was makeshift and unhealthy. With the reduced population it was now possible to set these matters right and to free the townships from the malarial mosquito.[11] Of deeper significance were the wider and long-term consequences. On the world industrial stage, the Copperbelt withstood the shock better than foreign producers owing to its cheap labour and the recent exploitation of rich sulphide ores. Emerging from the depression as low-cost producers, the Northern Rhodesian mines found an assured market in the United Kingdom whose consumption, already above world average, accelerated in the later thirties when rearmament began.[12] The decade was therefore one of spectacular expansion. At the beginning of 1935, when Nyasaland was still struggling in the trough of the depression and Southern Rhodesia was making a gradual recovery, Northern Rhodesia's prospects were beginning to soar. Mineral output in that year was valued at over £4 millions. By the outbreak of war in 1939 it exceeded £10 millions. This remarkable turn of fortunes did not go unnoticed south of the Zambezi.

During this period the small white population, strung out along the line of rail and with small communities at Fort Jameson and Abercorn, grew to over 11,000 in 1930 and then, after a sharp drop in 1931, more slowly to 13,000 in 1939. In the absence of self-government, politics had a different character from those of Southern Rhodesia, perhaps a more genuine one.

Between Unofficials and the colonial administration, the twenty years saw co-operation as well as antagonism. Both settlers and officials had an abiding interest in the development of the resources of the territory, but there was growing friction in debates about the future position of the European settlers vis-à-vis the Africans on the one hand and the Government on the other.[13]

Sir Herbert Stanley, the first Governor, did what he could to encourage a close partnership between the two sides of the legislature. This was easier during the first four or five years when all, Government included, expected a progressive advance towards independence. The publication in 1930 of a memorandum by Lord Passfield, the Labour Secretary of State for Dominion Affairs, defining British native policy in East Africa, thus caused a profound shock to settler opinion.[14] The interests of Africans in the territories concerned, stated the memorandum, must be paramount, 'and if those interests and the interests of immigrant peoples should conflict, the former should prevail'. His Majesty's Government 'regard themselves as exercising a trust on behalf of the African population, and they are unable to delegate or share this trust, the object of which may be defined as the protection and advancement of native races'. Although there was a proviso that the interests of the other communities, European, Indian or Arab, must be severally safeguarded, and unofficial members of legislative councils were regarded as 'equally responsible with Government members for the advice which they may tender . . . upon native affairs', it was considered essential that Governors should have overriding powers 'in case they should find it necessary to differ from their councils'.

This was in fact no more than a reassertion by the new Labour Government of the Devonshire Declaration of 1923; what distinguished it was its circulation to Livingstone and Zomba, hitherto seen as falling within the white-dominated southern African orbit.[15] Leopold Moore, in characteristically warm terms, expressed the opinion of this policy held by the average settler at the time: 'The Imperial Government says . . . the native race is paramount, it is supreme. If I were rude, I should say to that, bosh! . . . I intend to strive for my own survival and that of my race. The land should be occupied by those who can make the best use of it. I say, let the native take his chance with the whites.'[16] Sir Herbert Stanley tried long and patiently to explain to a deputation of unofficials that no real change in policy need be expected. He finally remarked: 'The objection by Mr Moore that people at Home have no idea what the native is like is really too futile for words. Great Britain was managing natives before any of us was born. There are many people at Home who know a very great deal more about the natives in this country than some Europeans whom I have met in this country.'[17]

The consequence of the memorandum, which held out little hope of self-government in the foreseeable future, but rather promised a Colonial Office administration with policies more irksome than hitherto, was a reversal of white settler opinion away from any Northern Rhodesia separatism and towards amalgamation with the south, so unpopular six years earlier. This inclination was fortified by the economic stringency of the trade depression, which showed clearly that Northern Rhodesia was at that stage less able to withstand such blows than Southern Rhodesia, whose gold on the new free market bolstered up the colony's economy. The Government's proposal to move the capital to Lusaka, against the wishes of the commercial interest at Livingstone, also aroused resentment. In November 1933 the unofficial members introduced a motion into the Legislative Council favouring amalgamation with Southern Rhodesia, and this aim remained an article of policy of the Northern Rhodesia Unofficials from that time forward.

The formation of a clearly defined land policy for Northern Rhodesia was delayed until after the Colonial Office assumed control in 1924. Under the Devonshire Agreement, the Crown recognized all alienations of land to Europeans made by the Company during its rule, though reserving the right to set apart a Native Reserve in the North Charterland Concession Company's area. This reserve was in fact demarcated in 1925. By 1 April, alienations totalled 11¾ million acres, including 2¼ million acres of B.S.A. Company estates at Abercorn, and six million acres along the line of rail south of Broken Hill. In July 1926 a Commission was appointed to examine what land should be set apart for native reserves, and in the following year these reserves were established by Order in Council. The object was to concentrate the African population for economic

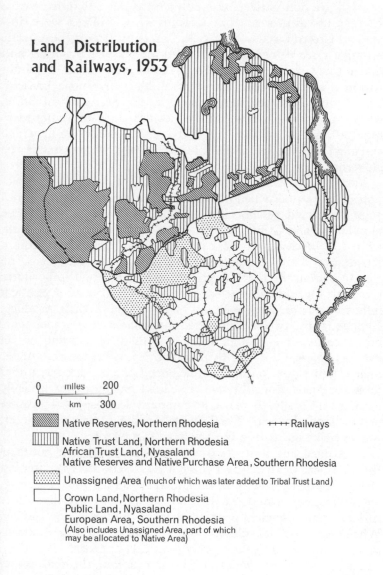

Land Distribution
and Railways, 1953

0 miles 200	
0 km 300	

▨ Native Reserves, Northern Rhodesia ++++ Railways

▥ Native Trust Land, Northern Rhodesia
African Trust Land, Nyasaland
Native Reserves and Native Purchase Area, Southern Rhodesia

⠿ Unassigned Area (much of which was later added to Tribal Trust Land)

☐ Crown Land, Northern Rhodesia
Public Land, Nyasaland
European Area, Southern Rhodesia
(Also includes Unassigned Area, part of which
may be allocated to Native Area)

and administrative purposes. No portion of a reserve could be granted to a non-native, except on a lease of less than five years. In 1929 it was decreed that Africans whose villages were situated on Crown Land or on B.S.A. Company estates (i.e. outside a native reserve) could be removed after a year's notice, and that no new native village should be erected on any land not within a native reserve, except with the Governor's consent. The Native Reserves were vested in the Secretary of State, whose approval for such grants or for any other alterations was required. Rights in Crown Lands, on the other hand, which extended over the remainder of the territory, were vested in the Governor on behalf of the Crown.

Northern Rhodesia thus appeared to be moving in the direction of its southern neighbour, which also at this time (until 1930) possessed reserves for the exclusive use of the native population, and Crown Lands available for alienation to both white or black on a basis of individual tenure. Southern Rhodesia's Land Apportionment Act, however, had no counterpart in the north. Agriculture was of small importance economically, though settlers engaged in it exerted a political influence out of all proportion to the value of their produce. In 1930, of the twelve million acres alienated only 70,000 were under cultivation, though more was used for grazing on an extensive basis. Of the cultivated land, 43,000 acres were under maize, and 2,300, mostly in the Fort Jameson district, under tobacco. Apart from the fact that land partition was unlikely in a Crown Colony, there was no comparable prospect of pressure on the land. Instead, Northern Rhodesia, twelve years later, was to strike out with a land policy of its own.[18]

In African administration also, policies north and south of the Zambezi drifted apart after 1924. Expressed in simplest terms, Southern Rhodesia remained a 'direct rule' territory, while Northern Rhodesia, like Nyasaland and Britain's other African dependencies, proceeded to an 'indirect rule' policy. When examined more closely, however, these methods of administration did not differ so widely as at first appears.

During the early years of the occupation, the features of native administration were common to most parts of Africa; direct rule through European officers was inevitable until the slave trade, forced tribute labour and certain abhorrent customs had faded from African memory. But to continue indefinitely along these lines might bring its own dangers. Sir Percy Girouard, Governor of Kenya, wrote in 1910: 'There are not lacking those who favour direct British rule; but if we allow the tribal authority to be ignored or broken, it will mean that we . . . shall be obliged to deal with a rabble. . . . There could only be one end, and that would be eventual conflict with such a rabble.'[19] So it appeared before the First World War when African society was still regarded as static, not capable of evolving into new forms. Already the authority of chiefs was fading; the reasons for their existence—service of the tribe in matters of war, land fertility and tribal religion—were being undermined by the enforcement of law and order, agricultural techniques and Christian missions. To meet this situation, Lord Lugard, proconsul in Nigeria, evolved the administrative method of indirect rule. Described in his book *The Dual Mandate* in 1922, it became a blueprint for British Colonial policy. 'Here then in my view lies our present task in Africa. It becomes impossible to maintain the old order; the urgent need is for adaptation to the new—to build up tribal authority with a recognized legal standing, which may oust social chaos. . . . The objective is to group together small tribes, or sections of a tribe, so as to form a single administrative unit, whose chiefs . . . may be constituted a "Native Authority". . . . The District Commissioner's task is to strengthen the authority of the chiefs, and encourage them to show initiative. . . . In brief, tribal cohesion and the education of tribal heads in the duties of rulers are the watchwords of the policy in regard to these backward races.'[20]

Inaugurated in Nigeria, this policy passed to East Africa in 1925 and was introduced to Northern Rhodesia by Sir James Maxwell, Governor in 1929. The Passfield Memorandum again declared the objective: 'The process now to be followed . . . is the development of native social and political institutions on native lines wherever such institutions exist, even in germ, in a form worthy of presentation. The African native thus . . . may gradually develop a political consciousness and a desire to take an increasing share, first in his tribal affairs . . . and ultimately also in the governance of the territory in which he lives.' This was very like the African half of the 'double pyramid' soon planned for Southern Rhodesia; the difference lay in the means of constructing the pyramid, and in the doctrine of paramountcy that lay beneath.

Northern Rhodesia's Native Authorities Ordinance and Native Courts Ordinance of 1929 brought the Indirect Rule policy down to the Zambezi. According to the first a chief designated as a Native Authority 'as far as possible according to tribal law and custom' was empowered to issue rules and orders for his tribe, and by the second he could enforce them, together with certain territorial laws, in the Native Court. The rudimentary character of the system was shown by the fact that the head of the Authority and the head of the Court were the same person, and would continue so until some 'separation of the powers' should take place.[21] The most radical feature was the power of the Native Court to deal with criminal cases and impose penalties, a right which had been broadly denied to chiefs from the outset of European rule. In 1936 the Native Authority was enlarged to include the appointment of councillors in some cases, and the Native Treasuries Ordinance gave Native Authorities power to collect the native tax and spend money from this and later other sources such as the Native Trust Lands Fund.

Indirect Rule had a difficult course ahead. Some of the problems were plain enough—chiefs were in most cases uneducated and often unsuitable for the exercise of this kind of responsibility and the appointment of councillors called for wide variety of practice. More serious was the growing evidence that the tribe was not capable of resuscitation as a modern institution. Northern Rhodesian administrators were trying to convert tribal government into rural local government, but the main support of the scheme, the hereditary chief, was a decaying power. Most serious of all, the policy failed to recognize the reality of a growing industrial African society along the line of rail, where the most serious problems of a changing society were to appear.

The phenomenon was soon to be forced on public notice, and indeed the companies were already faced with it. Ten tribal elders had been appointed in the Mufulira Mine Compound in 1931, but had been paid scant attention by the mineworkers. The 1935 disturbances, in which six Africans were killed and twenty-two wounded, took the authorities by surprise, particularly as the overt cause was an unheralded tax increase, though industrial grievances lay beneath. The district administration was not designed to cope with violence. The idea of bringing the Native Authority system into the town, though suggested, was quickly dropped. Various experiments with tribal assessors led to the formation of urban Native Courts in 1938–9, at last an official recognition that the town population was becoming stabilized. During the war urban Advisory Councils, consisting of Africans appointed by the District Commissioner, were set up in most Copperbelt towns. Meanwhile, Native Welfare Societies and Associations were springing up spontaneously all down the line of rail. After the war the Advisory Councils were reconstituted on an electoral basis which included representation of the welfare societies. The tribal elder system, a link with tribe, chief and village, had meanwhile fallen into abeyance. The urban councils were clearly more closely in contact with contemporary African opinion than the Native Authorities in the reserves. They were still only advisory however, and were not linked yet, except through the District Commissioner, with the township and municipal local government which continued in European hands.[22]

If Northern Rhodesia's administrative connections were with Britain's East and West African dependencies, those of Southern Rhodesia were with the Cape. To begin with the colony's native policy stemmed from Rhodes' Glen Gray Act of 1894 providing for taxation to compel Africans to work and to pay for their own development, 'industrial' education and control of the liquor traffic. The authority of the chiefs had been much more seriously interrupted by military conquest than in the north and indeed the Shona chiefs had never had the same authority in their communities as the Ndebele *zinduna*. Authority placed in the hands of Native Commissioners, themselves subordinate to Civil Magistrates, tended therefore to grow rather than, as in the north, to be transferred. In a sense this helped the chief to survive since his traditional and inherent powers, though greatly shorn, were not interfered with by the compulsory performance of modern responsibilities. It also, perhaps, created conditions in which a more genuine local government could emerge.[23] It was characteristic therefore that the Native Councils Act of 1937 was permissive in nature, Councils being set up only when the local people wished it. In 1943 when they were empowered to raise and spend local taxation (apart from the native tax) and encouraged to do so by the promise of a £ for £ grant from the Government, this power again was exercised voluntarily. The system was described by Huggins as a first step towards the African pyramid. 'It is like the old days in Athens when everybody met in the market square and fixed things up. We have only the beginning. We can develop from that to the elective councils, and when that principle has been mastered the councils themselves may elect delegates to the Central Parliament; and when they have done that these people can elect people to represent them in the Parliament of the country. It is a long way off, but we must have a plan. Why be in such a hurry?'[24] Ten and twenty years later, when the pace of the ox was rumbling into a stampede, this rhetorical question would not have been asked with such assurance. In the last months of the thirties, before war and social revolution shattered the illusions of an easy-going world, there seemed to be plenty of time.

A sister piece of legislation, the Native Courts Act, 1937, permitted the establishment of courts, consisting in each case of a chief or headman and two councillors, which could adjudicate in disputes between Africans that were capable of being decided according to native law and custom. Their powers were more limited than those of Native Courts in Northern Rhodesia and Nyasaland; in particular they had no jurisdiction in criminal cases and were subject to the supervision of the Native Commissioner, who could revise their decisions as he thought fit. None the less, the court system attracted support immediately. By August 1938, forty-five Native Courts had been established. Councils appeared more slowly, subject to the discouragement of additional taxation that usually followed; but in ten years there were over fifty in the Colony's reserves.

Northern Rhodesia's progress towards Urban Courts and Advisory Councils did not find its counterpart in the colony, whose urban populations continued to fluctuate and remained more directly under the control of the European administration. But if Northern Rhodesia showed more realism in this, the

Southern Rhodesian system permitted more flexibility. This was to become plain in the late fifties when the Indirect Rule system was faced with the irrevocable decline in the status of chiefs who had become officials of an unpopular government.

This digression on native administration serves to show differences of approach to the problem in the two Rhodesias. One point should not be overlooked. The problem in each case was different. In the south conquest, in the north, not. In the south land segregation and population congestion, but otherwise in the north. Differences of policy were not always a matter of choice but had their origins in the unalterability of past events.

When Northern Africans told commissioners of their dislike of the colony's native policy, it was not to direct rule that they were referring; indeed living mostly in the towns they had little experience of it. The main objection was to the pass system under the Native Registration Act of 1936 and the Native Passes Act of 1937. The combined effect of this legislation, which was reminiscent of the Union and had no comparable counterpart in the north, was that no African over the apparent age of fourteen could move outside his reserve without a visiting pass, a permit to seek employment in a town, or a current certificate of service. Migrants from outside the territory must obtain at the frontier a permit to seek work, which was valid for thirty days. This legislation and its consequences was regarded by Nyasalanders and Northern Rhodesians as a grievous restriction on their liberty. Beyond a slight modification after the war it remained unchanged till 1957.

The political history of Southern Rhodesia for the remainder of the thirties and during the war was marked by the steady consolidation of Huggins' authority.[24] The European electorate was on the whole well satisfied with the progress of native policy which, being out of sight, was also out of mind; it was also content with economic recovery and moreover with the prospect, as Northern Rhodesia's prosperity grew, of benefiting from the territory's mineral wealth and labour supply through closer association. Thus was Huggins' majority reinforced in the election of 1939; his authority continued undiminished till the end of the war. Efforts made by the Rhodesia Party wing led by Moffat and W. M. Leggate to regain control of the Government were of no avail, and in 1939 the remnants of the Rhodesia Party disappeared. Such real opposition as there was came from the Labour Party led by Jack Keller of the Railway Workers' Union. Profiting from the unemployment period, this group had won four seats in 1933 and had increased these to seven by 1939. But any hope of the Labour Party gaining a Parliamentary majority was illusory. Apart from the fact that its influence was bound to grow less with economic recovery, the real 'labour' of the colony was African. The policy of the party, apart from advocating a state social security system, was the prevention of African infiltration into areas of white employment. Co-operation with Africans, despite attempts, which split the party, to bring it about during the war, was politically impossible; and the European artisan class was insufficient numerically to overbalance the rest of the white electorate. The only other threat to Huggins' majority arose from the appearance during the war of a Liberal Party led by the former Minister of Finance, J. H. Smit. With a rather confused policy of 'Progress, Liberty and Planning', and attracting the Afrikaner vote in opposition to Huggins, the party gained twelve seats in the 1946 election, compelling the United Party to rely for the time being on Labour Party support. Rapid immigration, however, was swelling United Party ranks. Reaping advantage from fears of Afrikaner Nationalism after Malan's victory in the Union in 1948, Huggins dissolved Parliament and in the subsequent election, on a policy of loyalty to the Crown, closer association with the North, private enterprise, racial harmony and the retention of English as the sole official language, returned to power with an unshakeable majority. The United Party, though its name was to change, was not thenceforth to be challenged again until 1958.

The events of these years showed that a strong middle party, supported broadly by commerce, agriculture and the press, offering policies of security and opportunity to private business and of no nonsense towards the 'native', could have little to fear while the electorate remained predominantly British; and that the only serious threat that was likely to arise would come from the right.[25]

In Northern Rhodesia the political contest was between the

colonial government and the Unofficials whose demands became harder to resist as the territory became more solvent. Apart from the question of representation in legislature and executive, native policy was the main issue. It was taking on a new aspect with the growth of the urban African population, especially on the Copperbelt, which both multiplied opportunities for racial friction and aroused white fears of black labour competition. There was more talk of segregation. The miners' strike of 1935 presented a new spectre of co-ordinated African action that emphasized the smallness and isolation of the European community, and spurred on the amalgamationist movement. That year however the election of Colonel Stewart Gore-Browne, a settler with an estate in the heart of Bemba country, provided the Council with a member of independent mind, long experience in the country, and a real understanding of the rural African. He was the first leading settler in Northern Rhodesia firmly to reject racial segregation, and to look forward to an ultimate solution in co-operation and common citizenship.[26]

Gore-Browne stood equally firmly for an increase in the influence of Unofficials in the Government. In 1936, under his leadership, the Unofficials threatened to resign collectively 'as a protest against the waste of time and money involved in playing at Parliament' without the reality of power. The protest had its effect. The following year, Unofficials were represented on the newly formed Finance Committee. In 1938 the Official and Unofficial sides of the Council were equalized by reducing the nominated Official members from four to three, and by adding a nominated Unofficial member to represent African interests. Gore-Browne was appointed to the latter post, and during the next three years played a leading part in the establishment of Urban Courts and African Advisory Councils on the Copperbelt. Finally, in 1939, three Unofficials were admitted to membership of the Executive Council.

This swift political advance of the Unofficials was associated on the one hand with the growing demand for amalgamation, which now brought the Bledisloe Commission to Rhodesia, and on the other with the economic revival, which swelled the power of the white trade unions, notably on the Copperbelt. Here the European Mineworkers' Union had been formed in

1936 after the scare caused by the African riots the previous year. Significant of growing union influence was the advent to politics of Roy Welensky, a young railway driver and the outspoken leader of the Railwaymen's Union, who took Gore-Browne's place as Member for the Northern Electoral Area in 1938. The Northern Rhodesia Labour Party was formed in 1941, bringing a new voice to discussions in the Council, hitherto dominated by farming and commercial interests. During the war the influence of both unions and Unofficials continued to increase. While the former took the opportunity of extracting closed shop agreements from the mining companies, the Unofficials found their authority so enhanced that there began to be talk of abandoning the campaign for amalgamation. A measure of self-government might yet be attained without subordination to Salisbury.

Equally if not more important in the long run was a new awareness of African progress in many spheres and its fundamental importance in the future of the territory. Opportunities were opening up for African leadership in social welfare, local government and political organization, though more slowly in business and the professions. The war, here as elsewhere, proved to be the watershed over which the African people passed from being a passive to being an active factor in the territory's political and economic development. The question of African advancement had been mooted by the Forster Commission after the 1940 strike, a portent of great changes in the fifties. In 1943 the system of Urban Advisory Councils was extended by the establishment of Provincial Councils not only in the Western Province but elsewhere in the territory, where they were based on the Native Authorities. From these Councils members were selected to form the territorial African Representative Council in 1946. This attempt to combine the framework of rural local government with a pyramid of indirect African representation was to run into increasing difficulties in the years ahead.

Meanwhile, concern was expressed about the overcrowding in some of the reserves due to the increase of population and the consequent threat of soil erosion. Since before the war this problem had faced the Imperial Government in many colonial territories, and in an endeavour to meet it the Colonial

Development and Welfare Acts, passed in 1940 and 1945, provided funds that formed the basis for Five- and Ten-Year Development Plans for African social and economic progress. African development in Northern Rhodesia's remote rural areas would most likely come with a wider dispersal of European enterprise, but the political climate was hostile to any sign of infringing African security in land. The territorial government was in fact about to limit more closely the area available for white settlement. After five years of study the Northern Rhodesia (Native Trust Land) Order in Council of 1947 limited Crown Land to 16,610 square miles. The existing native reserves of 100,200 square miles were confirmed, and the remaining area of 170,810 square miles was designated as Native Trust Land. Here land could be leased for ninety-nine years only to natives or non-natives after consultation with Native Authorities and provided that the benefit of the 'aboriginal inhabitants' would result. Rentals from such leases would be paid into a Native Trust Land Fund, from which grants would be paid to Native Authorities.

This legislation restricted Crown Land, which alone could be alienated more or less freehold at prices which for some time only Europeans would be able to pay, to six per cent. of the territory. It thus marked a contrast with policy in Southern Rhodesia, and set Northern Rhodesia on a course away from segregation in land. None the less, it did little to allay the fears of Africans, who remained suspicious of the Government's land and agricultural policy.

The new dynamic of African development was recognized by the Unofficials after the war, but contrasting opinions emerged concerning how best to meet it. Whereas Welensky and the Labour Party declared that African progress could take place more satisfactorily through amalgamation with Southern Rhodesia, Gore-Browne pressed for responsible government separately in the north. His position as leader of the Unofficials was destroyed by a speech in April 1946 warning of deteriorating race relations, and expressing the need for African representation in government and the formation of African trade unions. His place as chairman was taken by Welensky, but his great influence in government circles remained. In 1948, he and Welensky again joined forces, now calling for more Unofficial influence in the executive. The subsequent negotiations with the Colonial Office resulted in a measure of responsible government. The Executive Council was to consist of four Unofficials as opposed to three Officials, with an understanding that the Governor would submit to a unanimous expression of Unofficial opinion. The number of elected Unofficials in Legislative Council was increased to ten. On the other hand two Africans, selected from the territorial Representative Council, were now to sit in the Legislative Council, together with three Europeans nominated for African interests.

African leaders, who regarded responsible government as a step towards amalgamation, showed little enthusiasm for this settlement, and their confidence in Gore-Browne evaporated. Moreover they grew increasingly suspicious of the Government's programme for the reform of African agriculture which accompanied the Native Trust Land Order in Council and the Ten Year Development Plan. The post-war wave of immigration was bringing Europeans into the territory at the rate of three or four thousand a year, and the race problem along the line of rail was becoming more acute. In 1948 the Northern Rhodesia African Congress was formed by coalescing a number of Native Welfare Societies in the African townships under the leadership of Godwin Lewanika, a moderate of Lozi royal descent. This organization, which was taken over in 1951 by Harry Nkumbula, a former schoolmaster, and renamed the African National Congress, was increasingly to become the focal point of militant African opinion in place of the Representative Council. It was to be ten years, however, before Government was compelled to deal directly with the Congress leaders.

The years after 1948, in the political field, were chiefly taken up with the movement for closer association in Central Africa, the first Federation Conference being convened at the Victoria Falls in 1949. Welensky's stature among Europeans in the territory steadily increased, particularly after his personal triumph in the negotiations with the Chartered Company leading to agreement in 1949 for the ultimate transfer to the Northern Rhodesia Government of the Company's mineral royalties. His abandonment of amalgamation in face of the modified objective of federation was a statesmanlike recognition of realities that perhaps more than any other single political action made closer association possible. But it only served to intensify mounting African fears regarding their political future, and their dread of closer association with the south.

There, African political influence was negligible. Few Africans were qualified to vote, and fewer still—less than 400—were registered on an electoral roll which totalled 54,000. There was no concentration of Africans working within a single industry such as existed on the Copperbelt, where the nucleus of social or political forces might appear. In the towns, Africans were of diverse origin, many coming from Northern Rhodesia and Nyasaland. The Bantu Congress of Southern Rhodesia, despite its grand name, had only had 150 members in 1938, chiefly educated men such as ministers and teachers, clerks and peasant farmers. Its tone was moderate, and while objecting to the pass laws and the Maize Control Act, its representatives had informed the Bledisloe Commission that there was no complaint with the Land Apportionment Act. There might perhaps have been an attempt by Europeans to make contact with this incipient middle class movement, but it was not made. By the end of the war the atmosphere was changing. The Bantu Congress had altered its name to the African National Congress which, though hardly more formidable, was beginning to give more distinct expression to the African sense of frustration. The unofficial railway strike of 1945 evoked an unaccustomed co-operation among urban Africans. Resentment grew against low wages and poor living conditions as well as against unpopular legislation such as the Urban Areas Act of 1946. The Congress movement, however, did not yet develop into a powerful force. It was not until 1957 that a militant Congress comparable with those north of the Zambezi became a factor to be reckoned with in Southern Rhodesian politics.

None the less, the railway strike of 1945 and industrial unrest in Bulawayo in 1948 severely jolted the complacency of Europeans in the colony. Huggins was already aware that land segregation and all that it implied would soon become administratively unworkable; the Union's Group Areas Act of 1950 pointed, plain as writing on the wall, the dangers of that road. The United Party and European public opinion as a whole could not be expected to accept such a revelation at this stage, but Huggins' legislation in 1951 showed the trend of his thinking. The Native Urban Areas Act, requiring the registration of African employees and laying down regulations concerning their accommodation and living standards, was an open recognition of the permanence of the African urban population. More striking still, the Native Land Husbandry Act planned to accelerate, before it was too late, the revolution in African agriculture that should have come a generation before. While appearing to make the adjustments necessary if the segregation policy were to survive, Huggins had taken important steps towards stabilization, which must eventually bring segregation to an end.

A leading part in steering this Bill through the Assembly was played by R. S. Garfield Todd. A missionary for sixteen years, he had taken up politics in 1946, and had attracted the attention of Huggins who invited him to join the United Party. He entered Parliament in 1948. His political position was close to that of the Prime Minister, but he lacked tactical experience and skill. Warning that race relations would grow steadily worse without a radical change in land and native policy, he displayed an outspokenness on behalf of liberal policies that, save in education, did not materialize during his period of office, and that finally lost him the support of the party. At this time his relatively advanced opinions were less noticeable beside Huggins' powerful authority. They indeed gave a liberal appearance to the United Party that served its own purpose.

The party as a whole was much further to the right. Its 1950 Congress seriously discussed a proposal to remove Africans from the common voters' roll. They were dissuaded by Huggins, who realized that such a step could founder plans for federation with the Protectorates, and explained that the colony could not afford to flout world opinion in such a way. The explanation, if Huggins believed it himself, did not satisfy the colony's right wing, increasingly aware that events were driving them in a direction they disliked. An intensive campaign developed for the preservation of a White Rhodesia, and against the movement, now well under way, for closer association with the 'black north'. Southern Rhodesian Africans, on the other hand, had nothing to lose from such an association, and on the subject of federation had little to say.

The Nyasaland Protectorate

Sir Harry Johnston had always hoped that the Shire highlands would provide the environment for one of the European 'nuclei of civilization' in East Africa. Though Nyasaland and Northern Rhodesia fell within the Africa north of the Zambezi that he regarded as having an essentially African rather than European future, his encouragement of white settlement in the highlands proved the basis of a government policy that continued into this century. Not until the 1930s did Nyasaland's future as an African country with an all-African government begin to emerge clearly in the public mind.

The story might indeed have been different but for the slow progress of railway construction that dominated the first three decades of the century. The development of the plantations, the growth of a European community, the trend of constitutional development, all depended on this vital factor. Had the country been 'opened up' to European influence before the First World War, as railway development made possible in Southern Rhodesia and to a lesser extent Northern Rhodesia and Kenya, events would have followed another course. The continuous rail link with Beira was not completed till 1935. At that time, economic advance was still delayed. The European population was only 1,781, of whom over half belonged to the administrative and missionary sections, whose influence therefore predominated. True it was that African progress had been equally slow, that native education, which had made a good start compared with Southern Rhodesia, was soon lagging behind, and that opportunities for local employment remained small. But when development came more quickly after 1935, the Imperial Government's colonial policy had hardened along definite lines. The key position held by Europeans in the economic enterprise of white-settled Africa has until recently always been their ace card, but it must be played at the right time; that is, before the Imperial Government's cumbersome machine has moved, not after. From Rhodes onwards, Rhodesian leaders, sustaining the founder's financial impetus through good times and bad, managed to keep the initiative even to the present day. From the beginning, the few European settlers in Nyasaland lacked the means for this initiative. Historically the reasons for this were diverse, but the immediate one was the delay in completing the railway.

The construction of the line from Chindio on the Zambezi to Blantyre in the highlands between 1906 and 1916 had by-passed much of the unreliable river route, and had brought the highland estates within reach of the lower Zambezi by rail, though all supplies and passengers still depended on the slow and inconvenient river steamers making their way up river from Chindio. Further construction had to await necessary capital, hard to obtain because no rich mineral deposits had been found in the Protectorate, and because of the expense involved in bridging the Zambezi, over two miles wide at Sena. The small revenue, limited by restricted economic development, was depleted by annual payments towards the public debt incurred by building the Shire railway and later (1922) that from Beira to Muraca on the Zambezi opposite Chindio. The Government had guaranteed the payment of interest on the debenture stock, and as the line did not pay its way until after the great bridge was erected in 1935 and the railway extended north from Blantyre the following year, this was an added burden upon public funds. In the 1920s Nyasaland was already being called the 'Cinderella of Central Africa'.[1]

The struggle to balance expenditure during the first generation of settlement accounted for the favourable bias shown by the colonial administration towards planters in the working of the 'tangata system'.[2] Owing to the return of Africans to the Shire highlands after the pacification of the nineties, many holders of estates under Certificates of Claim found Africans living on their land. In order to overcome the labour shortage, money rent was not accepted and the 'squatters' were compelled to work for one month, usually in the rainy season. Combined with the month's work necessary to earn for the hut tax, this made it hard for Africans to manage their own gardens. The consequent trouble helped to account for the Chilembwe rising. In 1917 the Government sought to remove the worst abuses of the system by the Native Rents (Private Estates) Ordinance that forbade exaction of service in lieu of rent, and exempted altogether Africans who had lived on the estate for longer than twenty years. This was difficult to establish and by various means estate owners managed to evade the working of the regulation for many years.

A considerable amount of land had been acquired with freehold rights in the grand old pioneering days, and Johnston's Certificates of Claim had been upheld in the constitution of 1902. Thereafter, however, the Administration was careful to grant no more freehold rights in land, but only to lease it on terms of not more than ninety-nine years. By the Crown Lands Ordinance of 1912 leases were to be generally for twenty-one years only, though long leases could be obtained when such slow-growing crops as tea, coffee and rubber were to be planted. When an estate was opened to lease it was held up for auction, and applicants wishing to bid must first be approved by the Government. There was a good deal of grumbling about the short leases, and in 1931 a new Crown Lands Ordinance revised the first by making the ninety-nine-year lease general, rents to be revised at least every thirty-three years. A land improvement clause was now included, which demanded a minimum of development, including cultivation and afforestation, to be carried out by the occupant.

Although in 1920 a total of nearly 3¾ million acres were held by European planters freehold, less than half a million acres were sold or leased during the next ten years. In part this was the consequence of the strict control exercised under the Crown Lands Ordinances, but two other factors go further to explain this disparity between the large tracts bought outright in the early years and the relatively small area leased later. In the first place, as in Southern Rhodesia, syndicates and land companies had acquired large blocks for resale. In 1919, for example, the British Central Africa Company started a private settlement scheme for ex-officers on sections of its large estates. More significant, secondly, the policy of reserving the bulk of the Protectorate's land for the African population was crystallizing during the late twenties and early thirties, and by 1935 practically all the Crown Land intended to be made available for alienation had been taken up.

European immigration had in any case always been slow. At the end of the war the total white population including officials was 724. Three years later, with the sharp rise induced by post-war immigration it reached 1,486 but at this point tobacco prices fell. Since coffee had slumped in 1904, tobacco had become the main hope for post-war settlers. But it was a notoriously unsteady crop. Prospective planters were discouraged by a warning that in case of failure the chances of obtaining employment in the Protectorate were slight. Many of the older settlers sold their estates at this time, and by 1924 the European population was less than in 1920. The Rhodesians by contrast did not meet with a similar reverse at this time.

The operation of the railway from Beira to Muraca since 1922, the recovery of prices with Imperial preference at one and fourpence a lb, and the growth of internal communications brought a revival in 1925. In that year the north road was being cut towards Kasungu, boma offices and civil service accommodation were being built or enlarged, bridges were being improved and existing roads drained and realigned. Cash cropping among Africans in the south increased and ploughs were now being sold in the native stores. This made labour again hard to find, and legislation limited the amount of cash cropping which African tenants on a European estate could carry out on their own; the European side of the economy, being the principal source of revenue, was still the first consideration of Government. Thirty-five thousand acres of land were leased out between 1926 and 1929.[3]

This gradual progress was expected to accelerate with the completion of the Zambezi bridge, whose construction had been approved by the Colonial Office in 1929, and upon which all hopes were now concentrated. The revenue had almost doubled since the end of the war, to nearly £400,000; though the public debt, now over £900,000, was a constant drain on resources, and annual grants-in-aid from Britain were still needed to balance the budget. The trade depression of 1930–32 came as a sad blow to these hopes. A grant from the Colonial Development Fund helped the Protectorate over a difficult period, but the setback had profound effects. Leases of land dwindled and the European population, which formed a graph of the country's potential prosperity, fell to 1,380 in 1933. There was a lot of distress among the small white community, and immigrants were forbidden to enter the Protectorate in search of employment, a restriction that was not lifted till 1937.

It was in these hard times, before recovery had shown signs of beginning, that work at last commenced on the two and three-quarter mile long bridge, and also on the northward extension of the line from Blantyre to the Lake. The latter project might have been carried out earlier, but with the bottle-neck at the Zambezi ferry already congested, it would have been ill-advised to increase the rail traffic north of the river. Because of the liability of the marshy country round Fort Johnston to flood, and because of the need to serve the plantations in the west around Dedza, Lilongwe and Fort Jameson, the line took a westerly course, the railhead being ultimately established at Salima a few miles inland from Domira Bay.[4]

The opening of a through railway on 1 March 1935 from Beira to Lake Nyasa, with regular passenger and freight services, coincided with the Protectorate's recovery from the trade depression, of which there were clear signs in 1936–37, to create conditions for a revival in fortune. By 1939 the white population exceeded two thousand and the revenue stood at over £1 million. An important source of this increased prosperity was the development of tea estates. Tea planting had started as an experiment in 1903, when Acting Commissioner Pearce reported lugubriously that the product, when brewed, 'can scarcely be said to reach the usual standard of ordinary tea, though it possesses a characteristic and pleasant taste of its own'.[5] Since the war, skill had improved in the growing and curing of tea and large estates were spread across the southward slopes of the Mlanje massif. During the thirties, tea replaced tobacco as the dominant crop in the country's economy.

By this time, however, any dreams that may have existed of Nyasaland as a 'white' colony, with the Shire highlands playing the part of the White Highlands in Kenya, had long faded. The late twenties had witnessed a turning point in African policies on the part of the Imperial Government as well as of locally self-governing administrations. Lugard's writings had had their effect. The Hilton Young Commission on East Africa had taken stock, and had forced the necessity for a policy on a world slowly awakening to the dynamism of Africa. The Native Reserves Ordinance in Northern Rhodesia, the Morris Carter Commission, to be followed by the Land Apportionment Act in Southern Rhodesia, the introduction of indirect rule in the northern territory, and the Passfield memorandum in 1930 were all signs that, one way or another, the Imperial and colonial governments were turning away from a policy of drift.

Apart from the perennial friction over the working of the 'tangata' system relating to African 'squatters' on European estates, land distribution had not presented a serious problem in Nyasaland. Owing to the African population density, the question of setting aside native reserves did not attract the early attention that it had done in the Rhodesias. It was confidently stated as late as 1930 that Africans felt little apprehension about their future security on their lands. 'For some years it has been the invariable practice of Government before alienating land to non-natives first to secure the acquiescence of the chiefs and headmen in the area, and this has done much to allay the apprehension of natives in regard to their land.' The Provincial Commissioner in Central Angoniland (a tobacco planting area) expressed the opinion that 'European settlement as such is not objected to by the natives'. . . .[6]

In 1936, after long deliberation and the consideration of several drafts, legislation was passed on this subject. The Nyasaland Protectorate (Native Trust Lands) Order in Council provided that there should be no further alienations of land freehold. All land not already alienated was to be Native Trust Land, vested in the Secretary of State and administered by the Governor for the direct or indirect benefit of the natives of the Protectorate. Native Trust Land could be 'subject to rights of occupancy' (leased), but the Native Authority of the area was first to be consulted, and the proceeds of the lease were to be paid into Native Authority funds. There were to be no native reserves; relative to the Rhodesias the Protectorate was densely populated, and the removal of African communities to restricted areas was impracticable; while to have all Nyasaland outside Crown Land areas closed entirely to European enterprise would hamstring economic development. In 1936 ten per cent. of the Protectorate was Crown Land, mainly held under Certificates of Claim; of this area, one third has since been repurchased by the Government for the resettlement of Africans.

Later, in 1950, all lands acquired or occupied on behalf of the Crown were renamed 'Public Land', while the remainder was to be known as 'African Trust Land'.

This system amounted almost to the opposite of that prevailing in Southern Rhodesia under the Land Apportionment Act; for though the 1950 Order in Council envisaged that African interests should be paramount in African Trust Land, Europeans and Africans may in practice acquire land on the same terms in the same areas. It was a course similar to that outlined by Lord Lugard in 1922, when he wrote: 'The Government should prohibit the transfer of lands to aliens, and reserve to itself the right to grant leases to them, and to appropriate the rentals to public revenue, paying full compensation. The Government may also develop, for the public good, lands which are not in beneficial occupation, and not likely to be required for such purpose.' He added that 'lands which are beneficially occupied may be appropriated for any public purpose, or for lease to aliens, if justified for the encouragement of trade or mining, and in the interests of public revenue'.[7] Lugard's thesis, which was largely adopted as its policy by the British Government, would not have countenanced the six per cent. of Crown Land in Northern Rhodesia, nor the forty per cent. of European land in Southern Rhodesia, not being intended for territories of permanent white settlement. Northern Rhodesia's was a dual position as a tropical dependency and a European colony, but the Native Trust Lands, suited to the former role, exactly fitted Lugard's idea of land policy.

Nyasaland, like Northern Rhodesia, fell under the influence of the British colonial policy of indirect rule; but there it began to take effect a good deal earlier. British rule had been established in the Shire highlands eight years sooner than in North-Eastern and North-Western Rhodesia; and it had come from the outset direct from Downing Street. There was no intervening period of Company rule during which, as in the Rhodesias, the situation in Southern Rhodesia coloured the general field of policy. In 1924 the District Administration (Natives) Ordinance was replaced by another, giving the District Councils a certain amount of executive responsibility. The system met with considerable success, but 'without some financial responsibility, no real share in the work of government is possible'. Progress in this respect was more marked in Tanganyika Territory, and in 1930 the Nyasaland Secretary for Native Affairs, returning from leave, broke his journey at Dar es Salaam. In his subsequent report he declared his conviction that Nyasalanders had the intelligence and capacity for similar responsibilities. In 1933 were passed the Native Authorities and Native Courts Ordinances drafted along the lines of the Northern Rhodesia legislation of 1929. There was in this case no separate Native Treasuries ordinance, for financial responsibilities—the right to levy taxes and spend funds—were written into the constitution of the Native Authorities.[8]

On the whole, meanwhile, conflict between the planter community and the Government was slight. The political problem was simpler than in the two Rhodesias. From the first there had been continuity of Imperial control. Moreover, with only a small part of the country really suitable for white settlement, and with a high density of African population, the European community never tried to claim the predominant influence in the councils of government that the handful of Europeans in Northern Rhodesia, for instance, were demanding as early as 1924. Sources of conflict were fewer. There were none of the almost empty lands, save in the inaccessible north, that were elsewhere to provide a bone of contention between black and white; nor any large concentrations of population that might give rise to a colour bar and arouse racial antagonisms.

It is therefore not remarkable that no elected member sat in the Nyasaland Legislative Council till 1953. The form of the Council remained substantially unchanged from its inception in 1902, apart from the addition of one Official and one Unofficial member from time to time. By 1946 it contained six Officials and six Unofficials, the latter all nominated and all European; one was appointed to represent African interests and was always a missionary. Dr Hetherwick of Blantyre performed this task with distinction for many years. The leading Unofficial from 1932 until the war was R. Tait Bowie, who was active in pressing the cause of Nyasaland's association with the Rhodesias.[9] On the whole, political discussion was evenly peaceful till 1948. The Council was then further enlarged to eighteen members by the addition of three Officials and three Unofficials; of the latter, two were Africans and one an Asian member.

But if the impermanent nature of European settlement in Nyasaland and the high proportion of official and missionary elements meant an absence of political controversy and of constitutional change until after the war, African interest in the affairs of the Protectorate was displayed by contrast earlier than in the Rhodesias. This was not because the education system was more advanced; such was not the case. There had indeed been a good start at the turn of the century, but the poverty of the Protectorate prevented this early momentum from being maintained. The explanation lies chiefly in the migrant labour system. Whether on the Copperbelt, in Southern Rhodesia or on the Rand, Nyasalanders found on the one hand higher wages and better material facilities for Africans, and on the other more restrictive and discriminatory laws. They would thus return discontented with conditions at home, yet proud of the relative absence of the colour bar, and anxious to extend their social freedom. The Protectorate was looked upon as a haven of security in a white man's world.[10] Many gained experience in minor administrative posts on the Copperbelt and in Lusaka, where ciNyanja was for a time the *lingua franca* of the African population. The self-confidence thus gained found expression in Native Associations, formed at a number of provincial centres during the inter-war years. These took an active interest in such subjects as cash-cropping, the working of the migrant labour system, and education. During the thirties, Africans were appointed regularly to the Education Advisory Board. The Associations were neither antagonistic nor servile towards the administration, and were on easy terms with the more traditional Native Authorities set up under indirect rule.[11] In 1938 their strong consistent opposition to amalgamation weighed powerfully with the Bledisloe Commission. Their significance was recognized by leading European settlers who, before the war, were tolerant of these signs of African aspiration, and conscious of the Protectorate's enlightened native policy.

The war period brought a rapid change in this atmosphere of contented relationships. African fears were aroused by the continued demands for amalgamation by white leaders in the Rhodesias. Nearly a third of the able-bodied male population was enrolled on active service, many being drafted overseas.

A more marked sense of distinct national unity appeared. Nyasa leaders kept in touch with Hastings Banda in London. In 1943 James Sangala, a former Native Association official, published a letter addressed to all Nyasaland Africans enjoining them to struggle for their freedom.[12] In 1944 there were vehement complaints of missionary paternalism, and talk of African representation in the Protectorate's Management Boards and Legislative Council. In May of that year the Nyasaland African Congress was formed. Branches were set up rapidly throughout the country, care being taken from the outset to ensure co-operation with the chiefs. Apart from a determined objection to any possible permeation of Southern Rhodesian native policy, the principal demands of Congress were for direct representation in Government and the rapid extension of African education.

The new atmosphere of impatience did not at once destroy the deep fund of goodwill existing between the African people generally, including their leaders, and the colonial administration. The latter went some way to meet the new movement. The African Protectorate Council was established in 1946, from which two members were selected to sit in the enlarged Legislative Council of 1949. In 1948 the first African Trade Unions were formed. The post-war Ten Year Development Plan allocated nearly £1½ million for education. By 1950 the first enthusiasm for the Congress had slackened off, and the political future of the Protectorate was beginning to present a favourable outlook, though economic prospects were less encouraging.

Affairs took a very definite turn for the worse, however, with the publication of the white paper on Closer Association in 1951. To a far greater extent than in Northern Rhodesia, this event alienated the sympathies of Africans, Congress and people alike, from the Government of the Protectorate. In 1951 the Nyasaland African Congress issued a declaration which stated in plain terms the position it thereafter undeviatingly maintained: 'We oppose Federation not only because of the oppressive racialistic policies of Southern Rhodesia. . . . We oppose Federation because we are a *Protectorate*. Our country is not a colony for European settlement, as Southern Rhodesia is. That is why we cannot accept the partnership of Europeans. Our political goal and the political goal of Europeans are poles apart. Ours is African self-government (that is, government by ourselves) and the establishment of a sovereign state when we have passed through our tutelage. To obtain that self-government and sovereignty we must develop without let or hindrance. Our destiny is like that of our fellow Africans in the Gold Coast, Nigeria and the Sudan. The goal of the European settlers is the establishment of a Central African Dominion, like South Africa, Australia, New Zealand and Canada, in which they will have an imperium over the African people, doing with them as they please, and denying them equal political and economic rights'.[13]

The African Recovery

Although the 'cursory glance' of a native commissioner might observe no more than the 'passive strength of immemorial custom' among Africans in 1929, the period between the war and the trade depression had seen the first stirring of African, as opposed to merely tribal, political consciousness. Native Associations appearing in the Protectorate and the Rhodesias were beginning to voice the African desire for a place in the political community and their concern at discrimination, levels of pay and land availability.

The associations were however generally too local in range or just simply too isolated to make any impact on the administration. Moreover, outside Nyasaland, literate Africans were too few for the effective organization and expression of disquiet. Indeed, since Nyasaland had almost a generation start over the other territories in education, several of the leaders of early native associations in Northern and Southern Rhodesia were expatriate Nyasas, while others were even Fingos or Sothos from South Africa. Such leaders, out of touch with the mass of local opinion and traditions, were not able to appear as convincingly representative either among their own community or before the white administration. On the other hand this extraneous leadership helped to turn incipient African movements away from the tribal revivalisms that had been expressed before the war in, for example, renascent Lozi nationalism, the Nyamanda movement among the Ndebele, and dreams among the Shona of new revolt. Thus the Rhodesia Bantu Voters' Association, formed in January 1923 with both Shona and Ndebele staff and membership, was led and inspired by South Africans Abraham Twala and Martha Ngano. Trade union activity reached Southern Rhodesia in 1927 in the form of an extension of the South African Industrial and Commercial Workers' Union, inspired by a Nyasa working in the south, Clement Kadalie, and brought north by another Nyasa, Robert Sambo.

Some new leadership also appeared in connection with the churches. The missions had been somewhat discredited by the war, a fact which helps to explain the 'prophet movements' of the 1920s and the secessionist churches of South Africa. On the other hand this ill wind brought valuable indirect consequences. The lack of enthusiasm for mission enterprise in disillusioned post-war Europe caused a shortage of staff in Africa when it was greatly needed. Some missions, notably the U.M.C.A., met their requirements by training Africans for pastoral duties. This trend was one of the most important features of the inter-war years; without it the churches would have been more seriously embarrassed by race politics after 1945. Another feature was the growing spirit of unity among the denominations, marked by the General Missionary Conference of Northern Rhodesia inaugurated in 1922. Roman Catholic societies attended this conference for eleven years, and thereafter remained as associate members.[1]

Effective political organization from the grass roots would however have to await slow-moving developments in the background. Most important were the growth of population, and the slow spread of literacy. The mortality rate began to fall sharply with the spread of medical facilities early in the century. For example, the rate in Southern Rhodesian townships averaged over fifty per thousand in 1910; by 1920, after a sharp rise on account of the post-war influenza epidemic, it was only twenty per thousand.[2] Formerly the highest proportions of deaths had been among young children. The population now began to increase rapidly in all territories and was in fact to double itself in twenty-five years; though this did not become fully known till the 1931 census showed the increase since that of 1911.

The progress of education was consequently unbalanced by the huge 'bulge' in the child population of the twenties and thirties. The missionary societies were hampered by the shortage of satisfactory teachers, and even more as these began to come forward, by lack of adequate funds. Nyasaland had made the best start—Livingstonia schools were attended by 5,000 pupils by 1896—but in the first decade of the century the size of the problem was overtaking available resources. By 1918 missions in Nyasaland were spending over £30,000 a year, while the Government would only double its grant of 1908 to £2,000. This provided something over 2,000 schools, attended by about 70,000 pupils, not all of them children. The number of children of school-going age must then have been some 300,000. The typical feature as in Northern Rhodesia was the 'bush school', a mud-walled building with mud floor and benches, crammed with young and old. The rate of wastage was high, and few pupils persevered to the upper primary standard. In Northern Rhodesia where missions arrived later and where the population was scattered over great distances the picture was even less favourable; for a similar population, there were 1,500 schools in 1924, attended by about 50,000 pupils. In Southern Rhodesia, government grants totalled the much larger sum of £23,000; 77,000 pupils attended some 1,200 schools which were often larger and more solidly constructed establishments than in the north.

The year 1925 saw public recognition of the size and urgency of the education problem and more active co-operation between Government and missions. The Phelps Stokes Commission, appointed by a charitable organization in the United States to tour East and Central Africa, published a report which was closely studied by the authorities. Its main recommendation was the use of a wider curriculum. Evangelism and literacy could not by themselves meet the challenge of a changing society. Community development, girls' education, agricultural and industrial training were needed.[3] There was quick response. In Northern Rhodesia a sub-department of Native Education was formed at once, to become a separate department in 1930. A training centre was opened at Mazabuka that year for Jeanes Teachers who would stimulate village communities towards more hygenic living and more scientific farming. A similar centre was started at Domasi, Nyasaland in 1926. Southern Rhodesia, not visited by the Commission but influenced by its findings, established a Native Education Department in 1927, followed by the Native Development Act 1929 which aimed to link education to rural needs.

The momentum of this new drive was not maintained, being interrupted by government economies during the trade depression; not till 1937 did a new increase begin. The slow advance did not arouse much criticism at this stage when Europeans were observing clearly, even anxiously, the advancing tide around the shores of Huggins' 'white island'. The view was often expressed that the limited education policy was a wise one; it would be dangerous for academically qualified Africans to be knocking on the doors of a society which could not find suitable work for them to do. But African education was not seriously impeded by the war. The Imperial Parliament's Colonial Development and Welfare Act, passed in 1940, acted as a stimulus. Northern Rhodesia's five-year plan brought government expenditure in 1948 to £300,000, 4½ per cent. of the total budget. Southern Rhodesia, spending over £500,000 or 6½ per cent. of its budget in that year was still ahead while Nyasaland lagged behind with £134,000 or 3¾ per cent. The bulk of the attendance however, was in primary, especially lower primary schools. In 1950 in all three territories together there were less than three hundred Africans attending secondary classes. The African population of the area in that year was five and a half million. This was slow progress in fifty years of European rule. But a dramatic advance was to come in the following decade.

It was thus not till after 1945 that African education began to affect the externals of life in Central Africa. The inter-war period had been one of slow build-up during which the majority of those who attended school stayed for too short a time to be permanently affected, while those who persevered became teachers themselves or took junior posts in government departments. The rural areas were least affected of all, since a boy with any schooling preferred to try his fortune in the town than to remain in the dusty outworn village community.

It is therefore not surprising that African agricultural methods were slow to change. In 1926 it was estimated that 27,500 ploughs were in use in the Southern Rhodesian reserves. This was more than were to be found north of the Zambezi, but still few in a principally rural population of over a million.

The plough, besides, was doing more harm than good in default of crop rotation and conservation practices. The Native Affairs Department had recognized, even before 1914, that improvements could only come through the conversion of land tenure from a communal to an individual system. Such a revolution would be difficult to bring about, and little effort was made. The need derived from the prospect of land shortage which before long would render impossible the traditional system of shifting agriculture, and make imperative the culling of herds; also from the fact that the most fertile land was no longer available to Africans, since it lay in the area alienated to Europeans. Africans considered that these factors being consequent on the European occupation, it was adding insult to injury when they were asked to abandon age-old traditions of land use with all their social implications. In Northern Rhodesia and Nyasaland, by contrast, where the land had not been appropriated on so large a scale, efforts to convert Africans to intensive farming methods were regarded often enough as being for the benefit of Europeans who would subsequently take over the 'improved' land. Either way, interference with African farming and land tenure was received with resentment and suspicion.

The first attempts to cope with this vital problem were made by mission schools such as that at Mount Silinda in Southern Rhodesia, where an agricultural course was based on the rotation of crops and soil conservation methods. The London Missionary Society ran a similar centre at Senga Hill near Abercorn. Soil and farming conditions varied widely, and these isolated efforts were slow to spread their effects, particularly as they received little positive encouragement from the authorities. In Southern Rhodesia the Agricultural Officer, E. D. Alvord, developed the use in the reserves of agricultural demonstrators trained at Domboshawa Government School, but they were still few in 1929. Government intervention in African farming was mainly felt through maize marketing controls, a Maize Marketing Board being set up in Southern Rhodesia in 1931. These controls were intended to maintain the quality of the maize grown as well as to supervise its distribution, but by assuming that African grain was inferior to European produce, which at this time was generally but not invariably true, they created a bias against the African farmer. Still less understood were the regulations restricting the size of cattle herds, essential in the interests of soil conservation. Cattle in the Southern Rhodesian native reserves increased in number from 330,000 in 1911 to 1,555,000 in 1938. Cattle held a traditional place in the social as well as the economic life of the African, and administrative efforts towards the culling of herds aroused opposition from the beginning, which was made no less by the ever present spectacle of the wide ranch lands in the neighbouring European areas.[4]

In fact the standard of living of Africans in the rural areas was declining during the inter-war period. With the population doubling itself every fifty years the ratio of children to adults increased. The shortage of cultivable land was already being felt in parts of Nyasaland and Southern Rhodesia. At the same time able-bodied men were increasingly in short supply in the villages as the custom of seeking work in distant towns became general throughout Southern Africa. Those tribes which had shown greatest resistance to the European demand for labour now suffered least from the decline in rural life and loss of tribal cohesion. Others, especially in Nyasaland and North-Eastern Rhodesia, were seriously affected. The publication of Dr Audrey Richards' *Land, Labour and Diet in Northern Rhodesia* in 1939 revealed the decay of rural life among the Bemba, one of the largest tribal groups in the territory. Frequently more than half of the men would be away from the village at one time, creating an atmosphere of decay and frustration. Old men, dispirited women and hungry children lived depressing lives among poor gardens, neglected granaries and dilapidated huts. The heavy work in cutting trees, opening new gardens and repairing buildings could no longer be performed satisfactorily. Men back from the town were reluctant to work, having brought gifts, and having as they saw it earned a rest. Growing boys no longer learned by working in the gardens with an older relative. Cash presents that found their way into the village community did little to increase its productivity and were spent on clothing rather than on food.

Not all tribes suffered equally from this deterioration in social and economic conditions. The Lozi, for example, were able to export annually large numbers of cattle for the growing beef industry in surrounding territories, and especially in Southern Rhodesia. Kazembe's Lunda on the Luapula and the Tonga on Lake Nyasa's west shore began to find markets for dried fish further afield. Communities close to the line of rail were able to sell their local produce at European centres. Lenje villagers grew vegetables for the mining population at Broken Hill; thus it was estimated that only a quarter of the Lenje taxpayers were absent from the village at any one time. Moreover Lenje women generally accompanied their menfolk to the townships, so that the loss of productive labour was less serious. Similarly, Lala beans were sold to a Lusaka firm, while Tonga maize supplied African urban workers' rations as far away as the Copperbelt.[5] But the great majority of the African population was less fortunately placed.

The decline of Bemba society was chiefly caused by the departure of its labour force in the thirties and forties with growth of the copper mining industry some two hundred miles distant. Over most of the country, the migrant labour system was at least as old as the occupation. Its early effects in Nyasaland have already been noted. The Pass Law of 1909 and other measures had failed in their object and every year tens of thousands of Nyasa Africans were away, chiefly in Southern Rhodesia and South Africa. An estimated twenty-five per cent. of those who left never returned home. Anxiety concerning this fact, concerning fraudulent contracts and excessive transport charges, besides the adverse effect on the Nyasaland economy, prompted a public enquiry in 1935. Its report went beyond official expectations. 'As our investigation proceeded,' it ran, 'we became more and more aware that this uncontrolled and growing emigration brought misery and poverty to hundreds and thousands of families and that the waste of life, happiness health and wealth was colossal.' The easily accepted dictum that the Nyasa African was an adventurous, even a nomadic spirit who loved to travel far from his home was exploded, and a state of affairs revealed which constituted 'a flagrant breach of the ideal of the trusteeship of native races'.[6]

If the Committee by strong words hoped to stimulate the Nyasaland Government to effective remedial measures it was to be disappointed; indeed such a task was hardly within its resources at that time. The report's revelations, however, were a notable commentary on conditions in the Protectorate. The principal cause of a man's departure in search of work which might take him a thousand miles from home was the need to pay tax. There was also the need to pay the school fees at the mission for himself or for a dependant, besides the wish to buy a blanket, saucepan, bicycle or clothes at the local store. But the tax alone could prove an embarrassment particularly in the poorer parts of the Protectorate. In the Northern Districts of some 1,600 square miles there was in 1934 a European population of 109 including sixteen government officials. The Africans numbered 328,314, on whom the total tax assessment amounted to £18,379. The impossibility of finding sufficient employment was manifest; in fact only 2,800 Africans could obtain work locally at wages which varied from 4s. to 30s. a month. The local market for cash crops was negligible. Practical difficulties excluded the acceptance of produce in lieu of cash. Inevitably thousands must seek to earn elsewhere. Nyasas showed little inclination to work in a neighbouring district, the chief reason being that higher wages were paid in other territories. The Commission, while pointing out that the individual gained in physical fitness, with ambition heightened by wider experience, the family and village community, not to speak of the tribal organization as a whole on which the new local government was intended to rest, were damaged beyond repair. The report recommended economic development for the benefit of the indigenous community—aid for cash cropping and mineral surveys—besides a modification of the tax law. The control of recruitment and interterritorial agreements were also recommendations which were carried out in due course but failed to stem the tide.

Nyasaland's problem, apart from the Protectorate's own special lack of minerals and other opportunities for industrial development, was that of Central Africa as a whole. It was an economic problem. The indigenous sector of the economy, in contact with a superimposed exchange economy exporting to the wider world, was being disrupted by it before it could adapt and become part of the new system. Dr Godfrey Wilson, in an essay on *The Economics of Detribalization in Northern Rhodesia* in 1942, described the 'disequilibrium' between rural African communities and the urban centres along the line of rail.

Migrant labour was depriving the rural area of its productive force in order to manufacture primary products for export; but the wealth thus caused was not flowing back into the rural area on a scale sufficient to raise it above the subsistence level; nor could it raise itself above that level by its own efforts, even were government investment forthcoming, since it had been deprived of its labour force. The conclusion is inescapable that African industrial wage levels on any basis were too low.

These wage levels were arrived at by the operation of the law of supply and demand, and consequently remained about the subsistence level. In Northern Rhodesia before the war an unskilled labourer working on a farm or on road construction could earn 10s. a month; a driver or other semi-skilled worker 15s.; while a cook in a European household might earn 20s. In parts of Southern Rhodesia wages were as much as fifty per cent. higher. The minimum wage in the building industry in Salisbury was 26s. a month. In Bulawayo, where it was not the practice to provide food or accommodation, the minimum was 47s. 8d. On the Copperbelt too they were higher: unskilled surface workers on the mines earned 12s. 6d., underground workers 22s. 6d., though deductions were made at some mines for the issue of personal equipment. In considering such rates it should be borne in mind that in most occupations it was the practice to issue a ration of food sufficient to feed an individual; in 1943 the value of a miner's monthly ration was assessed at 44s. 7d.; in other jobs it would have been considerably less.[9] On the other hand no account was taken of a man's family, whether in the urban location or in the reserve. Most African town workers in Southern Rhodesia, it was estimated by the Secretary of the Native Welfare Society in 1943, were living on or below the 'poverty datum line'.[10] The Howman Committee appointed the following year to investigate the economic, social and health conditions of Africans in urban areas generally confirmed this. 'Few builders', stated the report, 'appeared to realize the economic importance of well-nourished labourers.' This attitude was not confined to employers. The Prime Minister told the Native Welfare Society in Bulawayo in 1946: 'The economic wage for a native living with his family in an urban area is about £5 a month, and you also know that few natives, with their indolent habits and lack of training, are worth that amount.'[11] During the next few years, with trades training and the coming of collective bargaining, wage limits were to rise sharply, particularly in skilled grades and on the Northern Rhodesian Copperbelt. None the less in 1960 it was still possible for distinguished authorities to justify the contention that the real incomes of the great majority of the population had not appreciably risen during fifty years of contact with European economy.[12]

The basic assumption underlying the low wage level was that the African employee was not integrated in the exchange economy, would only stay temporarily in the urban area, and would shortly return to his subsistence economy in the rural area. This was generally true in the first three decades of the century. In Nyasaland the period of absence varied widely, but averaged between two and three years, the original object being to earn money and settle down to married life in the village. Migrants who worked in South Africa in any case were not allowed to have their families in the mine compounds, and though the companies did not enforce this rule in the Rhodesias, a similar practice was expected, indeed encouraged, to prevail. The rapid increase in copper production in the thirties brought a change on the Copperbelt, and by the end of the war the tendency was for a man to go back to the village to get married, and return to the mining town to live with his wife as a semi-permanent resident. More marriages were taking place in the town, and of these about a third were inter-tribal. A social survey conducted in Ndola after the war revealed that four per cent. of the African population were completely urbanized, having been born and brought up in the town, while a further fifty-four per cent. intended to spend the rest of their lives there; about half of these might return to the village in old age. Only the remaining forty-three per cent., less than half, were in close touch with their villages and could be regarded as migrant labour.[13]

This more permanent urbanization, which was most advanced on the Northern Rhodesia Copperbelt, was a feature of development throughout Central Africa. Three processes marked the change. The African was ceasing to rely for his basic security on the village. As long as he could fall back on the village in time of stress, he was not committed to urban life and would

never wholeheartedly strive to better his interests there. Together with this trend appeared the true participation of urban
Africans in the exchange economy. Demands for higher wages
and for commutation of rations into cash were combined with
increased diversification of African economic activity in town
locations and mine compounds. In a community of thousands,
differing in tribe and language, the African earned his livelihood
as a labourer in a copper mine or engineering works, as a
bricklayer or carpenter, a tradesman or owner of a transport
service. Government departments employed an increasingly
wide range of teachers, clerks and technical assistants. Although
the great majority of unskilled workers still earned scarcely
more than a subsistence wage, growing opportunities for the
few joined with increasingly close acquaintance with the white
man's world to arouse new demands for consumer goods and
higher living standards. Linked with this development appeared the third process, that of more permanent employment
leading to a higher level of average skill, to a more rapid
acquisition of basic technical understanding, and so to the
enhancement of the value of labour.

These trends in African urbanization found expression in
the development of machinery for voicing African opinion in
mine compounds and town locations; in active agitation for
advancement in industry and for higher wages; and thirdly, on
the part of the responsible authorities, in belated efforts to
reform African housing and tenure by Africans of property in
urban areas.

Since permanent urbanization was furthest advanced on
Northern Rhodesia's Copperbelt, it was there, as we have seen,[14]
that representation of African interests first appeared. In the
matter of collective bargaining and industrial advancement it
was again Northern Rhodesia, and mainly the Copperbelt,
which gave the lead. Until the end of the war there had been no
thought of providing for African trade unions anywhere. The
Southern Rhodesian Industrial Conciliation Act of 1934 had
not extended to African workers. In Northern Rhodesia
there was no legislative bar, but African miners lacked the
necessary training and experience to form an industrial organization of their own. However, a European miners' strike on the
Copperbelt in 1940 leading to a pay increase was followed by

violent disturbances in which seventeen Africans were killed and sixty-nine wounded.[15] The subsequent committee of enquiry stated firmly that African wages were too low. The Forster Commission was appointed to devise machinery by which African grievances could be represented to the management. War held things up but the British Labour Government after 1945 resolved that the trade union system must be made to operate in the African territories, and advisers were sent out to Northern Rhodesia to help African mine workers to organize. The first union to be formed was that of the Copperbelt Shop Assistants in 1948. The European union, anxious about these portents, invited the African miners to join them in 1947, but the proposal was rejected. The African Mineworkers Union was formed under the presidency of Lawrence Katilungu, to be recognized by the Companies in 1949. In Nyasaland also African unions appeared after the war, the first to be registered being the Association of Nyasaland African Motor Transport Workers in 1948.

The Dalgleish Commission had meanwhile been appointed to inquire into the transfer to Africans of jobs, principally in the mines, then being performed by Europeans. Its report recommended that Africans were capable immediately of filling certain European-occupied posts on the mines, and others in the near future after training. Transfers should only be carried out as jobs fell vacant; no European should be displaced. The European union refused to co-operate with the Commission, relying on its 1942 agreement with the Companies, which effectively prevented the transfer of jobs. A clause in this agreement stated: 'The work of the class or grade that is being filled by an employee at the time of the signing of this agreement, shall not be given to persons to whom the terms and conditions of this agreement do not apply.'[16] Nothing was done to implement the Dalgleish proposal. In 1951 the white union further strengthened its position by coming to an agreement with the inexperienced African union and with the Companies, that if an African took over a job from a European he should be paid and housed at the same level. This agreement postponed African advancement for five or six years. During that time, however, the African union gained in strength, as was plainly demonstrated by the prolonged strike late in 1952, bringing copper production to a standstill, and resulting in the Guillebaud award with a substantial pay increase in January 1953. By 1954 the A.M.U. had increased its membership to over seventy-five per cent. of the Africans employed on the mines, so that when advancement negotiations recommenced, they were able to exert their influence with renewed effect.

In 1953 Ronald Prain told the Royal African Society in London that the new policy of the Rhodesia Selection Trust was to break the industrial colour bar before the Africans decided to take matters into their own hands and try to break it themselves.[17] In November the following year, the Rhodesia Selection Trust gave notice of their intention to end the equal pay agreement with the European union, and with this announcement the advancement question, already the subject of a government report earlier in the year, was out in the open. Two plans emerged in February 1955—Anglo American offering a transfer of European jobs to Africans at the rate of one per cent. for five years, the Rhodesia Selection Trust proposing the dilution of European jobs to provide a ladder for African advancement without any fixed ratio. In September an agreement was reached amounting to a compromise between the two proposals. Twenty-four kinds of job were to be transferable immediately, and a survey was to be undertaken for further advance. Ronald Prain, chairman of R.S.T., won a concession by insisting that the European union should not have a veto in specific cases of African promotion. The agreement was a real step forward towards industrial partnership.[18]

It did not, however, bring industrial peace to the Copperbelt. The African union resented the Companies' determination that 'advanced' African workers should be pressed into the Salaried Staff Association, thus depriving the union of much of its leadership. The year 1955 was consequently punctuated by African strikes that more than once paralysed the industry, a wave of shop boycotts began, and mob attacks on Europeans occurred. In 1956 the African union's industrial campaign coincided with the revival of political activity by the Northern Rhodesia African Congress; in the latter part of the year the Government resorted to a state of emergency on the Copperbelt, and the rustication of the younger and more militant African union leaders, that lasted until January 1957. Thereafter Lawrence Katilungu, the union's capable president, who had been absent overseas, returned to restore his influence. Meanwhile the constitutional question was increasingly occupying the attention of Congress leaders.[19]

In fact, as might have been expected, the advancement agreement, itself commendable, had opened up a vista of new problems. Industrial partnership is inseparable from social and political integration. If Africans were to share European skills and earn European rewards, they could hardly be denied European amenities and responsibilities. Yet these same Africans were not usually 'educated' in the accepted European sense, did not live by those social customs and beliefs that make up the 'white man's standard' so often proclaimed by European politicians in Central Africa as inviolable. Hence, in part, the weight of obstruction from the European union. More than simply their economic security lay at stake in face of African industrial competition. The Northern Rhodesian Copperbelt differed perhaps from most other urban centres in the Federation both in the more rapid turnover of its white population and in the higher proportion of Afrikaner to Briton. It was, nevertheless, proving the anvil upon which many of the social and political as well as industrial solutions to the Central African problem were to be forged.

African union activity in Southern Rhodesia was slower to make itself felt, one reason being that in the colony there was no large concentration of African labour in a single industry such as existed on the Copperbelt. In 1945, at which time the Industrial Conciliation Act continued to confine the term 'employee' to Europeans, the African was still regarded as a more or less primitive servant without any claim to the rights of an emancipated worker. Unofficial combinations, however, unrecognized under the Act, were being formed. In 1945 African railway workers went on strike, and in 1948 there was a general stoppage among African workers in commerce and industry. These events, together with the forming of African trade unions north of the Zambezi, persuaded the Southern Rhodesian Government to provide some system of determining African conditions of employment. The Native Labour Board Act of 1948 provided for a National Labour Board which fixed minimum conditions of employment from time to time throughout the country. It was later amended in order to set up separate boards for individual industries. On none of these boards, however, were Africans represented.

The boards found in practice that representations were constantly made to them by unofficial groups of Africans claiming to be trade unions. In 1954 the Government resolved to recognize these unions, and thus by bringing them within the law to establish some control. The Native Industrial Workers' Unions Bill was however criticized by a Select Committee of Parliament, which considered that to legislate for separate African trade unions was to invite racial conflict. It was not until 1957 that the matter was finally settled by a new Industrial Conciliation Bill, passed in 1959 and in operation in 1960. Africans were now to be included in the term 'employee', a simple but major stroke of policy that was to lead to the formation of multi-racial trade unions, and the provision of conciliation machinery which applied equally to workers of all races. But the internal structure of industry could not be expected to alter immediately. In few industries, in Southern as in Northern Rhodesia, were Europeans yet prepared to relinquish jobs to Africans; though the inauguration, following the 1959 Act, of multi-racial apprenticeship schemes was an important step in this direction.

A consequence of the appearance of collective bargaining was a marked rise in the wage levels of skilled and semi-skilled African workers; though for the unskilled mass on such work as farming and road construction earnings remained at the subsistence level. The average wage of Africans employed in industry doubled between 1945 and 1955, when it was seventy-two pounds a year. In 1951, of the total African population of the three territories, amounting to some 5½ millions, 588,000 were employed in the European economy, representing an annual rate of earning of over £40 millions. Southern Rhodesia was the largest employer of African labour with a total of about 400,000, of whom 86,000 came from Nyasaland and 48,000 from Northern Rhodesia. The latter territory employed 228,000, of whom the great majority were drawn from within its own borders. It may be added that a further 70,000 Africans from the Central African territories were employed in the

Union, a proportion of whose earnings also found its way home. By 1956 the number of Africans employed had increased to a million, their earning capacity to £70 millions; sale of local produce was earning a further £10 millions.[20]

These figures, impressive in their own sphere, should be set against the aggregate personal money incomes of the European population of 215,000, which totalled £172 millions in 1956. The highest-paid African worker on the Copperbelt, who was a rare case, could earn £540; the income of the lowest-paid European mine-worker was £1,858.[21]

The slower emergence of African trade unions in Southern Rhodesia was partly due to the more gradual stabilization of its urban population. In 1948 it was estimated that eighty per cent. of the colony's African employees changed their jobs each year.[22] In part this could be explained by the more balanced development of communications and the wider pattern of European settlement in a colony whose area was only two-thirds that of Northern Rhodesia. The Southern Rhodesian labourer seldom worked so far from his home as did the Bemba or the Lozi on the Copperbelt or at Broken Hill. This partly accounts for the long delay on the part of Southern Rhodesian employers and local authorities in providing for African families in urban locations; a further explanation lies in the limited life of many gold reefs being worked. There were, in addition, political grounds for this reluctance to recognize the African as a permanent member of urban society.

The Plewman Commission, directed to report on African urban housing in 1958, pointed to a still deeper cause. A town was an organic economic unit and could not grow from a plain administrative decision. 'So long as African housing is seen simply as a housing problem and not as a problem of urban growth it cannot, in our opinion, be solved. The solution lies in a determined effort to throw off the shackles which prevent Africans from becoming normal urban dwellers with the same security for property which is afforded to other citizens in urban areas. . . . Much of the housing problem will then be solved through the normal channels of building activity and finance.'[23]

The Commission proposed sweeping reforms, to be spread over a ten year period. The payment of rents, at present as elsewhere in southern Africa the responsibility of the employer, should be passed to the employee. African wage limits should be increased, not only to absorb this extra burden, but to give scope for higher incomes which would not only expand the consumer market but also create possibilities of saving and home ownership. Meanwhile married accommodation should be subsidized. Such wage increases should not be allowed to upset the balance between the rewards for skilled and unskilled work; and the attraction of too many from the reserves should be offset by increasing the agricultural productivity of the rural areas.

This study of urban housing was important not for the results it achieved—its recommendations were mostly brushed aside by the Government—but because it revealed in a clear light the key problem: the productivity of the rural areas. As long as the majority of the population remained there, and as long as their productivity remained low, the increase in basic wage rates for urban employees and all that would follow from this was impossible.

In spite of the clear prospect of a rise in population, in Southern Rhodesia and Nyasaland particularly, which would make reform of African agriculture essential in the long run, however the land were distributed, it was not until after 1945 that full-scale programmes were launched by the territorial governments, aided in the case of the two northern territories by Colonial Development Funds. By that time it was dangerously late, both because pressure on the land was becoming serious while it would still be years before instruction became effective, and because by that time African political organizations were appearing which would make persuasion of a suspicious and conservative peasantry doubly difficult. This missed opportunity had indeed been one of the most serious blunders of the inter-war years.

In Nyasaland no sweeping attempt was made to interfere with the traditional system of land tenure. The Protectorate was not faced with its own urban problem. But pressure of a growing population led the agricultural department to intensify its efforts towards conservation of the soil, improved agricultural methods, and a balance between the production of food and cash crops along lines common to all Britain's East African territories. Population pressure was less in Northern

Rhodesia but the rural economy was threatened by urbanization along the line of rail and the Copperbelt. Soil conservation measures were undertaken in the maize belt and the Eastern Province. In 1946 an Improved Farming Scheme offered special privileges and loans to Central and Southern Province Africans who would farm according to correct principles.[24] In remoter districts peasant farming schemes were based on security of tenure through leases from Native Authorities. These efforts were partially effective but the much greater amount of land available to Africans in the huge territory removed the sense of urgency necessary for dramatic success. A revolution in African farming impelled from above was to be reserved for Southern Rhodesia where the disruptive influences of urbanization and land shortage were combined in the same territory.

Encouragement of intensive farming in the colony had begun after the war and by 1950 there were 3,000 plot holders in the reserves practising proper crop rotation, of whom 1,600 qualified as master farmers. But this progress was far too slow, as leading Southern Rhodesian statesmen were clearly aware. The Native Land Husbandry Act of 1951, unique in Africa, sought to convert parts of the reserves from communal land to individual plots with permanent private title. The size of the plots would vary according to the quality of the land and population density, and several years' work, including survey and the construction of dams and dip-tanks, was necessary before the Act could be implemented. Plots would be taken over gradually by selected farmers and proper farming practice would be compulsory.[25]

Apart from its effect on productivity, this measure carried implications of the utmost consequence. In the first place, it must finally and irrevocably destroy the tribal system, which was rooted in the historic link between the tribe and its communal land. Secondly, it would drive many people to the towns who were at present able to subsist on the overstocked and cultivated veld. Thirdly it would stabilize the urban population, whose members would no longer be able to wander back at will to the village and be sure of a garden to subsist upon. For all these reasons it aroused African opposition. European critics of the Bill, for various reasons, fastened on the inevitably small size of the African plots, which varied between one and a half and twenty acres in different reserves. In neighbouring European areas individuals owned thousands of acres, while thousands more were not developed at all. If African farmers were not to form an increasingly congested peasant society living on the subsistence level, the whole Land Apportionment system was going to be threatened.

The Bill passed through a legislature in which no African was a member. By 1955, after intensive preparatory work, its implementation was going ahead. By 1960 it was clear that its consequences for the colony's land policy could no longer be evaded.

The eruption of African political movements in the later fifties, caused at once by the speed of the economic revolution and the slowness of political advance, is described later. It demonstrated the failure of the 'pyramid' system of African representation, differently designed as it was in each of the Rhodesias, and even in Nyasaland. The 'pyramid' in Southern Rhodesia had hardly proceeded beyond Huggins' 'first step' in 1937; the 1957 Act was more truly local government legislation and not really intended as a rung in the ladder of African representation. In Northern Rhodesia the system rising from the Native Authorities through Provincial and African Representative Councils to the elected members of Legislative Council had ceased by the fifties validly to act as a channel of African opinion. In Nyasaland the Congress and the Chiefs— and therefore the Provincial and Protectorate Councils—had always been in closer accord. This gave greater weight to the nationalist movement. Yet the Government found it necessary to withdraw recognition of Congress in 1957, and sought to restrict discussion in Councils to a clearly defined list of local issues.

It might still be possible to cast grave doubts upon the 'responsibility' of African opinion, but no longer upon its existence or coherence. Once 'the baffling domain of the administrative officer', it had become not only as in 1939 a factor that could not be ignored, but an issue of the greatest moment in world affairs. The subject which aroused it to coherence, and upon which it was most strenuously expressed, was that of closer association between the northern and southern territories.

IX

MID CENTURY DECISIONS

Towards Closer Association

THE size of the area should be considered. From Beit Bridge, where the road from Pretoria to Bulawayo crosses the Limpopo river, to Mpulungu at the southern end of Lake Tanganyika, the distance is as great as that from Rome to Copenhagen. From the Barotseland border in the west to the shore of Lake Nyasa in the east, it is almost as far as from London to Poland's border with the Soviet Union. Not only was a community of spirit unlikely among the indigenous groups scattered over this wide region; among some of them existed long traditions of hostility and war. The common factor now superimposed, European settlement and economy, was an alien one. Through accidents of history as well as of geography, three distinct political units had evolved. Any attempt to combine these units must spring from alien influence, the more so since the question of closer union was linked directly with that of European-controlled self-government. In the nature of things, African support for, let alone initiative in, any movement towards closer union was unlikely. The advocates of such a union could hope, at best, for African passivity. The end of the Second World War saw the prospects of such a passivity vanishing for ever, but strong reasons had prevented the achievement of closer union at an earlier time.

The relationship between economic development and political independence has inevitably aroused discussion in recent years. It is axiomatic that for genuine political independence a society should be able to produce enough for consumption or for export to pay for the essential requirements of its population in the way of public order, health, communications and other necessities of progressive social life. What are regarded as necessities must indeed vary between one society and another. In Central as in South Africa it has been the

European community that determined not only its own standards but those to which the African population might rise. During the first three decades of the occupation, when Africans were generally looked upon as a source of cheap labour and little more, the minimum requirements of an independent state were fewer. Southern Rhodesia was thus able to pay its way by 1923, ignoring the vast expenditures that the next generation was to consider essential for social services. Northern Rhodesia similarly was balancing its budget in the early thirties, thus giving rise to the clamour for combined amalgamation and self-government that culminated in the Bledisloe Commission of 1939. It is possible that, accepting the limited standards of those days, the two Rhodesias at least, despite their small educated population, might have successfully formed an independent dominion at that time.

The world-wide social revolution that resulted from the war created new sets of criteria both for self-governing states and for the administration of backward communities. One was that power should not be handed over to privileged minorities. This implied the need for a broad distribution of the national income among the various racial, cultural or otherwise distinctive groups in society. On these terms self-government for a multi-racial state was not permissible anywhere in Africa in the post-war decade, though it existed from earlier days in Southern Rhodesia and the Union. However, the economy of Central Africa now began to change rapidly. Until the war its character had been mainly that of a frontier community. All three territories had depended chiefly on the exports of primary products such as minerals and tobacco for their income, and on imports for the supply of consumer goods. During the post-war phase the export of primary products continued to expand as before, though including a greater variety; but the industrial scene now witnessed the advent of secondary industry on a wide scale. A fully differentiated economy was emerging.[2]

A feature of this economy, one which in fact helped to make it possible, was the development of a home consumer market which rivalled the export market in significance. An important characteristic of this home market was the large part played in it by the African population. Though African wage rates rose slowly, the number of Africans in paid employment, as we have seen, increased rapidly. African money incomes by 1953 were four times as high as the assessed value of total subsistence production, and amounted to nearly half the total of European money incomes.[3] This development presented the prospect of a growing and potentially enormous domestic consumer demand.

Such a prospect was an asset to the long-term cause of self-government, whether for separate territories or for a larger union, in that it augured for an integrated economy and therefore for an integrated political community. On the other hand it was a threat to the aspirations of white minorities who could still hope to retain a dominant place in the economic and political structure. This helps us to understand the haste of Rhodesian settler politicians to achieve federation as a preliminary to independence during the fifties, before African economic development on the one hand, and British public opinion on the other, could catch up with them.

The cause of closer union in Central Africa has thus over half a century presented a picture of a duel between the hare and the tortoise—the hare of white domination, subjected to enforced halts by the accident of war or trade recession, overtaken by the slow-moving but inexorable advance of African awareness and overseas opinion. It is to an account of this procession of events that we now turn.

The first step towards greater unity was taken with the junction of North-Eastern and North-Western Rhodesia in 1911. By 1914 it was widely assumed that the union of Northern and Southern Rhodesia would follow as a logical conclusion. Two years later the Company prepared a plan for the legislative union of the two Rhodesias. When hostilities ended, however, the issue of self-government not only became more important than that of amalgamation, but conflicted with it. For whereas advocates of amalgamation dwelt on the similarity of interests of the white populations north and south of the Zambezi, and the opportunity it would provide for the harnessing of that river's water power, its opponents raised the insuperable objection that it would postpone indefinitely the coming of responsible government in Southern Rhodesia. Settlers in the south moreover were perturbed by the administrative deficits of the North, and also feared another land case with further compensation to be paid.

Political leaders preferred to put the horse before the cart and seek responsible government in the south first and amalgamation, or as some would have it, union with South Africa, afterwards. This was a recently formed point of view. Before 1923, though the administrations were separate, they were not dissimilar. Both were the responsibility of the Chartered Company. The British Government was represented by the same man as Resident Commissioner for each territory. Many officers had experience of service on both sides of the Zambezi. Though Southern Rhodesia had further developed representative institutions, an Advisory Council had recently been set up in Northern Rhodesia. After 1923 the two territories became politically much more distinct, Southern Rhodesia gaining virtual independence with a parliamentary constitution of its own, Northern Rhodesia the following year being placed firmly in the harness of Crown Colony status. The different controlling authorities were bound to bring, and as we have seen did bring, divergent policies. Unity in Central Africa, which had been physically impossible in the 1890s, was politically rejected in 1923–24, and long postponement was now inevitable.

For the time being, that is during the 1920s, Nyasaland did not enter the calculations of those who foresaw a greater dominion in Central Africa. Never a part of the Chartered Company's administration, the Protectorate continued economically separate, lacking any rail link with the Rhodesias; while the road from Lusaka to Fort Jameson was not opened till 1929 and even then provided a long and hazardous journey.[4] Secondly, whereas the cost of the railway, the principal item of public works expenditure in the early stages, had in the Rhodesias been borne by subsidiaries of the Company, in Nyasaland it was financed by the Imperial Government, to which the Protectorate was now tied by the burden of a heavy debt. The Rhodesias besides were linked together and with the Union by a customs agreement in which Nyasaland, being wholly within the regions covered by the Congo basin treaties of 1885 and 1919, was prevented from joining. Lastly, the impetus towards amalgamation in the Rhodesias sprang from the white settler population; but the Europeans in Nyasaland continued few in number, being still less than 1,500 in 1930, and containing a high proportion of missionaries and government officials.

The inclusion of Nyasaland was first discussed when, after 1930, a new demand for the union of the Rhodesias began to disturb the political air. The reasons for the revival of interest were various. The first arose out of events south of the Limpopo. The South African Party of General Smuts, whose bid for the incorporation of Southern Rhodesia in 1923 had gone a fair way towards success, was replaced in the 1924 Union election by the Nationalist Party led by General Hertzog. The new party had an Afrikaner bias, and while not expressly anti-British, was not concerned as Smuts was with the solidarity of the British Empire, and moreover soon began to follow a native policy which was out of keeping with the views of Southern Rhodesian leaders, heirs to the old Cape liberalism. People in the colony who had inclined towards union with South Africa now began to change their opinion, and to look once more towards amalgamation with Northern Rhodesia as a means of consolidation.

Meanwhile the British Government was groping its way towards a clearer and more positive policy in its African dependencies, and in 1928 sent out the Hilton Young Commission to inquire into the possibility of closer union between the East African territories.[5] In the course of its work the Commission visited the Rhodesias and Nyasaland. Its recommendation that Northern Rhodesia should be more closely linked with Nyasaland, and the suggestion that both should be connected with East Africa in the north, brought home to Europeans in Rhodesia the fact that the 'black' dependencies to the north-east, already close, might become even closer neighbours. The point was further hammered home with the publication in 1930 of the Passfield memorandum announcing the policy of paramountcy of native interests, a policy that was to be applied not only to East Africa and Nyasaland, but to Northern Rhodesia as well. The result was a reaction in favour of solidarity among the European communities in Central Africa, and from 1930 onwards a stream of petitions and recommendations for some form of closer union was directed to London, particularly from Northern Rhodesia.

Some of the findings of the Hilton Young Commission are of

interest in illustrating the views prevailing at the time. Opinion in Southern Rhodesia was reported to favour union with Northern Rhodesia, but to be anxious about the financial liability of that territory and its association with dependencies further north which were 'predominantly native in outlook'. Northern Rhodesian Europeans on the railway belt also sought union with the south, though Fort Jameson farmers were more interested in union with Nyasaland. Views in the Protectorate were more divided. The commercial and trading interests looked towards closer association with Tanganyika and Kenya 'when improvement of communications renders this possible'. But the smaller farmers and planters were generally in sympathy with the policy of 'white' Southern Rhodesia and opposed any link with Tanganyika. Union with Northern Rhodesia was considered to be the necessary first step. On the latter question, the Commission stated that the arguments in favour of administrative union between Nyasaland and the eastern area of Northern Rhodesia were numerous and strong. 'The line of communications and trade route from Fort Jameson and the Luangwa valley is at present through Zomba to Beira, and is likely to remain so. The export tobacco crop of N.E. Rhodesia and the Nyasaland Railway are necessary to each other. ... The Nyasaland/Northern Rhodesia border is drawn without any relation to tribal distribution. It cuts through the Cewa and Ngoni tribes. It would be better for both tribes and administrators to include them under one government.' Political differences existed between the two territories, notably concerning land tax, land tenure, and election to the legislature, but these were not insuperable obstacles. The Commission went on to suggest that should this union be carried out, the central railway belt of Northern Rhodesia might amalgamate with Southern Rhodesia, and Barotseland be constituted a separate Protectorate. The latter proposal is one which, like the proverbial bad penny, has persistently been turning up ever since. No action was taken on the Report, however, and the British Government, though pressed by the Labour opposition, declined to express its opinion about it.

The tidal wave of the world trade depression reached Central Africa early in 1931. Its effects, described elsewhere,[6] shook the confidence of Southern Rhodesians in their position as a separate economic unit, and contributed to the rise to power of Godfrey Huggins and his Reform Party, pledged to amalgamation of Northern and Southern Rhodesia. This policy received further impetus when Huggins' hand was strengthened by the steadily increasing output of the copper mines on the Katanga border. The average amalgamationist in Southern Rhodesia was less concerned with realizing Rhodes' grand concept of a 'United North' than with the progress of his own colony. Many saw Northern Rhodesia as no more than a huge copper mine whose potential millions could swell the Southern Rhodesian revenues; while a retired Chief Native Commissioner was bold enough to declare that 'Northern Rhodesia's only value to Southern Rhodesia is as a big native reserve to supply labour'.[7] These extreme views did the cause more harm than good and received the censure of moderate opinion; but *The Times* was able to say in 1938 that 'invariably during times of prosperity in Northern Rhodesia, the demand for amalgamation in the south becomes a clamour, while if Northern Rhodesia is in a bad way, it dies down'.[8] By that year the fact that the Northern Rhodesian Government had at its disposal an estimated surplus of £500,000 served to bring the Southern Rhodesian isolationists into the same camp with the more statesmanlike amalgamationist movement.

Viewed in retrospect the consequences of the trade depression were indeed incalculable for Central Africa. Not only was the economic balance between the two Rhodesias sharply altered in favour of Northern Rhodesia whose climate and land distribution none the less still postulated an African dominated country; but in Nyasaland the prospects of European settlement were set back at a critical juncture. It might be said that while the cause of closer association was visibly advanced by these events, so also were the troubles that must ultimately beset such an association.

The Imperial Government was slow to respond to the growing pressure for amalgamation that was boiling up in the Rhodesias during the 1930s. In 1931 J. H. Thomas, Labour Secretary of State for Colonial Affairs, refusing a request from the Southern Rhodesian Government supported by Northern Rhodesia elected members for a conference, said that 'while His Majesty's Government is not opposed to amalgamation in principle, Northern Rhodesia has not yet progressed far enough, and must continue to develop as a separate entity for some time to come'.[9] The elected members vigorously expressed the opposite view in resolutions passed in 1933, 1935 and 1936, but in the latter year the Secretary of State was still adhering to his predecessor's opinion. Northern Rhodesian agitation arose out of two circumstances. With an economy almost exclusively dependent on copper, concerning whose liability the crash of 1931 had aroused misgivings, it was considered that attachment to the South's more varied mineral and agricultural wealth would bring greater security. This opinion decreased in force, however, as during the thirties the copper ventures advanced with accelerating momentum. More powerful appears to have been the political consideration that union with Southern Rhodesia would free Northern Rhodesian settlers from Colonial Office control and give them more influence in their own affairs. In London for the coronation celebrations in 1937, Sir Leopold Moore expressed the dissatisfaction of 'the people' with the existing regime, and urged that their only hope lay in amalgamation. Ormsby Gore, the Colonial Secretary, asked him: 'You would rather be in subjection to the people in Salisbury than to Downing Street?' Moore could probably have replied safely in the affirmative, but remarked instead that it was not a question of subjection but of having the vote.[10]

But the British Government was preparing, if not to open the door, at least to release the catch. In June 1937 the Secretary of State, while not agreeing with Huggins' view that the territories, if not forced together, would drift apart, conceded that they were linked through communications, history and tradition, and added, 'I believe they are destined to be closely associated in all their future activities'.[11] Six months later the appointment was announced of a Royal Commission which, 'with due regard to the interests of the native inhabitants', should consider the promotion of closer co-operation or association between Southern Rhodesia, Northern Rhodesia and Nyasaland.

The Commission, headed by Lord Bledisloe, a former Governor-General of New Zealand, spent three months during 1938 in the Central African territories, and published its report early in 1939. Though Lord Bledisloe himself was in favour of some form of closer union, a number of minority opinions were attached to the Report, and the sum of its conclusions was that amalgamation could not be achieved immediately. The obstacles enumerated were the contrasting native policies between which it was yet too soon to choose, the general African opposition that had been discovered in the north, the limited size of the European population and the differing constitutional status of the three territories. The positive recommendations of the Commission were three. First, that Northern Rhodesia and Nyasaland might be combined under a single government without delay. Second, that the Nyasaland debt to the Imperial Government, amounting to £1½ millions, should be settled forthwith. Thirdly, that an inter-territorial advisory council should be set up, consisting chiefly of the Governors of the two northern territories and the Prime Minister of Southern Rhodesia, to co-ordinate economic and financial development in the whole area.[12]

A notable feature of the report was its emphasis on the striking unanimity of African opposition north of the Zambezi, 'a factor that cannot be ignored'.[13] One of the personal notes appended to the Report expressed the rather advanced view that, though the average African was yet ill-equipped to appreciate all that might be involved in a major question such as amalgamation, 'nevertheless he possesses a knowledge and shrewdness, in matters affecting his welfare, with which he is not always credited. It would be unwise to assume that his opposition is based, to a very large extent, on ignorance or prejudice, or to an instinctive dread of change.'[14]

The discussion aroused considerable interest in Britain, more remarkable because of the shadows cast in Europe by the gathering thunderclouds of war. The grim course of world events was to postpone any action along the lines of the Bledisloe proposals, but the Report was none the less significant. It brought Nyasaland, from the point of view of future planning, away from the East African and into the Central African orbit. It clearly expected that the three territories were to be closely bound up with one another in the future. Most important of all, its own conclusions and the public debate that followed them made it plain that native policy, and the responsibility of the

United Kingdom for Africans in the Northern territories, were the chief stumbling blocks to closer union. In the House of Commons Arthur Creech Jones reiterated the left-wing view that Northern Rhodesia was 'essentially a black man's country', and Sir John Harris of the Aborigines Protection Society declared roundly that nothing less than Britain's whole colonial policy was at stake. The veteran Lord Lugard, while defending the policies of the Southern Rhodesian Government, expressed misgivings for the future when the time should come for Huggins to retire and 'his powerful influence on behalf of the natives' be withdrawn.[15]

In Central Africa the Report was given a varied reception. In Southern Rhodesia it was generally approved as a step in the desired direction, but Northern Rhodesian Europeans were more impatient. On 8 June Unofficials in the Legislative Council deplored the 'indeterminate nature' of the conclusions reached. Gore-Browne criticized the proposed inter-territorial Council as unworkable, and the Northern Rhodesian Government was accused of bias against union with the colony. Moore resigned his seat as a protest, to be returned again unopposed in the ensuing by-election.

The coming of war prevented further discussion on the official level, but amalgamationists were determined to keep the issue alive. Huggins (now Sir Godfrey) declared in 1941 that he had not agreed to defer amalgamation for the duration of the war, and Roy Welensky in the same vein pressed that the principle at least should be accepted at once. It was decided however not to force the Imperial Government unduly. By 1943 a certain lack of solidarity on the subject was becoming evident among the Northern Rhodesian elected members. This was partly due to an awareness of the prosperity that wartime demands on copper were bringing to the territory, and to a growing appreciation of the influence that the Unofficials were now able, since the constitutional changes of 1938, to exercise in the Government. Some members recognized, besides, that African advance in the urban areas was creating a force that must in future be contended with.

On the African side, time was not standing still. Africans in Southern Rhodesia were enrolled in the armed forces, and Northern Rhodesia's eight battalions of Askari, drawn from all parts of the territory, were sent to fight in Abyssinia and Burma, and to guard the imperial communications from Palestine to Ceylon. Most of them were to go back to their homes at the end of the war with their minds broadened by travel and hardened by military discipline, and with an increased pride in Northern Rhodesia as their own territory under the Crown. Askari from Nyasaland similarly returned with widened horizons and heightened ambitions. They were to resume their life in territories in which new provision had been made for the expression of their political opinions through the creation of Provincial Councils, to which were soon added the African Representative Council in Northern Rhodesia and the African Protectorate Council in Nyasaland. These developments were accompanied by the formation of African nationalist organizations which derived much strength from the swelling number of urban workers along the Northern Rhodesian line of rail. African opinion, influential against amalgamation even in 1938 when it lacked an organized means of expression, was ten years later to become a great deal more vocal and effective.

Meanwhile, war conditions had increased the number of activities requiring combined operation, and in 1941 an interterritorial secretariat was created to organize the war effort. This became the forerunner of the Central African Council that the Bledisloe Commission had recommended. In 1944 the formation of the Council was announced. It was to consist of the Governors of Northern Rhodesia, Southern Rhodesia and Nyasaland, and three ordinary members nominated by the government of each territory; these were in practice the leading political figures in each case. The first meeting was held in June 1945, and the Council continued to meet twice a year until 1953. Useful work was done in extending Southern Rhodesian services to the other two territories, encouraging research, and co-ordinating communications and migrant labour. The Council was criticized for having no executive power and for being out of touch with the public. On the whole, however, it was accepted with tolerance, and some, like Welensky, were even prepared to regard it as the cornerstone of amalgamation.[16]

But it soon became apparent that the cause of amalgamation was likely to be a lost one. In the British election that followed the end of the war in Europe, the Labour Party was swept to power, pledged to prevent amalgamation unless and until the African inhabitants desired it. Huggins persisted none the less, and was fortified by a succession of events in 1948. In the Southern Rhodesian election of that year his United Party was given an unshakeable vote of confidence, gaining twenty-four seats out of thirty. By contrast the elections in the Union of South Africa brought Malan's Nationalists into office with the avowed intention of carrying out the policy of apartheid. The colony thus was able to stand out in sharper light as a bulwark of British liberalism in southern Africa. The British Government did not react as yet; but in Northern Rhodesia the formation of the first African Trades Union under the wing of the Colonial Office, and the recommendations in the Dalgleish report, emphasized the obvious fact that Africans were a coming economic as well as political power in the land. Once again, caught between the opposing policies of Pretoria and London, Rhodesian settlers north and south of the Zambezi were brought shoulder to shoulder.

On the initiative of Welensky, a meeting was held at the Victoria Falls in February 1949, to consider closer union.[17] The Colonial Office was not informed in advance. Huggins, Welensky and leading politicians from all three territories attended, but no Africans were invited to be present. It was at this first Victoria Falls conference that the plan for amalgamation was finally abandoned, and replaced by a proposal for some form of federation in which control of native affairs would be retained by the territorial governments. Thus it was hoped that the otherwise insurmountable bar presented by differing native policies would be overcome. Allowance could also be made for differing constitutional status, while with the northern territories continuing under the Colonial Office, the burden of staffing the public departments could be shared between the federal authority and the United Kingdom.

The omission to invite African members was later regarded as a serious error, though whether such an initial courtesy would have served to moderate the African attitude is doubtful. At any rate, when the proceedings were published, Africans and notably the Lozi showed themselves as hostile to federation as they had been to amalgamation. Arthur Creech Jones, visiting

Central Africa later in the year, declared that his Government was inflexibly opposed to the scheme, and regarded the Central African Council as sufficient for immediate needs. Faced with this check, the supporters of federation bided their time, knowing well that a British general election was not far off. They knew besides that any British government must pay attention to a public opinion that had been shaken by the abandonment of India in 1947. More recently Malan's demand for the High Commission territories, talk of a South African republic, and implementation of apartheid by the Group Areas Act of 1950 presented a new challenge to the integrity of empire. To many it appeared that the establishment of a strong British dominion in Central Africa would redress the balance.

In the event, the Labour Party was returned to power, but with a much reduced majority. Creech Jones was replaced by James Griffiths at the Colonial Office. Huggins at once returned to the charge. The new administration and indeed Parliament as a whole was now much more amenable to the idea of a strong British bloc in Central Africa, and Griffiths consented to a new conference, which met in London during March 1951. Although its objects were declared to be simply exploratory, it succeeded in reaching the unanimous conclusion that closer association in Central Africa had now become urgent, and that it should take the form of a federal constitution.[18]

Prospects were definitely improving for the supporters of federation, but the day was not yet won. Griffiths and Gordon Walker, Secretary of State for Commonwealth Relations, visited Central Africa and toured the country to sound opinion, black and white. They discovered strong African opposition to the plan which was rejected by the African Congress parties of Northern Rhodesia and Nyasaland, as well as the more moderate Nyasaland Protectorate Council. It was in fact with reluctance that the African Councils were persuaded to send representatives to the Second Victoria Falls Conference, which included the territorial leaders and the Secretaries of State, in September. The conclusions of this conference published in November showed however that all sides had gone a great part of the way towards agreement on closer union. Grave concern was expressed at the 'dangers which would flow from any weakening or dilution of the British connection and British tradition and principles in the three territories', which should be so strengthened as to ensure that these principles should continue to prevail.[20] There was general agreement that economic and political partnership between Europeans and Africans was the only policy under which federation could be brought about, and that any scheme of closer association would have to give effect to that principle. Further discussion was necessary before a constitution could be drafted, but the conference declared that in any federal scheme there should be enshrined the preservation of the protectorate status of the two northern territories, in which land policy and African advancement should remain the responsibility of Her Majesty's Government.

The term 'partnership', introduced to the conference by James Griffiths, speedily became a slogan that was widely used in public debate, and given various shades of meaning. The Colonial Secretary published a statement defining it as a principle according to which the interests of one section of the community should not be subordinated to those of any other, and which imposed on both Europeans and Africans the obligation to recognize the right of the other section to a permanent home in the country. 'In practice, partnership must ensure that Africans are helped forward by the Europeans . . . so that they may take their full part with the rest of the community in the economic life of the territory.'[19] This was clearly out of line with the doctrine of paramountcy enunciated in 1930, and was regarded by Africans with considerable suspicion. Partnership could mean senior and junior partners, without any definite term to the period of tutelage. Nevertheless, the Northern Rhodesian African representatives stated at the Falls conference that their people would be willing to consider the question of federation after the policy of partnership had been put into progressive operation. But so indefinite a principle could hardly be called a policy, no sudden change of policy could be expected or in fact materialized, and the general African attitude towards federation did not change.

A few months later the Labour Party fell from power in Britain. The new Conservative administration, with Oliver Lyttelton at the Colonial Office, announced its full agreement with the conclusions of the second Falls conference and repeated that federation was urgent and would be in the best interests of the African as well as the other inhabitants. A second London conference was called for April 1952. By this time African opposition had consolidated, and though the Northern Rhodesian African representatives had informal talks with the Colonial Secretary, both they and the Nyasalanders refused to attend the conference either as full members or as observers. The only Africans present were the two nominees from Southern Rhodesia. The outcome of the conference was a draft federal scheme produced with commendable speed in June, and commissions were appointed to examine fiscal, judicial and Civil Service questions.[20] In August Henry Hopkinson, Minister of State for Colonial Affairs, visited Central Africa to test African opinion, and reported that ninety per cent. of the African population knew nothing about federation, let alone understood it. Much of the opposition, he alleged, was a result of intimidation by extremist African groups. Meanwhile officials of the District Administration in the northern territories, acting on instructions to remain impartial, explained the scheme as best they could but refused to give advice about it to their anxious tribesmen, who were left to their own fears of Southern Rhodesian policies, and to the propaganda of African National Congressmen.

A final conference met in London early in 1953 to consider the draft federal scheme. This time no Africans were in attendance. The constitution agreed upon was to consist of a Governor-General appointed by the Queen, an executive council or cabinet responsible to the legislature, and a federal parliament of thirty-six members—eighteen from Southern Rhodesia, eleven from Northern Rhodesia, and seven from Nyasaland. The powers of this legislature were limited to a list including defence, trade, communications, industry and finance, while local government, African education, health, agriculture and land—in fact all matters either connected with native affairs or not common to the whole federation—were retained for the territorial legislatures. A common list enumerated items over which either federal or territorial governments might have control, though prior authority was given to the federal parliament. Revenue from customs duties apart from that on motor spirit was allocated to the federal government. Of income tax revenue, sixty per cent. was to be federal and forty per cent. territorial—more specifically seventeen per cent. to Southern Rhodesia, seventeen per cent. to Northern Rhodesia and six per cent. to Nyasaland. The territorial governments could themselves levy an income tax surcharge up to one-fifth of the federal rate.

The vexed question of African representation and the protection of African interests was finally solved by providing for the election of two African members and the nomination of one European member from each territory to the Federal assembly, and by the establishment of a standing committee of the assembly known as the African Affairs Board with the power to examine and veto if necessary bills which appeared to discriminate against Africans. The veto was not final, however, and could be set aside by the Governor-General or in the last resort by the Imperial Parliament. This committee was to consist of a nominated chairman, the three European members appointed for African interests, and three of the African members. A brief but important preamble to the constitution declared that Northern Rhodesia and Nyasaland were Protectorates of Her Majesty's Government and as such should continue to enjoy separate governments responsible for local and territorial political advancement 'so long as their respective peoples so desire'. The constitution could be changed at any time subject to a two-thirds majority of the Assembly and Her Majesty's approval, and in any case was to be reviewed within seven to nine years of its inception.[21]

The device of the Standing Committee did nothing to allay African fears, and the two-thirds majority needed to alter the constitution, while appearing a slender guarantee that such African political rights as had been included would be preserved, offered small hope of any amendment in their favour. Stronger than detailed criticism of the scheme, however, was the whole weight of emotional opposition. In the north this was steadily mounting. On 23 March Harry Nkumbula, president of the Northern Rhodesian African National Congress, ceremonially burned the White Paper before an enthusiastic concourse in Lusaka. The first two days of April were scheduled by Congress leaders as a national 'day of prayer' during which no African was to work for a white employer. The threatened strike fizzled out on the first day, as much for lack of organization as for lack of spirit; notably the Copperbelt Africans and the A.M.U. showed little enthusiasm for it. Matters were not improved by the Government's new fishing regulations on the Luapula, agitation over which led to the deposition of a chief. Many chiefs, notably Chitimukulu of the Bemba, were openly siding with Congress over federation. In Nyasaland the Rev. Michael Scott was providing a focal point for African opposition, and in March took three chiefs to London to support the African protest and to seek an interview with the Queen.

The British Government was by now fully committed to the scheme, which received the approval of the Imperial Parliament in April 1953. The constitution was then subjected to a referendum in Southern Rhodesia. The voting revealed a sixty per cent. majority in favour of federation, a proportion not greatly differing from that in support of responsible government in 1923. A week later the scheme was submitted to the Northern Rhodesia Legislative Council, and approved by seventeen votes to four, the minority consisting of the two African members and, to the surprise of the other Unofficials, the two Europeans nominated for African interests. The latter, John Moffat and the Rev. E. H. Nightingale, while approving of federation itself, took the line that it should not be forced against the wishes of the African people. In Nyasaland on 20 April the result was similar, the Asian member and one European voting against, while the two African members emphasized their hostility by walking out of the Council. It now remained for the Imperial Parliament to clear the last hurdle. In order to save time it was decided not to create the Federation by Act of Parliament, but to introduce a Permissive Federation Bill empowering the Queen to create the new constitution by Order in Council. The Bill passed in May, the final arrangements were completed, and on 1 August the Federation (Constitution) Order in Council received the assent of Her Majesty.

The inauguration of the new Federal state in October by the first Governor-General, Lord Llewellyn, diminished but did not end the intensity of 'the great debate'. On the one hand, the political parties forming to press their policies on the electorate and in the Federal legislature differed openly on the course the

Federation should pursue, the Confederate Party campaigning for partition into black and white areas with the Northern Rhodesian railway belt combined with Southern Rhodesia. On the other, the Labour Party in Britain now openly opposed the new constitution as having been forced through against the wishes of the majority of the inhabitants; and as the Federal constitution was to come up for review in 1960–62 a question mark as to its future hung faintly but unmistakably on the horizon. Meanwhile, African opposition in the Northern territories and especially in Nyasaland continued to smoulder, occasionally fanned to a blaze by nationalist leaders and foreign sympathizers.

Yet there was no violent outbreak, and little evidence even of deteriorating race relations. Dauti Yamba's claim that Africans in the north would continue to fight against Federation tooth and nail appeared an empty threat. It seemed that the builders of Federation had been right in their view that Africans needed only to be given a firm and determined lead for their antagonism to crumble. Certainly there was much African surprise when the Federal Party, pledged to partnership and a liberal programme, swept the board in the Federal elections of January 1954, leaving its segregationist Confederate opponents with only one seat.[22] Confederates however gained one-third of the votes cast in Southern Rhodesia, and African suspicions remained. Smuts, victor in the Union in 1919, had been replaced by Hertzog in 1924, and Hertzog had ultimately given way to Malan. What guarantee was there that events would not follow a similar pattern in Central Africa? That the Federation should have been allowed to be born in this atmosphere of mutual distrust was already seen to have been the great mistake of the statesmen who conceived it. Yet distrust was probably unavoidable. The deciding factor, once the British Government had been persuaded, was the predominantly white electorate of Southern Rhodesia. Huggins, whatever his own views, knew that to concede too much to African aspirations in the 'black north' would founder the scheme in his own colony. The supremely confident exponent of liberal white leadership, and inheritor of the Rhodes tradition of acting first and justifying afterwards, he and his followers were resolved to have a united Central Africa as the best hope for all its peoples, and as

African opposition, though regrettable, was not insuperable, it must be set aside.

Two questions remain to be considered: the urgency with which Federation was treated by its supporters, and the nature of African opposition to the scheme.

The sense of haste with which Federation was urged by its supporters in Britain as well as in Rhodesia derived principally from economic arguments. In the first place, both the Rhodesias and to a lesser extent Nyasaland were confronted by two inter-related problems—the communications bottleneck and the shortage of fuel and power. While the national product was over twice as large in 1956 as in 1946 and was increasing at a cumulative rate of over ten per cent. per annum, development in the fields of transport and power was stationary.[23] The single track lines traversing hundreds of miles from the ports of Cape Town, Beira and Lobito Bay could no longer cope with the traffic. In the early days they had been more than sufficient with the result that high freight charges had been an obstacle to development. Now the position was reversed. One solution was to construct new lines giving access to additional ports. Since the thirties, when trade relations with South Africa deteriorated, Huggins' Government had been pressing for a railway line through Northern Bechuanaland and South West Africa to Walvis Bay, but nothing had come of this proposal. More success attended the project for a line from Salisbury to Lorenço Marques, which was eventually opened in 1955, and relieved the pressure on Beira. In 1957 the weight of goods on the line south of the Copperbelt was reduced by the conclusion of an agreement with the Belgian and Portuguese Governments, permitting through transit at cheaper rates between Rhodesia and Lobito Bay.

Another approach to the rail traffic problem, however, was to reduce the amount of coal transported by providing alternative sources of power for mining. In 1953 the Copperbelt needed 80,000 tons of coal a month, but was receiving only 54,000 tons. The mines consequently had to burn wood, which was three times as expensive, and to import coal via Lobito Bay from South Africa and the United States. Hydro-electric power would help to solve this problem by taking the place of the thermal power stations in existence, and reducing congestion on the railways.[24]

The need for hydro-electric power was becoming paramount in its own right. From the point of view of the Copperbelt alone, the rate of expansion showed in 1950 that within ten years new thermal stations would be required, or much more hydro-electric power be imported from the Congo. The consumption of electricity had multiplied fivefold between 1940 and 1950, and the rate of increase was accelerating. The need for a large hydro-electric project on the Zambezi or the Kafue was increasingly apparent. The fact that this project would supply power to both Northern and Southern Rhodesia was, as it had been long ago in 1923, an argument in favour of closer association. In additional support, the view was constantly stressed that one large state would attract the necessary capital more easily than two or three small ones. So it came about that the Kariba Gorge, which Livingstone had looked upon with despair as a fatal blow to his hopes of an inland waterway, was now regarded as the power-source of Central Africa.

Quite apart from the Kariba project, the economy of Southern Rhodesia was causing some concern. There was a growing difficulty in balancing overseas trade, and domestic expenditure, including the outlay involved in the land revolution, seemed likely to prove enormous. Despite its higher revenue than that of Northern Rhodesia ($£16\frac{1}{2}$ millions in 1951 compared with $£11$ millions) its exports and revenues were expanding more slowly than those in the north.[25] Unable to stand alone therefore, the colony was once more in danger of falling within the South African orbit, from which fate only the copper revenues could reliably sustain it. This consideration weighed with the British Government also. The Union's demand for the High Commission territories, and for Bechuanaland in particular, could be more firmly resisted from the powerful stance that a Central African Federation would provide.

On the other hand the rising tide of African political expression was plain to see. If northern Africans were bound to oppose closer association with hitherto white-dominated Southern Rhodesia, the early fifties were the latest time at which their opposition could be safely overruled. This was even more true of Nyasaland, on whose manpower the two Rhodesias so largely drew, and expenditure on whose development was proving an increasing burden on the British exchequer. Territories in East as well as West Africa were moving towards independence but Nyasaland at this stage could hardly stand alone. Its people might fervently echo Sir Charles Coghlan's dictum of 1922 about 'liberty in rags' but this was a sentiment with which the British Government could hardly be expected to agree.

The British Government was in fact facing an acute dilemma, having to choose between the trusteeship principle and imperial economic and strategic considerations.[26] The debate resolved itself along party lines by raising the issue of the rightness of imposing a political system on a reluctant majority. The right wing in Britain tried to deny the existence of African opinion, thus questioning the application of democratic principle which requires that authority should wait on the consent of the governed. The left wing, possessed of a burning conviction that the uninformed mass does have an opinion, attacked Federation on this issue. 'To force through Federation', declared a Labour peer in the House of Lords, 'would be a betrayal of all that we as a people stand for.' Behind the debate, and explaining its acrimony, was the assumption that Federation would lead to a self-governing dominion. Hence the reservation in the preamble to the constitution, an 'entrenched clause' which more than any other single factor provided the way out of the dilemma.

The other question arising out of the events of these critical months was the motive for African opposition to the Federal scheme.[27] There was more to it than an instinctive fear of change imposed from without. African spokesmen at the time of the second London conference declared in the press that their hostility rested on two premises: the fear that Southern Rhodesian native policy would be extended to the two Northern territories, and anxiety lest self-government should be granted to one race before the other was able to play at least an equal part.[28] Great stress was laid on the treaties signed between the old chiefs and Queen Victoria's representatives which were believed to hold the political future of the African peoples in trust till they should enter independence in their own right. Federation was regarded as a betrayal of this trust. In fact the treaties, as people acquainted with the facts had been quick to point out, contained no such meaning, except possibly Lochner's treaty, being expedients for the moment rather than blue-prints of the future. It was maintained, however, that these objections were rendered superfluous by the clauses of the pre-amble, and by the fact that native affairs were to remain the concern of territorial governments subject to Imperial control. This could weigh little with African opinion, to which en-trenched clauses were notoriously fragile, and which regarded Federation as a disguised step towards amalgamation for the sole purpose of maintaining white supremacy as they saw it existing in Southern Rhodesia. The way to apartheid, they considered, was evidently to be paved with partnership. While the compilers of the 1951 white paper had declared that the differences in native policies were 'more apparent than real'; to Africans, many of whom had lived and worked on both sides of the Zambezi, they were real enough.

Behind it all was the fact of more white people in Southern Rhodesia. The spirit of the colony was the spirit of a white man's country, and was a spirit which no African nationalist in the north could be expected to tolerate. 'Black nationalism' had become a term of political abuse to European Rhodesians, who were prone to overlook the fact that some of their own par-tisans frequently displayed a white nationalism that was no easier to justify. True it might be that white supremacy meant 'civilization' while black nationalism did not, and that Africans in the Rhodesias and Nyasaland had not yet reached a stage at which, even had they the opportunity, they could form a work-able African state like those now mapped out for the British West African dependencies. But Rhodesian leaders overlooked the fact that African peoples, excluded from the society of the ruling class, were bound to react as a community with an ethos of its own; a community in which self-respect and pride of race would surely and rightly create a deep desire for self-expression and self-assertion. This is a law of nature and to impose the chains of the police state on its manifestation might appear an inevitable, but would certainly be a dangerous way out of the dilemma. The Federal Government had no police of its own, and African advancement was a matter for the territories; but policies in the different parts of the Federation were bound to approximate as the Africans in all three territories made common cause. Because the Federal legislature at least when it was born represented a largely European electorate, and most of the Europeans were in Southern Rhodesia, the attitude of the colony's whites would predominate in its counsels.

Southern Rhodesian Africans, however, were more confident in themselves in the memory of having put up a stiff fight at the beginning, and, having learned at closer quarters to trust and co-operate with their rulers, were more amenable to their situation and the future hope it offered. It was otherwise with Northern Africans, who considered that they had never been conquered and had never submitted to trial by battle. Honour and pride are among the mainsprings of human effort. African peoples, passing from the submissive, passive and sometimes pitiable condition to which the occupation, following on earlier disasters, had rendered them, were awakening to a new consciousness and dynamism which called for new and positive European thinking. The proclaiming of a meaningless partnership would hardly meet the case.

These things northern African leaders in 1953 foresaw. While they knew that they could not do without Europeans for a long time to come, the hope they had conceived of ultimately taking a leading part in running the show, if not of running it altogether, now burned more dimly. If the Federation were to be justified, if it were even to survive at all, means must be found whereby this hope could be revived.

The Attempt at Federation

An uneasy and expectant calm settled over the political scene in the three territories of the Federation in 1954. For the present, the conflict was over. Further efforts from those who had resisted the new development could be of little avail for the time being. The force of the *fait accompli* had again triumphed. Africans, having surrendered to an ingrained tradition of white leadership, waited with some pessimism for the Federal Party's policy of partnership to prove itself an honest reality or a political device. Northern Civil Servants resigned themselves to co-operation with and probably growing subordination to a Federal authority that was from the outset dominated by southern influence. Sir Godfrey Huggins and the architects of Federation, fortified by a large majority in the Federal Assembly and by a strong United Party administration in Southern Rhodesia led by Garfield Todd, prepared to consolidate their gains.

Two important decisions that had to be made early on did little to abate fears that southern voices would speak loudest in Federal counsels. The first was the placing of the new capital at Salisbury. The possibility of siting it at Lusaka or Livingstone, or even at some other Southern Rhodesian township, had been mooted but was brushed aside for reasons that were administratively sound but which weighed not at all with African opinion in the northern territories, particularly in Nyasaland. About the second decision, the question of the alternative hydro-electric schemes of Kariba and Kafue, Africans were less concerned. Northern Rhodesians, especially commercial interests in Lusaka, were particularly anxious for the latter plan, which would cost less and be completed in a shorter time, to be adopted. After much debate the advice of engineering consultants was accepted, and in 1955 the decision to build the Kariba dam was made. It was a sound decision, for though the credit resources of the Federation were to be strained to the utmost, the power requirements of the Copperbelt for which tremendous investment programmes were in train, as well as of industry elsewhere, would need the Kariba potential; but once again it appeared that the Southern Rhodesians were having things all their own way. Northern Rhodesian Europeans, and African leaders, aware that the great and growing wealth of the territory's mineral output was no longer being wholly ploughed back into their own development, were restive; but discontent was quietened by the boom in copper, reflected in building and other construction enterprise, which created an aura of prosperity during the first two years, and which appeared to augur well for the Federation's economic future.

This was a piece of good fortune which well suited the leaders of the Federal Party, who had all along made economic progress the main plank of their political platform. They still tended to overlook the fact that in the long run the Federation must stand or fall by African support. Africans were and are dubious about the value of economic benefits brought to them by the new order.[1] African opinion in Southern Rhodesia was still not clearly voiced. In the north economic progress reflected in the construction of social amenities had been a feature of development prior to Federation, and there had been no apparent reason why it should not accelerate in any case. Nyasalanders, who had most to gain, were accustomed to slower progress and had no wish to surrender, as they supposed, their nationalist aspirations to European domination in exchange for material benefits. Political freedom and social equality mattered, for the rising African élite, more than all else. That was what partnership promised. But during the first two years little was done to implement the promise. A great opportunity was missed. Five years were to pass before the United Federal Party, faced with the imminence of the constitutional review, made any real effort to win over moderate African opinion. By that time it was dangerously late.

None the less, steps were taken during these two years towards more liberal policies, which should not be overlooked. It is important to bear in mind that African affairs were nowhere the direct responsibility of the Federal Government. The Federal Party professed partnership but except in the public service and the Federal constitution, the burden of social and political reform was to be borne by the territorial administrations.

In Southern Rhodesia, reform of the trade union law was discussed, but the proposals were not to bear fruit till 1957. A progressive home ownership scheme for town Africans received favourable comment abroad. Most striking perhaps were minor amendments to the Land Apportionment Act, with the object of providing for the forthcoming establishment of a multi-racial University College in the European area of Salisbury, of which the foundation stone had been laid in 1953. Multi-racial attendance at clubs and hotels was also provided for, and professional men were permitted to practise in Salisbury irrespective of race. For these small inroads into the structure of the Act to be really effective, a change of heart among the European population was necessary, but this was not forthcoming in so short a time. The amendments were in fact passed in the teeth of strong opposition.

In Northern Rhodesia the Colonial Office had determined to accompany its partial abandonment of responsibility with a measure of political reform. Talks, which began before Federation, had nearly foundered on the rocks of European settler disapproval led by Roy Welensky. The latter was transferred to the Federal arena as Minister of Transport and Development in September, but local opposition continued and the final change was small enough. Two more elected Europeans were added to the Legislative Council making a total of twelve, while there were to be four nominated Africans instead of two. These, with two nominated Europeans to represent African interests, supported by eight Officials, left things much as before with a Government/African majority of two over the settler 'opposition'. In the Executive Council also the Official majority was preserved though reduced.[2]

The Northern Rhodesian franchise remained almost a hundred per cent. European, since only British subjects, among which there were perhaps ten Africans in the territory, might vote. Even the liberal resolutions introduced in the Council by Sir John Moffat, and passed with only one dissentient in July 1954, did not envisage any immediate change, but rather a 'period of transition' during which mutual fears of racial domination should be removed. Harry Nkumbula, President-General of the African National Congress, welcomed the resolutions, but any hopes of rapid change in the public attitude to the colour bar were disappointed. As the result of Congress action, segregation was ended in some of the territory's post offices late in 1955, and a campaign against the treatment of Africans in butchers' shops led in 1956 to the ending of the objectionable 'hatch' system in Lusaka butcheries and some other shops as well, and to the setting up of Race Conciliation Advisory Boards, to investigate cases of racial discrimination.

In Nyasaland, with its smaller European population, relations between Government and people had generally been good, and the outburst against Federation early in 1953 was followed by a return to normal conditions. The land question provided Nyasalanders with their abiding political anxiety, and the first months of the new order exploded the nationalist myth of large-scale European acquisition of African land. Fear lingered, however. Wellington Chirwa, the outspoken Nyasaland African in the Federal Parliament, continued to denounce Federation in terms which European politicians held up as evidence all too plain of African political immaturity. A radical advance in the Protectorate's constitution might have persuaded African opinion that their hopes of an all African government were consistent with the Federal framework, but the modest step forward in 1955 was hardly likely to achieve that object. The Legislative Council, hitherto of twenty members, with the Governor as Chairman, half Official and half Unofficial, was increased by raising the African membership from three to five. Their choice was still determined by indirect election and Government nomination, as in Northern Rhodesia. European and Asian members were now to be elected instead of being nominated as previously. There was still no provision for Africans on the Executive Council. Disappointing though these provisions might appear in retrospect, however, they were on the one hand denounced by the right-wing Europeans in the Federation as too radical, and on the other accepted by the African leaders in Nyasaland as sufficient for the time being. The Nyasaland African Congress, while not abating its perennial hostility to Federation, co-operated to the extent that three of the five Africans in the new Council were Congress members. Trouble was stored up for the future.

It is doubtful whether a larger measure of African representation at this stage would have altered the outcome, unless accompanied by a more sympathetic treatment of African grievances, particularly about land. None the less, it was only at this stage that a bid for Nyasaland African support for Federation might successfully have been made.

Taken all round, this was a modest record indeed of progress towards social and political partnership during the first two vital years. Perhaps more could hardly have been expected in view of the forces in the field. On the one hand was the Colonial Office, hampered by a tradition of gradualism. Facing it in Central Africa were ranged a dominant political party whose electorate was bemused by the success of Southern Rhodesian white paternalism; an influential press; and the financial power of large industrial concerns, of whom the copper companies significantly moved their headquarters from London to Salisbury during 1954. Behind these again was the general settler belief that immigration was all the time serving to redress the balance, and that to give the Africans too much too soon was to lose tricks in a vital stage of the game. At the same time, the tragic events in Kenya appeared to many as a warning against too rapid an acceleration of African advance.

Towards the end of 1955 all parties were beginning to take stock. The Federal review conference was still five years away but it was clearly in sight on the horizon. The events of the intervening period would determine the course the Federation would take thereafter. European political leaders of all parties were bent on independence in one form or another in 1960. But no British Government was likely to concede any measure of independence, unless a substantial increase of African representation had been granted in the meantime. The prospect of the conference therefore bestirred all four administrations to consider new steps in African participation in government. African opinion, on the other hand, began to be aroused from the torpor induced by its defeat in 1953, and once more active opposition to Federation, stimulated by talk of independence which would spell doom for African nationalist hopes, began to appear in the northern territories. This was particularly evident during the Nyasaland elections of 1956.

Between the two extremes, new forms of liberalism emerged. Distinct among these was the Capricorn Africa Society. Founded in 1949 by David Stirling to advocate inter-racial conciliation in British East and Central African territories, this was essentially an aloof and expatriate organization. Expressly its aim was not to descend into the arena of politics, but to bring influence to bear on the leaders of all parties and all races towards the idea of a common citizenship. Its first real appearance on the Central African scene was with the publication of a handbook in July 1955, outlining policy.[3] An intensive campaign for recruiting members followed, culminating in a conference of delegates for all races at Salima on the shores of Lake Nyasa in 1956. Delegates at the conference signed a contract outlining the principles of Capricorn policy, including multi-racial trade unions, land reform, and a qualitative franchise based on the multiple vote. The contract evoked some liberal approval, but the Society's rejection of universal suffrage, and its association with Federation in the African mind, failed to win it wholehearted African support.

In the meantime, other minds were addressing themselves to

the critical problem of the franchise. The Federal Party, under fire from critics of the swollen Kariba estimate, of rising prices and lack of leadership, needed a new tactic with which to recover waning prestige. In March 1956, Sir Godfrey Huggins, now Lord Malvern, shrewd as ever, presented the public with his conception of two multi-racial common rolls, with a higher and a lower qualification. On this and subsequent occasions it became clear that the 'two tier' proposal was framed with the object of reconciling two principles: that the political domination of Europeans by Africans must never come about; and that party divisions along racial lines must at all costs be avoided. The Federal Government now planned to draft a new franchise law within the next few months. In May 1956 the Southern Rhodesian Government moved in the same direction with the appointment of a Commission under the chairmanship of Sir Robert Tredgold, to investigate a new franchise system for the colony 'under which the Government is placed and remains in the hands of civilized and responsible people'. The remainder of the year 1956 was thus taken up with much debate on the subject of varieties of communal representation, amid rumours of disagreement between Garfield Todd and Welensky who had succeeded Malvern earlier in the year.

The Tredgold Report was published in March 1957.[4] Its recommendations were based on a system of two voters' rolls in single member constituencies. The upper roll was confined to people of either race who were British subjects, and who satisfied a fairly high standard of combined education and property qualifications. The lower or special roll gave votes to those with an income of over £15 a month, provided that the total number of special votes should never exceed in value more than a third of the total votes cast. Neither roll was exclusively confined to one race, though to begin with the upper roll would be predominantly European, and the lower predominantly African. The Commission adhered to the principle that though every man had a right to a say in his own government, this did not imply an inalienable right to vote; that the qualification of twenty-one years in a universal suffrage system was itself an arbitrary one; and that the vote called for an exercise of responsibility and skill. The Report was a weighty document, and will probably prove of abiding interest to students of constitutional law particularly in multi-racial societies. All three members of this commission were former chief justices, the Chairman himself having had long experience in Central Africa and having political connections that were liberal rather than otherwise. Their conclusions were to form the basis of European political thinking in the Federation, especially in Southern Rhodesia, for some years ahead; while even in Northern Rhodesia it became generally accepted that 'democracy', if not itself a questionable shibboleth, was certainly inapplicable to African states, and above all to multi-cultured societies. It looked as though the principle of the qualified vote had come to stay.

In reaction to this principle African nationalists, criticizing not quite accurately the relegation of Africans to the position of second-class citizens, and with their eyes on developments in West Africa, increasingly declaimed their insistence on universal suffrage, and 'one man—one vote' became a slogan of the African political platform.

The first outcome of the Tredgold Report was the publication by the Federal Government of a Constitution Amendment Bill in May 1957. This was followed in June by the announcement by Sir Roy Welensky of a scheme for a new Federal franchise. Only three months later, in September, did the Southern Rhodesian Franchise Bill, for the purpose of which the Tredgold Commission had presented their report, come before the Southern Rhodesian Parliament. It was apparent that the Southern Rhodesian and Federal Governments were acting in concert, and the steps being taken were associated in the public mind with Sir Roy's negotiations in London during April. It had then been agreed that the Federal Assembly was unmanageably small, and should be enlarged, though the future racial balance had not been specified. The franchise was to be altered, and Welensky's major concession had been that a reasonable number of British Protected Persons, in other words Northern Rhodesian and Nyasaland Africans, should be allowed to vote. This concession, and the shelving of the status question till 1960, caused an outcry among right-wing critics in Rhodesia, which abated little with the publication of the Constitution Amendment Bill on 22 May. In June the significant by-election at Mrewa near Salisbury, hitherto a safe

Federal Party seat, resulted in a victory for Winston Field, leader of the segregationist Dominion Party. It appeared to the British Government that in negotiations over the coming constitutional legislation, it would be wiser not to keep Welensky, hitherto regarded by many as the white hope of realistic liberalism in Central Africa, on too tight a rein.[5]

The Constitution Amendment Bill passed the Federal Parliament on 31 July 1957, increasing the membership of the Assembly to fifty-nine, of whom twelve would be Africans and three Europeans representing African interests. The African Affairs Board reported the Bill as a differentiating measure since it reduced the proportion of effective African representation. The sister piece of legislation, the Federal Electoral Bill, introduced in September, became law in January 1958. It provided for two rolls with qualifications similar to those recommended by the Tredgold Report; but whereas the forty-four elected members of any race could only be chosen by voters on the upper roll, the eight African members were to be chosen by members of both rolls. This would mean that, with the possible exception of Nyasaland, African members would be elected principally by European voters, a feature intentionally designed to prevent African 'extremists' from entering the Assembly.[6] To this, however, the African Affairs Board objected, and once again reported the Bill as a differentiating measure.

Both Bills were debated in the House of Commons, and in both cases motions of amendment from the Labour Party were defeated, and the objections of the African Affairs Board were overruled. Africans had from the outset doubted the effective force of the Board. Their doubts now appeared to have been fully justified. The British Government was evidently in league with Sir Roy Welensky. Though the elections of 1958 were still to come, African opinion hardened towards non-cooperation in Federal affairs and resistance to Federal policies.

Meanwhile in Southern Rhodesia Garfield Todd's United Rhodesia Party Government had announced its own proposals in June. These were more closely in line with the Tredgold Report, in that voters on the special or lower roll would join with ordinary voters in electing members of Parliament. But special voters could only be registered in number up to one-sixth of the total number of ordinary voters in the colony—a restriction which the Tredgold Commission had not envisaged. Thereafter the special income qualification of £20 a month was to be raised to £60. Todd's object had been to ensure the registration of Africans with ten years' education, and he had threatened to resign if a Bill giving effect to this aim were not passed. But the outcome was hardly enough to evoke enthusiastic African support, while the Prime Minister's stand for liberalism undermined his position in his own party.[7]

The rift between Todd and the rest of his cabinet (as much a question of personalities as of policies) was indeed widening. It had been accompanied by a move to co-ordinate the work of the United Rhodesia Party operating in Southern Rhodesia, and Welensky's Federal Party. In November 1957 the two groups combined into the United Federal Party, in which was included that branch of the Federal Party led by John Roberts, a Lusaka farmer, in the Northern Rhodesia Legislative Council. Todd, becoming increasingly isolated, returned from holiday in January 1958 to face a cabinet crisis and a demand for his resignation. At a party congress in February a new government was established under Sir Edgar Whitehead, a former civil servant now recalled from embassy duties in Washington. Todd was included in the cabinet, but in April left the U.F.P. to revive the old United Rhodesia Party, this time based on Liberal and African support. In view of the realignment of parties, a general election was clearly necessary, and in May the Southern Rhodesian Parliament was dissolved. The election of 5 June was based on the new franchise, but less than 1600 Africans had registered and not all of these took part. The result was a moderate victory for the United Federal Party, which won seventeen seats against the Dominion Party's thirteen. The United Rhodesia Party returned no member, and Todd himself was defeated. His fate exposed the dilemma of white liberals in Central Africa. 'Mr. Todd', wrote the *Economist*, 'has never learnt the basic lesson mastered years ago by Sir Roy Welensky and Lord Malvern, that a Rhodesian politician can put a significant amount of liberal and progressive legislation on the statute book, and still be re-elected, provided that he does not shout about it, and that when he does make a public statement, he emphasizes his conservatism and his determination to maintain the high standards of white civilization.'8

African opinion, resentful of interference in rural life through the new Land Husbandry Act, disappointed in Whitehead's refusal to act on the Plewman Commission's recommendations for reform in the urban locations, proceeded to further disillusionment. Support grew for the new African National Congress. This organization had been formed by the amalgamation in 1957 of the African National Youth League with the last surviving branch, at Bulawayo, of the old S.R. Congress. Its president was Joshua Nkomo, a former social welfare worker on Rhodesia Railways, who had attended the London Conference of 1952 and strongly opposed the Federal scheme; but the most powerful force was George Nyandoro, an able speaker and dynamic leader who roused rural Africans against the new land laws.

The Federal elections followed in the autumn of 1958. Here the issue was not the pace of African advancement, but the question of independence for the Federation and how to achieve it. The general confidence of the predominantly European electorate in the experience and leadership of Sir Roy Welensky and his superior ability to negotiate gave the United Federal Party an overwhelming majority with forty-six seats. The Dominion Party gained eight, and the new liberal Central Africa Party, led by Todd in Southern Rhodesia and Sir John Moffat, who had resigned from the African Affairs Board, in the north, won three seats, all of them in Northern Rhodesia. Few Africans took part, the Nyasaland African Congress and extremist Zambia Congress in Northern Rhodesia boycotting the election altogether. Opinion in Britain generally showed relief that the comparative success of the Dominion Party in Southern Rhodesia had not been repeated in the Federal sphere.

Meanwhile in Northern Rhodesia also a fresh constitutional advance took place in 1958. Elected members in the Legislative Council had been pressing for this since 1957, and in March 1958 two sets of proposals were published by the Government and United Federal Party respectively. They were similar in principle, based once again on the Tredgold two-tier pattern, though the U.F.P. plan was more favourable to European interests. When the Colonial Secretary, Lennox Boyd, published the British Government's scheme in a white paper in September, it amounted to a compromise between these two; subsequent concessions were made to U.F.P. pressure. The essence of the scheme was that there should be not only special and ordinary voters' rolls, but special as well as ordinary constituencies, the latter being along the line of rail. There were also to be four extra constituencies, in two of which Africans would elect Europeans, while in the other two Europeans elected Africans. The probable outcome would be a Legislative Council membership of fourteen Europeans and eight Africans, the latter supported by two nominated Africans and six Official members. The executive council would have an Unofficial majority, but at least two ministers must be African.[9]

African opinion has always been more clearly voiced north of the Zambezi than in the south. During recent years, African solidarity had been forcefully demonstrated during the wages and advancement negotiations on the Copperbelt. The National Congress now reacted sharply against the constitutional proposals, that denied any prospect of parity, and would sustain a high qualification for the ordinary voter for a long time to come. In June the white paper was burned at a Congress meeting. The African Representative Council demanded secession from the Federation. At an emergency Congress meeting in Lusaka, a powerful wing, led by Kenneth Kaunda and Simon Kapwepwe, passed resolutions strongly critical of Nkumbula's leadership. Kaunda and some of his supporters were expelled, and subsequently formed the Zambia African National Congress. Zambia's policy was to be uncompromising—a complete boycott of the new constitution and an unrelenting demand for secession from the Federation.[10]

Thus by the end of 1958 attitudes in Central Africa were hardening. The United Federal Party, determined on some form of Dominion status within three years, was established with secure majorities in three of the four governments—majorities that were based on electorates intended to be predominantly European for a long time to come. It was able to present a firm front alike to the right-wing Dominion Party, strongest in Southern Rhodesia, to the liberal opposition, most effective in the north, to African nationalism prowling at the gates, and to the British Government, whose gaze was already being diverted by the prospect of a general election in 1959. African organizations, on the other hand, despairing at last of partnership, dreading the outcome of the 1961 conference on the status of the Federation, and hoping to imprint their views indelibly on the minds of those who would form the forthcoming new administration in London, were growing increasingly militant, above all in Nyasaland.

Since the moderate constitutional reform of 1955, the Nyasaland African Congress leaders had grown steadily more outspoken. Chipembere in Legislative Council took the lead, in demanding the resignation of Chirwa and Kumbikano from the Federal Assembly; in calling for the return of Dr Banda to Nyasaland to lead the national movement; in resisting every measure that served to strengthen the administrative and economic links between Nyasaland and the Federation; and finally in February 1957 in walking out of the Council when the proposal to federalize European agriculture was discussed. Soon after this the Nyasaland Government withdrew its recognition of the Congress, explaining that circumstances had changed since recognition was first accorded in 1944.

There followed an increasing bitterness in the attitude of Congress and a growing atmosphere of potential violence. The two Nyasaland members of the Federal Assembly, refusing to resign their seats, were expelled from the party and Lord Home, visiting the Protectorate in October, was told that no compromise was possible. African members boycotted the Council meeting of April 1958 which approved the Federal Electoral Bill. In July 1958 Dr Hastings Banda, who had been out of the territory for thirty years but had been in continuous contact with African leaders, arrived in Blantyre to assume leadership of the African Congress. Banda started by demanding universal suffrage and an African majority in the Legislative Council. During five months his tone became increasingly extreme. In December 1958 he left the territory to attend the first pan-African Congress at Accra in company with other African leaders including Nkumbula and Kaunda from Northern Rhodesia. At this conference the Central African delegates together signed a declaration pledging them to break up the

Federation. Returning via Salisbury, where he introduced an African crowd to his infectious cry of '*Kwacha!*'—'the Dawn!'— Banda arrived back in Nyasaland to find that his policy of arousing the maximum emotional opposition to Federation was succeeding beyond his hopes, perhaps beyond his powers of control. He was in fact absent from the emergency Congress meeting held in the open air on 10 January at which there was much wild talk threatening a campaign of violence and bloodshed. During February destructive and disorderly incidents, ranging from the setting up of road blocks to the destruction of government property, were reported from all parts of the Protectorate. The projected visit of Lord Perth for constitutional discussions was postponed.

A threatening situation was in fact developing in all three territories. It was true that the respective African nationalist movements were not yet closely concerted. The Southern Rhodesian Congress was chiefly concerned with policies in the colony, notably the Land Husbandry Act, and was even anxious to maintain Federation. Many Northern Rhodesian Africans resented Banda's attempt to take Nyasaland out of the Federation, since it would weaken the overall balance of black against white; Nkumbula had denounced Banda on this question in December. But all three movements were mounting powerful emotional campaigns.

Sir Edgar Whitehead's Government was the first to act. Preferring as he afterwards explained to forestall violence rather than to wait for it to occur, the Prime Minister declared a state of emergency in the colony on 26 February. Some five hundred Africans were arrested. During the following weeks six Bills were passed, notably the Unlawful Organizations and Preventive Detention Bills which were to last five years, empowering the Government to detain people without trial for lengthy periods. The Congress Party was proscribed. The objects of these measures, whose interference with the rule of law was so blatant that they had to be modified in face of a spirited protest from the churches and the Bar Association, were both immediate and long term. A five-year plan for the implementation of the Land Husbandry Act was under way and was arousing African opposition. George Nyandoro was touring the rural areas inciting the people against the Govern-

ment's cutting and grazing regulations, and insistently contrasted the crowded reserves with the spacious ranchlands of
the white farmer beyond the demarcation line. A pressure was
clearly building up that could crack the framework of Land
Apportionment from within, and with it the whole basis of the
colony's policy of parallel development that had not yet been
overtly disowned. Whitehead's action, generally supposed to
have the purpose of freeing Southern Rhodesian troops for
service in Nyasaland if necessary, was as much concerned with
the vital need for a few clear years to master the land revolution,
that could be paralysed by political opposition, as with the
wider crisis in the Federation.

A week after the Southern Rhodesian declaration, Sir
Robert Armitage declared a state of emergency in Nyasaland.
A situation had been reached there in which, as the Devlin
Report later remarked, the Government had 'to act or abdi-
cate'. Over six hundred Africans, including Banda himself, were
detained, some of the arrests being accompanied or followed by
scenes of violence, notably at Nkata Bay, where twenty Africans
were killed. At the Government's request, Federal troops from
Southern Rhodesia were drafted to the Protectorate to assist
in the maintenance of order. The decision caused an outburst
of protest from liberals within the Federation and overseas.
Critics, particularly the Labour Party in London, declared that
the Nyasaland Congress had never intended to achieve its aims
by violence, and that Sir Robert Armitage had been
dragooned into taking the action he did by Sir Roy Welensky,
alleged to be anxious for a showdown with African nationalism in
all three territories. The Devlin Commission, however, reporting later in the year, while outspokenly describing Nyasaland
as a 'police state', firmly rebutted both these charges.[11]

The Government of Northern Rhodesia, though managing to
avert a declaration of emergency, none the less had to face its
own crisis. Elections under the new franchise were due in
March. Kaunda, returning in December 1958 from the Accra
conference, continued to lead his Zambia Congress Party in an
uncompromising attack on the new constitution, and proposed
to boycott the election. The old National Congress under
Nkumbula, on the other hand, while opposed to the constitution, was prepared to work with it for the time being. This

division in the African ranks weakened the nationalist force in the territory, but intimidation by Zambia was expected.[12] The authorities were particularly anxious for African co-operation, and on 11 March the Zambia Congress was proscribed, its leaders being rusticated to remote parts of the country. The elections which followed in April were without incident. The new Central Africa Party, led by Sir John Moffat, who had resigned his seat in the Federal Assembly after the failure of the African Affairs Board's attempt to stay the Federal Constitution Bill, won four seats. Nkumbula was returned on an African National Congress ticket. The United Federal Party with thirteen seats, while unable to outvote the liberal/official forces, provided an opposition which the Government could not afford consistently to overrule.

The dry season of 1959 saw a reaction of calm after the storms of March. The forces of order were on the alert, and African organizations were disarrayed by the detention of their leaders. Despite talk in Southern Rhodesia and Nyasaland of keeping dangerous elements behind bars for years if necessary, detained Africans were being released by stages later in the year. Kaunda was allowed freedom of movement in January 1960 and Banda, mainly owing to pressure from the new Colonial Secretary, Iain Macleod, was released the following April. Meanwhile in November 1959 the return to power of Macmillan's Conservative Party dashed African hopes of a reversal of policy from a Labour administration.

The events of February and March had none the less had profound effects. On the African side, policies of disorganized violence were discredited, and tendencies emerged on the one hand of subtler intimidation to close the ranks and on the other of explicitly non-violent propaganda. New parties replaced those that had been proscribed—the Malawi Congress in Nyasaland, the National Democratic Party in Southern Rhodesia, and the United National Independence Party in Northern Rhodesia. These were not rivals to the former parties, but were rather the old organizations revived in a more disciplined, better organized and more legitimate guise. Closely watched by the authorities, they now had the qualified support of liberals at home and most of world opinion abroad. The National Democratic Party, quickly recovering a militant spirit, continued to attack the Southern Rhodesian constitution and to organize opposition to the Land Husbandry Act in the reserves. Outbreaks of violence in 1959 in Salisbury and Bulawayo brought the deaths of African rioters, and the colony had to drop its proud claim that no blood had been shed in racial conflict since 1896. National Democratic Party organizers were detained; though Joshua Nkomo, who did not return from England until the following year, was then able to assume leadership of the party. The Malawi Congress, on the other hand, and to a lesser extent the United National Independence Party, with Banda and Kaunda once more in the field, moderated the tone of their politics and showed themselves prepared to co-operate in the northern territories where new constitutions were inaugurated in 1960 and 1961.[13]

On the side of Government and of most European opinion, the effects of the crisis were equally far-reaching. In Southern Rhodesia, the ferment produced some reluctant reappraisal from the moderate wing of the United Federal Party. On 10 February 1959 Burrows declared in Parliament that 'we have abandoned parallel development, we can forget it; it is outmoded, it is finished. We are now agreed on a policy of partnership, which is an entirely different thing.'[14] He was not contradicted, but that a leading politician should have felt the need for so emphatic a statement six years after the colony entered the Federation indicated the reservation with which many Southern Rhodesians had all along regarded the partnership principle. Even now powerful forces were prepared to fight a rearguard action over land segregation. Everything, it was contended, must still be done to retain the European area intact. Large private estates must be subdivided, immigration encouraged. The Government, whatever its views, had to handle this situation delicately; the Dominion Party now had the weapon it had been waiting for, and used it effectively during the debates on the moderate Land Apportionment Amendment Bill in 1959, which permitted hotels in the European area to become multi-racial. The Prime Minister was even now constrained to deny that he was one of those who wanted to do away with the Land Apportionment Act.

Meanwhile, rising hopes of independence for the Federation in 1960 had been blown away like smoke before a gale. The

Federal Government in the coming negotiations with Britain was thrown inevitably on the defensive. As always, however, it had two powerful assets, already used with constant effect by Huggins before 1953—the danger to British influence in Southern Africa which would ensue upon a dissolution of the Federation, and the blow to all hopes of a successful multi-racial state. Disintegrating forces were powerfully at work. Apart from the irreconcilable northern African parties, the liberal Central Africa Party was calling for a modification at least of the Federal structure. The Dominion Party as always aimed at a 'Central African alliance' of black and white states, but its Southern Rhodesian wing was soon to form splinter groups demanding separate independence for the colony. Against these movements the powerful but battered United Federal Party alone stood for perpetuation of Federation in its present form. Beyond doubt the only course lay in the conciliation of African opinion, and in the pursuit of this almost vain hope the party's propaganda machine in 1959 and 1960 commenced a country-wide campaign of wooing the African electorate and attracting African membership. It was mostly ineffective.

The immediate handling of African affairs was the responsibility of the territorial governments, and during 1959 the progress towards the old ideal of partnership, sluggishly implemented since 1953, was rapidly accelerated. In Southern Rhodesia Todd, who had startled the public by calling for British troops to protect Africans during the emergency, demanded a 'massive and immediate' end to the colour bar. Whitehead, who had first satisfied his countrymen by displaying a firm hand, plunged into a fresh programme designed to improve the social position of the African. A new Education Act planned to bring every African child into elementary school by 1964. The Trade Disputes Act, passed at length in March 1959, was to allow multi-racial trade unions by 1960. Separate counters in post offices were abolished, discrimination in the betting laws was removed, and the urban African housing programme accelerated. Most significant of all, perhaps, was the appointment of a Select Committee of Parliament to inquire into land policy. Its report in 1960, while defending the protective aspects of Land Apportionment, suggested that segregation might be relaxed in urban areas where new development was taking place; even more radical was the proposal, in a second report, that in due course the Act should be repealed altogether.[15]

In the other territories legislative activity was comparable. In Northern Rhodesia the Central Race Relations Advisory Board made recommendations leading to legislation which in 1960 put an end to racial discrimination in shops, cinemas, hotels and restaurants. The Nyasaland Government, while strengthening its police forces, continued its policy of resettling Africans living on private estates, permitted freedom of action to the Malawi Congress Party under Orton Chirwa and later Hastings Banda, and introduced an interim measure of constitutional reform which brought African representation on the legislature to seven, thus providing an African majority on the official side for the first time, and introduced two Africans to the Executive Council.

Such was the situation when the Royal Commission headed by Lord Monckton, appointed to make recommendations for the forthcoming conference to review the constitution of the Federation, arrived in the country in February 1960. Its membership and terms of reference had for many weeks been the subject of controversy. The main question at issue was whether the right of secession by a member territory should be a subject for consideration at the conference. Harold Macmillan, during the African tour which culminated in his address to the South African Parliament at Cape Town, had passed through the Federation in January and had then assured Welensky that the Commission would not be authorized to discuss the possible break-up of the Federation. None the less the Commission's report, when finally published in October after months of careful preparation, made it plain that its task had been impossible without recognizing secession as a political possibility.

Considering the force of opposing opinions and the urgency of the issues at stake, the Commission achieved a remarkable degree of unanimity, its report being signed by all but two of its twenty-five members. Recognizing that the dissolution of the Federation was undesirable on economic grounds, it stated in clear terms that if the association were to continue, African hostility must be overcome. There was therefore a need for 'drastic and fundamental changes' in the structure of the Federation and in the racial policies of Southern Rhodesia. The main recommendations were, first, that Africans should have a higher proportion of seats in the Federal Assembly and that the franchise should be extended in order to make the Assembly representative of 'the broad mass of both African and European opinion'; second, that the structure of the Federation should be altered by devolving powers on the Territorial Governments, leaving the Federal Government with responsibility only for external affairs, defence, and the control of the economy; third, that 'unfairly discriminatory legislation' should be removed in all territories, the Southern Rhodesian Pass Laws and Land Apportionment Act being particularly mentioned. Such equitability of laws between the races should be guaranteed by a Bill of Rights to be entrenched in the constitutions of the Federation and of the member territories, and by the establishment of Councils of State which would replace the African Affairs Board in which the people had lost confidence. Lastly the Commission advised that 'a declaration of the intention of Her Majesty's Government to permit secession by any of the Territories, if so requested after a stated time or at a particular stage of constitutional development, would have a very favourable effect, and might be decisive in securing a fair trial for the new association.'[16]

This last recommendation provoked indignant protests in Central Africa. Welensky, complaining that the British Premier had broken faith, declared bluntly that the proposal to permit secession by an individual territory would sound the death knell of the Federation. In the House of Commons debate on the report its defenders pointed out, however, that Lord Monckton had honoured his terms of reference by recommending that Federation should continue, and that a secession clause in the constitution would be a measure most likely to make its continuation possible. Here in fact lay the core of the difference between the points of view of the Federal and Imperial Governments. While the former considered that the Federation, whose survival was regarded as essential to the preservation of civilization in Central Africa, was the product of European leadership and could only be maintained through such leadership, the latter, observing the 'wind of change' in Africa, recognized that the initiative was passing to the African peoples. To deny this initiative its expression was to court disaster. To give it scope might be a 'leap in the dark', as Lord Derby once described the electoral reform of 1867, but such a revolutionary concession, if made in time, could reap a comparable reward.

The End of the Colonial Phase

The Federation was in fact doomed before the members of the Review Commission ever set foot on African soil. The final watershed had been crossed between 1956 and 1958. No such association can survive without the support of the mass of the people. The Africans in the north not only denied their support, but were by this time pathologically opposed to the whole system. The inability of the European leaders to recognize this fact was due to the dichotomy in Rhodesian society, and to the vast ignorance of contemporary African life and thought that was maintained by most of the white electorate. Many Europeans still spoke slightingly of Africans in their common speech. In the upper echelons of white society, moves towards liberalism were often marred by paternal condescension. These things damaged relationships and undermined attempts to create goodwill.

Beneath the surface the tide was beginning to run fast, while in the rest of the continent it was in full flood. Following the independence of the Sudan in 1956 and of Ghana in 1957, a rush of independent states appeared in 1960, including Nigeria, the Congo Republic and several former French territories. British East Africa was set on the same course. Against this tide the white minority of Southern Rhodesia, unshakably convinced of the rightness of their cause, resolved to make a stand. Their determination was stiffened by the course of events in the Congo, a vast, cumbersome and ill-prepared country in which orderly administration collapsed when the Belgian Government precipitately withdrew. The Congo disaster also influenced members of the right wing of the Conservative Party in Britain who, anxious to preserve this last bastion of empire, continued to give Welensky their marginal but vital support.

Following on the Commission's report, the conference to

review the constitution of the Federation met at Lancaster House in December 1960. It could according to statute have met at any time between 1960 and 1963, but Federal leaders, set on independence and aware that trouble was brewing, preferred to face the difficulties before the full storm burst. At this point was felt the force of Macmillan's policy, declared two years before. The future of the association must rest with the member states, and no decision on Federal independence could be taken until African-supported governments were established, especially in the northern Protectorates. After a fortnight of empty discussion the conference was therefore adjourned, pending the outcome of the territorial conference which had opened at the same time; that for Northern Rhodesia in Lancaster House, London, and that for Southern Rhodesia in Salisbury. A new constitution for Nyasaland, creating an African majority in the legislature, had already been enacted in July.

In the months ahead, Nyasaland was the pacemaker. Welensky had foreseen that Banda's release from detention in April would reopen the floodgates of Malawi nationalism, and that the Protectorate was as good as lost to the Federation. He was proved right. The elections under the new constitution in August 1961, while taking place in an orderly atmosphere that was in strong contrast to the turmoil of 1959, showed a very high percentage poll. Many walked up to ten miles to register their votes in the ballot box—a black rooster was the sign for Banda's Malawi Congress Party, while a leopard stood for the United Federal Party. The result was an overwhelming victory for the M.C.P., which returned twenty-two members against five U.F.P. and one Independent.

The succeeding twelve months saw an irresistible campaign for secession. The amount of intimidation exerted by M.C.P. agents was exaggerated by U.F.P. propaganda. Nevertheless there was intimidation and violence, mainly perpetrated by the extreme wing of the party led by Henry Chipembere, which even discouraged villagers from co-operating in the vaccination programme sponsored by the Federal Ministry of Health. Chiume, while denying this discouragement, admitted that the party would not support the Ministry's campaign. The number of deaths from smallpox increased sharply during 1961.[1] Banda, absent in London, sent a cable denouncing these methods and reminding M.C.P. supporters that they would soon have the best club with which to hit their opponents: their votes in the ballot box. The split between Banda and Chipembere was now openly visible. Banda himself insisted that Europeans were welcome to remain in the country provided that they would accept an African government, but he continued to denounce the association with the Rhodesias. The financial viability of an independent Malawi was secured when Britain agreed to finance the Protectorate's running deficit. In July 1962, rather than permit a new Federal link to be forged, the Nyasaland Government terminated negotiations with Salisbury for the financing of the Nkula Falls hydro-electric scheme.

Meanwhile, without pausing in his stride, Banda was negotiating for the next stage in the Protectorate's constitutional advance. Agreement was reached in November. There was to be a legislature elected on the basis of one man, one vote, with a limited number of seats reserved for Europeans. A predominantly African cabinet would be led by a Prime Minister who could appoint members from outside the Legislative Assembly; these could attend, but not vote in, Assembly debates. A Bill of Rights would guard the interests of minorities and the freedom of the individual. Internal self-government on the basis of this constitution was promised for February 1963, while in December Nyasaland's right to secede from the Federation was at last recognized.

The Federal Government fought these decisions step by step. The loss of Nyasaland would not, in itself, be fatal to the Federation; Sir Roy Welensky had always regarded the Protectorate as something of an embarrassment, with its small settler element and limited economic potential. The real significance lay in the precedent provided for copper-rich Northern Rhodesia, towards which the main effort of the U.F.P.'s rearguard action was therefore now directed. The day could yet be largely won if the two Rhodesias could be held together, welded to the axis of Kariba whose lake would provide no mean substitute for the scenic waters of Lake Nyasa.

The longer that Federation continued, the more difficult the 'unscrambling' would be; Welensky liked to assert that it would be impossible. He therefore played, sometimes desperately, for time. There were two fields of action open, in Central Africa and London. Despite their propaganda activities, the Federal Government were still out of touch with the realities of African opinion, as was shown in March 1963 when customs duties were raised on cheap clothing and footwear and dried milk. The response to pressure from Southern Rhodesia's white industrialists, this measure inevitably increased the Africans' cost of living. The attempt to win African support by an intensified propaganda campaign, and by removing more of what were euphemistically described as the 'pinpricks' of racial discrimination, were even less effective north of the Zambezi than in the south. Apart from this, Welensky's policy was twofold. First he must convince opinion in Britain, and especially in the Conservative Party, that the maintenance of the Federation was possible after all and that it was in the best interests of the African people. Secondly he must delay, and if possible prevent, the establishment of an African majority in the Northern Rhodesian legislature.

The first part of this policy met with considerable, indeed surprising, success. From the beginning of 1961 the Federal Government employed its publicity agents in London, 'Voice and Vision' Ltd., to conduct a costly propaganda campaign in the British press. African progress and welfare in the Federation were blazoned across the pages of national newspapers and in glossy brochures. The Federal Prime Minister himself made frequent visits to London, where he broadcast on radio and television, and spoke in public on a number of occasions, notably to the Institute of Directors at the Albert Hall in November 1961. It is difficult to assess the effect of these efforts but, in spite of Fleet Street's critical attitude, it seems to have been considerable. Right wing opinion continued to give qualified support to the Federation, and in view of this Macmillan's government more than once had to trim its sails.

This was nowhere more evident than in the case of the new Northern Rhodesian constitution. Welensky saw clearly that the future of the Federation now depended on the shape that this constitution would take. The proposal for a change aroused from the outset the fierce antipathy of the U.F.P. The existing constitution dated only from 1958. As recently as March 1960, Macleod had denied contemplating a new one. Kaunda's increasingly powerful United National Independence Party, however, was now demanding an advance comparable with that achieved by Nyasaland, in order to give Africans a stronger voice at the review conference table. In October Government House in Lusaka announced that a new constitution was under consideration. The news served to soothe the African nationalists, but did nothing to calm the fighting mood of the Northern Rhodesian whites, whose anxieties were being increased by observation of bloodshed and anarchy in the Congo.

The Northern Rhodesian conference opened at Lancaster House in December 1960 alongside the larger conference to review the Federation. Behind scenes of incompatible statements and dramatic walk-outs, Sir Roy Welensky fought the real battle with Macmillan and Macleod, whose open aim was now to achieve parity of European and African representation. Welensky revealed his awareness that here lay the real crux of the battle by personal intervention outside the rights of a Federal minister and by bitter exchanges with Macleod. He hinted darkly at unspecified action, and intensified his propaganda in London and Rhodesia. Following an injudicious threat of violence by Kaunda, who promised action which would 'make Mau Mau look like a picnic' if Britain did not concede an African majority, he called up the white Territorials in Northern Rhodesia on February 12, without the Governor's request required by the Federal Constitution. Further precautionary call-ups took place during ensuing weeks on the pretexts of possible disturbances and of events in the Congo.

Through this game of bluff and brinkmanship the discussions on Northern Rhodesia's constitution went on. The White Paper known as the Macleod plan was issued on 20 February, providing for a legislature of forty-five members including fifteen upper roll, fifteen lower roll and fifteen 'national' constituencies.[2] U.N.I.P. accepted the plan with extreme reluctance, Kaunda protesting that Africans would be unable to obtain the required percentage of votes on the upper roll for the block of 'national' seats. Welensky on the other hand bitterly denounced the proposals, and immediately set out to obtain their revision. At this time the new Southern Rhodesian constitution, agreed upon in February and to be confirmed by referendum in July, was arousing strong Dominion party opposition in the Colony. Welensky could now argue that unless the Macleod Plan were modified, white Rhodesian opinion would swing to the Dominion Party, the referendum would fail and the U.F.P. majority collapse. The British Government, under pressure from its right wing on the Common Market issue, and from the Katanga lobby over U.N. policy in the Congo, paid probably needless heed to this argument and agreed to modify the proposals.

This decision became known in Rhodesia on 23 June 1961. Kaunda at once denounced the alterations as a British betrayal, and the U.N.I.P. 'passive resistance' campaign began. Despite their leader's genuine insistence on non-violence, his inflammatory speeches led to a growing number of disturbances in July and August, lasting until October. Bridges were blown up in rural areas, roads blocked, buses attacked, village schools burnt down. U.N.I.P. agents were responsible for widespread intimidation. Twenty-one Africans were killed by the security forces, mainly in the Northern and Luapula Provinces.

Wearily the British Government agreed to reconsider its alterations to the Macleod Plan provided that the campaign for violence was brought to an end. In November the Governor, Sir Evelyn Hone, reported that the territory was again quiet, and a new conference was convened at Lancaster House by Reginald Maudling, who was Macleod's successor. At last in February 1962, despite Sir Roy's now ineffectual protests that Britain was surrendering to the 'violence and extremism' of U.N.I.P. and was 'indifferent to the fate of the Federation', a final arrangement was made. A compromise between the original plan and the June modifications, it reduced the proportion of votes required for Africans on the upper roll in the 'national' constituencies.

During twelve months, little had been achieved. Neither side was satisfied. On the one hand Welensky, fast losing face in Rhodesia, dissolved the Federal Assembly in an effort to reinforce his position with a new mandate; the attempt proved futile owing to apathy (see p. 357). On the other, the constitutional problem in Northern Rhodesia was still far from being solved; when the elections were held eventually in September 1962 they were conducted almost entirely on racial lines, the 'national' constituencies failing to achieve their object. More serious, the intervening months witnessed increasingly violent conflict between U.N.I.P. and the A.N.C. This conflict was largely a matter of personal loyalties. However the older Congress, led by Harry Nkumbula, attacked U.N.I.P. for its terrorism, and was more prepared for gradual change. Kaunda denounced Nkumbula for right-wing tendencies, and for supporting Tshombe in the Katanga. Clashes were frequent in the Copperbelt towns, where industrial unrest was added to political conflict. An independent report condemned both the actions of the police and the brutalities of African agitators. Much of the trouble was ascribed to the heightened tension resulting from the long-drawn-out delay in settling the political issue. This delay sprang in large measure from the effort to keep Northern Rhodesia within the Federation.

Early in 1962, soon after the Maudling constitution was promulgated, the British Government revealed that it still had hopes in this direction. In a late-hour attempt to discover a formula that would hold the crumbling Federation together, Duncan Sandys, Secretary of State for Commonwealth Relations, flew out to Central Africa. Little is known of his conversations in Blantyre and Salisbury, but the most remarkable feature of his tour was a brief visit to Lealui. The gentle Litunga of Barotseland, Mwanawina III, anxious about the growing influence of the young nationalists in his still feudal country, had for some months been requesting separation from Northern Rhodesia and a special status within the Federation. This suggestion had proved congenial to right-wing Rhodesians, who always preferred, in their relations with Africans, to deal with hereditary chiefs. Barotseland with its old-style monarchy would be a valuable substitute for Nyasaland as a Federal unit. In the end, however, the Litunga was advised not to seek separation from Northern Rhodesia. Instead the incident served to undermine his support and to increase the strength of U.N.I.P. in the Barotse constituencies, where in July they gained all fifteen elected seats on the Barotse National Council. The integrity of a future Zambia seemed to be successfully taking shape.

The Commonwealth Secretary's intervention, in a territory for which the Colonial Office was responsible, raised problems which were resolved by Macmillan's appointment of R. A.

Butler to a new Central African Office in March. Welensky publicly welcomed this move, for he misinterpreted it as a sign of London's solidarity behind the Federation. Already, however, cooler heads in Britain were recognizing the probability of dissolution and that negotiations would require clear judgement and a firm hand.

Meanwhile the new constitution had come into force in Southern Rhodesia. On 7 September 1961 the Salisbury Conference had agreed upon a new Legislative Assembly of sixty-five members elected on a dual-roll franchise (see Appendix II). Fifty members (in practice Europeans) would be elected from mainly 'A' roll constituencies, and fifteen members (in practice Africans) from mainly 'B' roll constituencies. A Declaration of Rights would be enshrined in the constitution, and a Constitutional Council of twelve members, mainly senior legal appointments, would guard against discriminatory legislation. As a concession to the right wing, practically all the reserve powers of the Imperial Parliament over the Colony's internal policy were now to be eliminated. This constitution, the first major change since 1923 and the first to provide for African members of the Assembly, could only be altered with the approval of the British Government or after a referendum of all races. A referendum of the existing electorate in July had supported the change by 41,919 votes to 21,846.

The preparation of the new constitution was accompanied by further progressive legislation. Whitehead's U.F.P. administration had already in January 1961 opened all posts in the Southern Rhodesian Civil Service to members of any race on the principle that 'irrespective of race and colour there shall be equal pay for equal work'. The discriminatory Immorality Act, a legitimate source of African resentment for sixty years, was repealed. Cinemas were to open their doors to members of all races. After a decision on appeal to the Federal Supreme Court, public swimming baths were opened to non-Europeans. In April the Land Apportionment Act was amended to permit Africans to obtain freehold title to land in African townships in the European Area. In June a further amendment created a new class of land, to be known as 'unreserved land', and covering about 5¾ million acres, which could be used by people of any race. In addition, 2 million acres were transferred from the European to the African (formerly Native) Area, now to be called Tribal Trust Land.[3] Meanwhile the repeal of the Pass Laws, which dated back to 1937, took effect in April; the only document now required to be carried by an African in any part of the Colony was an identity certificate. Sir Edgar Whitehead declared that the possibility of continuing white supremacy for very much longer was 'as dead as the Dodo'.

Unfortunately none of this legislation mollified the National Democratic Party. In February, indeed, the situation had appeared hopeful. Nkomo and Sithole had attended the constitutional conference, and at its conclusion had joined in the invitation issued to the United Kingdom and Southern Rhodesian governments to work out the details of a draft constitution on the lines proposed. Nkomo, however, had subsequently received a cable from N.D.P. agents in London describing the draft scheme as 'disastrous' for Africans. His position now changed. Claiming that his attitude at the conference had been misunderstood, he declared that Africans could not accept the proposals concerning the legislature and the franchise. When the Salisbury conference was resumed in May, Nkomo and Sithole walked out of the opening session, and subsequently conducted an unofficial plebiscite among Africans alone.[4] This abrupt change of front and the clear repudiation of Whitehead's progressive legislation exasperated the partnership-minded U.F.P., aroused widespread indignation amongst the white electorate, and was a major factor in the subsequent swing to the right.

African objections to the constitutional proposals were allied to grievances about land. Modifications in the Land Apportionment Act had not reduced the resentment caused by the continued implementation of the Land Husbandry Act. The Government's agricultural service had come into head-on collision with the human factor, for this had not been sufficiently taken into account. The whole scheme was slowing down. In 1961 the decision was taken to proceed with the allocation of land and grazing rights 'only in areas where this was specifically requested by the tribesmen'.[5] At the same time the land revolution was being dislocated by the economic difficulties in which the collapse of the Federation had placed Southern Rhodesia. The decline in the rate of industrial expansion was causing urban unemployment by 1962. Thus, instead of the rural African being encouraged to take up permanent residence in the towns, a reverse drift from the towns to the villages was occurring. In many places this served to make good the shortage of male labour in rural communities where, in prevailing conditions, work had been mainly carried out by women, children and old folk; it also intensified the clamour for more land. However, the land demanded was not the individual plots of the Land Husbandry Act but gardens to work freely under the old system. Reluctantly the Government was having to permit grazing land to be ploughed. There was still plenty of land in the European Area. The Government insisted that there would be no shortage in the African area if only Africans would farm properly. The consequent tensions provided abundant opportunity for nationalist propaganda and agitation.

The African repudiation of the constitution marked the beginning of a series of disturbances in the main Southern Rhodesian centres; they persisted through the dry season and coincided with Kaunda's 'passive resistance' campaign in the north. N.D.P. intimidation was mainly directed at discouraging Africans from registering on the new electoral rolls. In December there were riots in Salisbury during which police, who were being stoned, opened fire on the crowd killing one African and wounding others. As a result the party was banned. A week later Joshua Nkomo formed a new organization, the Zimbabwe African People's Union (Z.A.P.U.). Among its leaders was Dr Parerenyatwa, a respected member of the Colony's Medical Service and a newcomer to the political scene, who was to lose his life three months later when his car was struck by a train at a railway crossing. Other leaders were George Nyandoro and John Chikerema, who were both still under restriction orders, and Leopold Takawira. The new party was to prove even more militant than the old. Serious disorders broke out in Salisbury in May 1962 and Z.A.P.U. leaders refused to meet R. A. Butler when he made his first visit to the Federation that month on the grounds that Britain had not agreed to alter the constitution.

These events formed the climax to the career of the U.F.P. in Southern Rhodesia and of its leader Sir Edgar Whitehead. Sometimes criticized as arrogantly incommunicative, Whitehead had hitherto displayed a mind of his own. The middle-of-the-road liberalism to which he had faithfully adhered now began to be crushed out between the extreme wings. Despite renewed protests from the Churches and the Bar Association, he turned once more to emergency legislation. The Unlawful Organizations Act was strengthened and the Law and Order (Maintenance) Act was extended for a further five years. Z.A.P.U. was banned. Nkomo, declaring that his party would not follow the N.D.P. into oblivion but would remain in being, left the country to seek support abroad. Other leaders went underground. Arson, minor acts of sabotage and intimidation of Africans who showed signs of co-operating with the new franchise spread through the colony.

Whitehead, in fact, had been driven back to the position of 1959, in spite of his efforts to 'kill by kindness' the nationalist front. Since 1959, however, the U.F.P. had lost ground and the Federation, the *raison d'être* of the party, was already in the shoals of dissolution; meanwhile in Southern Rhodesia a vigorous right wing was setting its face against the policy of compromise and preparing to mount an offensive.

During the weeks before the elections the Prime Minister strove to regain confidence at home and abroad in his government's ultimate intentions. The issue had been taken up at Westminster, in the Organization for African Unity, and, above all, at the U.N. Whitehead now crossed the Atlantic to New York, whither Nkomo also led a delegation. In vain he pledged an end to land segregation and an African majority in the legislature before many years were past. His reception was cool. Sir Hugh Foot, permanent British delegate, resigned in protest against British policy in Rhodesia. Meanwhile at home white opinion was moving fast towards the other extreme. The European electorate, restive now at the attachment to the emergent African states across the Zambezi, were in no mood to be humoured by Sir Edgar's promise to repeal the Land Apportionment Act. At the polls on 4 December 1962 the U.F.P. was defeated, winning only 29 seats against 35 gained by the Rhodesian Front. A new administration led by Winston Field took office in Salisbury. Whitehead took over the leadership of the opposition until his retirement a year later.

The collapse of the U.F.P. in Southern Rhodesia marked the

end of the moderate liberal experiment which had its origin in the colony's brief association with the northern territories. From this time forward the tide of reform began to ebb disastrously. The Rhodesian Front was the successor to the Dominion Party, which had combined with other right-wing groups earlier in 1962. Its policy favoured the maintenance of white supremacy 'for the foreseeable future', the continuance of land segregation and the independence of Southern Rhodesia. Field denied that his party's policy was *apartheid*; in fact, except that the work of a decade could not be undone, it resembled the out-dated 'double pyramid' of the thirties. A Tribal Trust Land Act was planned to make the Chiefs, who were to be known as 'Tribal Authorities', responsible for the working of the Land Husbandry Act in the African Areas; an incongruous move, for the Land Husbandry Act was simultaneously disrupting the tribal system. Later the Dominion Party and its successor the Rhodesian Front were to make increasing use of the Chiefs in their relations with the African population. The Chiefs mostly proved willing to co-operate, since they were glad of this chance to shore up their declining prestige. Meanwhile, popular African movements were to be eliminated. Students at the University College of Salisbury were forbidden to debate political questions. The national broadcasting system was brought under government control. An early indication of the new resolve to take a strong line was the introduction of a mandatory death penalty for attempted arson in the Law and Order (Maintenance) Act.

Thus at the end of 1962 all three territories were headed by governments bent on the break-up of the Federation. Meanwhile, in the Federal Government offices in Salisbury, Welensky with his ministers still reigned supreme. For months, however, his position had lacked foundation. His appeal to the Federal electorate in April had misfired. The Africans had boycotted the election. Dominion Party voters had also stayed away. In an exceptionally low poll, U.F.P. members had been returned in fifty-four out of fifty-nine constituencies, in many cases unopposed. Armed with this meaningless majority, Sir Roy prepared to make his last stand. It came over Britain's concessions to Nyasaland at the end of 1962. Supplied with promises of secession and internal self-government, Banda returned from London to Blantyre to receive a tumultuous welcome from an unprecedented concourse of 40,000 Africans. Welensky's cup of bitterness now flowed over. He asserted that the British Government had broken its 'solemnly pledged word', thereby dishonouring 'firm and specific pledges which were given at the end of the 1953 conference and constitute a binding undertaking on the contracting parties'. Thus began a ragged dispute which cannot be said to have been concluded by the British publication in March of a White Paper recording a transcript of exchanges on the subject in 1953. The purport of the British argument was that no guarantee against breaking up the Federation had been written into its constitution; the understanding had been simply that no amendments to the constitution could be made unless all four governments in Central Africa were agreed. Since the Federation had been created by an instrument of the Imperial Parliament, it was implicit that the Imperial Parliament on its own had the power to end it.[6] The appearance of permanence had naturally been encouraged at the outset for obvious reasons, among them to ensure the attraction of capital investment. Sir Roy had grounds for complaint. These arguments were not wholly convincing. The British Government, though justified legally, had shifted its ground. Though it is in the nature of international politics for this to happen, there ought to be better communications and liason between friendly countries than existed between London and Salisbury. For the atmosphere of mutual mistrust that had existed since Federation began, both sides must bear a share of the blame.

Whatever the truth, Welensky's blustering denunciations were dust against the wind. The big copper mining groups now transferred their headquarters from Salisbury to Lusaka. In April the U.F.P. recognized the inevitable and disbanded; apart from a temporary Federal corps, its members in the territories set up new parties on a local basis. In Southern Rhodesia Whitehead's group, now the Rhodesia National Party, continued to demand an end to land segregation. Its influence steadily declined. In Northern Rhodesia John Roberts headed the National Progress Party which, while representing the European section of the community, aimed to co-operate with U.N.I.P. in the preparations for a new African state; their leader warned them against involvement in Southern Rhodesia's bid for independence. The National Constitution Party in Nyasaland, led by the former U.F.P. member Michael Blackwood, similarly sought to protect minority interests while building up an independent Malawi in co-operation with the Malawi Congress Party.

Finally the conference met at Victoria Falls in June to arrange for the dissolution of the Federation. Under Butler's chairmanship it performed its complicated task with harmony and speed. Arrangements were made for the joint management of the Rhodesia Railways, the Kariba power system, and the Central African Airways. The Federal public service was to be disbanded, 80 per cent of its members being expected to find re-employment in territorial departments. The Federation's military forces were reallocated in October; most notably the bulk of the R.R.A.F. with one squadron of parachute commandos would be taken over by Southern Rhodesia. The spreading of the Federal public debt caused the longest discussion. The debt amounted to £246 millions, which included territorial loans and £26 millions for Kariba, and the loans for the railways, which were to be shared equally between Northern and Southern Rhodesia. For want of any other means of assessment the remaining £118 millions were to be shared in the ratio of 52 per cent by Southern Rhodesia, 37 per cent by Northern Rhodesia, and 11 per cent by Nyasaland, since this was the basis of the respective share of the Federal assets which were allocated to each territory. The ratio in fact amounted to a considerable concession by the Northern Rhodesia government. Lastly it was agreed that the Federation should come to an end on 31 December 1963.

North of the Zambezi events now moved steadily towards their inexorable conclusion. Nyasaland obtained the final draft of its new constitution in May 1963. Dr Banda, now Prime Minister and still steadying his radical wing, obtained the promise of an independent Malawi for July 1964. In the first elections for the new Legislative Assembly in May 1964 the M.C.P. swept the board, winning all fifty seats in the common roll constituencies; the three seats in the reserved constituencies went to the National Constitution Party. Two months later on 6 July 1964 Malawi became an independent dominion within the Commonwealth. Speaking at the independence celebrations, the man who had led them to freedom was careful to warn his three million countrymen of hard times ahead and of salvation only through hard work and enterprise. He insisted that Malawi would take no part in controversies between east and west. Time was to show that non-alignment might prove difficult for a young country desperately in need of capital investment from abroad. On this subject Banda's dispute with his left wing was to grow in acerbity in the months to come; while Chipembere demanded closer contacts with Tanzania, the Prime Minister held fast to economic relations with more western-affiliated countries including Rhodesia and Mozambique.

Northern Rhodesia's advance to independence, though favoured with more security, was comparable at a few months' remove. The U.N.I.P./A.N.C. coalition took office at the end of 1962 and at once began a new campaign for secession. The right to secede was granted in March 1963, and the next few months were occupied in drafting yet another new constitution, the third in six years. The result combined British and American experience. Zambia was to be a republic within the Commonwealth. Its first President would be chosen by the existing legislature, and thereafter by the electorate at the same time as a general election. Sixty-five of the seventy-five members in the Legislative Assembly would be elected in common roll constituencies on a universal franchise. The remaining ten were to represent reserved, which were in fact European, constituencies. The President was empowered to appoint a further five members. The House of Chiefs, already a feature of the 1962 constitution, would continue to provide a second chamber. Barotseland was to be included in the republic, but the Litunga's Council could exercise a delaying veto over national legislation. A Bill of Rights and a Constitutional Council of judicial members would guard against discriminatory laws.

Even at this late stage, and especially on the Copperbelt, the territory was riven by an internecine feud between the main nationalist parties. Over a thousand violent incidents with political motivation were reported in Northern Rhodesia between August and October 1963, in spite of denunciations by both party leaders. In July 1964 more violence flared in the restless Northern Province, where U.N.I.P. sympathisers clashed with Alice Lenshina's Lumpa Church.[7] Lenshina, trying to bargain with Kaunda's government for special privileges for her organization, obtained support from the A.N.C. The government sent in troops and order was restored at the cost of heavy casualties.

Kaunda's government faced one other problem which had been long foreseen. Under the existing agreement between the Northern Rhodesian Government and the B.S.A. Company, the latter's royalties, currently worth £7 millions a year, were due to pass to the territory in 1986. In a White Paper in October the Government pointed out the anachronism of a chartered company, which itself took no part in mining operations, holding mineral rights which in almost every other part of the Commonwealth were vested in the Crown. Further, they challenged the validity of the treaties on which these rights were based, pointing out that Lewanika had had no justification for signing away rights in Lamba country; it is doubtful, in fact, whether Lewanika ever did so.[8] During half a century, millions of pounds had passed out of the country which were the rightful due of its people, and the White Paper declared 'a grave moral charge against the British Government in its capacity as protecting Power.' In an eve-of-independence settlement, the B.S.A. Company surrendered its rights to the new Zambian government in return for £4 millions compensation, half of which would be paid by Britain. Thus was swept away an anomaly dating back to, and reminiscent of, the halcyon days of Rhodes.

On United Nations Day, 24 October 1964, Zambia became an independent republic within the Commonwealth. Fortunate in its immense wealth, having exports currently amounting to £130 millions a year, it was also blessed with harmonious race relations, and with a constitution which envisaged a non-racial rather than a multi-racial system. The European population had to a large extent accepted the transfer of power with good grace, while in Kenneth Kaunda the country had a leader who promised to become one of Africa's statesmen. A development plan, to be prepared with the aid of the United Nations Economic Commission, aimed at rural advance and the more even spread of wealth in a country where four-fifths of the population still lived at subsistence level. Plans were afoot for a £71 million rail link with Tanzania. This would open up the north-east with its lake fisheries and opportunities for cattle-ranching. At the same time it would give land-locked Zambia an outlet to the sea independent of the Rhodesian and Portuguese railway systems.

Relations with Rhodesia were in fact a major item of policy for both Zambia and Malawi. They were largely governed by the terms of the agreements reached at Victoria Falls in the latter part of 1963. These agreements represented the residue of the idea of closer association which dated back for thirty years. Mutual trade treaties, while not amounting to a customs union, secured for the time being a vital export market for Rhodesia's secondary industries. With doubtful prospects of permanence, the Rhodesia railways system continued to be controlled by a Board on which both Rhodesian and Zambian governments were represented. The governments of all three territories continued to share in the management of Central African Airways. An Agricultural Research Council provided for an exchange of technical knowledge and skill. These areas of co-operation had existed before the Federation had come into being. The sole legacy of the federal experiment, apart from the University College at Salisbury, some fine if costly hospitals in Malawi and the mushroom growth of Rhodesian secondary industry, appeared to have been the hydro-electric power from the Kariba dam. Kariba was expensive in capital cost, in present power rates and in past political antagonism. None the less it might prove, in the end, to be the decisive factor for unity and co-operation. The Zambezi had for centuries divided the peoples to the north and south, where a more hospitable inland waterway might have joined them. The Central African Power Corporation was an organization necessary both to Zambia and to Rhodesia or its successor state. Zambians and Rhodesians would sit together round its board room table, working for the prosperity of the region.

The degree of co-operation in the immediate future depended on the course of developments south of the river. Once the fate of the Federation had been sealed, events in Rhodesia began to dominate the stage. There, in marked contrast to the northern scene, Field's Rhodesian Front administration, its alert and efficient security services well-supplied with military equipment, acted vigorously against the nationalist movement. By mid-1963 that movement had split asunder. While Nkomo's position as charismatic leader was still building up in the country as a whole, doubts about his leadership had been growing within the party. More than once abroad during a crisis, he was also inclined to take decisions without reference to his colleagues. In July the more intellectual and radical wing of Z.A.P.U. broke away to form the Zimbabwe African National Union. Ndabaningi Sithole, leader of the splinter group, was already under restriction, and later received a sentence of twelve months' hard labour for calling on Africans 'to have axes, bows and arrows and other instruments ready to oppose physically unilateral independence'. Bitter hostilities, exacerbated by tribal divisions, developed between the two factions till 1964, when Nkomo, after cat and mouse treatment by the police, was sent to the new restriction camp at Gonakudzingwa in the south-east corner of the colony. African nationalism was at its lowest point of effectiveness in the past ten years.

The European right wing, meanwhile, was gaining momentum in its drive for control. After a cabinet split in April 1964, Winston Field was replaced as party leader and Prime Minister by Ian Smith. Formerly Welensky's chief whip, Smith had resigned from the U.F.P. in opposition to the 1961 constitution and had become a founder-member of the R.F.P. the following year; he was thus free from association with the federal break-up. Now he commenced an outspoken campaign for independence, if necessary by unilateral action. This received wide support among an electorate resentful at British connivance in the demise of the Federation and at the status now being attained by their recent northern partners. Naturally enough the Commonwealth leaders at their July conference in London, to which Smith was not invited, expressed strong disapproval of the proposal for unilateral action without the concurrence of the Rhodesian people as a whole. To the suggestion that the bulk of the population was opposed to independence under present conditions, the Rhodesian government replied with a Chiefs' Indaba and a referendum. Few non-Europeans voted in the referendum on 5 November 1964 which supported Smith by an overwhelming majority of 58,091 to

6,096. This was less remarkable than the Chiefs' decision at Domboshawa two weeks earlier, which gave unamimous support for the 'cutting of strings'. The use of Chiefs for such a purpose, described by Lord Malvern as 'a swindle', was viewed with profound scepticism abroad. It is doubtful whether politically aware Rhodesian Africans saw it any differently. The Rhodesian Front had merely demonstrated its persistent resolve to deny the existence of an African political movement by acting as if it were not there.

As the position momentarily stabilized early in 1965, three factors appeared to govern the coming phase. First was the line to be taken by the Organization for African Unity, still loud in its denunciations; second was the policy of the British Government, still ultimately the responsible power. It soon became evident that in neither case was direct intervention in Rhodesian affairs a likely occurrence at least for the immediate future. African states to the north, preoccupied with their own security and economic problems, and in most cases separated from Rhodesia by great distances, were in no position to take direct action. Zambia indeed, the only country so placed, was inhibited by its dependence on Rhodesia for electric power and for a railway outlet to the sea. The British Government, now led by Harold Wilson's Labour administration, was particularly anxious not to disturb the peace of South-Central Africa at this early moment in the career of its newly independent states. Moreover the only platform from which military intervention might be launched was, again, Zambia, with communications through Kenya and Tanzania. In taking such a step, Britain could not only do irreparable harm to what hopes were left for moderate opinion and for the growth of satisfactory race relations in Rhodesia. She could also set a precedent for warfare between the bulk of black Africa and the white-ruled south which was a long-term danger for the continent. From the first therefore Wilson set his face against a resort to arms, but gave clear warnings of economic and diplomatic sanctions if Rhodesia tried to break away on its own terms.

The British Prime Minister's pledge, given in a letter to Smith at the end of March 1965, not to use force against Rhodesia may have been decisive in resolving the R.F.P. government upon a unilateral course. When by clear implication the issue was put to the electorate on 7 May 1965, the

R.F.P. won all fifty of the 'A' roll seats. David Butler, the new leader of the Rhodesia Party, lost his place. Josiah Gondo became the leader of an opposition consisting of ten Rhodesia National Party members supported by five Independents, among all of whom only one, Ahrn Palley, was likely to carry weight. Nothing now stood in the way of unilateral action apart from the sanctions threat.

The third factor then, and the vital one, was the economy of Rhodesia. In 1964 its condition was still buoyant, even booming; exports exceeded £119 millions, giving a favourable trade balance of £35 millions. The situation, however, showed a decline in investment and, even more, in home consumption. The rate of white immigration had been steadily falling, and since 1961 the outflow of Europeans leaving the country had been exceeding the number of those coming in.[9] It was in these terms that the future of Rhodesia would be fought out.

Right-wing Rhodesians ascribed this decline in fortune to uncertainty about the status of the country. Pressure upon the R.F.P. administration to seek independence was intensified towards the end of the dry season of 1965. Business interests concerned about the shortage of investment, and tobacco farmers anxious to plan crops for the coming season, called for a speedy settlement. The British Government reiterated its stern warnings and invited Smith to London for talks in October. Five principles or conditions were there put forward by Harold Wilson, concerning which Britain must be satisfied before Rhodesia's independence could be granted. While professing in large measure to accept these principles, the R.F.P. leader insisted that they could be safeguarded within the framework of the existing 1961 constitution. British ministers demanded that this constitution be modified to provide a surer guarantee of African political progress. No agreement was reached. Smith returned to Salisbury amid the acclamations of his supporters. The former Rhodesian Premier Garfield Todd, now a nationalist supporter and a member of Z.A.P.U., was placed under house arrest and a unilateral declaration of independence (U.D.I.) appeared to be imminent.

In an eleventh hour attempt to avert the crisis, the British Prime Minister flew out to Salisbury. After five days of intensive negotiations, he proposed a Royal Commission to investigate constitutional amendments that might form the basis of a treaty between the two governments. Hopes for a solution along these lines were quickly dashed by disagreement on the Commission's terms of reference, and on 5 November a state of emergency was declared in Rhodesia. The last attempt to reach moderate opinion in the colony by direct confrontation with the facts had failed. Six days later, victims of their own propaganda, faithful to the spirit of Rhodes and Jameson, protesting to the last their loyalty to crown and flag, Smith's government unilaterally and illegally severed the political tie with Britain.

These events provoked world-wide controversy, for the consequences were incalculable for Africa and the world. In Britain the issue had struck deep chords in the national consciousness. This was no mere sentimental or ·abstract moral problem. To some extent attitudes were influenced by experience of immigrant race problems at home. Beyond this it was plain that British policy towards Rhodesia could profoundly affect the integrity of the Commonwealth. The twin streams of two centuries of colonial and imperial policy were coming unavoidably into collision. Ever since the debacle in America, Britain had been careful of the susceptibilities of her colonists abroad. In Canada, Australia and New Zealand a pattern had been set that, with modifications, had been followed in the case of the white settlements in Africa south of the Zambezi. Meanwhile in India the policy of trusteeship and of guidance towards independence of non-European peoples, transferred in the present century to Britain's tropical African dependencies, had been steadily and painstakingly evolved. The incompatibility of these policies south of the Zambezi had long been plain to see. The romanticism of the Rhodes era, the traumatic effect of the South African War, blindness towards the emergence of African political aspiration and the shock of world conflict had combined to inhibit intervention by the Imperial Government during the second quarter of the century. The failure of the federal experiment in multi-racial compromise at last now opened the eyes of the British public to the fact that here was a nettle painful to grasp but too dangerous to leave alone.

Nor was the danger only for the Commonwealth. The Rhodesian crisis would necessarily, unless it were speedily resolved, raise the whole issue of southern Africa. If force were not used at once, sanctions would have to be employed; and sanctions, to be effective, would need the co-operation of the Republic and Portugal, or else be turned against them. The blockade of southern Africa had been talked of as an outside possibility for years. Seen at closer quarters it was an operation of great magnitude that would test the integrity of the United Nations and whose consequences none could foresee.

It was easy to pass judgement on the white population, upon whom had been placed the heavy burden of trusteeship that was rightly an imperial responsibility. In many respects this burden had been borne with credit both before and since the war. Now circumstances not all of their own devising had placed the present generation in a situation from which it was difficult for them to extricate themselves alone. Isolated from the robust stimulus of social revolution that for two decades had gusted among the peoples of the world, socially divided from the proletariat within their own society, too close to the South African stream, they had been unresponsive to currents of contemporary thought and often antagonistic to them. Viewing with misgiving the course of events in Africa north of the Zambezi, most white Rhodesians believed that they were uniting self-interest with principle in resisting their southward march. Consequently, and as was almost inevitable among a privileged minority in control of its own affairs, the political leadership had moved consistently further and further to the right. No British government, in such a situation, and with the eyes of the world upon it, could abandon its ultimate control, tenuous though the link had become through years of unconcern.

White Rhodesians indeed could still learn to value Britain's involvement during the coming period of transition to majority rule. Their long term position could be dangerous on a continent whose peoples had for years been compelled to contain their resentment against the South African regime. Time would show whether, prompted perhaps by unconscious memories of the heroic but disastrous Shangani patrol, the desperate spirit of no compromise would prevail; or whether the shocks and pressures of world reaction to U.D.I., combined with an innate respect for the rule of law, would bring a new realism out of which better understandings could emerge, and moderate leadership, both black and white, revive.

X

THE HAZARDS OF INDEPENDENCE

Rhodesia Besieged

AT the end of 1965 it appeared doubtful whether the voice of moderation would be effectively heard in Rhodesia for several years to come. It was true that during the ill-judged violence and intimidation of 1963 many Africans had become disillusioned with the Z.A.P.U. and Z.A.N.U. leaderships. The disenchantment remained for some time, and helps to account for the reluctance of rural tribesmen to give much help to the guerillas entering the country from the north. This did not however amount to enthusiasm for the direction the country was taking. Africans on the 'B' roll still numbered less than 5,000 though many more were qualified for enrolment. Even smaller numbers voted in the elections which sent the fifteen African opposition members to the Legislative Assembly, who had thus little real basis of support in either urban or rural areas. The suppression of protest strikes against U.D.I. in Bulawayo and elsewhere, and the continuing activity of police spies and informers in the African suburbs under the emergency regulations, led to a slow recovery of support for the detained leaders of the nationalist organizations. These organizations however were no longer working strictly within the Rhodesian context, but were aligned with resistance movements elsewhere in southern Africa, and indeed against a background of African resurgence throughout the continent. Thus Joshua Nkomo, who had once been prepared to work for gradualism through the 1961 constitution, was now inescapably committed to the principle of immediate majority rule. Throughout these years he continued to be confined in the remote restriction camp at Gonakudzingwa. Though retaining the affection and loyalty of many Africans, he remained, by force of circumstances if no more, unreconciled with the Z.A.N.U. leadership detained hundreds of miles away at Wha Wha near Gwelo. This denial of effective representation to the 4½ million Africans did not foster the growth of a strong moderate wing. The Chiefs, of whom the government made so much, could speak usefully on some aspects of life in the Tribal Trust Lands, but were irrelevant as an expression of African political opinion among the 41 per cent of the African population who lived in the European area and above all among the 10 per cent who lived in the urban areas, where the true political issues were coming to the surface.

Meanwhile the European community of 230,000, with its electorate of some 80,000, continued to be ranged even more solidly behind the Rhodesian Front. The voice of moderation in this sector was silenced not so much by the censorship as by the nature of the crisis itself. Right wing opinions were therefore given free rein. Their influence was all the greater in that since 1962 the Rhodesia Front had not only displaced the discredited U.F.P. as the establishment party, but had infiltrated the hierarchies of the professional and commercial associations as well as local government councils, and brought them under party control.[1] Though public services and even private associations continued to be remarkably free from graft as such, they became much less free from political pressures. These factors, as much as the obtrusiveness of the independence issue, account for the total success of the Front at the polls in the elections of 1964 and 1969, as well as in all by-elections as late as 1971, both before and after the declaration of a republic. Backed financially by wealthy cattle ranchers and tobacco farmers who were determined at all costs to maintain Land Apportionment and the segregation that followed from it, sustained electorally by the 'new Rhodesians' of the clerical and artisan class who had most to lose from African competition, and supported, though more reluctantly, by the mining, industrial and commercial organizations, the R.F.P. could afford, in 1965 at least, to regard its opponents on either wing as small and eccentric minorities. Above all white Rhodesian loyalties were able to focus upon Ian Smith. As a born Rhodesian who had rarely visited Britain, a farmer who had graduated in business studies at Grahamstown and a man imperturbably possessed of his simply conceived opinions, he was able to represent nearly to perfection the white Rhodesian amalgam of settler, farmer and entrepreneur, with all its certainties, hopes and fears.

Opening his independence broadcast on 11 November Smith, without a shadow of embarrassment, had paraphrased a clause in the more celebrated declaration of 1776. If this oblique appeal to the new world to redress the balance of the old fell, for the time being, upon deaf ears, at least it was a gesture towards the importance of the occcasion. In a statement studded with Churchillian phrases, such as that 'the mantle of the pioneers' had fallen on the shoulders of 'a courageous people', Smith assured his listeners that Rhodesia had not rejected the possibility of racial harmony, that it was their firm intention to abide by the constitution, and that the protection of the rights of all peoples enshrined therein would not be abrogated or disregarded. In being the first 'Western nation' since the war to have the determination and fortitude to say 'thus far and no further', the Rhodesians had 'struck a blow for the preservation of justice, civilization and Christianity'. The latter assertion followed passages urgently referring to the shortage of foreign investment, and led to protests from church leaders such as that 'the declaration of independence was prompted not by Christian ideals but by Rhodesian Front policies'. To the British government, however, the issue at stake was not the degree of civilization, Christian or otherwise, within Rhodesia at the time, but the probable direction that events were almost bound to take over the years ahead. The apartheid policies south of the Limpopo were uppermost in the minds of observers overseas when judging the Rhodesian question, and in view of these policies Smith's assurances about 'the rights of all peoples' could carry little weight. Existing constitutional controls, frail as they were, provided the only means by which the drift towards apartheid might be avoided.

These controls were now struck away in the adjustments, consequent upon independence, that were drafted into the new structure, which was published on the same day and known thereafter as the 1965 Constitution. The Governor, then Sir Humphrey Gibbs, was to be superseded by an Officer Administering the Government, a post to which Mr Clifford Dupont, Minister for External Affairs, was appointed a week later. Other adjustments included the removal of all remaining powers of the Crown and the ending of appeals to the Judicial Committee of the Privy Council. Amendments to entrenched clauses, such as those relating to the judiciary, the franchise and the Declaration of Rights, were made subject to the safeguards of a 'blocking third' and of separate referenda of the four races; for the sake of appearances, the royal approval was retained as an alternative. Existing holders of public appointments were to continue in office, providing only that if required to do so they swore an oath of acceptance to the new Constitution. Despite Sir Humphrey Gibbs' perhaps necessarily ambiguous injunction to all citizens 'to refrain from acts which would further the objectives of the illegal authorities' but nonetheless 'to carry on with their normal tasks', civil service and forces personnel might have been in a difficult situation had Britain resorted to the use of force. However, ignoring the clamour from African states, the British government was to confine itself to economic sanctions as an extension of diplomacy, and the de facto authority of the 'Smith regime' became unquestionable before many months were past.

Diplomacy was to have a difficult passage. Among the odds ranged against it were not only the initially small size of the Labour government's majority, which both set a premium on early success and compelled a bipartisan and therefore compromise approach; but also the antipathy felt by the Rhodesian leaders for their socialist antagonists. Ian Smith was to sum up this antipathy in November 1966 on the first anniversary of independence: 'We are poles apart. They are socialists worshipping the idea of the welfare state, and we are individuals supporting a capitalist system, with the accent on individual initiative and enterprise. Earlier this year Mr Wilson said we Rhodesians lived in a different world, a different century. We do.' From this extended viewpoint it was easy for white Rhodesians, echoing the distortions of South African nationalism, to brand any left-wing opinion as 'communism'. 'Just as, ten years ago,' declared Smith in a broadcast in October, 'Hungary was in the forefront of this battle for men's freedom from the horrors of the communist system, so today we are in that position.' It was true indeed that Africa had witnessed plenty of horror during the past decade, and was soon to suffer a series of brutal civil wars in the Congo region, Nigeria and the Sudan; that for some years the continent had been exposed to ceaseless radio propaganda from Peking; that Rhodesia's own nationalist parties in exile were known to be seeking support respectively from Russia and China; and that as recently as June 1965 President Chou en Lai, on a visit to Tanzania, had remarked that Africa was 'ripe for revolution'. All this seemed to give substance to Clifford du Pont's description of the states to the north, 'where country after country is disintegrating into rudderless fragmentations which are easy prey to the unscrupulous ideologies which seek to exploit them'. Such judgements ignored the real problems of the post-colonial era, the progress already being made to overcome them, and the commitment to non-alignment of some African states. In the eyes of white Rhodesians, many of them fugitives from the collective society, socialism was responsible for the troubles of the continent. It boded ill for a negotiated settlement that it was a socialist government with whom they had to deal.

British leaders, while aware of this antagonism, were able to distinguish between the principles of socialism and self-determination. The first of the five principles, 'unimpeded progress to majority rule', summed up their whole case. Recognition of U.D.I., it was repeated again and again, would be a betrayal of responsibilities to 4½ million Africans. This rush of sensitivity, contentedly dormant for so many years, owed its sudden awakening partly to the collapse of the Central African Federation, partly to the return of a Labour administration to office in 1964, but in no small degree to the post-Bandung solidarity of the Afro-Asian states. In recent years this had been given powerful emphasis by the multiplication of non-white seats in the United Nations General Assembly and, as far as Britain was concerned, by the Afro-Asian majority in the Commonwealth. Harold Wilson, who had by then already attended two difficult Commonwealth conferences since U.D.I., told the House of Commons in September 1966 that 'the very existence and future of the Commonwealth as we know it today have been put in jeopardy by the illegal actions of a few politicians in Rhodesia'. This was a constant theme, to be repeated by the Foreign Secretary Michael Stewart four years later when he stressed the 'vital importance for good relations between the different races of mankind that the illegality of the Rhodesian regime should be firmly asserted', and by Lord Caradon the following year when he warned that the Douglas-Home settlement proposals would 'forfeit the possibility of British leadership in the third world . . . maybe for the rest of the century'.

Thus the whole significance of the Rhodesia crisis which, despite its relatively diminutive proportions in terms of economics, military logistics and population, managed to become the subject of Security Council resolutions and occupy the attention of great powers, must be seen in the context of world politics. The 1960s were the decade when the 'cold war' was being diverted from direct confrontation into a contest for the minds, and indeed for the markets, of the 'new' and uncommitted states of Africa and southern Asia. The United States, embarrassingly accused of aggression in Asia, and with its own civil rights struggle passing through a critical phase, could not afford to equivocate in Africa. China and the U.S.S.R., since 1960 pursuing divergent roads, were bound to compete for the support of African nationalism, both against each other and against the capitalist West. Britain, the country most directly concerned, was in the most difficult position of all. The fundamental reappraisals that had followed the Suez affair and the subsequent shedding of the colonial empire had not yet worked themselves through. The problems of Aden and Singapore were still unresolved, and Britain's strategic role in the Indian Ocean still undecided. Meanwhile immigration from the West Indies and Pakistan had created new problems for the humanitarian conscience at home that tended to project themselves into situations abroad and particularly towards southern Africa. Yet, struggling still with recurrent economic crises, Britain, on the one hand increasingly dependent on Nigerian oil, could not on the other afford to jeopardize vast investments in South African mining and industry, nor valuable export markets. It was not an easy basis for waging economic war.

The effectiveness of economic sanctions was an unknown factor in 1965. Ian Smith's optimistic pronouncement that they would be a 'nine days' wonder' was as unrealistic as Harold Wilson's repeated threats of appalling consequences and incalculable turmoil. The Rhodesian government, as during the Second World War, could nonetheless look with confidence to the proximity of South Africa, who had a vested interest in the failure of economic sanctions at any time. Portugal, neighbour to Rhodesia in Mozambique, with a guerilla war on its hands, had even stronger reasons for pursuing a friendly neutrality. Looking further afield, France, recently extricated from colonial commitments in Indo-China and Algeria, was busily developing its commercial interests in Africa. Businessmen in certain other capitalist countries, such as West Germany, the Netherlands, Switzerland and Japan, could be relied upon to find loopholes in any sanctions system.

In view of this the initial British moves against the rebel regime were mild in the extreme. The Prime Minister told the House of Commons on 11 November that 'we have no proposals to make on oil supplies', and repeated that 'we do not contemplate any national action (i.e. force) for the purpose of coercing the illegal government into a constitutional posture'. All aid to Rhodesia was, however, to cease. Rhodesians were denied access to the London capital market, and new exchange controls were set up. The purchase of Rhodesian tobacco and sugar was banned. Defending the moderate nature of these provisions, and anxious to preserve a bipartisan front, Wilson pointed out that while 'the aim must be to make this illegal act impossible', policy must be based on conciliation rather than coercion. Behind such a policy lay the view that U.D.I. was the work of a few extremists in the Rhodesian Front and Smith's cabinet. The threat of economic collapse would persuade the Rhodesian Parliament and electorate to topple the regime which had brought the troubles upon them. Stronger measures might have had this effect; it is doubtful. As it was, Rhodesian opinion tended to unite against intimidation from without.

The Rhodesian government soon responded with new controls over banks, commerce and industry and with a seven-point plan to counter the effects of sanctions. Black Rhodesian employees who became redundant would be placed in jobs held by aliens—there were 250,000 Zambians and Malawians working in Rhodesia—and these would progressively be repatriated.[2] Zambian imports from Rhodesia must be paid for in non-sterling currency, and the payment of interest to British nationals was blocked. In face of violent propaganda emanating from Z.A.P.U. agents in Lusaka,[3] and the plans announced in London for a radio transmitter in Francistown, heavy penalties were created for listening to subversive broadcasts. A fortnight later, press censorship was imposed. The *Rhodesia Herald*, and other publications of the Argus Press which had editorially opposed U.D.I. and stood for policies that in southern Africa passed as liberal, retaliated by producing blank spaces, which the government tried unsuccessfully to forbid.

Early in December, observing the negligible effect of their initial measures, the British government placed new bans on the purchase of Rhodesian minerals and foodstuffs, amounting to 95 per cent of Rhodesian exports to Britain. On 17 December the oil embargo was announced, though with explicit denials of any intention to blockade the port of Beira for the purpose. Meanwhile, following a United Nations resolution on 19 November, many countries broke off diplomatic relations and imposed selective sanctions. South Africa and Portugal were not among these. While regretting Rhodesia's impetuosity, President Verwoed denied any intention of interfering with private trade, while the Portuguese authorities explained that they could not refuse the use of their ports to a land-locked country. Before long foreign goods were entering Rhodesia from the south overstamped with South African trade names. Rhodesian exports secured passage the same way. By the end of February 25,000 gallons of petrol a day, much of it in the form of gifts, was crossing the Limpopo at Messina by road, while far greater amounts, reimported from South Africa via Lorenço Marques, were entering Rhodesia by rail.

The decision of the Rhodesia-Mozambique Oil Pipeline Company to continue pumping crude oil from Beira to Umtali, and the announcement early in March of work on six new oil storage tanks at Beira, decided the British government to go back on its previous decision and to blockade the port. Although this blockade failed to prevent Rhodesia from obtaining petroleum, it had important indirect consequences, for in the test cases of the *Joanna V* and the *Manuela*, tankers under the Greek flag chartered to a South African Company, Britain found it impossible to enforce the blockade legally without recourse to the U.N. Security Council. The Council resolution of 10 April declared that the supply of oil to Rhodesia constituted a threat to peace, called on all states to prevent such supply, and required the United Kingdom government to use force if necessary to prevent tankers from going to Beira. Wilson was attacked by the Opposition not only for breaking pledges about the use of force but for taking the dispute to the United Nations; and though the Prime Minister was able to argue a diplomatic success in that the use of force was confined to Britain and only authorized at Beira, this event marked the beginning of the end of bipartisanship on Rhodesian policy in Britain. The Labour government, abandoning conciliation, was now resolved with international support to bring down the rebel regime by destroying the Rhodesian economy, if possible before the next Commonwealth Prime Ministers' Conference in September.

By May 1966, however, Rhodesia was clearly weathering sanctions. Despite a decline in the import of consumer goods and some local disruption of trade, there was no overall increase in unemployment. Petrol, rationed since 27 December, was in adequate supply. Much of the recent tobacco crop, sold secretly in March, had gone to South Africa for storage and re-export. Reduced crops, to be sold at guaranteed prices, were planned for the future; the government would buy surplus leaf and store it in hangars at Salisbury airport. A £5 million government loan was fully subscribed by June. By the end of the year the economy no longer faced serious difficulty. Tobacco farmers, especially in Mashonaland and Manicaland, turned to the production of more beef, maize and cotton.[4] Mining continued to flourish in an atmosphere of confidence that was promoted by world demand and by the discovery during 1968 of valuable new nickel and chrome deposits. The development of light industry helped to meet the shortage of consumer goods, besides creating a class of entrepreneur that was increasingly reluctant to see a settlement come about. Linked to South Africa, Rhodesia did not devalue its currency in 1968, but in 1970 decimalized with a Rhodesian dollar that was the equivalent of the South African rand. Though exports did not regain the 1965 total until 1971, a considerable economic growth amounting to 8 per cent per annum was maintained by investing in domestic enterprise. Much of all this was due to the skill of the Finance Department led by John Wrathall, and even more to the ingenuity of Rhodesian businessmen. A price had to be paid in that markets were harder to find, so much commerce had become underhand dealing, and by 1969 Rhodesian passports were acceptable nowhere in the world outside southern Africa.

The progressive 'tightening' of the embargo during 1966, leading after the rejection of the *Tiger* proposals in December to the Security Council resolution calling for selective mandatory sanctions, followed by another in May 1968 for comprehensive mandatory sanctions, was of little apparent effect. Despite hopeful statements in London early in 1967 that sanctions were at last beginning to 'bite deeply', African and Commonwealth leaders became increasingly sceptical. Use of the metaphor doubtless inspired the remark of Ali Simbule, Zambian High Commissioner designate to London in May 1968, that Britain was a 'humbled toothless bulldog', which being reported in British newspapers caused a delay of some weeks in Simbule's arrival.

It would be untrue however to say that the sanctions operation was a complete failure. By 1971 it was clear that there were three areas of major concern within Rhodesia to which only the ending of sanctions could bring relief. The first lay in the aggravation of rural unemployment, already mounting due to natural and rapid population increase. Desmond Frost, chairman of the R.F.P., told the party congress in October 1971 of 'the ever-increasing African population explosion, and the tremendous uncontrolled African influx into the towns, with all its unnecessary implications'. By this time, more Africans were born every year than there were Europeans in the country. Each year more Africans left school than there were European workers in employment.[5] Quite apart from the hope of increasing the rate of white immigration, if white Rhodesians were to avoid taking the road to hard-line apartheid, there would have to be a rapid growth of the rural economy, in both European and African areas, which only the reopening of export markets could make possible. The 1961 Land Husbandry Act had failed in its purpose. New roads, dams and irrigation were called for, involving heavy capital expenditure with little immediate return. The aid that Britain was offering in exchange for a settlement would prove invaluable here. More immediately urgent, secondly, was the need for the replacement of capital equipment, particularly locomotives and rolling stock on the railways. Lying behind all else, however, was the third major source of anxiety, the shortage of foreign exchange. Here, rather than in the attempted blocking of specific items such as oil, lay the true effectiveness of sanctions, slowly though the mills might grind. Leading industrialists had all along been concerned about this. In November 1968, exasperated by the failure of the *Fearless* talks, the Chairman of the Rhodesian Iron and Steel Corporation in a letter to the *Rhodesia Herald* had warned of 'faster economic deterioration' to come; a fortnight later the Chairman of the Rhodesian board of the Standard Bank wrote of the need for a 'massive injection of external capital', which only a settlement could bring. The year 1969, with an excellent rain season and the exploitation of new high-grade chrome deposits, saw a revival of confidence, but the underlying anxiety remained. In November 1970, at the time of the new Conservative government's first exploratory steps, Ian Smith told the Legislative Assembly that 'the best thing that could happen for Rhodesia would be for sanctions to come to an end now,' because although the economy was buoyant, 'this would help us as far as our foreign exchange is concerned'.

Compared with these slow but inexorable pressures, the efforts of the Zimbabwe nationalists to disrupt the country by means of guerilla attacks were of small effect. These attempts had two objectives. The first, that of arousing the African population whether by example, exhortation or intimidation, to bring about the breakdown of law and order which, according to the Wilson formula, would justify British military intervention, never had the least chance of success. Apart from the efficiency of the well-organized and equipped security forces, the local inhabitants south of the Zambezi belonged to tribes that had been driven north by the Shona in past centuries, and were among the most pacific of Rhodesia's African population. More important was the propaganda value flowing from guerilla activity. It remains yet to be determined how far the inspiration for this campaign came from the nationalist parties themselves, and how far from further afield. The Organization for African Unity, though divided on the Rhodesian question right at the start in 1965, maintained a Liberation Committee at Dar es Salaam to act as a clearing house for volunteers and equipment. The arms came from various sources, principally China. Volunteers—known as freedom fighters to their supporters, guerillas to the rest of the world, and terrorists in Rhodesia—had been variously trained in Moscow, Peking and Pyongyang, in Cuba, West Africa and Algeria. From transit camps in southern Zambia they made regular forays between 1965 and 1970 across the Zambezi. Attacks generally commenced during the long grass period of February and March towards the end of the rains, and continued through the dry season till the grass-burning in September. During 1966 and 1967 the most serious threat took the form of sabotage within Rhodesia itself, consisting of attempts on railway lines, the maiming of cattle and the destruction of crops. The peak period of guerilla activity extended for twelve months from early August 1967, at which time the exiled African National Congress of South Africa announced an alliance with Z.A.P.U. with the declared aim of overthrowing the white governments of both countries. A large number of 'freedom fighters' was believed to be gathering north of the Zambezi. On 8 September President Vorster, commenting that 'it is our downfall that is being sought', admitted that South African police had been sent to operate in support of the severely stretched Rhodesian army. Ten days later the Law and Order (Maintenance) Act was amended to include the mandatory death penalty for 'unlawfully possessing arms of war'. The expected infiltration, which took place north of the Wankie game reserve, proved less dangerous than expected; but in February 1968 some 150 guerillas, having crossed the Zambezi east of Kariba, spent over two months in concealed camps before they were found and hunted down with the loss of a third of their number. A third wave met a similar fate in July.[6]

It was in face of these pressures that the Rhodesian authorities proceeded to the execution in March 1968 of three Africans whose death sentences for murder, passed before November 1965, had been held up pending appeal. In finally refusing to allow the appeal to the Judicial Committee of the Privy Council in London, and in declaring that the Rhodesian government was a fully de facto government, the Appellate Division of the High Court at last came down on the side of independence.[7] Strong and widespread reactions overseas reflected anger at the carrying out of the executions after so long a delay, but also concern over the fate of other condemned Africans, by then numbering about a hundred. At the United Nations a new twenty-three clause resolution called for comprehensive mandatory sanctions. It is possible that in this instance world protest had some effect; in September the mandatory death penalty for carrying arms was repealed, and over the next three years there was a steady commutation of death sentences into life imprisonment. The guerilla offensive of 1967–8 thus had undoubted indirect effects, notably the bringing of South Africa and Rhodesia closer together and, on the other hand, the stiffening of economic sanctions. Ultimately perhaps it contributed to the meeting of Wilson and Smith aboard H.M.S. *Fearless* which, despite the British premier's disclaimer in March that there could be no more dealings with this 'essentially evil' regime, took place early in October.

The collapse of the *Fearless* talks did not however lead to an intensification of guerilla activity, the main impetus of which appeared indeed to be on the wane. This was due not only to the fate of the 1968 operations but also to disputes among the leadership. Throughout these years the endemic quarrel between Z.A.P.U. and Z.A.N.U. had smouldered on, embittered by military failure. It was now compounded in March 1970 by a split within Z.A.P.U. between its Shona members, including Chikerema and Nyandoro, who wanted to join forces with Z.A.N.U., and its Ndebele wing, notably Jason Moyo and Edward Ndhlovu, who were opposed to this course. The Zambian government, exasperated by these disputes and by the violence between the factions that frequently arose, deported 129 Zimbabwe nationalists, mostly from guerilla camps, to Rhodesia, and threatened to close the offices of the exiled movements. More than a year later, elements of both parties who favoured unity combined to form the Front for the Liberation of Zimbabwe. Organized by Sultan Siwela, a twenty-nine year old graduate of Boston University and a newcomer to the political scene, Frolizi at this stage constituted a third force rather than a real merger between the two main parties. Most of the Z.A.P.U. and Z.A.N.U. leaders stayed away, still unreconciled.

If Rhodesian Africans were to exert any positive influence upon coming events, with which they were so vitally concerned, some attempt to make up their differences, inside as well as outside the territory, was becoming a matter of urgency, for less than two months after Frolizi was announced in Lusaka a new draft settlement was signed by Ian Smith and Sir Alec Douglas-Home in Salisbury. This was the outcome of the latest in a long series of negotiations between the British and Rhodesian governments going back for nearly six years, and it is to a brief account of these exchanges that we now turn.

Late in February 1966, three months after U.D.I., the Conservative opposition at Westminster began pressing the government to reopen talks with Smith. The Prime Minister's statement on 21 April that 'there is a great deal we are prepared to forgive and forget, but we are not prepared to legalize an act of rebellion' revealed what was to prove an outstanding obstacle to agreement—the British insistence on constitutional propriety. His following remark, 'nor are we prepared to compromise on points laid down by two successive governments', pointed to the second obstacle, the five principles. To these a sixth, more an aspiration than a principle, that there should be no oppression of majority by minority or vice versa, was now added. Visits to Salisbury by senior civil servants and junior ministers only emphasized the differences that were to bedevil talks for five years: whereas Smith, who Wilson now realized was the only man he could deal with, expected immediate recognition of his government, the British wanted a face-saving interim administration headed by the Governor; and whereas Britain sought for entrenched guarantees, with external safeguards, for unimpeded progress to majority rule, the Rhodesians hoped to be able, by use of a 'braking mechanism', to adjust the franchise and the number of 'A' roll seats at will. Committed at the Commonwealth Conference in September to go to the U.N. for mandatory sanctions if a settlement was not reached by Christmas, Wilson flew to meet Smith aboard H.M.S. *Tiger* at Gibraltar on 2 December.

During seventy-two hours cruising off the Moroccan coast, a 'working document' was produced in three parts: first, a new constitution was to include a bicameral legislature, 'A' and 'B' roll franchises with cross-voting, strong safeguards against amendment and a justiciable Bill of Rights; second, a Royal Commission was to make recommendations for reducing racial discrimination; and third, a complicated procedure was devised for the 'return to legality'.[8] The *Tiger* talks failed not only because Smith refused to make a decision on the spot which the British, somewhat unreasonably, expected him to do, but because the 'legality' procedure was both unrealistic and open to misinterpretation. On Smith's return to Salisbury the Rhodesian cabinet, reluctant to settle in any case, seized upon the interim administration proposals as 'repugnant' and on 6 December issued a distorted version referring quite incorrectly to a quisling government supported by British troops and Whitehall administrators, and including African 'extremists'. The British government, in accordance with its September commitment, now requested the U.N. for selective mandatory sanctions, and announced the policy of 'no independence before majority rule', or NIBMAR, at once condemned as disastrous by the Conservative opposition.

The months coming after the *Tiger* debacle indeed witnessed a progressive backstepping by Britain from this untenable position. Following a visit by Lord Alport, a former Federal High Commissioner, to Salisbury in June 1967, Wilson told the House of Commons that 'we fully reserve our position' on NIBMAR. Edward Heath told the Tory party conference in October that Britain had blundered and misjudged. There had been 'a fundamental psychological misunderstanding of the nature of the Rhodesian people, both European and African'. By an overwhelming majority the conference voted for a settlement without insisting on a return to legality. The Labour party conference was more reserved, but in November Wilson sent George Thompson to Salisbury. Three months later, in February 1968, Sir Alec Douglas-Home made the same journey. At this point the March executions appeared to make reconciliation once more impossible, but the check proved to be only temporary. By October Wilson could point to the modification in the Law and Order (Maintenance) Act and also to the removal of certain 'intransigent racialists' from Smith's cabinet, a reference to the resignations of William Harper in July and of Lord Graham in September. In the background the continuing Nigerian civil war was diverting attention away from Rhodesia; there would be less to fear from the next Commonwealth Conference due in January 1969. All things considered, Wilson felt free to make a new attempt at a settlement as soon as the annual party conferences were out of the way. In September 1968 yet another civil servant made a confidential visit to

Salisbury. In October Britain abstained from a NIBMAR resolution in the Security Council. Finally on 9 October, nearly two years after *Tiger*, the British premier faced Smith once more across the wardroom table of a British warship, this time the *Fearless*, anchored throughout the talks in Gibraltar harbour.

Although the Rhodesians were treated with greater courtesy on this occasion, the discussions proved as barren as before. The new British proposals were very close to the *Tiger* document, but the absence of the complex procedures for return to legality, to which the Rhodesians had so strongly objected before, marked a definite retreat.[9] None the less on his return to Salisbury Smith found that the constitutional safeguards written into the proposals were 'fundamentally and completely repugnant'. These safeguards included not only a blocking third in the Legislative Assembly for all ordinary amendments, and a blocking quarter of the elected members of both houses sitting together for amendments to the entrenched clauses, but also an appeal to the Judicial Committee of the Privy Council against any such amendment which should be adversely reported on by the Constitutional Council as being either discriminatory or contrary to the Declaration of Rights. Since a similar, though less precise, 'second safeguard' had been written into the *Tiger* document two years before and had then met with no objections from the Rhodesian leaders, the British government had reason to suppose that Smith and his colleagues were prevaricating. A subsequent visit by Thompson to Salisbury in an attempt to find a way round Rhodesian objections on this and other items was of no avail. Broadcasting on 19 November Smith declared that an external second safeguard 'would derogate from the sovereignty of Rhodesia' and would mean a 'second-class independence' in which 'we are not masters in our own house'.

Once again it seemed to be a final end of 'talks'. Already on 11 November, the third anniversary of U.D.I., a new green and white Rhodesian flag had replaced the Union Jack. Desultory exchanges between London and Salisbury during the next few months revealed unchanging attitudes. On 21 May President Vorster stopped for two days of private talks with Smith before proceeding to visit Portugal, Spain, France and Switzerland.

On the same day the Rhodesian government published its own proposed new constitution which, together with the question of whether Rhodesia was to become a republic, was to be the subject of a referendum in June.

The decision to proceed to a new constitution, and probably to a republic, was only one step, though an important one, in the series of political manoeuvres that had been going on among Europeans in Rhodesia since 1967. During the twelve months that followed U.D.I., Ian Smith's position had been unquestionably strong both in the country and within his party. The moderate opposition to his left, ill-organized and at best half-hearted, closed ranks with the government in face of the unprecedented wave of sabotage and the sanctions threat. Extensions to the state of emergency, censorship of the press, police intervention against the University and a Constitutional Amendment Bill undermining the Bill of Rights were mostly accepted without serious demur. On the right the small but influential minority, content with the signal victory of independence, was biding its time. The *Tiger* affair however had changed all this and from that time Smith's position was increasingly in danger of being undermined, not so much in the country as a whole as within the powerful organization of the R.F.P. For *Tiger* had shown that Smith was prepared to accept a constitution with Africans in the legislature, even ultimately holding a majority of seats. His oft repeated 'not in my lifetime' was designed to calm the fears of his own white countrymen rather than to defy opinion abroad. This was a prospect which the hard core R.F.P. right wing would never accept.

The consequent stresses within the party began to appear during the following eighteen months, and came to a head when the R.F.P. constitutional proposals were published in July 1968. Based on the Whaley Commission report of the previous April, these proposals aimed at eventual parity of black and white representation in the central legislature but also at a provincial structure, to be reached after a delay of five years, with separate administration of the races. The implied objective of quasi-Bantustans was plain enough, but the 'two-stage' nature of the plan was still too tentative for the Rhodesia National Party, a new breakaway group from the R.F.P. formed in March. William Harper had already resigned from the cabinet on 4

July, and another right-winger, Lord Graham, left on 12
September. Next day the bulk of the Salisbury Central branch
of the R.F.P. resigned their membership in like-minded protest.
These moves expressed long-gathering discontent with Smith's
policies in view of continuing guerilla activity and the state of
the economy, and reflected a desire for the abandonment of
compromise and for the definitive separate development that
could only lead ultimately to closer union with South Africa.
Meanwhile on 29 August a new Centre Party, heir to the old
Rhodesia Party and supported by liberal organizations such as
the Rhodesia Action Association and the Rhodesia Constitutional Association, was formed to oppose this drift to apartheid.
Smith, aware that the ground was shifting under his feet, saw
the danger greatest on the right, and warning his followers
against 'racialists and extremists' exhorted them to uphold the
principle of fair play for all.

It was in these circumstances that the Rhodesian leader
flew to Gibraltar in October to meet Harold Wilson on H.M.S.
Fearless, knowing that he could not afford to accept the 'second
safeguard'. None the less the failure of the *Fearless* talks was a
defeat for Smith as well as for Wilson. In order to survive, he
must now swim with the tide that was taking Rhodesia out of
touch with Britain and ultimately towards South Africa. The
government's constitutional proposals, which at last appeared
on 21 May 1969, therefore went a long way towards meeting the
demands of the right wing, though they stopped short of confining African political activity to provincial councils.[10] A
republic was envisaged, subject to a referendum. There were to
be separate African and European voters' rolls, and cross-
voting was abolished. Ultimate parity was to be extended to
Africans, but never more than parity, and even this was to be
dependent upon the level of income tax that Africans paid.
The safeguard against amendments was to be a blocking third
only. The Declaration of Rights was no longer to be justiciable
in the courts and the use of preventive detention was, in any
case, excluded from it. Despite condemnation by the Constitutional Council and opposition from the Chiefs' Council,
African parties, business organizations, trade unions, the
Churches and elder statesmen, this uninhibitedly white supremacist constitution was approved in the referendum on 20

June by 54,724 votes to 20,766. On the same day an even larger majority of the predominantly white electorate voted for a republic. All this was still not enough for the extreme right. A week later the Conservative Alliance was formed, calling for the re-introduction of the old pass laws and for separate amenities for the races. But Smith had managed to bid high enough for the present. On 2 March 1970 Rhodesia was declared a republic, and in the elections ten days later the R.F.P. won all fifty European seats. Of the elected African places the Centre Party won seven, the eighth going to Josiah Gondo of the National Political Union.

This constitutional drift to the right was matched by other segregationalist legislation which resolutely stopped up the inroads in racial discrimination pioneered during the early sixties. In November 1967 the Municipal Amendment Act empowered local authorities to segregate amenities in public places such as parks, playing fields and swimming pools. Salisbury City Council immediately implemented these provisions. An even longer stride towards overall apartheid was taken with the Land Tenure Act of November 1969 which replaced existing Land Apportionment Acts and set out to be a final definition of segregation in land.[11] Apart from some 6½ million acres of national land, the country was divided almost equally between a European area of 44,952,900 acres and an African area of 44,944,500 acres; it was to be illegal for white or black to live or to own property in the contrary area. Furthermore the Act provided for differentiation in the European area between the European, Asian and Coloured races. The latter section foreshadowed the passage at last of the Property Owners' (Residential Protection) Bill. This notorious measure, first introduced in June 1967 to protect property values, would allow the inhabitants of predominantly white suburbs to petition the Minister for the removal of members of other races, in practice Asians and Coloureds, from the district, and would establish a 'denominational tribunal' to determine the race of the individuals concerned. Held up by the old 1961 Declaration of Rights, this bill now became feasible under the truncated Declaration of the new republican constitution.

The Churches in Rhodesia protested vigorously, even desperately, against these laws; on 25 April the Christian

Rhodesia: Land Distribution, 1969

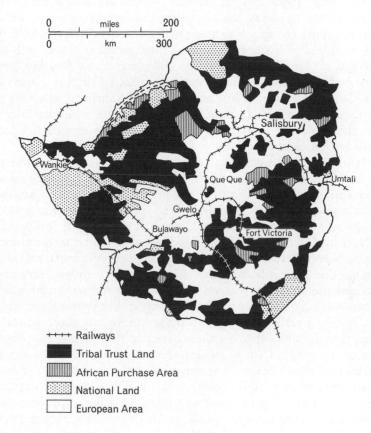

0   miles   200
0   km   300

Salisbury
Wankie
Que Que
Umtali
Gwelo
Bulawayo
Fort Victoria

+++ Railways
Tribal Trust Land
African Purchase Area
National Land
European Area

Council affirmed that the new constitution and the Land Tenure Act could not be reconciled with the Christian faith 'because they entail separation and discrimination solely on the basis of race . . . in direct contradiction to New Testament teaching'. The Roman Catholic bishops threatened to close all their institutions. It was of no avail. The government went ahead with economies in African education which involved reducing the primary school course from eight years to seven and reducing the grant to missions for teachers' salaries by five per cent.[12] The Tangwena tribe, under pressure since 1968 to leave their lands in the Inyanga hills, were now forcibly and repeatedly evicted. In February 1971 Cold Comfort Farm, a multi-racial institution on the outskirts of Salisbury, was closed and put up for sale. In October a similar fate was announced for the Epworth Methodist Mission which supported 3,500 Africans on European land.

It was at this eleventh hour that the Conservative government in London, holding office since June 1970, made Britain's third and apparently final bid to check the drift to apartheid and to re-establish the now time-honoured principle of unimpeded progress to majority rule. The draft settlement proposals signed by Ian Smith and Sir Alec Douglas-Home in Salisbury on 24 November, by abandoning the second safeguard, marked yet another retreat by Britain.[13] Although the Foreign Secretary assured the House of Commons that the proposals were consistent with his own five principles of 1964, the White Paper was assailed in Parliament and the press mainly on three counts: first, that the new settlement was based on the existing supremacist constitution of 1969; second, that the improvements which it claimed were measured against that 1969 constitution rather than against the 1961 constitution which was the original context of the five principles; and third, that the improvements themselves were pitiably small, were prospective rather than immediate in effect, and were dependent entirely upon the good faith of the white minority. Thus, U.D.I. and subsequent legislation would be legalized. The R.F.P. would continue in power. Though the income tax formula for increasing African representation was abolished, the new formula based on the percentage of Africans on the higher voters' roll would allow an increase so gradual as to delay African parity, let alone majority rule, until well into the next century. Membership of the African lower roll was to be greatly enlarged by its extension to those who had completed their primary education, but this was not reflected in any increase in the number of directly elected Africans in the House of Assembly, which still stood at eight. The new Declaration of Rights, though to be made justiciable, was hedged about with restrictions, could not affect existing law, and could be overriden by a state of emergency. The new amendment procedure, which would require a majority of the European and a majority of the African members of the House of Assembly voting separately, was an advance on the 1969 situation but not on that of 1961. It was in any case achieved at the expense of the second safeguard and in a constitution in which only half of the African members of the legislature were directly elected.

It was less than surprising therefore that the Pearce Commission, which spent two months in Rhodesia between January and March 1972 testing the acceptability of the proposals in accordance with the fifth principle, should conclude with an emphatic negative in its report, published in May.[14] Nonetheless the outcome came as a considerable shock to white Rhodesians, perhaps because this was the first time that mass African opinion had been sought outside the medium of the tribal leaders. Ian Smith subsequently described the report as 'naïve and inept'. It was certainly true that much in the complex proposals could not have been comprehensible to most of the African public, particularly in the rural areas where rejection was most overwhelming, and that interpreters could find no equivalent in Chishona or Sindebele for many essential terms. Nonetheless, those of the more politically conscious urban Africans who were able to be interviewed in small groups or as private individuals recorded a vote of 68 per cent against the proposals and only 15 per cent in favour, while 17 per cent were undecided.[15] The Rhodesian government blamed these results upon intimidation; but the Commission found that though there was 'a limited number of cases of serious intimidation' during the disorders that accompanied the first fortnight of their visit, notably at Shabani,[16] Gwelo, Fort Victoria, Harari and Umtali, this state of tension subsequently subsided and had 'no lasting or overwhelming effect' upon the outcome.[17] The African verdict appears to have been based rather upon suspicion that a deal, in which their own leaders had not been consulted, was being made over their heads; upon a reluctance to trust white minority governments not to adjust the franchise qualifications to their disadvantage from time to time, as had been done several times before; upon their views on the land question; and perhaps even more upon the wish, now that an opportunity had at last come their way, to express a will of their own.[18]

In doing so, they were undoubtedly influenced by the propaganda of the African National Council, an organization formed in December 1971 to 'explain and expose the dangerous implications' of the proposals. Its leader, Bishop Abel Muzorewa of the American Methodist Church in Rhodesia, waged an active campaign safeguarded by the government's guarantee of normal political activity while the Commission's work was in progress,[19] and made a favourable impression during his visit to the United Kingdom in March. There can be no doubt that the success of the A.N.C., and the verdict of the Pearce Report, gave a powerful impetus towards reviving African political morale. This impetus might in the long run prove to be irreversible, and to have been the most significant effect of this third British attempt to resolve the Rhodesian problem. Most European, and some African, critics argued that in securing the rejection of the proposals the A.N.C. had repeated the error of African leaders in 1961, exasperated what sympathetic white opinion still remained, and condemned the African people to political ineffectiveness for a long time to come. This view overlooks the fact that whereas in 1961 the Africans took part in the original discussions, in 1971 they did not; nor had a decade of Dominion Party/R.F.P. policies and public statements raised their hopes of a fair deal in the long run. Meanwhile the whole political structure of the continent had radically changed: the white-ruled redoubts of 'fortress southern Africa' seemed unlikely to surrender to pressures from outside or from within; but rather, from their economic strength, to be in a position to exert contrary pressures on the independent tropical zone.

For the time being at least, a settlement was thus ruled out. The sanctions programme, six-and-a-half years old, was wearing thin and had been seriously breached in January when the

United States under its new Strategic Materials Act recommenced the import of Rhodesian chrome. To outward appearances at least the supposedly beleaguered republic was one of the stablest, indeed one of the most prosperous, states in Africa south of the Sahara. Perhaps its greatest strength lay in the time being taken, far longer than originally expected, by the independent states to the north to resolve their enormous problems of economic, cultural and ethical change. Its greatest vulnerability in the long run lay in the built-in, almost irreversible white superiority syndrome leading necessarily to race separation and, given the manifest imbalance of the land distribution, to race antagonism. The peaceful solution to this intractable problem could enable the communities of Rhodesia to raise new hope for southern Africa, perhaps for the rest of the world.

Zambia Emergent

Some of the most damaging consequences of U.D.I. lay in its effects upon the newly-fledged republic of Zambia. Among these can be counted the deterioration of relations between the races, the decline of commercial farming, the disruption of Zambia's natural economic links with southern Africa and the development, at great cost, of new communications with the north, and the acceleration towards a presidential type of one-party state. It must be conceded, however, that these trends were being foreshadowed before U.D.I. As early as December 1964 the new Zambian government gave notice of the ending of its trade agreement with South Africa, and introduced a bill providing for the deportation of British or Rhodesian subjects, hitherto protected, if they 'frustrated government policy' or 'promoted racial animosity'. A further bill created penalties for insults to the President, to the national flag or to the national anthem. Adjustments in the relationship with the mining companies were also forecast. Indeed, a surge of self-assertion following the period of colonial rule and the association with Rhodesia during the federal period was bound to come, while the tribal divisions within the country were bound to be exacerbated by self-government and would inevitably give rise to measures designed to emphasize the central authority. It was unfortunate, however, that that authority should be so manifestly challenged by the confrontation with Rhodesia at such an early stage. The government was compelled to take an uncompromising line. Broadcasting from Lusaka on 11 November 1965, President Kaunda declared that Zambia would not hesitate to meet force with force if its territory should be violated and, warning that a 'racially bloody war', even a third world war, might not be far distant, appealed for British troops to guard the Kariba dam. Recognizing that Rhodesia had inherited the bulk of the former Federal air force and that Zambia lacked airborne defences, and impressed by the sabotaging of a Copperbelt power pylon, the British government quickly dispatched a squadron of Javelin fighter bombers to Ndola together with a detachment of the R.A.F. Regiment. Though Wilson stated that Britain 'would not stand idly by' if Rhodesia cut the power supply to the Copperbelt, the Javelin operation was equally intended to forestall any Zambian appeal elsewhere. The squadron remained in Zambia for nine months until August 1967, by which time the Rhodesian threat was less apparent and Kaunda's alarmism was being discounted.

Meanwhile the imposition of sanctions against Rhodesia had some awkward consequences for Zambia. The Rhodesian insistence on payment in advance in convertible currency for imports through Rhodesia was extended in May to the through carriage of Zambian exports, including copper. Though the Zambian government challenged this decision in the courts, the rail outlet through Rhodesia was effectively closed from 23 May. By purchasing from the United States the consignment of 26 diesel locomotives originally destined for Rhodesia, Zambia was able to augment the use of the Benguela railway and of the Congolese rail system; but by the end of July these alternative routes were still only carrying 50 per cent of the monthly copper output. Italian Fiat had by this time agreed to supply 800 lorries for use over the Great North Road to Dar es Salaam. In March Herculese airfreighters began lifting copper out of the stockpile. The most critical transport problem arose from the Rhodesian ban on the transit of oil to Zambia, which immediately followed the British oil embargo of 27 December 1965. A British airlift of petroleum products from Dar es Salaam was supported in January by American contractors flying from Leopoldville to Elizabethville. Use was also made of the railway from Beira to Selima, and thence of the Great East Road. By May 1966 it was possible to discontinue the airlift; but the fuel shortage was not fully ended until the opening of the 1,058-mile oil pipeline from Dar es Salaam to Ndola two years later. Meanwhile, compared with the problems of copper exports and petroleum imports, the assurance of coal supplies caused less anxiety. The Rhodesians rapidly thought better of a new and prohibitive export tax on coal, but during 1966 the Zambians commenced open-cast mining of just usable coal at Nkandabwe and Siankondobwa. By May coal imports from Wankie had fallen from 60,000 tons a month to 40,000 and continued to decline. Kaunda was able to announce on 3 May that Zambia's imports from Rhodesia had been cut by 75 per cent.

Thus by mid-1966 Zambia had managed, with largely British assistance and in association with Tanzania and the Congo, to dispense with most of its commercial and communications links with Rhodesia. Mainly this had been done by the use of short term expedients, but the preparation of permanent alternative systems was already under way. Tenders were out for the oil pipeline contract. In March 1966 an independent Zambian airline, operated by an Italian subsidiary of Alitalia, put an end to the use of the old Central African Airways. Later in the year, following the publication of the F.A.O. report on the Kafue basin, plans were announced for the construction of a hydro-electric scheme on the Kafue River that would free the Copperbelt from dependence on Kariba. Work on this project began in 1968, the contract having been awarded to a Yugoslav firm. Most ambitious of all, however, was the decision made in June 1967, in conjunction with Tanzania, to accept an offer from the Chinese government to build the Tan-Zam Railway and to finance it to the extent of £100 millions. This project had been under discussion since Chou en Lai's visit to Tanzania in 1965. Despite President Nyerere's professed indifference as to the source of the capital, the Africans would have preferred to obtain funds from an international consortium. The World Bank however decided that the railway would be uneconomic and require heavy subsidies. Britain would not go beyond offering half the survey costs. By 1967 therefore both Nyerere and Kaunda had decided to accept the Chinese offer, and after the Zambian President's visit to Peking, where he received an enthusiastic welcome, the agreement was signed. By 1968 hundreds, and by 1970 thousands, of Chinese technicians were working in Tanzania and Zambia.

This extrication of Zambia from much of her economic involvement with white-ruled southern Africa was in some ways to her advantage. Long-term benefits were bound to accrue from the development of new lines of communication, even though the routes to the south must some day be re-opened. The railway to the north-east had been mooted before 1900 and several times since.[1] The new oil pipeline not only freed the over-burdened railway for other freight, but even lowered the price of petrol. The Kafue hydro-electric project would soon make possible the exploitation of the Kafue plain that had been envisaged in the 1950s. New sugar plantations, new coal mines and new industry would now be forced ahead more rapidly than would have been the case had the links with Rhodesia been maintained.

The confrontation with Rhodesia nonetheless aggravated the problems facing the new republic while at the same time tending to distort or to obscure the real issues. These issues can be grouped under three heads: first, internal security, defence and foreign alignment; second, the strategy and consequences of economic growth; and third, the struggle for unity in the face of centrifugal tribalism.

The question of defence was not one with which the new government would have expected or wished to be faced, but within a year of independence Zambia found herself the front-line representative of the O.A.U., of the British sanctions programme and in due course of a United Nations' offensive. In Angola to the west and in Mozambique to the east, as well as in South-West Africa, African liberation movements were waging guerilla warfare in which they looked to Zambia for refuge and for passive support. While the Zambian government firmly refused to permit guerilla training to take place within its territory, it was neither able nor indeed willing to forbid 'freedom fighters' to travel through, and turned a blind eye to the existence of transit camps on the north bank of the Zambezi. Rhodesian counter-measures, including river patrols and air reconnaissance, were challenged by Zambia as a threat to her security. Early in 1968 a Portuguese aircraft dropped bombs on a village in the Eastern Province killing three people. Later the same year Portuguese troops crossed the border from Angola and burned three Lovale villages to the ground. Following the laying of landmines in the Caprivi strip by Namibian or South-West African guerillas allegedly operating from Zambian soil, South African police began occasionally to patrol inside the Zambian border south of Sesheke. Though such measures were inherently defensive or retaliatory rather than aggressive, there was open talk in the south of a pre-emptive strike. When added to intermittent acts of sabotage such as the destruction of a Benguela railway bridge in 1966, of the Luangwa road bridge in 1968, and of a pumping station on the oil pipeline in 1969, they combined to create a feeling of defencelessness in Zambia. Her enormous area and 4,000 miles of frontier were guarded by a brigade of three battalions, still trained and led by officers on secondment from the British Army, and her tiny collection of unarmed reconnaissance planes could be no match for the air forces to the south.[2] Neighbouring Malawi, with its growing economic and diplomatic ties with South Africa, gave little comfort. Kaunda had denounced Dr Banda as a traitor to the African cause, diplomatic missions were closed, and any hope of improving relations were dashed in 1967 when Malawi announced large territorial claims in Zambia's Eastern Province. This was to be followed by Banda's acceptance of a massive South African aid programme and his own state visit to the Union in 1970.[3] To the north, Congo (Kinshasa) with its turbulent record and heavy dependence on foreign capital was at best an unreliable friend, and by 1970, like Malawi, was drawing closer to Pretoria. In these circumstances, Kaunda's drive for closer links with Tanzania were all the more explicable. U.D.I. had in fact placed Zambia in greater immediate isolation than Rhodesia which, despite sanctions, could rely on close economic and military support from a powerful neighbour.

The sense of isolation goes some way to explain Kaunda's persistent but increasingly unrealistic demands that Britain should put an end to the Rhodesian revolt by force. Such an eventuality would in fact have been disastrous for Zambia, whose strategic installations were hopelessly vulnerable to retaliation. Kaunda however had to take into account a volatile public opinion and a critical opposition. Denied British intervention, and facing a general election at the end of the year, he asked for and in 1969 obtained a Rapier ground-to-air missile system, a weapon of sophistication unique in black Africa. This concession, though it enabled the Zambians to indulge in an expensive gesture of defiance, did little to improve the now cool relations with Britain, or to silence the complaints from Lusaka that Zambia had been inadequately compensated for the cost of her economic turnabout or for her part in the sanctions operation. The accelerated Africanization of the Zambian army now followed, accompanied by the replacement of British officers in the Zambian Air Force with Italian personnel. Kaunda could not in fact free himself from ultimate dependence on British support. Committed publicly and privately to non-alignment, he knew that to call for example on China for assistance in a crisis would be disastrous.[4] This made the restraint of British policy all the more irksome. Race relations were adversely affected. Just as Rhodesians suspected the British of supporting the guerilla operations, the Zambians accused them of being in league with the southern whites.

Kaunda had foreseen this danger at the outset of the U.D.I. crisis in November 1965 when he had turned in fury on the Rhodesian African nationalists for the violence of their anti-European broadcasts over Lusaka radio. During 1966 opinion turned against Europeans generally, especially on the Copperbelt where, at Kitwe, a serious stoning incident occurred. The expulsion of two expatriate staff of Anglo-American convicted of espionage in April 1967 did not improve matters. In May the European officers of the police special branch were given a month's notice to quit the country, and in the prevailing climate many other Europeans, mostly British, resigned from the administrative services and left. This exodus was one of the most serious blows suffered by the young republic. The hundred or so Zambian graduates at the time of independence could have been absorbed many times over in the administrative departments, let alone elsewhere, and it would be some years before the accelerated secondary education programme, and the new University of Zambia which opened near Lusaka in 1966, could make up the balance. Until that time Zambia needed not only to hold as many expatriates as possible but also to attract others both to fill existing posts and to train the young Africans who would ultimately replace them.[5] Instead the reverse happened. Making a virtue of necessity, the President proceeded to a policy of deliberate Zambianization. Inevitably such appointments often went to U.N.I.P. supporters whose career of political activism did not always suit them to public service. Standards in transport and public administration began to decline.[6] Meanwhile the crime rate was on the increase. This was partly due to the presence of 'freedom fighters' making their way through the country to the transit camps, and partly to the wave of immigration from the rural areas to the burgeoning shanty towns along the line of rail. It was natural that the Zambian government should blame its difficulties on Britain's failure to suppress the Rhodesian revolt.

In spite of these difficulties, however, the first of the new development plans, scheduled for the five years from 1966 to 1970, achieved a remarkable degree of growth in certain areas of the economy, notably in secondary industry. At that time the copper mines still accounted for 95 per cent of the country's exports, provided 56 per cent of its revenue and made up 38 per cent of its domestic product. Foreign investment would take care of mineral expansion. The government now poured massive funds, derived from the sequestration of the B.S.A. Company royalties and from the booming copper tax revenues, into diversification away from copper. Important new projects included the sugar estates at Nakambala, a textile factory at Kafue, where a new industrial complex was planned, a new cement works at Ndola and a huge poultry-rearing scheme outside Lusaka, not to mention the gigantic though less productive international airport outside the capital. At the same time an ambitious education programme raised annual expenditure from £4 millions to £29 millions a year, envisaging the opening of 40 new secondary schools by 1970. Primary school enrolments nearly doubled in a phenomenal leap from 378,000 in 1964 to 694,000 in 1970. Much of this made sense on paper only. In a country where 45 per cent of the population was aged under 15, herculean remedies were called for, but figures of this order were only attained by the abbreviation of training courses and by compromising on standards. At the same time much of the object was lost when many rural children, upon leaving school, at once set off for the line of rail. Despite the growth rate of 10 per cent attained over the five-year period, there had not been, as was proudly claimed, an economic revolution, but only a marked acceleration of the uneven development that had been going on more slowly before.

By 1968 Kaunda and his advisers were becoming aware of this. They also knew that the giant mining industry, on which the bulk of Zambia's economy still rested, was a thriving capitalist complex closely linked with that of South Africa and paying dividends to a host of shareholders in that country and overseas. The same was true of much of secondary industry and the distributive trades. Three motives now prompted Kaunda to convert his country's rapid economic development into something more like a genuine economic revolution. The first of these was the continuing wish to be free of white dominion in any and every form and to match political with economic independence. The second derived from the view that a degree of public ownership would make more effective direction of the economy possible, and by this means overcome the imbalance between urban and rural development. 'From the measures we have taken leading us to economic independence,' the President was to write in 1970, 'we hope to succeed in bringing the fruits of independence to our people, especially in the rural areas where 80 per cent live in great poverty.' Thirdly was the need, as Kaunda saw it, for the government to lead more firmly, to integrate and to consolidate what was more and more often referred to as 'the nation' at a time when inter-tribal and inter-racial mistrust were beginning to threaten the coherence of the state.

In seeking for a new economic pattern, Kaunda was chiefly influenced by the examples of Tanzania, with its philosophy of 'ujamaa', a form of co-operative socialism and national self-reliance inaugurated by Julius Nyerere in the Arusha Declaration of January 1967,[7] and of Chile, whose President, Dr Allende, was experimenting with a new form of non-Marxist socialism. Speaking as a guest at the annual U.N.I.P. conference later that year, Nyerere seemed to be warning the Zambians that with very different economies there was no need for their countries' policies to coincide.[8] Kaunda indeed realized that Zambia could not, as Tanzania proposed to do, dispense with foreign investment, which was the breath of life for a mineral-rich territory. Nonetheless his new policy, announced at Mulungushi on 19 April 1968, envisaged restrictions on trade by expatriates—Europeans and Asians—in order to increase Zambian participation in the economy and the share to Zambian businessmen of the funds available for loan. Principal among the measures announced to Parliament in January 1969 was the 'request', under threat of compulsory acquisition, to twenty-six major foreign-owned companies that they should sell 51 per cent of their shares to the government. New trading and road-transport licences would only be granted to Zambian-controlled companies, and existing trading licences would be forbidden to non-Zambians outside the ten main urban centres. An immediate consequence was the closing of 850 Asian-owned stores up and down the country, which few Zambians came forward to buy even at knock-down prices. These measures amounted to Zambianization rather than nationalization. The mining companies were spared interference, merely being required, like other privately-owned companies, to limit the remission of dividends abroad to 50 per cent of profits. As much as 80 per cent had formerly been going overseas, and the balance of 30 per cent was now to be spent on developments within Zambia.[9] Any intention of nationalizing the mines was however repeatedly denied.

Kaunda's next step, announced at a U.N.I.P. National Council meeting at the Matero suburb of Lusaka on 11 August, therefore came as a surprise to the two large copper-mining groups as well as to world financial interests. The new proposals involved the taking over by the state of all mineral rights in the country, and replacing them by 25-year exploitation leases; meanwhile the mining companies were to be 'invited' to sell 51 per cent of their shares to the government. The pill was sugared however by the device of an improved mineral tax, and by the ending of the recent restriction on dividend payments overseas; logical enough, as the mines were no longer private companies, and most necessary, as the restriction was threatening to damp down foreign investment in Zambian mining enterprise. The new measures were accompanied by the setting up of two public authorities, the Industrial Development Corporation (INDECO) and the Mining Development Corporation (MINDECO) to manage the new responsibilities.[10] Though checked by a serious mine disaster at Mufulira in September 1970, a considerable increase in production now took place, and though this had been planned for months earlier, the government was able to claim much of the credit.

Indeed the effect of the new policy on Zambia's economy was less than might have been expected. Growth continued into 1970 at a steady rate, and was only to be slowed by the collapse in the price of copper, from £700 to £400 a ton, in 1971. On the one hand, government purchase of majority holdings in large companies did not deprive those companies of skilled management. On the other, the attempt to Zambianize medium-scale enterprise could not in any case succeed at the stroke of a pen. Thus, a resolution of the U.N.I.P. National Council in March 1972, deploring 'the failure on the part of some sections of our population to take full advantage of the economic reforms in their entirety' noted that the requirement for builders to sub-contract to Zambians only 'has been largely frustrated by the inadequacy and lack of enthusiasm of Zambian would-be sub-contractors'. It added with regret that to most Zambians the term 'economic reforms' meant 'shops, bars and tea-rooms, and not the wider spectrum'.[11]

Such problems were an inevitable and common experience in communities attempting by a combination of planning and expenditure from above to change their peoples' way of life and economic motivation. Of more immediate danger to the Zambian revolution was the price of copper in world markets. The second National Development Plan, outlined by the President on 12 January 1972 and designed to cover the five years 1972–6, took this into account by reasonably assuming an average price of K740 per ton.[12] This still allowed for the enormous proposed outlay of K2,161 millions. Though most of this money was to be spent on mining, industry and transport development, including an 'integrated iron and steel industry', with the aim of increasing Zambia's self-sufficiency, much of the space in this new Plan was devoted to an urgent call for a rural renaissance. The disequilibrium between the stagnant rural areas and the booming line of rail, now usually referred to as the 'rural-urban gap', had doubled since independence. Considerable expenditure was now to be devoted to agricultural extension units and loans. Villagers were exhorted to build themselves new houses of sun-dried brick, to plant fruit trees, to dig wells, rear more chickens and even rabbits. Schemes were announced for the re-grouping of villages in productive areas and for the organization of co-operative farms, two of which, on an Israeli pattern, had already been set up close to the Copperbelt in 1971. The initial effect of all this was slight. The rural renaissance would have to await the necessarily slow penetration of modern transport systems into the outlying areas. Meanwhile an attempted incomes policy in operation since 1970 had done little to check mounting urban wage levels.[13]

In spite of the motto 'One Zambia—one nation', Zambia was in fact rapidly building itself into two societies at a speed only made possible, ironically enough, by its huge copper resources. There were, however, other grave divisions and of these that between the races was less threatening than that between the tribes. In 1963 Kaunda had proclaimed a non-racial policy for the new republic, but by 1970 non-tribalism had become much more urgent. This fact lay behind the President's newly-minted philosophy of 'humanism'[14] as well as behind the subsequent moves towards the establishment, in 1972, of a one-party state.

Much of the trouble lay within the United National Independence Party itself, and went back to the year before independence. The use of violence during 1963 by local party leaders both against the colonial administration and against groups opposed to them, notably the Lumpa sect, had set a dangerous pattern for political method. Many of these local leaders now held senior posts in local and central government. Since then political contests such as by-elections and especially the election campaign of December 1968 continued to be marked by inter-party and inter-tribal fights in the crowded townships. Such events followed the precedents of other African countries, where the first elections after independence were likewise the signal for dangerous political unrest. More serious was the development of an almost Bismarckian type of struggle for the eradication of religious sects who seemed through their beliefs to challenge the integrity of the state. By 1969 some 20,000 Lumpas were refugees in the Katanga, while an unknown number of Jehovah's Witnesses had been driven from their homes, some to their death, for their refusal to salute the flag or to sing the anthem. These things happened in a country whose constitution safeguarded the rights of individuals, the interests of minorities and liberty of worship. As in 1962, Kaunda denounced the violence but was not able to restrain provincial officials. Meanwhile regular extensions of the emergency regulations, as in Rhodesia, authorized restriction without trial to selected areas.[15]

Although the emergency regulations in any case set aside some of the constitutional safeguards, the constitution was itself progressively modified to suit the requirements of Kaunda's strategy by strengthening both the executive and the Party. Executive control over the parliamentary party was increased in September 1966 by a constitutional amendment requiring members of the House who resigned from or were expelled from their party to contest their seats again in by-elections. A year later the size of the House was increased by 30 members to 105. By 1968 however communal antagonisms were threatening the integrity of both party and state. The shock of the President's threatened resignation in February pulled the dissidents within the government together for a time, but regional issues were meanwhile beginning to run on party lines. Nalumino Mundia, a former Lozi minister, had formed a United Party late in 1967 to promote Lozi interests. Violent political clashes involving the U.P. led to its proscription in August 1968. During the year however U.N.I.P. lost four southern by-elections to the A.N.C. which, still led by the veteran Harry Nkumbula, now began to obtain Lozi support. The violent election campaign of December led to a U.N.I.P. victory of 81 seats to A.N.C.'s 23; but the A.N.C. had won 8 of the 10 seats in Barotseland.[16] Although these results confirmed U.N.I.P.'s dominant position in the legislature, they also gave a startling emphasis to separatist tendencies in Barotseland, to some extent in the Mwinilunga district of the north-west, and also in the Southern Province. These areas, especially Barotseland, had gained less from the 'Zambian revolution' and from the new transport links to the north-east. Work on the new West Road being constructed from Lusaka to Mongu was incomplete and at a standstill. The banning of labour contracting to

South Africa, a system of which the Lozi had formerly made much use, was a further grievance. The government now added insult to injury by renaming Barotseland the Western Province and by terminating the special rights accorded to the Litunga by the treaty of 1897.

Angered by the Barotseland election results, Kaunda threatened to cancel the trading licences of A.N.C. supporters there, and to dismiss A.N.C. members from the police and the civil service. 'We bow to the feelings of the people,' he said, 'and the feelings of the people are that it must pay to belong to the U.N.I.P.' Tension was maintained by violent incidents at Mumbwa and Livingstone at the turn of the year. The law, upheld in the last resort by the High Court, stood in the way of official persecution, and the wrath of the executive began to be turned towards the judiciary. When the crisis came in July 1969, however, it was over a different matter altogether. Two unarmed Portuguese soldiers, invited across the border by the Zambian customs officer at Feira, had thereupon been arrested and subsequently jailed for two years by the local Zambian magistrate. In the High Court Mr Justice Evans upheld their appeal, ordering their release after eighteen days' imprisonment, and criticizing the Zambian authorities concerned. Kaunda, aware of the imminence of his radical statement on the copper mines, misinterpreted these comments as being a reflection upon the Presidential authority, and denounced the theory that the judiciary had the right to criticize the executive power. When Chief Justice Skinner supported Evans' judgement, a Lusaka mob including five hundred uniformed members of the Zambian youth service stormed the High Court, damaging furniture and destroying documents. Courtrooms on the Copperbelt were also attacked. Judges Skinner, Evans and Wheelen, with regret and good wishes for Zambia, left the country.[17] The President announced that he would 'change the structure of the constitution' to allow lawyers of only five years' standing, or less 'if they did their work efficiently', to sit in the High Court, and proceeded to Zambianize the judiciary.

Such an important modification to the constitution presented no difficulty because only a month earlier, on 17 June, the referendum procedure required for a step of this nature had been abolished. The abolition had itself required a referendum, but it had been explained to the public that a favourable vote would make it possible to disappropriate absentee landlords without recourse to special procedure. Many European farmers had left Zambia since 1965, but without selling their farms, and the price of land had consequently slumped. The government wished to take over this land and either re-allocate it to Zambians or create government ranches. This, it was claimed, required an amendment to the Bill of Rights, an amendment which was used for doing away with the referendum procedure altogether. The way ahead for further changes was now open.

During his Matero speech on 11 August, the President warned that 'if we wanted, we could make Zambia a one-party state today. We have all the necessary instruments, including the will of the majority of the people'. It was to be over two years before that step was taken, but during that time the structure of U.N.I.P. was adapted and extended for the purpose, mainly in response to challenges from centrifugal forces both inside and outside the Party. In August 1969, immediately after Matero, violent incidents on the Copperbelt followed by Simon Kapwepwe's resignation as Vice-President on the grounds that the Bemba were suffering discrimination presented Kaunda with a crisis long foreseen. Many Copperbelt workers, especially at Mufulira, were Bemba. Communal antagonisms involving these 'tough and assertive northerners' could have more immediately inflammatory consequences than those involving the relatively peripheral Lozi and Tonga groups. Kaunda swiftly demonstrated his powers of leadership by dissolving the central committee, by assuming for himself the position of secretary-general of the Party, and by persuading Kapwepwe to stay on as Vice-President for the life of the existing Assembly. In November 1970 the post of secretary-general was given wider powers, while new party principles and a new code of discipline were laid down. The re-elected central committee had been increased in size so that the balance of communal representation could be improved. This move however appeared to give more rather than less scope for communal disputes within the U.N.I.P. hierarchy. In April 1971 Kaunda had to outlaw two unofficial tribal committees representing Bemba and Tonga factions, and Justin Chimba, Minister of Trade and Industry, was dismissed for breaching the principle of collective responsibility. Worse still Kapwepwe finally broke away in August to form a United Progressive Party in alliance with the A.N.C. against the U.N.I.P. and Kaunda. Though the U.P.P. was banned early in 1972,[18] there could now be little hope of the one-party state coming to pass in the natural course of events.

At Mulungushi on 4 March 1972 Kaunda therefore announced his decision to proceed to a 'one-party participatory democracy' in Zambia.[19] A constitutional commission had already been appointed; Nkumbula and Mundia had been invited to serve, but had refused. The President emphasized that the decision was not designed to suppress opposition. 'We are permanently set against dictatorship.' Nonetheless 'the one-party democracy will help us to weed out political opportunists and people who have become professionals at manufacturing lies and pretending to oppose what they inwardly welcome.' Perusal of the Daily Parliamentary Debates would prove that 'there are no grounds for organized parliamentary opposition in the country. We can deal with all our problems within the same family.'

At the time of the 1968 elections, a Copperbelt youth leader had expressed the idea more concisely to the London *Times* correspondent by saying that in the old days 'we only had one Chief, and he had no opponent'.[20] However there was more to the new policy than a reversal to African tradition, natural though it might be for Zambian Africans to recognize and understand the one-party state in this light. Rather it was a realistic acceptance of the fact that the transitional stage was likely to be longer drawn out than the constitutional theorists of the colonial period had envisaged. Many African states had acknowledged the same realities, not least those closest to hand. Most powerfully there was the example of Tanzania. There the one-party state had come about naturally; it had been necessary to institutionalize it in order to give scope for democratic criticism within T.A.N.U. In Zambia it had not come about so easily, and it was necessary to establish it in order to resist communally inspired criticism outside U.N.I.P. There were other differences. Whereas Nyerere could address the National Assembly in Swahili, the Zambians had no African common language. Nor was Tanzanian society riven into two, as Zambia's was, by an ever-growing urban-rural disequilibrium. In neighbouring Malawi on the other hand President Banda was adapting his own highly assertive personality to his own set of circumstances. In a country that was proportionately even more rural yet tribally and linguistically more homogeneous, he had adopted the trappings of traditional paramountcy more openly, even brazenly to western eyes, and by November 1970 had accepted the Presidency for life. Such a step Kaunda, in his vast and variegated land with its increasingly detribalized industrial society along the line of rail, consistently and wisely refused to take. Short of this however the charisma and energy of his personality were providing a focus during its first decade of independence that Zambia could not easily have spared.

One-party states were not of course confined to Africa. Several Zambian leaders had visited both Moscow and Peking. Zambian government literature, as if in emulation of the Chinese booklets of which English versions were increasingly on sale in Lusaka and Copperbelt bookshops, spoke of U.N.I.P. as 'the Party' in terms which had an ominous ring. 'The unity of the Party', declared Kaunda on 8 May 1971, 'is the unity of the people.'[21] U.N.I.P. must be synonymous with unity and peace, with development and prosperity, with defence and security, and with discipline. The rejection of dictatorship was nonetheless sincere enough. Kaunda's homespun 'humanism', though sometimes discredited as a utopian form of socialism, was distinguished as sharply from Marxist communism, which set one class against another, as from apartheid, which set one race against another. Kaunda in fact sought to lead his country down the middle road. This was a lonely road and a perilous one in a world where the realists were taking sides. With foreign-trained freedom fighters drifting through to the Zambezi and beyond, and with Chinese technicians committed to railway construction for years ahead, the danger from the left was ever present. Alarmed at attempts to promote a proletarian movement among African workers on the Copperbelt, the government in August 1971 had had to close the East German consulate in Lusaka and to recall students and trade missions from the German People's Republic. Meanwhile the pull from the right was equally, perhaps more insidious. The siren tones of Dr Hilgard Muller's outward-looking *verligte* policy towards black Africa were reaching well north of Zambia's borders. It was undeniable that the South African broadcasting system provided the most popular listening for the Zambian public. If it was mortifying to have to depend in emergency on Rhodesian maize,[22] the time might come when copper prices fell so low that Zambia would have to turn to South Africa for assistance. If these things should come to pass, and if the counter-revolution should prove successful in Angola and Mozambique, it was not inconceivable that Zambia might yet become economically if not politically subordinate to a white-ruled southern African complex.[23]

The immediate objective of non-alignment, of humanism and of the one-party state was the avoidance of these extremes, and the cultivation of the new kind of nationalism that was emerging in Zambia, as elsewhere in Africa. This went beyond the old African nationalism, largely race-orientated, which struggled against colonial control, to the new spirit which sought against all the forces of urban distortion and communal separatism, to give full scope to the African personality, to create a nation where there was none before, and to train its people in the enthusiasms and compromises, the loyalties and restraints, which the functioning of democracy of whatever kind requires.

APPENDIX I

A summary of the views of the various political groups in Southern Rhodesia on the franchise question, January 1961.

(1) The Dominion Party advocated (*a*) that there should be no change in so far as this would involve a lowering of existing standards; (*b*) that the present Lower Roll should be eliminated; (*c*) that the monetary qualifications should be related to the value of money.

(2) The United Federal Party (in power at the time), while recognizing that Africans must over the years play an increasing part in the affairs of the country, stressed the importance of not lowering the qualifications for the franchise.

(3) The Central Africa Party advocated a simple franchise qualification of literacy in English, and the inclusion of additional categories of persons holding responsible positions in the public service, who would not necessarily be literate in English.

(4) The National Democratic Party maintained that 'one man—one vote' was the only realistic solution to the question of the franchise.

(5) The Coloured Community asked that two special seats in the legislature should be reserved for them since they considered that this was the only practical way of safeguarding their political status as a minority group.

(6) The Asian Organization accepted universal adult suffrage as the ultimate objective, but considered that this should be achieved by stages.

APPENDIX II

Summary of the franchise qualifications in the 1961 Constitution for Rhodesia.

The following categories qualified for the franchise, provided that they

  (a) were over 21 years of age,
  (b) were citizens of the Federation of Rhodesia and Nyasaland,
  (c) had resided in the constituency or electoral district concerned for three months prior to the election, and
  (d) had sufficient knowledge of English to complete the registration form.

'A' Roll:

  (a) Those who had been in receipt of an income of £720 for the previous two years, or who had ownership of immoveable property worth £1,500, or
  (b) Those who had completed a course of primary education and had been in receipt of an income of £480 for the previous two years, or had ownership of immoveable property worth £1,000, or
  (c) Those who had completed four years secondary education and had been in receipt of an income of £300, or had ownership of immoveable property worth £500, or
  (d) Chiefs or headmen.

'B' Roll:

  (a) Those who had been in receipt of an income of £240 for the previous six months, or who had ownership of immoveable property worth £450, or
  (b) Those who had completed two years of secondary education and had been in receipt of an income of £120 for the previous six months, or had ownership of immoveable property worth £250, or
  (c) Those who, being over 30 years of age, had been in receipt of an income of £180 for the previous six months, or had ownership of immoveable property worth £350, or
  (d) Kraal heads with a following of 20 heads of families, or
  (e) Ministers of religion.

Married women could vote on either roll provided their husbands were qualified.

APPENDIX III

Summary of the five principles on which the British Government required to be satisfied before granting independence to Rhodesia in October 1965.

(1) The principle and intention of unimpeded progress to majority rule enshrined in the 1961 Constitution would have to be maintained and guaranteed.

(2) There would also have to be guarantees against retrogressive amendment of the Constitution.

(3) There would have to be an immediate improvement in the political status of the African population.

(4) There would have to be progress towards ending racial discrimination.

(5) The British Government would have to be satisfied that any basis proposed for independence was acceptable to the people of Rhodesia as a whole.

Commenting on these principles, the Rhodesian Government replied:

(1) The 1961 Constitution already provided for an increasing number of Africans able to vote. Guarantees against retrogression would be a question of mechanism.

(2) It was proposed to add a Senate, consisting of twelve chiefs elected by the Chiefs' Council, to vote together with the Assembly on any question affecting the revision of the entrenched clauses. This would replace the referendum procedure provided under the 1961 Constitution.

(3) Such a Senate would represent a major political advance for Africans. None other was contemplated, apart from increasing the number of voters on the 'B' Roll to include all taxpayers.

(4) The Rhodesian Government hoped that segregation would disappear by an evolutionary process, but refused to repeal the Land Apportionment Act.

(5) The desire of the majority of the population for independence on the basis of the 1961 Constitution had already been demonstrated by consultation with tribal opinion and by a referendum of the electorate.

APPENDIX IV

Summarized extracts from the 1969 Constitution of Rhodesia.

LEGISLATURE

The House of Assembly

Composition:

50 European members

16 African members (8 directly elected, 8 indirectly elected by electoral colleges of Chiefs, Headmen and Councillors—4 each in Mashonaland and Matabeleland)

Total 66 members

Increase in African representation:

When the proportion of income tax assessed on Africans exceeds sixteen sixty-sixths of the total income tax assessed on Europeans and Africans the number of African members will be increased so that it bears the same proportion to the total number of members as the proportion of income tax that is assessed on Africans. The first two additional Africans will be indirectly elected and the next two additional seats will be filled by direct election; additional seats thereafter to be allocated in this sequence. When parity of representation with the Europeans is reached there is to be no further increase in African representation.

The Senate

Composition:

10 Europeans chosen by the European members of the House of Assembly

10 African Chiefs—5 each from Matabeleland and Mashonaland chosen by the Council of Chiefs in each Province

3 members appointed by the President—one Coloured and two European

Total 23 members

ELECTORAL SYSTEM

Franchise Qualifications

All voters must be citizens of Rhodesia over 21 with an adequate knowledge of English and able to complete the application form in their own writing.

European roll:

> *Either* income £900 or property value £1,800; *or* income £600 or property value £1,200 plus four years' secondary education.

African roll:

> *Either* income £300 or property value £600; *or* income £200 or property value £400 plus two years' secondary education.

AMENDMENTS

Entrenched clauses dealing with the Legislature, the Judicature, amendment procedures, the Declaration of Rights and fundamental land laws cannot be amended without a two-thirds majority of each House.

APPENDIX V

POPULATION (thousands)

	S. R.			N. R.			Ny.		
	African	European	Asian & Col'd	African	European	Asian & Col'd	African	European	Asian & Col'd
1900 .	500	11·7		770			830		
1905 .	622	13		790			880		
1910 .	734	20·8		820	1·5		950	·7	·5
1915 .	822	27·3	1 / 2	860	2	·1	1,080	·8	·4
1920 .	860	32·5	1·2 / 2	950	3	·2	1,200	1·5	·5
1925 .	922	38·2	1·4 / 2·1	1,050	4	·3	1,350	1·7	1
1930 .	1,048	47·9	1·7 / 2·4	1,310	11·1	·6	1,500	1·9	1·5
1935 .	1,223	54·4	2·1 / 3	1,370	10·7	·8	1,600	1·8	1·4
1940 .	1,390	65	2·5 / 3·8	1,500	14·3	1·4	1,850	2·1	2
1945 .	1,640	80·5	2·9 / 4·4	1,630	20·8	1·7	2,100	2·3	2·8
1950 .	2,100	125	3·6 / 5·2	1,700	36	3·1	2,300	3·8	5·2
1955 .	2,400	165	4·9 / 7·6	2,085	65	6·6	2,550	6·3	9·4
1960 .	2,830	223	6·7 / 9·9	2,340	76	10·3	2,810	9·3	12·8
	R			Z			M		
1965 .	4,020	219	8 / 12·7	3,600		10·5	3,841	7·4	11·5
1969 .	4,847	228	8 / 15	4,003	45	11	4,050	6·5	10·5

NOTES

CHAPTER I SECTION 2: THE DAWN OF HISTORY IN CENTRAL AFRICA

1. J. Desmond Clark: *The Prehistory of Southern Africa*, p. 105. But see K. P. Oakley: 'Earliest Use of Fire', *Proceedings of 3rd P.A.P.C.*, pp. 385–6, 1957, suggesting a later date.

2. Clark, op. cit., Ch. 4 describes the different types of proto-Boskopoid man of which the Early Stone Age in Southern Africa gives evidence. See also Clark's article in 'Early Man in Northern Rhodesia' in *N.R. Journal*, Vol. II, No. 4. For the relationship between Bushmanoid man and these early antecedents, see P. V. Tobias: 'Bushmen of the Kalahari', in *Man*, March 1957.

3. Clark, op. cit., Ch. 7.

4. C. Wrigley: 'The Economic Prehistory of Southern Africa', *Jnl. of African History*, Vol. I, No. 2, p. 200.

5. Clark, op. cit., p. 260.

6. Consecutive phases of Later Stone Age occupation have been found in a cave at Nachikufu, south of Mpika, including earlier semi-naturalistic paintings and later schematic designs.

CHAPTER II SECTION I: IRON AGE PEOPLES AND THE NEW ERA

1. B. Davidson: *Old Africa Rediscovered*, Chs. 1, 2.

2. B. Davidson, op. cit., pp. 139 f. The absence of the use of copper meant that tropical Africa was to pass direct from the Stone to the Iron Age, without an intervening Bronze Age in between. This has its own significance, for the manufacture and working of bronze has had its part to play in the technical evolution of human societies. It does not explain the non-appearance of the wheel. This revolutionary discovery was made in Asia during its Bronze Age, but did not appear in barbarian Europe until the Iron Age. That its use did not spread into tropical Africa, despite early and occasional passage of the Saharan 'cart trails', is most likely due to the dry phase and the widening of the desert belt; wheeled vehicles cannot pass easily through soft sand. The consequent lack of basic mechanical devices and techniques was to prove a great handicap, and to this source the 'primitiveness' of most African cultures can largely be traced. See also R. F. H. Summers: 'Possible Influences of the Iron Age in Southern Africa', in *S.A. Jnl. of Sc.*, Vol. 52, 1955, and B. Fagan: 'Pre-European Iron-working in Central Africa', *Jnl. of African History*, Vol. II, No. 2, 1961.

3. J. D. Clark: *The Prehistory of Africa*, p. 216.

4. J. Hiernaux: 'Bantu Expansion: The evidence from physical expansion, confronted with linguistic and archaeological evidence', *Jnl. of African History*, Vol. IX, No. 4, pp. 505–15. Also R. Oliver: 'The Problem of the Bantu Expansion', *Jnl. of African History*, Vol. VII, No. 3, pp. 361–76.

5. Uncertainty regarding the origins of the Negro race is caused by lack of skeletal remains. The earliest evidence in Africa is provided by a skull exhibiting negroid features unearthed at Khartoum, and dating back to Mesolithic times, some 10,000 years B.C. Similar and roughly contemporary remains have been discovered at Timbuktu. S. Cole: *The Prehistory of East Africa*, pp. 104, 114–16.

6. J. D. Clark, op. cit., pp. 208–9.
7. B. Fagan: *Southern Africa*, p. 106 f.
8. R. Coupland: *East Africa and its Invaders*, p. 17.
9. B. Fagan in *The African Iron Age*, ed. P. L. Shinnie, pp. 229–30. See also a clear summary of the Iron Age in Mashonaland by E. Alpers in *Aspects of Central African History*, Ed. T. O. Ranger, Ch. 1.
10. L. Fouché: *Mapungubwe: Excavation Reports*, 1937.
11. B. Fagan, op. cit., pp. 230–1.
12. A. Whitty: 'Origins of the Stone Architecture of Zimbabwe', *Proceedings of the 3rd P.A.C.P.*, 1957, p. 377. For the results of the most recent research, ascribing the elliptical building the Rozwi period between the fourteenth and fifteenth centuries, see R. Summers: *Zimbabwe: A Rhodesian Mystery*, 1964.
13. Fouché, op. cit., pp. 43–5.

Chapter II Section 2: Early Shona Kingdoms

1. I am indebted to Mr R. Summers for this information.
2. H. von Sicard: 'Derivation of the name Mashona', *African Studies*, Vol. IX, No. 3, 1950.
3. J. Walton: 'Some Features of the Monomotapa Culture', *Proceedings of the 3rd P.A.C.P.*, 1957.
4. D. P. Abraham: 'The Monomotapa Dynasty', *Nada*, No. 36, 1959, p. 62.
5. A useful account of this period is in A. Alpers: 'The Mutapa and Malawi Political Systems' in *Aspects of Central African History*, Ed. T. O. Ranger.
6. D. P. Abraham: 'The Early Political History of the Kingdom of Mwene Mutapa', *Leverhulme History Conference*, 1960.
7. A. Alpers, op. cit., pp. 10–11.
8. D. de Goes: 'Chronicle of the Most Fortunate King Dom Emanuel', in G. M. Theal: *Records of South-Eastern Africa*, Vol. III, p. 129.
9. J. de Barros: 'Asia' in Theal: *Records*, Vol. VI, p. 267.
10. J. dos Santos: 'Eastern Ethiopia', in Theal: *Records*, Vol. VII, p. 199.
11. Dos Santos, op. cit., p. 204.
12. Ibid., p. 289.
13. B. Fagan: *Southern Africa*, p. 122.
14. F. P. Mennell and R. Summers: 'Ancient Workings of Southern Rhodesia', *O.P.N.M.S.R.*, Vol. II, No. 20, p. 768.
15. J. Wainwright: 'The Jaga and their Name for Iron', *Man*, April 1955.
16. E. Alpers, op. cit., pp. 15–16.
17. R. Summers et al.: *Inyanga*, pp. 255–6.
18. J. N. Andrada: *Report of Trade Conditions, 1789*, quoted by Abraham, op. cit.
19. For the later fortunes of the Rozwi/Shona kingdom, see T. O. Ranger: 'The Nineteenth Century in Southern Rhodesia' in *Aspects of Central African History*.

Chapter II Section 3: The Portuguese Settlements

1. R. Coupland: *East Africa and its Invaders*.
2. Coupland, op. cit., pp. 36–40.
3. E. Axelson: *South-East Africa 1488–1530*, p. 108 f.
4. Axelson, op. cit., p. 149.
5. Ibid., p. 147 f.
6. D. Livingstone: *Missionary Travels*.
7. W. F. Rea, S.J., in *Rhodesiana*, No. 6, 1961.
8. G. M. Theal: *Records of South-Eastern Africa*.
9. G. M. Theal: *A History of Southern Africa*.

10. Dos Santos, op. cit., in Theal: *Records*, Vol. VII, p. 218.
11. A. Bocarro in Theal: *Records*, Vol. III, p. 367 f.
12. Dos Santos, op. cit., p. 75.
13. Dos Santos, op. cit., p. 274.
14. Bocarro, op. cit., p. 415 f.
15. E. Axelson: *Portuguese in South-East Africa 1600–1700*, p. 97.
16. Axelson, op. cit., p. 99.
17. B. de Razende: 'The State of India' (1634), in Theal: *Records*, Vol. II, p. 413 f.
18. Axelson, op. cit., p. 6.
19. Dos Santos, op. cit., p. 271.
20. Axelson, op. cit., p. 161.
21. Coupland, op. cit., pp. 67–72.
22. Livingstone, op. cit., p. 631.

CHAPTER III SECTION 1: THE NYASA TRIBES

1. See above, p. 38.
2. J. Bruwer: 'Note on Maravi Origins and Migration', *African Studies*, Vol. 9.
3. T. Cullen Young: *Notes on the History of the Tumbuka-Henga Peoples*.
4. E. H. Lane Poole: *Tribes of the Eastern Province of Northern Rhodesia*, pp. 39–40. This version has doubt cast upon it by R. Apthorpe: 'Problems of African History: the Nsenga of Northern Rhodesia', in *H.P.C.A.*, No. XXVIII (1960), suggesting an independent origin.
5. Dos Santos: 'Eastern Ethiopia', in Theal: *Records*, Vol. VII, p. 309. See also T. Cullen Young, op. cit., p. 143 footnote, suggesting that 'Zambezi' may be derived from 'Amachembezi', the name accorded to those inland tribes who file (kuhemba, kuchemba) their front teeth. The Portuguese knew the Zambezi and its deltas as the 'rivers of Cuama'.
6. J. Clyde Mitchell: *The Yao Village*, p. 22.

CHAPTER III SECTION 2: THE LUBA DISPERSAL

1. C. M. N. White: 'The Balovale Peoples and their Historical Background', *H.P.C.A.*, No. VIII, (1949), p. 33.
2. J. Desmond Clark: 'A Note on the Pre-Bantu Inhabitants of Northern Rhodesia and Nyasaland', *S.A. Jnl. of Science*, Vol. 47, No. 3, (1950), p. 80 f.
3. See V. W. Turner: 'A Lunda Love Story', *H.P.C.A.*, No. XIX, (1955), based on Dias de Carvalho, 1890.
4. Turner, op. cit., p. 13.
5. I. G. Cunnison: *The Luapula Peoples of Northern Rhodesia*.
6. Mwata Kazembe: *Ifikolwe Fyandi*. Cunnison, op. cit., suggests that Nkuba's people were Bemba. Cunnison: 'Kazembe's Charter', *N.R. Journal*, Vol. III, p. 220, translates extracts from 'Ifikolwe Fyandi' notes.
7. V. W. Brelsford: *The Tribes of Northern Rhodesia*.
8. A. Jalla: *History of the Barotse Nation*, an unpublished manuscript, by courtesy of the *Paris Evangelical Mission*.

CHAPTER III SECTION 3: THE RETURN OF THE SOUTHERN BANTU

1. A. T. Bryant: *Olden Days in Zululand and Natal*. I am indebted to Mr R. Summers for the derivative meaning of the name 'Zulu'.
2. A. Jalla: *History of the Barotse Nation*.
3. D. Livingstone: *Missionary Travels*, p. 59.

4. F. Coillard: *On the Threshold of Central Africa*, p. 59.
5. Bryant, op. cit., Ch. 42.
6. For the fate of Mzilikazi's sons and the question of the succession, see W. C. Tabler: *The Far Interior*, p. 307.
7. T. O. Ranger in *Aspects of Central African History*, pp. 125–130.
8. E. H. Lane Poole: *Native Tribes of the Eastern Province*, p. 4.
9. T. O. Ranger, op. cit., p. 120.
10. J. A. Barnes: *Politics in a Changing Society*, p. 9.
11. Lane Poole, op. cit., p. 7. Also T. Cullen Young: *Notes on the Speech and History of the Henga-Nkamanga People*, p. 197.
12. Barnes, op. cit., p. 16.

CHAPTER IV SECTION 1: VIAGEM À CONTRA COSTA

1. F. de Lacerda: 'Diaries', translated by R. F. Burton in *Lands of the Cazembe*, p. 3.
2. De Lacerda, op. cit., p. 55.
3. Ibid., p. 73.
4. Ibid., p. 101.
5. Ibid., p. 96.
6. F. D. Pinto: 'Diaries', in Burton, op. cit., p. 125.
7. Baptista, op. cit., p. 188.

CHAPTER IV SECTION 2: THE SLAVE TRADE

1. Recorded by Masoudi, the Arabian geographer, who travelled down the coast that year. The Greek *Periplus* of A.D. 80 mentions slaves 'of the better sort' being exported from Somalia.
2. Sir R. Coupland: *East Africa and Its Invaders*, p. 500.
3. F. Moir in the Scottish Geographical Magazine, April 1885. *C.O. Pamphlet*, No. 8479A.
4. D. Livingstone: *Narrative of an Expedition to the Zambezi*, p. 356–7. Cf. H. H. Johnston: *British Central Africa*, p. 159.
5. C. 7504: British Central Africa Protectorate Annual Report, 1895.
6. L. H. Gann: 'The End of the Slave Trade in British Central Africa', *H.P.C.A.*, No. XVI, (1954), p. 31.
7. Livingstone, op. cit., p. 40.
8. C. Harding: *In Remotest Barotseland*, p. 124.
9. Harding, op. cit., p. 207.
10. Livingstone: *Last Journals*, Vol. I, p. 104.
11. H. T. Harrington: 'The Taming of North-Eastern Rhodesia', *N.R. Journal*, Vol. II, No. 3, p. 12.
12. Gann, op. cit., p. 34.
13. Ibid., pp. 37–9.
14. CO/417/309.
15. Sir R. F. Burton: *The Lake Regions of Central Africa* (1860). See also Coupland, op. cit., pp. 136 ff.
16. Quoted by J. Simmons: *Livingstone and Africa*, p. 61.
17. Livingstone: *Last Journals*.

CHAPTER IV SECTION 3: LIVINGSTONE

1. D. Schapera: *David Livingstone—Family Letters*, p. 18.
2. D. Chamberlin: *Some Letters from Livingstone*, p. 122.

3. D. Livingstone: *Missionary Travels and Researches in South Africa* (1857), p. 92.
4. Ibid., p. 294.
5. Ibid., p. 434.
6. Ibid., p. 441.
7. Ibid., p. 637–8.
8. For Livingstone's geographical achievements, see F. Debenham: *The Way to Ilala*.
9. Livingstone, op. cit., p. 28.
10. D. Livingstone: *Narrative of an Expedition to the Zambezi*, p. 128.
11. Ibid., pp. 110–114. A useful sketch of Iron Age society.
12. Ibid., p. 178.
13. Livingstone: *Missionary Travels*, p. 213.
14. See below, pp. 102–3.
15. D. Livingstone: *Last Journals*, Vol. I, p. 177.
16. Ibid., p. 267.
17. Ibid., p. 199.
18. Ibid., p. 250.

CHAPTER IV SECTION 4: THE PIONEER MISSIONS

1. D. Thompson: *England in the Nineteenth Century*. Already in 1839 the new Society for the Extinction of the Slave Trade and for the Civilisation of Africa, known later as 'Exeter Hall', had given its unanimous opinion that 'the only complete cure for all these evils (the slave trade) is the introduction of Christianity into Africa.' C. P. Groves: *The Planting of Christianity in Africa*, Vol. II, pp. 7–8.
2. C. Northcott: *Robert Moffat, Pioneer in Africa*, pp. 141–6.
3. Quoted in H. C. Dann: *Romance of the Posts of Rhodesia*.
4. R. U. Moffat: *John Smith Moffat*, pp. 84–5.
5. Quoted in Northcott, op. cit., p. 292.
6. 'Matabele Mission of J. S. and E. M. Moffat'. S. R. Archives, p. 225.
7. F. Coillard: *On the Threshold of Central Africa*, p. 44.
8. Northcott, op. cit., p. 297.
9. Ibid., p. 296–308.
10. O. Chadwick: *Mackenzie's Grave*, for a full account.
11. See C. W. Mackintosh: *Lewanika of the Barotse*, pp. 8–10.
12. C. W. Mackintosh: *Coillard of the Zambezi*.
13. Coillard, op. cit., p. 478.
14. Mackintosh: *Lewanika of the Barotse*, p. 39.
15. Mackintosh: *Coillard of the Zambezi*, p. 397.
16. C. W. Mackintosh: *Some Pioneer Missions of Northern Rhodesia and Nyasaland*.
17. W. P. Livingstone, op. cit., p. 162.
18. J. van Velsen: 'The Missionary Factor among the Lakeside Tonga of Nyasaland', *H.P.C.A.*, No. XXVI (1959), p. 5.
19. A. J. Hanna: *The Beginnings of Nyasaland and North-Eastern Rhodesia*, pp. 23–32.
20. See below, p. 118 f.
21. C. Gouldsbury and H. Sheane: *The Great Plateau of Northern Rhodesia*, p. 241.

CHAPTER IV SECTION 5: THE TRADERS

1. G. Tabler: *The Far Interior*, Ch. 9.
2. Ibid., Chs. 5, 6.
3. Ibid., Ch. 9.
4. T. Baines: *Goldfields Diaries*, S. R. Archives Oppenheimer Series, p. 553.

5. Ibid., p. 695.
6. F. C. Selous: *A Hunter's Wanderings in Africa.*
7. A. J. Hanna: *The Beginnings of Nyasaland and North-Eastern Rhodesia*, p. 20.

CHAPTER V SECTION 1: EUROPE AND AFRICA IN THE NEW PHASE

1. M. Perham: *Lugard—The Years of Adventure*, p. 479.
2. Quoted in W. L. Langer: *European Alliances and Alignments*, p. 493.
3. S. E. Crowe: *The Berlin West African Conference*, pp. 108–9.
4. R. Robinson and J. Gallagher: *Africa and the Victorians*, pp. 238 f.
5. J. A. Froude: *Oceana, or England and Her Colonies* (1886), p. 8.
6. F. Whyte: *Life of W. T. Stead*, p. 112.

CHAPTER V SECTION 2: THE CONVERGING FORCES OF IMPERIALISM

1. E. A. Walker: *A History of Southern Africa*, pp. 309–321.
2. B. Williams: *Cecil Rhodes*, p. 41.
3. F. Gross: *Rhodes of Africa*, p. 62.
4. Williams, op. cit., pp. 80–1.
5. Walker, op. cit., p. 398.
6. Williams, op. cit., p. 119.
7. R. U. Moffat: *John Smith Moffat*, pp. 378–9. Also C. 5524, p. 13.
8. African (South), No. 369.
9. P. Mason: *The Birth of a Dilemma*, p. 118.
10. C. 5198, p. 126.
11. Gross, op. cit., p. 150.
12. Moffat, op. cit., p. 221.
13. C. 5918, pp. 174–5. Shippard however expressed the view that 'some of the older Matabele indunas are confessedly sick of carnage and desire nothing so much as a peaceful government with security for life and property, not to be obtained under the present regime'.
14. C. 5918, p. 139. The Concession is also reproduced in H. Marshall Hole: *The Making of Rhodesia.*
15. African (South), No. 372, p. 25.
16. Williams, op. cit., p. 130.
17. R. E. Robinson in *C.H.B.E.*, Vol. III, p. 174.
18. C. 8773. See Williams, op. cit., p. 137–8.

CHAPTER V SECTION 3: SETTLEMENT AND CONQUEST

1. B. Williams: *Cecil Rhodes*, pp. 147–9.
2. Quoted in P. Mason: *Birth of a Dilemma*, p. 142.
3. R. Robinson and J. Gallagher: *Africa and the Victorians*, p. 247.
4. Quoted by Gross: *Rhodes of Africa*, p. 207.
5. C. 6212.
6. C. 6495.
7. C. 7171, pp. 8–9.
8. R. U. Moffat: *John Smith Moffat*, p. 258.
9. Lobengula's claim to 'own' Mashonaland had been described by Selous in 1889 as 'utterly preposterous'. See T. O. Ranger in *Aspects of Central African History*, p. 129. Also above, p. 65.
10. Quoted by Neville Jones in *Rhodesian Genesis*, p. 74.
11. African (South), No. 454. See S. Glass, *The Matabele War*, for a full account.
12. Quoted by Gross, op. cit., p. 235.
13. Quoted by Jones, op. cit., p. 89.
14. C. W. Mackintosh: *Coillard of the Zambezi*, p. 398.

15. N. Jones, op. cit.
16. B.S.A. Company Director's Report, 1894.
17. C. 8773. See E. A. Walker: *A History of Southern Africa*, pp. 423–4.
18. C. 8130: Report of the Land Commission, p. 10. Report also deals with cattle settlement. See Mason, op. cit., pp. 383–9.
19. F. C. Selous: *Sunshine and Storm in Rhodesia*, p. xi.
20. For the causes of the rebellion, see Sir R. Martin's *Report on the Native Administration of the B.S.A. Company together with a letter from the Company commenting on that Report*, C. 8457, 1897. See also T. O. Ranger in *Aspects*, pp. 142–52, 210–15.
21. Selous, op. cit., p. 24.
22. 'Vindex': *Cecil Rhodes: Political Life and Speeches*, various extracts.
23. N. Rouillard: *Matabele Thompson*, p. 193.

CHAPTER VI SECTION 1: LEWANIKA AND THE NORTH-WEST

1. C. W. Mackintosh: *Coillard of the Zambezi*, p. 381.
2. C. 5198, p. 215. See T. W. Baxter: 'The Barotse Concessions', *N.R. Journal* Vol. I, No. 1, p. 40.
3. Baxter, op. cit., p. 47.
4. R. Bradley: 'Coryndon and Lewanika in North-Western Rhodesia', *N.R. Journal* Vol. IV, No. 2.
5. African (South), No. 559, p. 129.
6. Concession reproduced in L. H. Gann: *Birth of a Plural Society*, p. 215 f.
7. African (South), No. 552, p. 151.
8. African (South), No. 552, pp. 159–60.
9. Cd. 2584: *Award of H. M. The King of Italy respecting the Western Boundary of the Barotse Kingdom.*

CHAPTER VI SECTION 2: THE ARAB WAR

1. Sir R. Coupland: *The Exploitation of East Africa*, pp. 222–6.
2. Quoted by Hanna: *The Beginnings of Nyasaland and North-Eastern Rhodesia*, p. 59.
3. Hanna, op. cit., p. 78.
4. M. Perham: *Lugard—the Years of Adventure*, p. 110. For the attitude of the Foreign Office towards the Missions at this time, see R. Robinson and J. Gallagher: *Africa and the Victorians*, p. 224.
5. F. D. Lugard: *The Rise of our East African Empire*, Vol. I, p. 151.

CHAPTER VI SECTION 3: JOHNSTON AND THE BRITISH CENTRAL AFRICA PROTECTORATE

1. For Johnston's early career, see R. Oliver: *Sir Harry Johnston and the Scramble for Africa*, Chs. 1–3.
2. Oliver, op. cit., p. 151.
3. Those Kololo and their descendants who had worked with Livingstone on his second expedition, and had settled in positions of authority among the Shire tribes.
4. C. 5904.
5. C. 6370.
6. A. J. Hanna: *Beginnings of Nyasaland and North-Eastern Rhodesia*, p. 150.
7. See J. van Velsen in *H.P.C.A.* No. XXI, 1955.
8. Hanna, op. cit., p. 157.
9. Ibid, p. 157.
10. I. Cunnison: *The Luapula Peoples.*
11. 'Alfred Sharpe's Travels' (Edited Despatches), *N.R. Journal* Vol. III, p. 210.
12. R. Robinson and J. Gallagher: *Africa and the Victorians*, p. 283.

13. C. 6046. See Anderson's comment, pp. 1–3.
14. Robinson and Gallagher, op. cit., p. 296.
15. For Stairs' account, see his letter reproduced in F. S. Arnot: *Missionary Travels*.
16. Oliver, op. cit., p. 189. Hanna, op. cit., p. 182.
17. F. D. Lugard: *The Rise of our East African Empire*.
18. C. 8103.
19. C. 8103, C. 7925.
20. Johnston was awarded the K.C.B. in 1895. He returned to Africa in 1898 as Commissioner for Uganda.

CHAPTER VI SECTION 4: PACIFICATION OF THE NORTH-EAST

1. See above, p. 145.
2. J. A. Barnes: *Politics in a Changing Society*, p. 73.
3. Barnes, op. cit., p. 78.
4. T. W. Baxter: 'The Angoni Rebellion and Mpezeni', *N.R. Journal* Vol. I, No. 2, p. 19.
5. A. J. Hanna: *Beginnings*, p. 237.
6. H. C. Dann: *Romance of the Posts of Rhodesia*, pp. 51–2.
7. Dann, op. cit., p. 54.
8. B.S.A. Company Administrative Reports, 1898–1900.
9. T. W. Baxter: 'Slave Traders in North-Eastern Rhodesia', *N.R. Journal* Vol. I, No. 1, p. 15.
10. See Young's account. *N.R. Journal* Vol. II, p. 68.
11. R. Codrington in B.S.A. Company Administrative Reports, 1899–1900.

CHAPTER VII SECTION 1: MINING AND LAND SETTLEMENT

1. B.S.A. Company Annual General Meeting, 1893.
2. E. Tawse Jollie: *The Real Rhodesia*, pp. 168–9.
3. K. Bradley: *Copper Venture*.
4. Bradley, op. cit., Ch. 5.
5. For the history of the railway north of the Falls, see H. F. Varian: *Some African Milestones*, Ch. 6.
6. B.S.A. Company Report of Extraordinary General Meeting, Jan. 1908, p. 25.
7. CO/417/284.
8. B.S.A. Company Report of Company's Proceedings 1889–92, p. 25.
9. CO/417/320.
10. Cd. 8674.
11. Southern Rhodesia Legislative Council Debates, 1950.
12. L. H. Gann: *Birth of a Plural Society*, p. 221.
13. Gann, op. cit., p. 146.
14. CO/417/309.
15. CO/525/7.
16. H. H. Johnston: *British Central Africa*, pp. 112–13.
17. CO/525/11.

CHAPTER VII SECTION 2: ADMINISTRATION

1. C. 9138. Order in Council No. 20, October 1898.
2. C. Leys: *European Politics in Southern Rhodesia*, p. 191.
3. E. Tawse Jollie: 'The Real Rhodesia', pp. 52–3. For a summing up of settler attitudes and grievances at this time, see also R. C. Hawkin: 'Rhodesia', in the *Contemporary Review*, August 1903.

4. B.S.A. Company: Report of Annual General Meeting, 1908.
5. See biographical article by R. Summers and L. H. Gann in *N.R. Journal*, Vol. III, p. 44.
6. African (South), No. 559, p. 321.
7. African (South), No. 656, p. 120. Cd. 1200, p. 36.
8. B.S.A. Co. Administrative Reports, 1900–1902.
9. Cd. 1200.
10. African (South), No. 694, p. 172.
11. R. Gelfand: *Northern Rhodesia in the Days of the Charter*.
12. Cd. 786–26, p. 13.
13. Nyasaland Legislative Council Debates, quoted in report of Commission on Emigrant Labour, 1935.
14. B.C.A. Protectorate Annual Report, 1905.
15. C. 7504, p. 29.
16. H. C. Dann: *Romance of the Posts*, pp. 44–5.
17. B.S.A. Company: Reports on Administration 1897–8, p. 108, 1900–2, pp. 148–9.
18. Ibid., 1900–2, pp. 104, 424.
19. H. T. Harrington: 'The Taming of North-Eastern Rhodesia', *N.R. Journal*, Vol. II, No. 3, p. 17.
20. W. V. Brelsford: *The Story of the Northern Rhodesian Regiment*, p. 13.
21. B.S.A. Co. Administrative Reports, 1902.
22. For early history of the B.S.A. Police in Southern Rhodesia, see C. Harding: *Frontier Patrols*, Ch. 22.
23. CO/517/320.
24. CO/417/309.
25. Ibid.
26. CO/417/283.
27. Dann, op. cit., p. 74.
28. African (South), No. 559.
29. P. Mason: *The Birth of a Dilemma*, pp. 279–80. See also Lord Hailey: *Native Administration in the British African Territories*, Part II, p. 83 f, Part IV, p. 20–21.
30. Harrington, op. cit., p. 17.
31. C. 7504, p. 29.
32. The immediate effect was to lessen the power of the chiefs and increase that of the D.O., since the new councils of headmen were in the nature of things under the D.O.'s close supervision. Some resulting discontent has been associated with the Chilembwe rising of 1915 (below, p. 231.).
33. CO/417.
34. B.S.A. Company: Reports on Administration, 1898–1900.

CHAPTER VII SECTION 3: THE AFRICAN SUBMISSION

1. J. A. Barnes: *Politics in a Changing Society*, p. 172.
2. W. V. Brelsford: *Tribes of Northern Rhodesia*, Appendix.
3. J. A. Barnes: 'History in a Changing Society', *H.P.C.A.*, No. IX, 1951.
4. G. Shepperson and T. Price: *Independent African*, p. 190.
5. G. Wilson and M. Hunter: *The Study of African Society* (R.-L. I. Paper No. 2), p. 16.
6. R. Oliver: *The Missionary Factor in East Africa*.
7. G. Wilson and M. Hunter: *The Analysis of Social Change*, p. 119.
8. Shepperson and Price, op. cit., p. 189 f.
9. Nyasaland Legislative Council Debates, 11 March 1915.

10. W. V. Brelsford: 'Aspects of Bemba Chieftainship', *R.-L. I. Communication* No. 2, 1944.
11. J. Taylor and D. Lehmann: *Christians of the Copperbelt*, pp. 24–7.

CHAPTER VII SECTION 4: THE GREAT WAR

1. R. Williams: *German Penetration in Central Africa*—Address to the London Chamber of Commerce, June 1918. Central Africa Pamphlets, No. 11. In 1913, during a temporary improvement in Anglo-German relations, a secret treaty between London and Berlin arranged for the partition of the Portuguese African territories in the event of the collapse of the regime in Lisbon. In December 1914, William II made a tentative offer to buy the entire Congo Free State as the price of German withdrawal from Belgium.
2. W. V. Brelsford: *The Story of the Northern Rhodesian Regiment*, p. 29.
3. H. Moyse-Bartlett: *The King's African Rifles*.
4. Brelsford, op. cit., pp. 53–57.
5. Moyse-Bartlett, op. cit., p. 412.
6. G. Shepperson and T. Price: *Independent African*, p. 935. The authorities were sufficiently concerned to confiscate the offending edition of the newspaper.
7. C. P. Groves: *The Planting of Christianity in Africa*, Vol. IV, pp. 74–81.

CHAPTER VIII SECTION 1: THE PASSING OF COMPANY RULE

1. B.S.A. Company Report of 25th Ordinary General Meeting, March 1923.
2. J. P. R. Wallis: *One Man's Hand*, p. 180.
3. B.S.A. Company, 25th O.G.M., March 1923. For the Company's viewpoint at this stage, see D. O. Malcolm's speech to shareholders at the Extraordinary General Meeting on 28 July 1922. Also Malcolm in the Quarterly Review, January 1924.
4. Cmd. 1129: Cave Commission.
5. Cmd. 1984.
6. C. Leys: *European Politics in Southern Rhodesia*, pp. 39–41.
7. Leys, op. cit., pp. 134–5.
8. L. H. Gann: *Birth of a Plural Society*, pp. 164–5.
9. Gann, op. cit., pp. 166–8. See also S. R. Denney: 'Leopold Moore versus the Chartered Company', *N.R. Journal*, Vol. IV, No. 3.
10. Cmd. 1471.

CHAPTER VIII SECTION 2: DIVERGENT POLICIES IN THE RHODESIAS

1. H. Clay: 'Enquiry into Industrial Relations in Southern Rhodesia', *C.S.R.*, 3–1930.
2. Chief Native Commissioner, Southern Rhodesia: Report, 1929.
3. B.S.A. Company: Director's Annual Report, 1927.
4. C. Leys: *European Politics in Southern Rhodesia*, pp. 135–8.
5. *The Times*, 31 March 1938. See also Bledisloe Report, p. 170.
6. Morris Carter Report, *C.S.R.* 3–1926.
7. *The Times*, 24 June 1926.
8. See retrospective view of Land Apportionment Policy in Plewman Commission Report, 1958, p. 20 f.
9. *C.S.R.* 26–1936.
10. L. H. Gann: 'The Northern Rhodesia Copper Industry and the World of Copper 1923–52', *H.P.C.A.*, No. XVIII, 1955.
11. Colonial Office Annual Report, Northern Rhodesia, 1931, pp. 10–11.
12. Gann, op. cit.
13. J. W. Davidson: *The Legislative Council of Northern Rhodesia*.

14. Cmd. 3573.
15. See also Hilton Young Commission Report, 1929, Introduction.
16. Northern Rhodesian Legislative Council Debates, 21 March 1930.
17. Governor's Address, 27 October 1930: *Rhodesian Pamphlets*, No. 40.
18. See below, p. 271.
19. Colonial Office Annual Report, British East Africa Protectorate, 1910, p. 9.
20. F. D. Lugard: *The Dual Mandate*, p. 217.
21. Lord Hailey: *Native Administration in the British African Territories*, Part II. See also M. Perham: *Address to the Royal African Society of Arts*, Vol. LXXXII, No. 4252.
22. A. L. Epstein: *Politics in an Urban African Community*, Chs. 2 and 3.
23. R. Howman: *Report on Local Government for Southern Rhodesia*.
24. Southern Rhodesia Legislative Council Debates, 26 June 1941.
25. Leys, op. cit.
26. Ibid., pp. 174–5.
27. Davidson, op. cit., p. 72 f.
28. S. Gore-Browne: 'Legislative Council Twenty Years Ago', *N.R. Journal*, Vol. II, No. 4, p. 41.
29. Davidson, op. cit., p. 43.

CHAPTER VIII SECTION 3: THE NYASALAND PROTECTORATE

1. Hilton Young Commission Report, 1929. Cmd. 3234.
2. For an account of the system and its problems, see G. Shepperson and T. Price: *Independent African*.
3. Colonial Office Annual Reports, Nyasaland.
4. See 'Report on Nyasaland Railways and Proposed Zambezi Bridge', 1929. Also for comments on migrant labour.
5. Cd. 1772: B.C.A. Protectorate Annual Report, 1903.
6. Nyasaland Native Affairs Annual Report, 1931.
7. F. D. Lugard: *The Dual Mandate*, p. 300.
8. Nyasaland Legislative Council Debates, 6 June 1933.
9. Debates, 6 June 1933.
10. R. Gray: *The Two Nations*, pp. 340–1.
11. The accord between the chiefs and the new political movements in Nyasaland derived from the higher density of population in rural areas and from the absence of urban concentration. In Northern Rhodesia, where the political movement grew out of urban associations along the line of rail (see p. 265) there was antagonism between hereditary authorities and new leaders which only began to disappear during the federal years and which helps to explain the lesser degree of coherence in the Northern Rhodesian movement against Federation before 1953. This antagonism was even more marked in Southern Rhodesia where it continued into the mid-sixties to undermine African nationalism.
12. Gray, op. cit., p. 337.
13. Nyasaland African Congress: *Why We Oppose Federation* (typescript), Lilongwe, 1952.

CHAPTER VIII SECTION 4: THE AFRICAN RECOVERY

1. C. P. Groves: *The Planting of Christianity in Africa*, p. 133.
2. M. Gelfand: *Northern Rhodesia in the Days of the Charter*.
3. Groves, op. cit., pp. 108–12.
4. R. Gray: *The Two Nations*, p. 60 ff.
5. G. Wilson: 'The Economics of Detribalisation', *R.-L. Institute*.
6. Report of Committee appointed to enquire into Emigrant Labour, 1935.

7. D. Bettison: 'Factors in the Determination of Wage Rates in Central Africa', *H.P.C.A.*, No. XXVIII, 1960.

8. Howman Committee: Report on conditions of Africans in Urban Areas. Salisbury, 1944.

9. A. L. Saffery: 'Some Aspects of African Living Conditions on the Copperbelt of Northern Rhodesia', 1943. *Rhodesian Pamphlets*, No. 61.

10. P. Ibbotson: *Report on a Survey of African Urban Conditions in Southern Rhodesia*, 1943.

11. *Bulawayo Chronicle*, 21 August 1946.

12. D. Bettison, op. cit. Also W. J. Barber: *Economy of British Central Africa*, p. 207.

13. J. Clyde Mitchell: *African Urbanisation in Ndola and Luanshya*, 1944.

14. See above, pp. 264–5.

15. Report of the Commission appointed to enquire into the Disturbances on the Copperbelt, Northern Rhodesia, 1940.

16. Quoted by A. L. Epstein: *Politics in an Urban African Community*, p. 104.

17. Epstein, op. cit., p. 107.

18. *The Economist*, 17 September 1955.

19. See below, p. 332 f.

20. U.N.E.S.C.O.: *Structure and Growth of Selected African Economies*, 1956.

21. T. M. Franck: *Race and Nationalism*, pp. 277–8. The African average was £123 p.a., the European £2,390 p.a. See also E. Clegg: *Race and Politics*, pp. 202–3.

22. Inter-African Labour Institute: *Preliminary Survey of the Human Factors of Productivity in Africa*.

23. Report of the Urban African Affairs Commission (Plewman Commission) 1958.

24. C. E. Johnson: 'African Farming Improvements in the Plateau Tonga Maize Areas of Northern Rhodesia', *Agricultural Bulletin* No. 11, Lusaka 1956.

25. *What the Land Husbandry Act Means to the Rural African*, Salisbury, 1955. See also Gray, op. cit., p. 297 f.

CHAPTER IX SECTION 1: TOWARDS CLOSER ASSOCIATION

1. Notably the Victoria Falls Conference on Amalgamation, 1936.

2. U.N.E.S.C.O.: 'Structure and Growth of Selected African Economies', 1956, p. 29 f.

3. Ibid., p. 10.

4. See H. Ridley: 'Early History of Road Transport in Northern Rhodesia', *N.R. Journal*, Vol. 11, No. 5.

5. Cmd. 3234: Hilton Young Commission Report, 1929.

6. See above, pp. 252, 257–8, 278–9.

7. *The Times*, 22 March 1938.

8. Ibid.

9. *The Times*, 22 June 1937.

10. Ibid.

11. Cmd. 5929: Bledisloe Commission Report, Conclusions.

12. Ibid., p. 218.

13. Ibid., p. 250.

14. *The Times*, 1 August 1939.

15. D. Taylor: *The Rhodesian*, p. 88. Clegg: *Race and Politics*, p. 116.

16. Clegg, op. cit., pp. 148–50.

17. Cmd. 8233: Report of Conference on Closer Association.

18. Cmd. 8411: 'Closer Association in Central Africa'—Statement by H.M. Government, November 1951.

19. East Africa and Rhodesia, 17 April 1952. See Clegg, op. cit., pp. 195–6. The term 'partnership' in this context had first been coined by Sir Stewart Gore-Browne in 1936.

20. Annual Register, 1952.

21. Cmd. 8573. See Cmds. 8671–3 for reports of judicial, fiscal and civil service commissions.

22. Annual Register, 1953.

23. U.N.E.S.C.O., op. cit.

24. W. Hance: *African Economic Development*, p. 137. Also Sir Gilbert Rennie: 'Power in the Federation' in *Rhodesia and East Africa*, 1958, pp. 120–2.

25. Cmd. 8234: 'Central African Territories: Historical, Geographical and Economic Survey', pp. 46–7.

26. D. S. Rothchild: *Towards Unity in Africa*, p. 128.

27. Ibid., p. 129 f. Also Clegg, op. cit., p. 176.

28. *The Times*, 5 February 1953.

CHAPTER IX SECTION 2: THE ATTEMPT AT FEDERATION

1. Hazlewood and Henderson: *Nyasaland. The Economics of Federation.*

2. Legislative Council (Amendment) Ordinance, December 1953.

3. P. Mason: *Year of Decision*, pp. 63–5.

4. Tredgold Commission Report.

5. P. Mason: *Year of Decision*.

6. *The Economist*, 12 January 1959.

7. C. Leys, op. cit., p. 142–4.

8. Mason, op. cit., p. 73.

9. Cmnd. 530, 1958.

10. Report of an enquiry into all the circumstances which gave rise to the making of the Safeguard of Elections and Public Safety Regulations, 1959 (Ridley Report), p. 7.

11. Cmnd. 814: Report of the Nyasaland Commission of Enquiry (Devlin Commission).

12. Ridley Report, pp. 11–13.

13. Younger rank and file U.N.I.P. associates, however, were responsible for acts of violence and one European death during 1960.

14. Southern Rhodesia Legislative Assembly debates, *Hansard*, 10 February 1959.

15. Report of the Committee on the Resettlement of Natives, 1960. Salisbury.

16. Cmnd. 1148: Report of Advisory Commission on the Review of the Constitution of the Federation (Monckton Commission), 1960.

CHAPTER IX SECTION 3: THE END OF THE COLONIAL PHASE

1. Deaths from smallpox in Nyasaland were as follows:

    1 in 1958.
    23 in 1959.
    64 in 1960 (42 of these during November and December).

2. One of these fifteen was to be a territorial constituency for electing an Asian member. The franchise approximated closely to that for Southern Rhodesia, which is shown in Appendix II; the chief difference being the greater number of additional categories on the lower roll including membership of Native Authorities and Courts and Township Management Boards.

3. Land distribution in Southern Rhodesia in 1963 was as follows:

Tribal Trust Land	40,123,000
African Purchase Area	4,284,200
National Land	10,524,200
Unreserved Land	5,876,900
European Land	35,710,400

4. This plebiscite was quietly attended. Its verdict, recorded by the N.D.P., was: For the constitution, 235. Against, 152,277.

5. Report of the Secretary for Internal Affairs, 1961.

6. Duncan Sandys, however, told the House of Commons in December that Britain did not take responsibility for the break-up of the Federation. It was 'already breaking up of its own accord'. Hansard, 17 December 1963.

7. For the Lumpa Church, founded in the Chinsali District in 1955, see Taylor and Lehmann: 'Christians of the Copperbelt', p. 248 f.

8. See above, p. 166.

9. The European proportion of the population rose to its peak level in 1960, when it was 6·0 per cent. By 1964 it had fallen to 5·1 per cent. See *The Times*, 17 November 1965.

CHAPTER X SECTION 1: RHODESIA BESIEGED

1. D. J. Murray: *The Governmental System of Southern Rhodesia*, pp. 365–6.

2. The Pearce Commission considered that most of these foreign workers regarded Rhodesia as their home. In the event the proportion repatriated was small.

3. An example of this propaganda is printed in F. Clements: *Rhodesia: the Course to Collision*, pp. 634–5.

4. See the Report of the Secretary for Agriculture, Salisbury, 1971.

5. John Parker: *Rhodesia, Little White Island*, p. 162.

6. Some details of the guerilla activities can be found in K. Maxey: *From Rhodesia to Zimbabwe*, Fabian Research Series 301, 1972.

7. Mr Justice Fieldsend resigned from the bench in protest at this decision. A second High Court resignation came in June when Mr Justice Dendy Young gave up his office following a Judicial Committee ruling in the case of Daniel Madzima-buto.

8. Cmnd. 3159.

9. Cmnd. 3793.

10. It is possible that this rejection of the Provincial Council solution and adherence to the principle of an all-racial national assembly will be seen as a turning point of some significance.

11. A useful summary of the history of land apportionment can be found in George Kay: *Rhodesia: a Human Geography*.

12. For the year ended June 1970, expenditure on education was: European $17,143,945, African $17,104,380. Enrolment in European schools in 1970 totalled 65,857, of whom 39,725 were in primary schools and 26,132 in secondary schools. Enrolment in African schools in 1970 totalled 694,865, of whom 671,457 were in primary schools (133,951 of them in the initial grade), 2,378 were in junior secondary schools, and 21,040 were in full secondary schools.

13. Cmnd. 4835. An openly hostile, but nonetheless useful, critique of the proposals is summed up in the Southern African Research Office pamphlet *Rhodesia: Proposals for a Sell-Out*, 1972.

14. Cmnd. 4964.

15. Pearce Commission Report, p. 59. This figure has been selected from various regional and occupational categories of evidence as being one of the more significant. It should be noted that even the more educated class of African, such as the teachers, who would be most likely to benefit from the proposals, rejected them (e.g. Mashonaland North—60 per cent against, 19 per cent in favour, 21 per cent undecided; in Mashonaland South the majority of teachers against was much higher). The presumably independent-minded African farmers of the African Purchase Areas rejected the proposals by an overwhelming majority. Representatives of the Asian and Coloured communities, on the other hand, accepted the proposals by large majorities as offering an improvement on their present position. European evidence showed 98·4 per cent in favour, 1·5 per cent against and 0·1 per cent undecided.

16. The disturbances at Shabani on 12–13 January are considered to have been entirely industrial, though the fact of six African deaths no doubt contributed to subsequent unrest elsewhere.

17. The Report expressed the view that 'the upsurge of political activity—so long banned—coinciding with the arrival of the Commission led to situations in which agitators urged people to take part in violent demonstrations against authority' and that 'threatening or pressing a man to join one of these riotous crowds had everything to do with a strong confrontation with authority but little or nothing to do with a man's attitudes to our enquiry'.

However, the Commissioners for Matabeleland North were convinced that in their rural areas 'all public meetings and not a few individuals were influenced to a considerable extent by fear engendered by that section of the population actively advocating rejection of the proposals. This fear—recalling lively memories of events in the early sixties when reprisals were taken against families and property—was a definite factor in dissuading some from saying "Yes" to the proposals and deterred many more from attending meetings.' Pearce Report, p. 179.

18. See the Pearce Report, Appendix G, p. 192 for a breakdown of African attitudes.

19. The arrest and detention of R. S. Garfield Todd and of Miss Judith Todd raised doubts about the effectiveness of this pledge. Nkomo and other African leaders remained in detention, though with the exception of N. Sithole who was serving a prison sentence they were allowed interviews with the Commission. British M.P.s were denied entry into Rhodesia.

CHAPTER X SECTION 2: ZAMBIA EMERGENT

1. By C. J. Rhodes for example. See p. 160.

2. R. Hall in *The Times* special report on Zambia, 24 October 1969.

3. Malawi's far greater dependence than Zambia's on communications through white-ruled territory (Mozambique and Rhodesia) only partly explains President Banda's foreign policy. During his visit to the Union in 1970 he stated publicly and emphatically that such a policy of co-operation could do more to improve race relations, and the position of the African in southern Africa, than the antagonistic policies of other states.

4. D. K. D. Kaunda: *Africa in the Sixties*, p. 6. In 1970 Zambia acted as host country for the Conference of Non-Aligned Nations. See also R. Hall: *The High Price of Principles*, p. 24.

5. The number of expatriates working in the copper mines fell from 7,621 in 1964 to approximately 5,000 in 1969. The number of Africans working at jobs formerly held by whites rose from 704 to 3,671 during the same period.

6. See M. Wright: *Zambia—I Changed My Mind*, pp. 130–2. The line from

Livingstone to the Copperbelt was experiencing 'a crash a day' in 1969, 80 per cent of the accidents being caused by 'irresponsibility, drunkenness and carelessness'—rail crash enquiry report, *Times of Zambia*, 28 April 1970.

7. Dr J. Nyerere: *Ujamaa: Essays on Socialism*, pp. 13–37.

8. Dr J. Nyerere: *Freedom and Socialism* (Speeches).

9. Between 1964 and 1968 Zambian Anglo-American, one of the two major copper-mining groups, provided the government, in royalties and taxation, with 62 per cent of their gross mining profits, i.e. £168 millions, retaining 17·3 per cent or £46 millions, to finance development. Shareholders thus received only 21 per cent of the total, itself taxable. H. Oppenheimer, Managing Director of Anglo-American, admitted on 18 December 1968 that 'the balance between retaining domestically generated funds in Zambia by restricting remittances abroad, and maintaining a satisfactory climate for investment from abroad, is not easy to strike'.

10. A third public authority, the Finance Development Corporation (FINDECO) was established when the banks were similarly taken over in 1970.

11. From the official U.N.I.P. publication *The Nation is You*, March 1972, p. 59.

12. The new currency of 1 Kwacha = 11s. 8d. was introduced on 16 July 1968.

13. Since independence the annual increase in earnings greatly accelerated, averaging 18 per cent per annum for Africans and 9·3 per cent for non-Africans over the period 1964–9. By 1969 the average earnings for Africans in wage-earning employment was about K875, and for non-Africans about K5140.

14. Dr K. D. Kaunda: *Humanism in Zambia*, Zambian Information Services, 1968.

15. Alice Lenshina and her husband were confined to a restriction camp in Barotseland.

16. Three cabinet ministers lost their seats in Barotse constituencies during this election.

17. An account of these events is in M. Wright, op. cit., Ch. 5. Judges Skinner and Evans obtained high judicial appointments in Malawi the following year; within six months Evans had left that country also in protest against President Banda's decision to place the determination of witchcraft cases in the hands of the local African courts. In Banda's view, strict application of the rules of evidence in the High Court allowed too many offenders to go free.

18. Kapwepwe and 121 others were arrested when the U.P.P. was banned on 4 February. Thirty-five of these, including Kapwepwe himself, were freed on 1 January 1973.

19. *The Nation is You*, March 1972. President Kaunda signed the bill converting Zambia into a one-party state on 31 December 1972.

20. *The Times* social report on Zambia, 7 November 1968.

21. *A Path for the Future*, Zambian Information Office, July 1971, p. 7.

22. The crop failure of 1969–70 compelled the Zambian government to import 1·5 million bags of grain from Rhodesia. Recovery measures, including a massive expansion of mechanized farming in the Lusaka district, were expected to produce a surplus of 7 million bags by 1973, enough to render Zambia free from any dependence on her southern neighbour. At the same time it inevitably diminished further the opportunities and incentives of the rural African to raise his production and break into the cash sector. See Ruth Weiss in *The Guardian*, 7 December 1972.

23. See R. Hall: *The High Price of Principles*.

BIBLIOGRAPHY

Place of publication is London unless otherwise stated.

Works marked with an asterisk(*) contain comprehensive bibliographies for their own subjects.

GENERAL

FAGE, J. D., *An Atlas of African History* (1958).
OLIVER, O. and FAGE, J. D., *A Short History of Africa* (1962).*
WALKER, E. A., *A History of Southern Africa* (1957).*

PREHISTORY

ALIMEN, H., *The Prehistory of Africa* (1957).
CATON-THOMPSON, G., *The Zimbabwe Culture* (Oxford, 1931).
CLARK, J. D., *The Prehistory of Africa* (1970).
CLARK, J. D., *The Prehistory of Southern Africa* (1954).*
CLARK, J. D., et alia, Ed. *Proceedings of the Third Pan African Conference on Prehistory* (1955).
COLE, S., *The Prehistory of East Africa* (1954).*
DAVIDSON, B., *Old Africa Rediscovered* (1959).*
FOUCHÉ, L, *Mapungubwe: Ancient Bantu Civilization on the Limpopo. Reports on Excavations 1933–35* (1937).
JONES, N., *The Prehistory of Southern Rhodesia* (Cambridge, 1949).
ROBINSON, K. R., *Khami Ruins. Report of Excavations 1947–55* (Cambridge, 1959).
SHINNIE, P. L. (Ed.), *The African Iron Age* (1971).
SUMMERS, R., et alia, *Inyanga* (Cambridge, 1951).
SUMMERS, R., *Zimbabwe: A Rhodesian Mystery* (1964).

TRIBAL HISTORY

BARNES, J. A., *Politics in a Changing Society—the Fort Jameson Ngoni* (R.-L. I., Manchester, 1954).
BRELSFORD, W. V., *The Tribes of Northern Rhodesia* (Lusaka, 1956).
BRYANT, A. T., *Olden Times in Zululand and Natal* (1929).
BULLOCK, C., *The Mashona* (1927).
CUNNISON, I. G., *The Luapula Peoples of Northern Rhodesia* (R.- L. I., Manchester, 1959).
CUNNISON, I. G., *History on the Luapula* (Cape Town, 1951).

GLUCKMAN, M. and COLSON, E., *Seven Tribes of British Central Africa* (R.-L. I., Manchester, 1951).
HOLE, H. M., *Lobengula* (1929).
HOLE, H. M., *The Passing of the Black Kings* (1932).
JALLA, A., *History of the Barotse Nation* (Unpublished. By courtesy of the Paris Evangelical Mission).
KAZEMBE, MWATA, *Ifikolwe Fyandi* (1951).
MACKINTOSH, C. W., *Lewanika Paramount Chief of the Barotse* (1942).
MITCHELL, J. CLYDE., *The Yao Village* (R.-L. I., Manchester, 1959).
OMER-COOPER, J. D., *The Zulu Aftermath* (1966).
POOLE, E. H. LANE, *Notes on the Tribes of the Eastern Province of Northern Rhodesia* (1941).
RANGER, T. O. (Ed.), *Aspects of Central African History* (1968).
READ, M., *The Ngoni of Nyasaland* (1956).
SMITH, E. and DALE, A., *The Ila-speaking Peoples of Northern Rhodesia* (1920).
STOKES, E. T. and BROWN, R., *The Zambezian Past* (1966).
YOUNG, T. CULLEN, *Notes on the History of the Tumbuka-Henga Peoples* (1932).

THE PORTUGUESE

AXELSON, E., *South-East Africa 1488–1530* (Cape Town, 1940).
AXELSON, E., *Portuguese in South-East Africa 1600–1700* (Johannesburg 1960).
BURTON, SIR R. F., *Lands of the Cazembe*—mainly a translation of the travel diaries of Lacerda, Pinto, the Pombeiros, Monteiro and Gamitto (1873).
COUPLAND, SIR R., *East Africa and its Invaders from the Earliest Times to the Death of Seyyid Said* (Oxford, 1938).
HALL, R. N., *Prehistoric Rhodesia* (1909).
THEAL, G. M., *Records of South-Eastern Africa*, Vols. I–VI (Cape Town, 1898).

LIVINGSTONE AND THE SLAVE TRADE

CHAMBERLAIN, D., *Some Letters from Livingstone* (1940).
COUPLAND, SIR R., *Livingstone's Last Journey* (1945).
COUPLAND, SIR R., *The Exploitation of East Africa* (1959).
DEBENHAM, F., *The Way to Ilala* (1959).
GELFAND, R., *Livingstone the Doctor* (1957).
LIVINGSTONE, D., *Missionary Travels and Researches in South Africa* (1855).
LIVINGSTONE, D., *Narrative of an Expedition to the Zambezi and Its Tributaries* (1865).

SEAVER, G., *David Livingstone: His Life and Letters* (1957).
SCHAPERA, D., *David Livingstone: Family Letters* (1961).
WALLER, J. (Ed.), *Last Journals of David Livingstone* (1874).

MISSIONS AND TRADE

ARNOT, F. S., *Missionary Travels in Central Africa* (1914).
BAINES, T., *Northern Goldfields Diaries, 1869–72* (Oppenheimer Series, 1946).
BALDWIN, A., *A Missionary Outpost in Central Africa* (1914).
CHADWICK, O., *Mackenzie's Grave* (1959).
COILLARD, F., *On the Threshold of Central Africa* (1902).
ELMSLIE, W. A., *Among the Wild Ngoni* (1899).
GOULDSBURY, C. and SHEANE, H., *The Great Plateau of Northern Rhodesia* (1911).
HANNA, A. J., *The Beginnings of Nyasaland and North-Eastern Rhodesia, 1859–95* (1956).
HARDING, C., *In Remotest Barotseland* (1905).
HETHERWICK, A., *The Romance of Blantyre* (1931).
LIVINGSTONE, W. P., *Laws of Livingstonia* (1921).
MACKINTOSH, C. W., *Coillard of the Zambezi* (1907).
MACKINTOSH, C. W., *Some Pioneer Missions of Northern Rhodesia and Nyasaland*, (R.-L. Museum, 1950).
MOFFAT, R. U., *John Smith Moffat* (1921).
NORTHCOTT, W. C., *Robert Moffat, Pioneer in Africa* (1961).
OLIVER, R., *The Missionary Factor in East Africa* (1952).
PINTO, S., *How I Crossed Africa* (Philadelphia, 1881).
SELOUS, F. C., *A Hunter's Wanderings in Africa* (1907).
SMITH, E. W., *The Way of the White Fields in Rhodesia* (1928).
TABLER, W. C., *The Far Interior* (1961).*
WALLIS, J. P. R., *Matabele Journals of Robert and Emily Moffat* (Oppenheimer Series, 1945).
WALLIS, J. P. R., *Thomas Baines* (1941).

THE SCRAMBLE FOR AFRICA

Cambridge History of the British Empire. Vol. III. *The Empire—Commonwealth 1870–1919*. Vol. VIII. *South Africa, Rhodesia and the Protectorates* (Cambridge, 1936).
CROWE, S. E., *The Berlin West African Conference* (1942).
LANGER, W. L., *European Alliances and Alignments* (New York, 1931).
PERHAM, M., *Lugard—The Years of Adventure* (1956).
ROBINSON, R. and GALLAGHER, J., *Africa and the Victorians. The Mind of Imperialism* (1961).
SLADE, R., *King Leopold's Congo* (1962).

RHODES

GROSS, F., *Rhodes of Africa* (1956).
MITCHELL, SIR L., *Life of the Hon. C. J. Rhodes* (1910).
PAKENHAM, E., *Jameson's Raid* (1960).
'VINDEX', *Cecil Rhodes: Political Life and Speeches* (1900).
WILLIAMS, B., *Cecil Rhodes* (1938).

OCCUPATION AND PACIFICATION

BARNES, J. A., *Politics in a Changing Society* (1954).
COLVIN, I., *The Life of Jameson* (1923).
GANN, L. H., *The Birth of a Plural Society. Northern Rhodesia 1894–1914* (Manchester, 1958).*
GLASS, S., *The Matabele War* (1968).
HANNA, A. J., *The Beginnings of Nyasaland and North-Eastern Rhodesia* (Oxford, 1956).*
HOLE, H. M., *The Making of Rhodesia* (1926).
JOHNSTON, SIR H. H., *British Central Africa* (1897).
JONES, N., *Rhodesian Genesis* (Bulawayo, 1953).
LEONARD, A. G., *How We Made Rhodesia* (1896).
MASON, P., *The Birth of a Dilemma* (1958).
MOFFAT, R. U., *John Smith Moffat* (1921).
OLIVER, R., *Sir Harry Johnston and the Scramble for Africa* (1957).*
ROUILLARD, N., *Matabele Thompson* (1936).
SAMKANGE, S., *Origins of Rhodesia* (1968).
SELOUS, F. C., *Sunshine and Storm in Rhodesia* (1896).

COMPANY RULE

BRADLEY, K., *Copper Venture* (1952).
BRELSFORD, W. V., *The Story of the Northern Rhodesian Regiment* (1954).
DANN, H. C., *Romance of the Posts of Rhodesia and Nyasaland* (1940).
GANN, L. H., *The Birth of a Plural Society* (1958).*
GELFAND, R., *Northern Rhodesia in the Days of the Charter* (1961).
HARDING, C., *Frontier Patrols* (1937).
JOLLIE, E. T., *The Real Rhodesia* (1924).
LONG, B. K., *Sir Drummond Chaplin* (1952).
MASON, P., *The Birth of a Dilemma* (1958).
PAULING, G., *Chronicles of a Contractor* (1926).
VARIAN, H. F., *Some African Milestones* (1953).
WALLIS, J. P. R., *One Man's Hand. The Story of Sir Charles Coghlan and the Liberation of Southern Rhodesia* (1950).

MALAWI

CLUTTON-BROCK, G., *Dawn in Nyasaland* (1959).
DEBENHAM, F., *Nyasaland: The Land of the Lake* (1955).
MOYSE-BARTLETT, H., *The King's African Rifles* (1956).
PIKE, J. G., *Malawi: A Political and Economic History* (1968).*
SHEPPERSON, G. and PRICE, T., *Independent African* (1958).

POST-1923: POLITICAL

ALLIGHAN, G., *The Welensky Story* (1962).
CLEGG, E., *Race and Politics: Partnership in the Federation* (1960).
DAVIDSON, J. W., *The Legislative Council of Northern Rhodesia* (1948).
EPSTEIN, A. L., *Politics in an Urban African Community* (1958).
FRANCK, T. M., *Race and Nationalism* (1960).
GANN, L. H., *A History of Northern Rhodesia* (1964).
GANN, L. H., *A History of Southern Rhodesia to 1934* (1965).
GRAY, R., *The Two Nations* (1960).*
HAILEY, LORD W. M., *An African Survey* (1956).
HANNA, A. J., *The Story of the Rhodesias and Nyasaland* (1960).
KEATLEY, P., *The Politics of Partnership* (1962).
LEYS C., *European Politics in Southern Rhodesia* (Oxford, 1959).
LUGARD, F. D., *The Dual Mandate: A Study of Policy in British Colonial Territories* (1922).
MASON, P., *Year of Decision* (1961).
SEGAL, R., *Political Africa* (1961).
WELENSKY, SIR R., *Four Thousand Days* (1964).

POST-1923: ECONOMIC AND SOCIAL

COLSON, E., *Marriage and the Family among the Plateau Tonga of Northern Rhodesia* (R.-L. I. Manchester, 1958).
BARBER, W. J., *The Economy of British Central Africa* (1961).
GROVES, C. P., *The Planting of Christianity in Africa*, Vol. IV (1958).
HALL, R., *Zambia* (1967).
HANCE W. A., *African Economic Development* (1958).
HAZELWOOD and HENDERSON, *Nyasaland: The Economics of Federation* (1960).
MULFORD, D. C., *Zambia: The Politics of Independence* (1967).*
MURRAY, D. J., *The Governmental System of Southern Rhodesia* (1970).
PALLEY, Dr C., *The Constitutional History and Law of Southern Rhodesia, 1880–1965* (1966).
RANGER, T. O. (Ed.), *Aspects of Central African History* (1968).
RICHARDS, A. I., *Land, Labour and Diet in Northern Rhodesia* (1939).
TAYLOR, J. and LEHMANN, D., *Christians of the Copperbelt. The growth of the Church in Northern Rhodesia* (1961).

U.N.E.S.C.O., *Structure and Growth of Selected African Economies* (New York, 1958).

WATSON, W., *Tribal Cohesion in a Money Economy: A Study of the Mambwe People of Northern Rhodesia* (R.-L. I., Manchester, 1958).

WILSON, G., *An Essay on the Economics of Detribalisation in Northern Rhodesia* (R.-L. I, 1941).

WILSON, G. and HUNTER, M., *The Study of African Society* (*Nyakyusa*) (R.-L. I., 1939).

WILSON, G. and WILSON, M., *The Analysis of Social Change* (Cambridge, 1945).

POST-1965

CLEMENTS, F., *Rhodesia: The Course to Collision* (1969).

HALL, R., *The High Price of Principles: Kaunda and the White South* (1969).

JOURNALS

In order to save space, recommended articles are not listed here, but a number have been mentioned in the text references.

Abbreviations used in the text references are placed here in brackets.

African Studies, Journal of the University of Witwatersrand.
Human Problems in Central Africa, Journal of the Rhodes-Livingstone Institute. (H.P.C.A.).
Journal of African History.
Man, Journal of the Royal Anthropological Society.
Nada, Native Affairs Department Annual, Southern Rhodesia.
Northern Rhodesia Journal. (N. R. Journal).
Occasional Papers of the National Museum of Southern Rhodesia. (O.P.N.M.S.R.).
South African Archaeological Bulletin.
South African Journal of Science. (S. A. Jnl. of Sc.).
Rhodesiana.

PUBLISHED PARLIAMENTARY PAPERS
(UNITED KINGDOM)

Correspondence on the affairs of Bechuanaland and Adjacent Territories (1888). C. 5524.
Correspondence on the Action of Portugal in Mashonaland and in the Districts of the Shire and Lake Nyasa (1890). C. 5904.
Further Correspondence on the affairs of Bechuanaland and adjacent Territories (1890). C. 5918.
Correspondence on the Anglo-Portuguese Convention of 20 August

1890 and the subsequent Agreement of November 14 1890. (1890). C. 6212.

Correspondence on the Anglo-German Agreement (1890). C. 6046.

Papers relating to the Anglo-Portuguese Convention of 11 June 1891. (1891). C. 6370.

Correspondence relating to Great Britain and Portugal in East Africa (1891). C. 6495.

Correspondence concerning the B.S.A. Company in Mashonaland and Matabeleland (inc. Lippert Concession) (1893). C. 7171.

Report by Commissioner Johnston on the first three years' administration of British Central Africa (1894). C. 7637.

Papers respecting the British sphere north of the Zambezi (1891), and agreements with the B.S.A. Company (1894). C. 7504.

Correspondence concerning Operations against Slave Traders (1896). C. 7925, 8103.

Report of the Land Commission for Southern Rhodesia (1897). C. 8130.

Report on the B.S.A. Company's Native Administration, together with a letter from the Company commenting on that Report (1897). C. 8547.

Correspondence on the Administration of the B.S.A. Company (1897). C. 8547.

Reproductions of B.S.A. Company Charter (1889), Mashonaland Order in Council (1891), and Matebeleland Order in Council (1894). C. 8773.

Southern Rhodesia Order in Council (1898). C. 9318.

British Central Africa Protectorate Annual Report on Trade and Conditions (1901), Cd. 896–26.

Correspondence on Southern Rhodesia's labour supply (1902). Cd. 1200.

British Central Africa Protectorate, Report on Trade and Conditions (1902–3). Cd. 1772.

Correspondence on the Proposed Introduction of Chinese Labour into Southern Rhodesia (1904). Cd. 2028.

British Central Africa, Report on Trade and Conditions (1903–4). Cd. 2242.

Award of H.M. the King of Italy respecting the western boundary of the Barotse Kingdom (1905) Cd. 2584.

B.S.A. Company's Supplemental Charter (1914). Cd. 7970.

Papers Concerning the Southern Rhodesia Native Reserves Commission (1915). Cd. 8674.

Papers concerning the Proceedings of the Cave Commission (1921). Cmd. 1129.

Agreement between the Secretary of State for the Colonies and the

B.S.A. Company for the settlement of Outstanding Questions relating to Northern and Southern Rhodesia (1921). Cmd. 1984.

First Report of the Committee appointed to consider certain questions relating to Rhodesia (Buxton Committee) (1921). Cmd. 1273.

Second Report of the Buxton Committee (1921). Cmd. 1471.

Letters Patent granting Responsible Government to Southern Rhodesia (1923). Cmd. 1573.

Memorandum concerning Indians in Kenya (Devonshire Memorandum) (1923). Cmd. 1922.

Report of Commission on Closer Union in East and Central Africa (Hilton Young Commission) (1926). Cmd. 3234.

Memorandum on Native Policy in East Africa (Passfield Memorandum) (1930). Cmd. 3573.

Report of Commission appointed to enquire into Disturbances on the Copperbelt of Northern Rhodesia (1935). Cmd. 5009.

Report of the Rhodesia and Nyasaland Royal Commission (Bledisloe Commission) (1939). Cmd. 5929.

Report of Conference on Closer Association in Central Africa (First London Conference) (1951). Cmd. 8233.

The Central African Territories: Historical, Geographical and Economic Survey (1951). Cmd. 8234.

Comparative Survey of Central African Native Policies (1951). Cmd. 8235.

Closer Association in Central Africa: Statement by H.M. Government (1951). Cmd. 8411.

Draft Federal Scheme (1952). Cmd. 8573.

Reports of Preparatory Commissions to consider Fiscal, Judicial and Civil Service Questions (1952). Cmds. 8671–3.

Report of the Conference on Federation (Second London Conference) (1952). Cmd. 8753.

Federation of Rhodesia and Nyasaland Constitution Amendment Bill (1957). Cmnd. 298.

Federation of Rhodesia and Nyasaland Electoral Bill (1958). Cmnd. 362.

Proposals for Constitutional Change in Northern Rhodesia (1958). Cmnd. 530.

Nyasaland, State of Emergency (1959). Cmnd. 707.

Despatch from the Governor of Nyasaland concerning the Declaration of Emergency (1959). Cmnd. 81.

Report of the Nyasaland Commission of Enquiry (Devlin Commission) (1959). Cmnd. 814.

Despatch from the Governor of Nyasaland commenting on the Devlin Commission's Report (1959). Cmnd. 815.

Report of Nyasaland Constitutional Conference (1960). Cmnd.
1132.
Report of the Advisory Commission on the Review of the Constitu-
tion of the Federation (Monckton Commission) (1960). Cmnds.
1148–1151.
Southern Rhodesia Constitutional Conference Report (1961).
Cmnd. 1291.
Southern Rhodesia Constitution Part I: Summary of proposed
changes. Cmnd. 1399.
Southern Rhodesia Constitution Part II: Detailed provisions.
Cmnd. 1400.
Report of the Nyasaland Constitutional Conference held in London
in November 1962. Cmnd. 1887.
Federation of Rhodesia and Nyasaland: Commentary on state-
ments relating to the establishment of the Federation and their
bearing on the withdrawal of Nyasaland (1963). Cmnd. 1948.
Correspondence between Her Majesty's Government and the
Government of Southern Rhodesia. Cmnds. 2000 and 2073.
Report of the Northern Rhodesia Independence Conference (1964).
Cmnd. 2365.
Barotseland Agreement (1964). Cmnd. 2366.
Southern Rhodesia: Joint Statement issued on 11 September 1964
by the Prime Ministers of Britain and Southern Rhodesia at
the conclusion of their talks in London on the subject of inde-
pendence. Cmnd. 2464.
Documents relating to the negotiation between the United King-
dom and Southern Rhodesian Governments (1965). Cmnd. 2807.
Documents relating to proposals for a settlement (1966). Cmnd.
3171.
Report on the Discussions held on board HMS *Fearless* (1968).
Cmnd. 3793.
Report on Exchanges with the Regime since the talks held in
Salisbury in November 1968 (1969). Cmnd. 4065.
Rhodesia Proposals for a Settlement (1971). Cmnd. 4835.

Further correspondence and memoranda are included in the
Colonial Office Prints, those relevant to South and Central
Africa being entitled *African (South)*. They are available at the
Colonial Office, and the relevant volumes can also be seen at
the Central African Archives in Salisbury.
Relevant volumes of original correspondence at the Public Record
Office are in the following series:
CO/417 South Africa, including the sphere of the B.S.A.
Company, 1884–1925.

FO/2   East Africa, including British Central Africa, until
         1903.
CO/525 British Central Africa, later Nyasaland, 1904–1936.

MISCELLANEOUS OFFICIAL PUBLICATIONS

Report of the Land Commission for Southern Rhodesia (Morris
  Carter Report) (1926). Salisbury, C.S.R. 3–1926.
Report on the Nyasaland Railways and the Proposed Zambezi
  Bridge (1929). Zomba.
Report on Industrial Relations in Southern Rhodesia (H. Clay,
  1930). Salisbury, C.S.R. 3—1930.
Correspondence relating to the Constitutional position of Southern
  Rhodesia (1936). Salisbury, C.S.R. 26—1936.
Report of the Committee appointed to enquire into Emigrant
  Labour (1936). Zomba, 500—7581.
Report of the Commission appointed to enquire into the Distur-
  bances on the Copperbelt (1940). Lusaka.
Report of the Committee appointed to investigate Urban Conditions
  in Southern Rhodesia (Howman Report) (1943). Salisbury.
Report on Some Aspects of African Living Conditions on the Cop-
  perbelt of Northern Rhodesia (A. L. Saffery, 1943). Lusaka.
Report of the Commission appointed to enquire into the Advance-
  ment of Africans in Industry (Dalgleish Report) (1948). Lusaka.
Agreement with the British South Africa Company on the mineral
  rights owned by the Company in Northern Rhodesia and for
  the eventual transfer of those rights to the Northern Rhodesian
  Government 1950 (1951). London, H.M.S.O., Col. No. 272
  (58–272).
Native administration in Central Nyasaland (L. P. Mair, 1952).
  London, H.M.S.O., Colonial Research Study No. 5.
The administration of justice and the urban African: a study of
  urban native courts in Northern Rhodesia (A. L. Epstein, 1953).
  London, H.M.S.O., Colonial Research Study No. 7.
Report of African Local Government in Southern Rhodesia (R.
  Howman, 1953). Salisbury.
Report of the Board of Enquiry into the Advancement of Africans in
  the Copper Mining Industry (Forster Report) (1954). Lusaka.
What the Native Land Husbandry Act means to the Rural African
  (1955). Salisbury.
Humanism in Zambia and a Guide to its Implementation (Dr K. D.
  Kaunda, no date). Lusaka.
A Path for the Future: an Address to UNIP (Dr K. D. Kaunda,
  1971). Lusaka.

INDEX